Promoting resilience in child welfare

Editors

Robert J. Flynn
School of Psychology
& Centre for Research on Community Services
University of Ottawa

Peter M. Dudding
Child Welfare League of Canada
& Centre of Excellence for Child Welfare

James G. Barber
Faculty of Social Work
University of Toronto

D0733147

The University of Ottawa Press gratefully acknowledges the support extended to its publishing programme by the Canada Council for the Arts and the University of Ottawa.

We also acknowledge with gratitude the support of the Government of Canada through its Book Publishing Industry Development Program for our publishing activities.

Library and Archives Canada Cataloguing in Publication

Promoting resilience in child welfare / editors, Robert J. Flynn, Peter M. Dudding, James G. Barber.

(Actexpress)
Includes bibliographical references and index.
ISBN-13: 978-0-7766-3553-8
ISBN-10: 0-7766-3553-0
   1. Foster home care. 2. Children—Institutional care. 3. Foster children.
I. Flynn, Robert J. (Robert John), 1942– II. Dudding, Peter M., 1951– III. Barber, James G., 1954– IV. Series.

HV715.P76 2006   362.73   C2005-902563-8

All rights reserved. No parts of this publication may be reproduced or transmitted in any form or by any means, electronic or mechanical, including photocopy, recording, or any information storage and retrieval system, without permission in writing from the publisher.

Cover design and layout: Leah Gryfe

ISBN-13: 978-0-7766-3553-8
ISBN-10: 0-7766-3553-0

Published by the University of Ottawa Press, 2006
542 King Edward Avenue, Ottawa, Ontario K1N 6N5
press@uottawa.ca/www.uopress.uottawa.ca

Printed and bound in Canada

Table of Contents

Part 2: Resilience and Foster Care Research, Policy, and Practice

List of Contributors

James G. Barber
Faculty of Social Work
University of Toronto
Toronto, Ontario
Canada

Julie Beaulac
School of Psychology
University of Ottawa
Ottawa, Ontario
Canada

Ivan Brown
Centre of Excellence
for Child Welfare
University of Toronto
Toronto, Ontario
Canada

Gabrielle Burke
Consultant
Melbourne, Victoria
Australia

Beverly A. Byrne
Prescott-Russell Services
to Children and Adults
Plantagenet, Ontario
Canada

Ruth Champion
Department of Human Services
State Government of Victoria
Melbourne, Victoria
Australia

Deirdre Cheers
Barnardos Australia
Sydney, New South Wales
Australia

Paul H. Delfabbro
Department of Psychology
Adelaide University
Adelaide, South Australia
Australia

Marie Drolet
School of Social Work
University of Ottawa
Ottawa, Ontario
Canada

Peter M. Dudding
Child Welfare League of Canada
& Centre of Excellence
for Child Welfare
Ottawa, Ontario
Canada

Angela Dumoulin
School of Psychology
University of Ottawa
Ottawa, Ontario
Canada

Elizabeth Fernandez
School of Social Work
University of New South Wales
Sydney, New South Wales
Australia

Robert J. Flynn
School of Psychology &
    Centre for Research on
    Community Services
University of Ottawa
Ottawa, Ontario
Canada

Hayat Ghazal
Department of Psychology
University of Rouen
Mont-Saint-Aignan
France

Robbie Gilligan
Department of Social Studies
    & Children's Research Centre
Trinity College Dublin
Dublin
Ireland

Pamela Gough
Centre of Excellence
    for Child Welfare
University of Toronto
Toronto, Ontario
Canada

Lisa Holmes
Centre for Child
    and Family Research
Loughborough University
Loughborough
England

Ulf Hyvönen
Umeå Research and
    Development Unit
Umeå Social Services
Umeå
Sweden

Helen Jones
Department for Education
    and Skills
London
England

Evelyn G. Khoo
Department of Social Welfare
Umeå University
Umeå
Sweden

Ross A. Klein
School of Social Work
Memorial University
    of Newfoundland
St. John's, Newfoundland and
Labrador
Canada

Kathleen Kufeldt
Muriel McQueen Fergusson
    Centre for Family
    Violence Research
University of New Brunswick
Fredericton, New Brunswick
Canada

Christopher E. Lalonde
Department of Psychology
University of Victoria
Victoria, British Columbia
Canada

Louise Legault
Institute of Population Health
University of Ottawa
Ottawa, Ontario
Canada

Raymond Lemay
Prescott-Russell Services
    to Children and Adults
Plantagenet, Ontario
Canada

Sophie Léveillé
Centre of Excellence for
    Child Welfare
University of Toronto
Toronto, Ontario
Canada

Lenora Marcellus
Faculty of Nursing
University of Alberta
Edmonton, Alberta
Canada

Ann S. Masten
Institute of Child Development
University of Minnesota
Minneapolis, Minnesota
USA

Shaye Moffat
Centre for Research on
    Community Services
University of Ottawa
Ottawa, Ontario
Canada

Jude Morwitzer
Barnardos Australia
Sydney, New South Wales
Australia

Simon Nuttgens
Salvation Army Children's Village
Calgary, Alberta
Canada

Lennart Nygren
Department of Social Welfare
Umeå University
Umeå
Sweden

Sarah Pantin
School of Psychology &
    Centre for Research
    on Community Services
University of Ottawa
Ottawa, Ontario
Canada

Julie Perkins-Mangulabnan
School of Psychology
University of Ottawa
Ottawa, Ontario
Canada

Andrew Pithouse
Social Work Studies
School of Social Sciences
Cardiff University
Cardiff
Wales

Scott Rideout
Muriel McQueen Fergusson
   Centre for Family
   Violence Research
University of New Brunswick
Fredericton, New Brunswick
Canada

Annie Robitaille
School of Psychology
University of Ottawa
Ottawa, Ontario
Canada

Vivien Runnels
Centre for Research
   on Community Services
University of Ottawa
Ottawa, Ontario
Canada

Melissa Sauvé-Kobylecki
School of Social Work
University of Ottawa
Ottawa, Ontario
Canada

Mike Stein
Social Work Research
   and Development Unit
University of York
York
England

Jessica Vinograd
School of Psychology
University of Ottawa
Ottawa, Ontario
Canada

Harriet Ward
Centre for Child and
   Family Research
Loughborough University
Loughborough
England

Preface

This book is composed of revised papers selected from those presented at the international conference, *Promoting Resilient Development in Children Receiving Care*, held at the University of Ottawa, August 16-19, 2004. The conference served as both the Sixth International Looking After Children Conference, part of a series held approximately every two years by the international Looking After Children initiative, and the Fifth National Child Welfare Symposium, part of an annual series organized by the Canadian Centre of Excellence for Child Welfare. The overarching theme of promoting resilience in children in care was chosen because its emphasis on positive development rather than on problems was timely and bridged the interests of the two child welfare audiences.

It has been almost two decades since conceptual work began, in 1987, on *Looking After Children* and a decade since publication, in 1995, of the first official version of the Looking After Children instruments. Developed and implemented in the United Kingdom under the leadership of Roy Parker, Harriet Ward, Helen Jones, Carolyn Davies, and their colleagues, and with the sustained financial support of the UK Department of Health, Looking After Children has been an important vehicle globally for the promotion of resilience, that is, positive patterns of functioning or development during or following exposure to adversity (Masten, chapter 1, this volume). Looking After Children promotes resilience by emphasizing the development of competence among young people in care through effective partnerships in the provision of care, good parenting, and high expectations. Looking after Children has been implemented to varying degrees in some 15 countries, in the UK, Europe, Scandinavia, and Australasia. Whether as part of the Integrated Children's System in the UK or as a "stand-alone" approach elsewhere, the Looking After Children philosophy will remain an important influence on child welfare services internationally for quite some time to come. The Ottawa conference was designed to take stock of the accomplishments of Looking After Children and to explore its links, on multiple levels, with the burgeoning area of resilience theory, research, practice, and policy. In presenting new studies from several countries on the relationship of resilience to Looking After Children or other child welfare innovations, the present book complements and considerably extends Newman's (2004) recent synthesis of the international literature on strategies for building resilience in young people in care.

The Canadian Centre of Excellence for Child Welfare organizes its ongoing series of National Child Welfare Symposia in order to contribute to the development of research, practice, and policy with children and families and to the transfer of knowledge among Canadian stakeholders. As part of the Ottawa conference, the Centre of Excellence organized a policy symposium entitled, *Is permanence necessary for resilience? Advice for policy makers*. The paper by Ivan Brown, Sophie Léveillé, and Pamela Gough (chapter 6, this volume) captures the key observations and policy suggestions made at this symposium.

The Child Welfare League of Canada (CWLC) was the lead agency in organizing and hosting the Ottawa conference, in close collaboration with the other co-sponsoring organizations: the Centre of Excellence for Child Welfare, the Centre for Research on Community Services at the University of Ottawa, the Ontario Association of Children's Aid Societies, Prescott-Russell Services to Children and Adults, and the Ottawa Children's Aid Society. Substantial financial support for the conference or this book was provided by Human Resources Development Canada (now Social Development Canada), the Centre of Excellence for Child Welfare, the Social Sciences and Humanities Research Council of Canada, and the Faculty of Social Sciences of the University of Ottawa.

The first five international Looking After Children conferences were organized by Professor Harriet Ward and her colleagues and held in England. Professor Ward invited people from the UK and a number of other countries to take part. The participants benefited greatly from listening to reports on how Looking After Children was being implemented in the UK and elsewhere, as well as from sharing their experiences with international colleagues. At the fifth international Looking After Children conference, held at Worcester College at Oxford University in 2002, the first two editors of the present book, Bob Flynn and Peter Dudding, requested that the sixth international conference be held in Canada, in 2004. We did so because several Looking After Children projects in Canada had produced considerable momentum for the approach. We wanted to make Looking after Children known to a wider audience in Canada, including policy makers from federal, provincial, and territorial governments and voluntary-sector organizations, young people in care, child welfare practitioners, middle and senior managers, foster parents and other caregivers, and researchers and academics. In the event, the Ottawa conference attracted a great deal of interest, in Canada and other countries. Some 350 participants attended, from each of Canada's 10 provinces and three territories and from Australia, Hong Kong, Ireland, New Zealand, Sweden, the United Kingdom, and the United States.

Bob Flynn and Peter Dudding brought to the conference and to the preparation of this book their knowledge of Looking After Children, gained from conducting or administering, respectively, evaluative research on the implementation and outcomes of the approach. Peter Dudding was also closely associated with the Centre of Excellence for Child Welfare. Jim Barber, the third editor, represented the Centre of Excellence on the conference planning committee and, as an Australian child welfare researcher who had recently moved to the University of Toronto, brought to the conference and book an international perspective on child welfare research, practice, and policy.

The editors acted as a peer-review committee in evaluating and selecting the present papers from a considerably larger number submitted by participants after the conference. We used two main criteria in choosing papers: the quality of the research, scholarship, and writing, and direct relevance to the conference theme of promoting resilient development in children in care. We strove to avoid conflicts of interest in reviewing the various papers, including our own. Space limitations prevented us from including a number of good papers that we judged to be less directly pertinent to the conference theme than those selected. Virtually all the papers included were revised in light of our editorial comments before final acceptance.

The book comprises three parts. Part 1 provides individual, service-system, cultural, societal, and cross-societal perspectives on resilience theory and its relationship to child welfare policy and practice. Three of the six chapters in this section, including the introductory one, are directly related to Looking After Children, and a fourth chapter presents observations and recommendations from the previously mentioned policy symposium. Part 2 consists of papers on resilience and foster care research, policy, and practice, ordered according to the ages of the young people studied, from infants to young people leaving care. Six of the 10 chapters in Part 2 have a direct link with Looking After Children. Part 3 presents a series of instructive case studies that describe the successful implementation of Looking after Children or related child-welfare innovations on the successively higher levels of the individual practitioner, single agency, network of collaborating agencies, state, and nation. Seven of the nine chapters in Part 3, including the concluding one, are based on or make explicit mention of Looking after Children.

One useful way to approach the book would be to begin by reading the first and last chapters. In the first chapter, Ann Masten provides an authoritative, up-to-date overview of resilience concepts and findings. She notes that we have recently entered upon a third, *intervention* wave in resilience research, focused on promoting resilience through practice and policy. Masten suggests that if fundamental human adaptive systems, on several levels, operate in an unimpaired fashion, then many children and young people may be expected to recover from the adversities and threats to development that they have experienced. In describing a new, dynamic resilience framework for child welfare, she links her introductory chapter to a number of other chapters in the book. In particular, she emphasizes the potential of Looking After Children to act as a vehicle for promoting positive missions, models, measures, and methods, such that a child welfare system based on Looking After Children would function like a fundamental human adaptive system, thereby increasing the likelihood of resilience for young people in care.

In the last chapter, Jim Barber provides a concise synthesis of the research findings and practice and policy suggestions found throughout the book. To organize his observations, he uses Bronfenbrenner's (1979) ecological framework. The latter fits well with Masten's resilience framework, because both are multi-level in nature, involving people and other resources on the individual, familial, organizational, community, cultural, and societal levels. Together, Masten's and Barber's contributions provide a coherent framework for reading the other 23 chapters in a systematic fashion.

We believe this book makes at least three significant contributions to the child welfare literature. First, it is the only volume composed of original papers that explore the specific relationship between resilience theory and child welfare research, policy and practice. Second, it is unique in providing extensive conceptual, empirical, or descriptive analyses (in 16 of 25 chapters) of the important role of Looking After Children in promoting resilient development among young people in care and in improving child welfare systems. Third, it has an international flavour, with contributions from authors currently residing in eight different countries: Australia, Canada, England, France, Ireland, Sweden, the United States, and Wales.

We wish to thank the following people and organizations for their collaboration: the 42 contributors; Ruth Bradley-St-Cyr (Director) and Marie Clausén (Managing Editor), University of Ottawa Press; Sue Sullivan, Centre of Excellence for Child Welfare; Neil Kelly, Creative Edge (copy editing); Leah Gryfe (cover design and page layout); and the organizations, mentioned earlier, that co-sponsored or co-funded the conference or book: the Child Welfare League of Canada; the Centre of Excellence for Child Welfare; the Centre for Research on Community Services, University of Ottawa; the Ontario Association of Children's Aid Societies; Prescott-Russell Services to Children and Adults; the Ottawa Children's Aid Society; Human Resources Development Canada (Social Development Canada); the Social Sciences and Humanities Research Council of Canada; and the Faculty of Social Sciences, University of Ottawa.

The Editors

References

Newman, T. (2004). *What works in building resilience?* Ilford, Essex, England: Barnardo's.

Bronfenbrenner, U. (1979). *The ecology of human development: Experiments by nature and design.* Cambridge, MA: Harvard University Press.

Part 1:

Resilience Theory and Child Welfare Policy and Practice

CHAPTER 1

Promoting resilience in development: A general framework for systems of care

Ann S. Masten

Introduction

The systematic study of resilience began over three decades ago, as developmental psychopathology emerged (Luthar, in press; Masten, Best, & Garmezy, 1990; Masten & Powell, 2003). Scientists searching for understanding of causes and pathways leading to psychopathology began to study children at risk for a variety of reasons, including the genetic risks of a mentally ill parent and the hazards of growing up in contexts of poverty, war, family violence and many other adversities. Some of these investigators noticed that a substantial portion of children with high-risk status appeared to be developing well and some were even flourishing; this observation piqued the scientific curiosity of a small cadre of pioneering psychologists and psychiatrists who set out to understand this phenomenon (Garmezy, 1974; Garmezy & Rutter, 1983, Murphy & Moriarty, 1976; Rutter, 1979; Werner & Smith, 1982).

The great insight of these pioneers was not simply in recognizing the diversity of outcomes among children statistically at risk for psychopathology, but in realizing that the study of resilience in these children's lives had the potential to inform practices and policies aimed at changing the odds for positive development. Three waves of resilience research ensued (Wright & Masten, 2005): the first wave focused on *what questions,* identifying the key components of resilience, the risks and adversities, the assets and resources, the vulnerabilities and protective factors that might account for good outcomes in some children and poor outcomes in others; the second wave shifted attention to *how questions,* the processes and systems involved in naturally occurring resilience, with more dynamic multi-level models of how resilience emerges from the interactions of multiple biological and social systems across many levels of analysis; and the third wave, now under way, addresses *intervention questions* about creating or promoting resilience through practice and policy.

Developmental resilience is a very broad topic, and much science remains to be conducted. Nonetheless, a resilience framework for conceptualizing intervention has begun to take shape as a result of the initial decades of resilience science (Masten, 2001; Masten & Powell, 2003). The purpose of this chapter is to delineate the outline of that emerging framework as applied to the design of services and interventions for children in care. In section one, basic concepts from resilience studies are concisely summarized. In section two, pertinent findings from the resilience literature are highlighted through a discussion of the *Short List* of factors associated with resilience in many studies and the *fundamental human adaptive systems* implicated by that list. Section three outlines a resilience framework for child welfare interventions, drawing on Looking After Children (LAC) (Parker, Ward, Jackson, Aldgate, & Wedge, 1991; Ward, 1995) as an international example of applied resilience theory (Flynn, Ghazal, Legault, Vandermeulen, & Petrick, 2004; Newman, 2004).

Resilience concepts and theory

Resilience refers to positive patterns of functioning or development during or following exposure to adversity, or, more simply, to good adaptation in a context of risk. In behavioral studies, resilience is inferred from two judgements about how well an individual is doing: one concerns the quality of adaptive functioning or development, and the other concerns the exposure to some kind of threat to functioning or development (Luthar, in press; Masten & Coatsworth, 1998; Masten, 2001; Masten & Powell, 2003). Very generally speaking, resilience is an inference about how well a system has responded to challenge. This concept can be applied to any living system or to a human organization, such as a family or school. If there has been no challenge, a person or a family or some other kind of system might be described as competent or successful but not (at least not yet) resilient.

The criteria for defining or operationalizing resilience for research have varied and there have been controversies about these criteria (Masten, 1999; Masten & Powell, 2003; Luthar, in press). In developmental science, resilience investigators have often judged how well children are doing in terms of their progress or success in age-salient developmental tasks, the benchmarks of psychosocial development in a given culture and time in history (Masten & Coatsworth, 1998). Some of these tasks are universal for the species, such as learning to talk and communicate in childhood, and others are common but not universal, such as academic achievement. During the school years, children in many modern societies are expected to do well in school, get along with other children, and follow the rules for conduct in the community. As they make the transition to adulthood, new developmental tasks emerge in the domains of work, romantic relationships, and parenting.

Some definitions of resilience focus additionally on how a person is feeling, in terms of psychological well-being or happiness (Luthar, in press). It is also reasonable to include additional domains of physical or mental health in the definitions of what it means to be "doing okay" in life (Masten & Coatsworth, 1998). Therefore, it is important when judgements about resilience are made (in research, practice, or policy) that the criteria for judging positive outcomes be clearly indicated.

Many kinds of risk or adversity have been included in studies of resilience, ranging from a single, acute event to a chronic situation characterized by ongoing danger or persistently high cumulative risk (Masten et al., 1990; Masten & Powell, 2003; Luthar, in press). *Risk factors* are predictors of undesired outcomes, a broad term for the elevated probability of a negative outcome, based on convincing evidence that the risk factor is a significant predictor of that negative outcome. Examples include premature birth, parents with low education levels, mental illness in a parent, child abuse or neglect, and poverty. Risk factors often co-occur or pile up in the lives of children, hence investigators have studied the impact of *cumulative risk* or *risk gradients*, where rising risk levels are associated with more problems (Luthar, in press; Masten & Reed, 2002; Masten et al., 1990; Masten & Wright, 1998). *Adversity* or *negative life events* are subtypes of risk factors, referring to direct negative experiences, ranging from acute disaster exposure to chronic interparental conflict. Research on resilience has focused on a wide variety of risk factors and adversities, including divorce, bereavement, war, disaster, surgery, adoption, neglect, abuse, etc. *Stressors* are events that typically disrupt the functioning of a system and may cause *stress*, which occurs when actual or perceived demand on a system exceeds adaptational capacity, at least temporarily. In individuals, stress has been studied at multiple levels, including the physiological processes that occur when the human body is responding to physical or psychological challenge, to the psychological experiences of distress or anticipated stress; however, the terms can be used to refer to any system (i.e., a family or a school or a health care system) that is currently disrupted in some way by overload, and demand is now exceeding adaptive capacity. Stress in a living system often produces both disequilibrium and efforts to restore adaptive functioning.

Resilience presumably involves many processes that result in positive adaptation over the course of development. Resilience research often has focused on differential predictors of good and poor outcomes, in an effort to discern what enables some people to function well or recover well while others do not. Direct predictors of better outcomes often are described as *assets* or *resources*. If predictors appear to play a special role under high-risk or high-adversity conditions, they are called *protective factors*. Some factors work both ways. Good parenting and higher IQ scores, for example, predict better academic achievement across all levels of adversity; however, under hazardous rearing conditions, these advantages appear to play a particularly important role in adaptation and development (Masten & Coatsworth, 1998; Masten, 2001).

Key findings on what makes a difference

There has been remarkable consistency in the findings on what makes a difference for children across diverse situations in studies of resilience (Luthar, in press; Masten, 2001, 2004; Masten & Powell, 2003). Many of the key correlates of good outcomes among children with high cumulative risk or adversity that were initially identified in early reviews of the literature continue to be corroborated (Garmezy, 1985; Rutter, 1979, 1990). As a result, it is possible to list widely observed correlates of good adaptation or development from resilience studies. Moreover, it is important to consider what such a list may mean.

The short list

A typical "short list" (Masten, 1998, 2004; Masten & Reed, 2002) of resilience correlates appears in Table 1. The list includes qualities of individuals, families, and other contexts in which children live that consistently have been observed to predict or accompany better adaptation under hazardous conditions. A close relationship with a caring and competent adult is widely considered the most important and general protective factor for human development, particularly for younger children who are highly dependent on caregivers. Good cognitive functioning, such as problem-solving skills or good attention regulation, are widely reported as well. This list reflects to some degree the factors that social scientists have studied and it also doubtlessly reflects the preponderance of research on Western cultures in the literature on resilience. Thus, while most of these factors have been observed in non-Western cultures, there may be other common correlates that will be added to this list as the international literature grows.

The big question that arises as one examines this list, is what it may signify. I have suggested that the short list provides important clues to the most fundamental protective systems for human adaptation and development (Masten, 2001).

Table 1. Short list of factors associated with behavioral resilience in children and youth

Relationships and parenting
Strong connections with one or more effective parents.
Parenting quality (providing affection, rules, monitoring, expectations, socialization).
Bonds with other prosocial adults (kinship networks, mentors, elders, teachers).
Connections to prosocial and competent peers.

Individual differences
Learning and problem-solving skills (intelligence).
Self-regulation skills (self-control of attention, emotional, arousal, impulses).
Positive views of the self and one's capabilities (self-efficacy and self-worth).
Positive outlook on life (beliefs that life has meaning, faith, hopefulness).
Appealing qualities (social, academic, athletic, attractive; engaging personality; talents).

Community context
Effective schools.
Opportunities to develop valued skills and talents.
Community quality (safety, collective supervision, positive organizations, emergency services).
Connections to prosocial organizations (clubs, religious groups).
Socioeconomic advantages.

Fundamental adaptive systems in human development

Table 2 presents a list of fundamental adaptive systems implicated by the short list of resilience correlates (Masten, 2001, 2004; Masten & Coatsworth, 1998). I have argued that these systems, the result of biological and cultural evolution, provide children with the capacity for adapting and recovering from a wide range of adversities in the course of development (Masten, 2001). Further, if these systems are operating normally, resilience is common and can be expected. The greatest dangers to children are posed by risks and adversities that damage or disable these protective systems, or prevent them from developing normally. Thus, children who lose or are separated from their parents, or whose brains are damaged as a result of a disaster, are in much graver danger than children who have well-functioning parents and central nervous systems. Similarly, it is possible that adversity interferes with the development of good self-regulation skills, as may happen with early neglect or maltreatment, or the mastery motivation system is "turned off" by an unresponsive environment, as may happen to an infant left alone too much in an orphanage (Masten & Gewirtz, in press).

These circumstances would leave a child highly vulnerable to adversity and poorly equipped for the developmental tasks that lie ahead.

Table 2. Adaptation systems for behavioral resilience implicated by the short list

Attachment relationships providing emotional security and protection.

A family with caregivers providing for survival needs, emotional and physical security, socialization, and social regulation of behavior until self-regulatory systems mature.

A brain in good working order, with information and learning systems operating normally.

Self-control systems working normally, providing for self-regulation of arousal, emotion, behaviour.

A mastery motivational system that is working normally to reward learning and adaptive behaviour.

Cultural systems of belief and practice, including religion and religious organizations.

Social systems that nurture and support fundamental developmental systems, including schools.

Community safety and emergency service systems.

Developmental windows of change—risks and opportunities

There is currently great interest in the possibility that there are windows of risk and vulnerability over the course of development, when many systems pertinent to adaptation are in flux and may be particularly primed for change, for better or worse (Masten, 2004). Some of these windows may arise from biologically driven developmental changes, resulting from pubertal processes or normal brain development, while others result from culturally based changes in context or expectations (Dahl & Spear, 2004; Steinberg et al., in press). The transitions of early and late adolescence, for example, including the transition to secondary schooling, puberbal changes, driving, becoming sexually active, or moving away from home, may convey vulnerability for some problems and risky behaviours, but also provide opportunities for positive change as well (Masten, 2004; Masten, Obradovic, & Burt, in press). As the brain matures, the full interconnectivity and efficiency of the executive systems become available to support self-regulation and planning in new and more adaptive ways, without the scaffolding of adults. The neurobiology of resilience is an exciting frontier of contemporary research and theory (Curtis & Cicchetti, 2003; Luthar, in press; Masten, 2004).

A resilience framework for promoting child welfare

Resilience research continues to accumulate rapidly (see Luthar, in press), although there is much work remaining, both to describe the many processes that may account for naturally occurring resilience and to experimentally induce resilience through intervention. Nonetheless, the consistency of the findings on resilience and the success of early experiments to promote competence and resilience in children and youth have yielded important clues about processes and a general framework for thinking about interventions to promote and protect resilience among children at risk for a variety of reasons (Masten, 2001; Masten & Powell, 2003). Indeed, it could be argued that a generation of attention to resilience in the lives of children and youth has had a transformational influence on the conceptual framework for many aspects of practice (Masten, 2001; Masten & Powell, 2003; Yates & Masten, 2004a, b). At the heart of this transformation is a shift to include more positive approaches in the mission, models, measures and methods of practice. Each aspect of this transformation can be observed across many web sites, books, and conferences on the LAC system, including the chapters of this volume and the conference which preceded it.

Mission: Framing positive objectives

In a resilience framework for practice, the goals of the intervention or program are stated in positive terms, often focused on promoting positive adaptation or development. Promoting resilience goes beyond the prevention of problems, setting positive outcome and process goals. Thus, a program to prevent delinquency or reduce school dropout may state goals in terms of promoting positive school involvement, prosocial friendships, academic achievement, or increasing high school graduation rates. Meeting these objectives can then be evaluated at the individual and aggregate level. The LAC system exemplifies this shift through positive mottos ("good parenting—good outcomes") and mission statements ("designed to improve the parenting experience of children looked after by welfare agencies"). As was noted in the first issue of the newsletter, *Looking After Children: Canadian Update*, published by the Child Welfare League of Canada (2002), "The LAC project also suggested a move away from the traditional goal of reducing harm to the more positive, pro-active concept of maximizing positive outcomes" (p. 1).

Positive goals are consistent with the evidence concerning the role of positive achievements and processes in resilience and problem prevention. Moreover, the marketing appeal to stakeholders of positive goals may be considerable (Masten & Powell, 2003). Programs to promote healthy development, academic achievement, work success or civic engagement are more appealing and less stigmatizing than programs to prevent violence or failure in high-risk children and youth.

Models: Including the promotive, adaptive, and protective

The models of change in a resilience-framed program emphasize positive predictors, processes, and outcomes, along with risks, vulnerabilities, and negative processes. Whether they are described as strengths, assets, resources, or protective factors, human or social capital, adaptive or protective processes, resilience-framed models include positive change agents and the possibility of positive change through intervention. Resilience models also encompass positive outcomes. LAC models convey a positive model of change through statements like this: "LAC promotes resilience by emphasizing the development of competence…through effective partnerships…good parenting and high expectations." The general LAC model reflects a theory of positive development that emphasizes the role of parenting quality and stability for children's success in achieving age-salient developmental tasks, and also the importance of partnership, consistency, and continuity of care in providing the quality of care children require for healthy development (Flynn et al., 2004).

Measures: Assessing resources, competence, and positive change

The positive goals and processes of a resilience-based program require measures that extend beyond symptoms, problems, disorders, and risk factors to assess progress on positive criteria of child development. Such criteria include success in implementing a positive change, building more capacity or assets in a child's life, mobilizing powerful protective systems, such as an individual's child's sense of mastery, attachment relationship between a child and a caregiver or mentor, faith and hope in the future, or bonding to prosocial peers or schools. It is particularly important to assess well-being and competence on age-salient developmental tasks, and not simply psychopathology.

One of the major features of the LAC system has been the commitment to assessment and the widespread dissemination of practical tools and processes by which to monitor progress and improvement in children and the systems of care designed to promote their welfare. The tools developed as part of LAC to provide consistent assessment and monitoring have focused on "seven developmental dimensions of well being" for six specific age groups. These dimensions (health, education, identity, family and social relationships, social presentation, emotional and behavioral development, and self-care skills) encompass many of the developmental tasks identified by developmental researchers as central to competence (Flynn et al., 2004). As evident in many chapters of this volume, there has been wide acceptance among multiple stakeholders (including young people themselves) of these dimensions as a meaningful framework for assessing children (and the systems that serve them), notwithstanding concerns about implementation and fidelity issues, such as completion rates in practice (Bailey, Thoburn, & Wakeham, 2002). In addition, it is becoming standard practice to judge the status and progress of children in care against population norms, rather than relative standing as compared to other high-risk children; increasingly LAC tools incorporate such population-normed items (Flynn, et al., 2004).

The LAC assessment tools and the comprehensive Assessment and Action Record (AAR) may also function as *facilitators of system change* by: directing attention and resources to important dimensions of child functioning and positive goals; providing a systematic way of documenting multiple dimensions of positive outcome; highlighting the promotive or protective factors that children need for positive development; and serving to systematically track progress, not only of children in care but also of the systems involved in their care. In their chapter, for example, Klein, Kufeldt and Rideout (this volume) describe the benefits of the AAR recording and monitoring system as a tool for encouraging good practice and also as a supportive system for the parents and clinicians who use the system. Similarly, in their respective chapters, authors Khoo, Nygren and Hyvonen, and authors Drolet and Sauvé-Kobylecki, have noted ways that AARs are showing utility for practice, management and policy, as well as for the assessment of outcomes for children in care. Even the research to improve and adapt the AAR tool has the potential to influence the quality of care, as the items become more sensitive and valid for assessing the needs and progress of children in care, as well as measuring their satisfaction with placements (e.g., see research on the second Canadian adaptation, the AAR-C2, in chapters 11 and 17 by Flynn and colleagues).

Methods: Reducing risk, increasing resources, and engaging powerful adaptive systems

Resilience data and models suggest the possibility of multiple strategies for promoting positive adaptation or development, differing in the targeted process, outcome, or timing. Many models of resilience include some combination of negative and positive influences, expressed as risks versus assets or resources, vulnerabilities versus protective factors, or more complex combinations of direct, mediating, and moderating effects (Masten, 2001; Masten & Shaffer, in press). These models suggest three basic strategies for intervention: reducing risk effects; boosting resource effects; and protecting, restoring, or engaging the powerful adaptive systems that normally protect human functioning and development. Efforts to reduce risk effects attempt to lower the exposure to negative events, experiences, or conditions, ranging from the prevention of premature births to the prevention of drunken driving accidents in teenagers. Efforts to boost assets and resources represent attempts to promote good outcomes by providing more of whatever may be needed for a child to adapt and succeed, varying from a stable home to a tutor or a college tuition scholarship to a case manager. Strategies that target major adaptive systems represent efforts to ensure that the most fundamental and often multifaceted protections are working for a child's benefit. Foster care and mentoring programs for high-risk children, for example, represent significant efforts to provide a child with a protective adult or attachment relationship; these kinds of programs are designed to provide children with a secure base and all of the potential positive influences afforded by an active adult who can function as advocate, role model, resource broker, emotional and behavioral regulator, etc. A variation on this strategy is to protect or promote the effectiveness of relationships or protective systems that are already part of a child's life. Risks and threats in life often harm children indirectly by damaging key adaptive systems for children, as when a parent is harmed or unable to function. Some of the most effective interventions for children have targeted their parents, in an effort to improve or protect the quality of the parent's functioning during a challenging time (Masten & Shaffer, in press).

Preventive interventions for children with high cumulative risk often adopt combined strategies that blend all three of these basic approaches. The LAC approach is designed around a model of good parental care that requires multifaceted efforts to reduce the risks of unstable or poor-quality care, improve access to resources based on needs, and to provide continuity of high-quality care and effective parenting. To do so, the LAC approach has focused on strategies to ensure that the integrated systems of care for child welfare are operating well through training, partnership, evaluation, and assessment. In essence, the LAC approach was designed to ensure that a child welfare system operates like a fundamental human adaptive system, so that taking a child into care would improve the odds for resilience, rather than increase a child's risk. It is too soon to evaluate how well that ambitious goal has been met in the many regions and nations around the world that have adopted the LAC approach. That is an empirical question. Nonetheless, the LAC approach provides a striking illustration of how a resilience framework might be applied in practice and also how its success might be evaluated.

Conclusion

As research on resilience accrues, a resilience framework for practice and policy is beginning to take shape. Positive goals, models, measures, and methods are included more systematically in interventions to promote child welfare. International efforts to implement more positive approaches to child welfare (including applications of the Looking After Children approach to systems of care) reflect both a profound transformation in approach to interventions for children that is better grounded in theories and evidence about positive human development and the adaptive systems that support the development of competence and resilience. Nonetheless, there is much work ahead to understand the processes of positive development and change, at multiple levels. Resilience research to date has focused predominantly on individual and family processes, particularly psychosocial processes, and very little on the role of biological, cultural or community systems, including systems for child welfare and education. Experiments to create resilience through interventions at many levels with diverse methods, including integrated systems of care, are just beginning—though progress can be observed in many spheres of activity, as evident across the chapters of this volume. We stand on the threshold of a new age of resilience-focused research and practice that holds the promise of deepening our understanding of what makes a difference in the lives of children and our effectiveness in promoting positive adaptive systems and healthy child development.

References

Bailey, S., Thoburn, J., & Wakeham, H. (2002). Using the "Looking After Children" dimensions to collect aggregate data on well-being. *Child and Family Social Work, 7*, 189–191.

Child Welfare League of Canada. (2002). Looking After Children. *Looking After Children: Canadian Update, 1*, 1–6.

Curtis, W. J., & Cicchetti, D. (2003). Moving research on resilience into the 21st century: Theoretical and methodological considerations in examining the biological contributors to resilience. *Development and Psychopathology, 15,* 773–810.

Dahl, R. E., & Spear, L. P. (Eds.). (2004). *Adolescent brain development: Vulnerabilities and opportunities* (Vol. 1021). New York: New York Academy of Sciences.

Drolet, M., & Sauvé-Kobylecki, M. (2006). The needs of children in care and the Looking After Children approach: Steps towards promoting children's best interests. In R. J. Flynn, P. M. Dudding, & J. G. Barber (Eds.), *Promoting reslience in child welfare.* Ottawa: University of Ottawa Press.

Flynn, R. J., Ghazal, H., Legault, L., Vandermeulen, G., & Petrick, S. (2004). Use of population measures and norms to identify resilient outcomes in young people in care: An exploratory study. *Child and Family Social Work, 9,* 65–79.

Flynn, R. J., Robitaille, A., & Ghazal, H. (2006). Placement satisfaction of young people living in foster or group homes. In R. J. Flynn, P. M. Dudding, & J. G. Barber (Eds.), *Promoting resilience in child welfare.* Ottawa: University of Ottawa Press.

Garmezy, N. (1974). The study of competence in children at risk for severe psychopathology. In A. Koupernik (Ed.), *The child in his family: Children at psychiatric risk* (Vol. 3, pp. 77–97). New York: Wiley.

Garmezy, N. (1985). Stress-resistant children: The search for protective factors. In J. E. Stevenson (Ed.), *Recent research in developmental psychopathology: Journal of Child Psychology and Psychiatry book supplement* #5 (pp. 213–233). Oxford: Pergamon Press.

Garmezy, N., & Rutter, M. (1983). *Stress, coping and development in children.* New York: McGraw-Hill.

Khoo, E., Nygren, L., & Hyvonen, U. (2006). Resilient society or resilient children? A comparison of child welfare service orientations in Sweden and Ontario, Canada. In R. J. Flynn, P. M. Dudding, & J. G. Barber (Eds.), *Promoting resilience in child welfare.* Ottawa: University of Ottawa Press.

Klein, R., Kufeldt, K., & Rideout, S. (2006). Resilience theory and its relevance for child welfare ptactice. In R. J. Flynn, P. M. Dudding, & J. G. Barber (Eds.), *Promoting resilience in child welfare.* Ottawa: University of Ottawa Press.

Luthar, S. S. (in press). Resilience in development: A synthesis of research across five decades. In D. Cicchetti & D. J. Cohen (Eds.), *Developmental psychopathology: Risk, disorder, and adaptation* (2nd ed., Vol. 3). New York: Wiley.

Masten, A. S. (1999). Resilience comes of age: Reflections on the past and outlook for the next generation of research. In M. D. Glantz, J. Johnson, & L. Huffman (Eds.), *Resilience and development: Positive life adaptations* (pp. 289–296). New York: Plenum.

Masten, A. S. (2001). Ordinary magic: Resilience processes in development. *American Psychologist, 56*, 227–238.

Masten, A. S. (2004). Regulatory processes, risk and resilience in adolescent development. *Annals of the New York Academy of Sciences, 1021*(1–11), 1–25.

Masten, A. S., Best, K. M., & Garmezy, N. (1990). Resilience and development: Contributions from the study of children who overcome adversity. *Development and Psychopathology, 2*, 425–444.

Masten, A. S., & Coatsworth, J. D. (1998). The development of competence in favorable and unfavorable environments: Lessons from research on successful children. *American Psychologist, 53*, 205–220.

Masten, A. S., & Gewirtz, A. H. (in press). Vulnerability and resilience in early child development. In K. McCartney & D. A. Phillips (Eds.), *Handbook of early childhood development*. Oxford, UK: Blackwell.

Masten, A. S., Morison, P., Pellegrini, D., & Tellegen, A. (1990). Competence under stress: Risk and protective factors. In J. Rolf, A. S. Masten, D. Cicchetti, K. Nuechterlein & S. Weintraub (Eds.), *Risk and protective factors in the development of psychopathology* (pp. 236–256). New York: Cambridge University Press.

Masten, A. S., Obradovic, J., & Burt, K. (in press). Resilience in emerging adulthood. In J. J. Arnett & J. Tanner (Eds.), *Growing into adulthood: The lives and contexts of emerging adults*. Washington, DC: American Psychological Association Press.

Masten, A. S., & Powell, J. L. (2003). A resilience framework for research, policy, and practice. In S. S. Luthar (Ed.), *Resilience and vulnerability: Adaptation in the context of childhood adversities* (pp. 1–25). New York: Cambridge University Press.

Masten, A. S., & Reed, M.-G. J. (2002). Resilience in development. In C. R. Snyder & S. J. Lopez (Eds.), *Handbook of positive psychology* (pp. 74–88). London: Oxford University Press.

Masten, A. S., & Shaffer, A. (in press). How families matter in child development: Reflections from research on risk and resilience. In C.-S. A. & J. Dunn (Eds.), *Families count: Effects on child and adolescent development*. Cambridge: Cambridge University Press.

Masten, A. S., & Wright, M. O. D. (1998). Cumulative risk and protection models of child maltreatment. *Journal of Aggression, Maltreatment & Trauma, 2*(1), 7–30.

Murphy, L. B., & Moriarty, A. E. (1976). *Vulnerability, coping, and growth: From infancy to adolescence.* New Haven: Yale University Press.

Newman, T. (2004). *What works in building resilience?* Ilford, Essex, England: Barnardo's.

Pantin, S., Flynn, R. J., & Runnels, V. (2006). Training, experience, and supervision: Keys to enhancing the utility of Assessment and Action Record in implementing Looking After Children. In R. J. Flynn, P. M. Dudding, & J. G. Barber (Eds.), *Promoting resilience in child welfare*. Ottawa: University of Ottawa Press.

Parker, R., Ward, H., Jackson, S., Aldgate, J., & Wedge, P. (1991). *Looking After Children: Assessing outcomes in child care.* London: Her Majesty's Stationery Office.

Rutter, M. (1979). Protective factors in children's responses to stress and disadvantage. *Annals of the Academy of Medicine, Singapore, 8,* 324–338.

Rutter, M. (1990). Psychosocial resilience and protective mechanisms. In J. Rolf, A. S. Masten, D. Cicchetti, K. H. Nuechterlein, & S. Weintraub (Eds.), *Risk and protective factors in the development of psychopathology* (pp. 181–214). New York: Cambridge University Press.

Steinberg, L., Dahl, R. E., Keating, D., Kupfer, D. J., & Masten, A. S. (in press). The study of developmental psychopathology in adolescence: Integrating affective neuroscience with the study of context. In D. Ciccheti & D. Cohen (Eds.), *Handbook of developmental psychopathology* (2nd ed.). New York: Wiley.

Ward, H. (1995). *Looking After Children: Research into practice. The second report to the Department of Health on assessing outcomes in child care.* London: HMSO.

Werner, E. E., & Smith, R. S. (1982). *Vulnerable but invincible: A study of resilient children.* New York: McGraw-Hill.

Wright, M. O. D., & Masten, A. S. (2005). Resilience processes in development: Fostering positive adaptation in the context of adversity. In S. Goldstein & R. Brooks (Eds.), *Handbook of resilience in children.* New York: Kluwer Academic/Plenum.

Yates, T. M., & Masten, A. S. (2004a). Fostering the future: Resilience theory and the practice of positive psychology. In P. A. Linley & S. Joseph (Eds.), *Positive psychology in practice.* Hoboken, NJ: Wiley.

Yates, T. M., & Masten, A. S. (2004b). Prologue: The promise of resilience research for practice and policy. In T. Newman, *What works in building resilience?* (pp. 6–15). Ilford, Essex, UK: Barnardo's.

CHAPTER 2

Promoting resilience and permanence in child welfare

Robbie Gilligan

Addressing issues of loss

On a recent holiday here in Ireland, my wife and I stopped at the local garage in a small village for some assistance with our car. The owner was friendly but subdued. He explained that the whole community was deeply affected by the death a day or two previously of a local 19-year-old in a car crash. The young man at one point had worked in his garage. The funeral was to take place that evening. Together the three of us contemplated the horror for the young man's parents of the loss they had endured. "They'll never be the same" this garage owner said. "They'll improve—but they'll never be the same." This is a very profound comment from an apparently simple, but clearly very sophisticated man.

Many children in care may never be the same—following the enormity of their loss. They may have to learn to endure the *ongoingness of withoutness,* to quote the memorable phrase of a woman writing about coping with life after the death of her 11-year-old son (Vincent, 1998). Life may never be the same after a grievous loss. And we must remember that the loss of parents who are still alive may actually be harder to accept or come to terms with than the more logical and legitimate loss of parents through death (Eagle, 1994).

Yet a young person in care may face a heightened risk not only of loss, but also of social isolation. The young person may end up with a smaller social network than an equivalent young person not in care. A restricted social network may lead to a reduced range of social roles. In the absence of additional or alternative social roles, the young person may develop a consuming and stigmatized master-identity as "young person in care" that comes to dominate their sense of self. Their in-care status may also lead to excessive reliance on formal services which may be both a cause—and consequence—of weaker access to informal social support. The young person may also have a narrower base of positive role models on whom to draw personally for guidance, inspiration and encouragement.

Those of us working with young people in care must be sensitive to the possible risk for these young people of being entrapped in a ghetto populated almost exclusively by young people in care or their carers—a ghetto that may lead on to longer-term social exclusion on many fronts. At worst, we must strive to protect young people in care or leaving care from an "endless tundra of aloneness and loneliness" to quote a telling phrase of the Irish playwright, Brian Friel.[1] This "endless tundra" of loneliness may be a real risk if we are not very active in promoting and preserving social connections for all young persons as they grow up.

I am reminded here of the young woman—let's call her "Annie"—at a little low-key leaving-care graduation party in her honour.[2] There was a very positive atmosphere and she joined in the speeches to say a few words reflecting on her experience. Looking around the room, she said, "All my friends are adults." Most of the people present were adults from the services who had helped her along the way. She meant the comment appreciatively and affectionately, but there was certainly another very telling way to read it. Her story illustrates the risk of restricted social networks, excessive reliance on formal services and the master identity of being in care. Immersion in professional service systems may risk cutting young people off from peers and natural networks.

A young adult who had grown up in the care system in Australia touches on the same issue. He was contemplating marrying the mother of his child, but he said he would have "no one to invite to the wedding" (Maunders et al., 1999). A challenge for those concerned with the lives of young people in care is to ensure that young care leavers do indeed have social networks that can yield up a potential list of invitees to their wedding. I want to suggest that a sense of "belonging" should become very central in thinking about the needs of young people in care.

Raymond Carver, the great American writer and poet, addresses this issue of belonging—a central question for all of us—in his poem "Late Fragment":[3]

And did you get what
You wanted from this life, even so?
I did.
And what did you want?
To call myself beloved, to feel myself
Beloved on the earth.

These are profound questions for every human being, but they seem especially challenging for those of us concerned with young people in care. Can they call themselves "beloved"? Do they *feel* themselves "beloved"? Is the legacy of our work with them that they are connected into such enduring relationships? Is the legacy of our work with them that they are able to sustain, and be nurtured in, these enduring relationships?

One of my key arguments in this paper is that we must be both humble and flexible in how we go about helping build this legacy of relationships for a young person in care. Humility makes sense because we quickly know how challenging this task is. Flexibility makes sense because one size will not fit all. Youngsters come in different sizes and different circumstances, and need different responses. To quote a mother making a good job of rearing her teenage boy in the unforgiving and violent streets of inner city Philadephia, "You have to be flexible, because life is flexible." She was talking to researcher Frank Furstenberg and his colleagues (1999) about her approach to parenting and the dilemmas she found. Her advice seems well suited to the challenges of providing well for young people in care.

Where are youngsters in care to find these relationships? It is hoped that they will find them with their primary carers, and possibly also in their family of origin. But they may also find positive and influential relationships in other settings—in school, for example. We should be open to finding such potential relationships wherever they may lie waiting to be tapped. We should look "wherever life pours *ordinary plenty*" to quote our much-loved Irish poet, Patrick Kavanagh.[4]

Part of the *ordinary plenty* that life may pour may include the example and encouragement of key role models in a young person's life and indeed of key relationships that the young person may observe. Yugoslav-Australian philosopher Raimond Gaita[5] has written a wonderful reflection on his life growing up in his migrant family in Australia and his relationship with his father, who for much of the time was a lone parent. His account has a great deal to say about resilient development in the face of much adversity. He was close not only to his father, but also to his father's best (male) friend. In the book, *Romulus My Father*, he acknowledges the debt he owes both men for their influence and for the quality of the men's friendship and its impact on him as a young boy:

> On many occasions in my life I have had the need to say, and thankfully have been able to say: I know what a good workman is; I know what an honest man is; I know what friendship is; I know because I remember these things in the person of my father, in the person of his friend Hora, and in the example of their friendship.

I think these powerful and moving lines from Raimond Gaita speak strongly to our work with young people in care. Through our efforts, are youngsters in care endowed with at least some abiding images and experiences that help to steer them through life?

The power of such relationships can reach beyond the grave as Irish poet, Seamus Heaney, reminds us in his short poem "1.1.87" (in *Seeing Things*). I suggest that it is in part an acknowledgement to his late father for the sense of being supported that he has inherited.

"1.1.87"

Dangerous pavements.
But I face the ice this year
With my father's stick

Life's *ordinary plenty* to be found in many places

Part of life's *ordinary plenty* may lie waiting to be tapped in school. And the benefits flowing from different aspects of school may be felt well into adulthood. A major New Zealand study of adult women who were victims of childhood sexual abuse found that positive school experiences in any one of the academic, sporting or social spheres were among the influences that helped those of the women who had largely recovered from the experience (Romans et al., 1995).

Clearly, such benefits from school experience extend to those enduring adversities other than sexual abuse, as the story of Debra Fearn testifies. Debra Fearn grew up in care in England and now lectures in a university there. In this quotation, she reflects on the help she received from a teacher, as she coped with life in care:

> …the intervention of my English teacher has helped shape the person I am today.
>
> She became a "surrogate" mother to me in many ways, with very little effort it seemed at the time. However looking back, she put in time and energy over and above what could be expected. She saw a "spark" in me and for the next seven years, ensured that the spark became a flame that did not extinguish itself. She believed in me, and gave me courage and a belief in myself that could have easily been lost along the way.
>
> When I failed Maths and French at "O" Level, she ensured that I received extra tuition after school, and she gave me the belief that I would be successful the second time around. In addition, she gave me extra handwriting lessons, and these were crucial in helping me to pass French especially. My handwriting was neat but very, very small, so these extra lessons made a vital difference.
>
> What makes her stand out in my mind is that she cared for me and she liked me. She was my friend, so even though she did not teach me

for two years, she had regular informal chats with me, and kept an eye on my progress. Other teachers were an important influence on me, too, and they played their part in making school an enjoyable experience, but Mrs. Hoole walked the extra mile that made the difference."[6]

I recount this story, not to imply that every teacher lies waiting to play such a role (though quite a few may do so), but more that Mrs. Hoole is but one example of the range of adults, beyond those in primary care giving roles, who may play a key role in a young person's positive development. What is also significant is that such a key role may need only to be played over a selected period. Enduring effect does not necessarily need very long-lasting involvement.

Relationships with other adults beyond home and school may also yield enduring benefits. For example, an adult from a young person's extended family or social network may play a mentoring role in helping the young person to develop a skill or interest. These opportunities often present unexpectedly—and the trick is to not let them pass by. One illustration of this involves a grandfather, who had been a French polisher (specialized polisher of fine furniture). He began to teach his skills to his grandson who was an adolescent living in a residential unit. The head of the household allowed the youngster to use "a shed out the back" to practise his newfound skill. He was able to get some work from staff and neighbours. This was an example of the professional—the head of the household—using his influence to release positive energy in the grandfather-grandson relationship and add a resource that assisted the fullest exploitation (in the best sense) of what the grandfather had to offer. Lending the shed seems to reflect professional practice of a very high standard, a practice sensitive to the layers of meaning in the grandfather's generosity to his grandson. This transmission of a skill was not only giving the young person a social niche, a meaningful role, a means of enhancing self-esteem and self efficacy. It was also helping the youngster to connect with traditions in his family of origin and thereby assisting his sense of belonging and identity as part of that family grouping. It was also helping the boy ease into the world of work. He ultimately found a niche as a French polisher in adulthood.

The value of hobbies/interest and associated social roles

As the story above indicates, part of life's *ordinary plenty* may also lie in hobbies/interests and activities that may attract the interest of a young person.

Another nice example of this comes from the story of a young boy who had been in residential care and at the age of 9 or 10 went to a foster family. He was a shy boy and inclined to be a loner in school and at home. It happened that the foster father was interested in tropical fish and soon the boy became interested too. He became so enthusiastic that he got other boys at school interested and they formed a tropical fish club; he began to write to pen pals abroad who were also tropical fish fans. And he also got himself a job over two summers in the local pet shop because he knew so much about tropical fish. After a few years the placement broke down. The social worker collected him in her car to move him to the next placement; and the foster father drove behind with the boy's tank of tropical fish.

If nothing else, the boy had acquired a potential lifelong interest and had been helped to tap into social relationships and social roles a long way from life in care. Clearly, the boy had gained from the placement in many ways, but the tropical fish seemed an especially important legacy. These fish—and the foster carers—had helped him to escape the ghetto of care. They helped him to shed the master identity of "boy-in-care," or perhaps more accurately "depressed-boy-in-care," if the truth were told. These fish and the foster carers also helped him to acquire the experience of roles as part-time worker in a pet shop, pen pal, tropical fish expert, club organiz-er in school, and friend. This set of new roles may have served to boost his morale, even temporarily, and offered him an important sense of what might be possible in the future. This story of minding goldfish reminds us of the potentially therapeutic power of what, on the surface, may seem sim-ple or mundane experience in children's daily lives.

This story illustrates that by managing to build on even one positive factor in a child's circumstances, this may prove a turning point onto a more positive pathway or into a positive upward spiral of change (Clausen, 1995). One thing going well may change a child's perception of him or her-self, and what is possible (Gilligan, 2001). More important even, it may challenge negative expectations of others about that child.

These stories of progress stemming from school, hobbies and part-time work chime with the research findings of Vaillant and Vaillant (1981). They found that what they termed "childhood industry" was associated with bet-ter mental health, better inter-personal relationships, and better work expe-riences for men who had grown up in high-crime neighbourhoods in inner-city Boston. By this they meant men who as children had showed a capacity to be active on a range of fronts, that is, in regular part-time work, household chores, school achievement, and involvement in extra-curricu-lar activities. So encouraging young people in care to be active and to dis-play initiative and self-efficacy at home, in school, and in the wider world may have an important later pay-off for them.

In thinking about how to help promote protective factors for young people in care, it is worth recalling that people live their lives in a number of domains: home, school, neighbourhood, peer group, recreational activities, part-time work. The challenge is to find and support positives in at least one of these domains. Supportive resources in even one domain may help the young person to cope with negative forces in another (Brodsky, 1999). Good times in school may, for example, help a child to cope with bad times at home. Doing well in a part-time job may help a young person to counteract negative experiences in school or home. What we have to do is help troubled youngsters to find what have been termed "arenas of comfort" in their lives (Simmons & Blyth [1987], in Thiede Call, 1996). It may well be that at times, the child's "arena of comfort" may lie outside the family or the residential unit or foster home. For many children, a key "arena of comfort" may be school or some part of school that works well for them.

These different domains or arena of comfort offer opportunities to play different social roles of, for example, neighbour, student, part-time worker, sports committee member. These roles help to generate relationships.[7] It is hoped that one or more of these relationships may yield up positive turning point experiences as in Debra Fearn's relationship with her teacher, Mrs Hoole. The role identity associated with each of these roles also helps to dilute any oppressive master-identity such as that of "young person in care."

Valuing children's capacity

Part of valuing life's ordinary plenty is also about recognizing and valuing the child or young person's own capacity or agency. Children and young people are active agents in their own development. They are not passive bystanders in their own growth and progress. They are not passive receptacles into which adults pour experiences. They are not wholly dependent. Children are active players in the search for their own destiny. Children help to shape the relationships they have with the people around them. We must avoid the trap of overlooking the child's capacity, the child's views and the child's concerns.

In a recent workshop I ran, a professional told a very personal story that underlines this point. She spoke of how she is a lone parent and of how a couple of years earlier she had received a diagnosis of cancer. She told her three children the news. They were obviously shocked but they put on a brave face. But what she didn't know, until six months later when the news about her condition was much brighter, was that the children had indeed been very worried. But they had judged it best to shield her from that worry. With better news about the cancer, they were now able to admit to her that they had talked a lot amongst themselves and with best friends about their concerns and fears. They had also discussed at length about who would mind them after she died. These three children were then aged between 7 and 11. The woman who told this story said she had learned deep lessons about how much is going on in children's minds beyond what adults can see, and about how resourceful children can be.

Let us not underestimate the impact of life events on children's inner worlds, nor their capacity to sometimes shield us from what is going on in that inner world. And further let us not underestimate children's capacity to come up with thoughtful, resourceful and intelligent responses to their predicaments. This is not to put the onus on the young person for his or her own salvation, but it is to say that we should not exclude the young person's expertise.

This story of the children's courage, self-reliance and good judgement also underlines the powerful support siblings may render each other in conditions of adversity. Preserving sibling ties may be a very important service to children in our care, as siblings are likely to be around for the "long haul" and probably understand the realities of a child's history and experience better than anyone else.

Reflections on the meanings of permanence

In thinking about permanence, it seems important to look at it from the child's perspective, rather than merely from that of the placing agency. Rather than thinking of permanence as a merely a legal or administrative concept or threshold, we should also think of it as a psychological state— and a state that must, crucially, be assessed by its incumbent. The child's subjective sense of the placement is critical. So also is the question of how isolated the child would be if the placement proves not to endure.

Permanence needs to be considered in terms of two different axes—stability (staying put) and continuity (staying connected). It also needs to be considered how accessible permanent placements actually are for the broad mass of children in care, and how sustainable permanent placements are for run-of-the-mill entrants to care from home, especially for those who are a little older. No one can reasonably challenge the intention of permanence, but it is prudent to ask questions about its coverage and durability, especially since it has been such a powerful paradigm in child welfare planning. What proportion of children benefit from a permanent placement? What proportion enjoy strong ties to their new family well into adulthood?

I would like to stress the continuity axis in thinking about permanence, about the significance of continuity of key connections in the child's life. In that regard, perhaps we should consider three dimensions to permanence or "connectedness": first, the child's *subjective sense* of whether it exists for him or her; second, the *cultural connectedness* between the child's background and the "permanence placement" and *social connectedness* between the child's original social network and the "permanence placement."

In my teaching, I like to rely on a horticultural metaphor to illustrate my argument. No attempt to transplant a tree or shrub is easy, and certainly (I speak as a purely theoretical gardener!) it can only be contemplated if a lot of original soil surrounding the roots goes to the new site of planting. Similarly, I propose that the child needs to bring a sufficient amount of emotional soil from the old site to the new, if the new placement is to have a chance of taking hold.

The basis of viable permanence lies in a sustainable combination of affection and obligation arising from psychosocial ties and/or from cultural roles and commitments. People have or develop a long-term commitment to a child arising from some combination of love and a sense of duty. But these may not be enough to see a placement through to successful permanence.

A key challenge in planning for permanence or "connectedness," I want to propose, is ensuring that there are second-tier supports—people who can step into the breach if the placement breaks down. By stepping into the breach, I do not necessarily mean becoming the new replacement primary caregiver, but at least by acting as some kind of "guarantor" for the child's well-being. Some commentators propose the goal of permanence as being a "family for life." In one sense, no one in his or her right mind could dispute the worth of that aim. My question is what happens if no family emerges or the family evaporates because of problems of whatever kind. My suggestions would be that we should be aiming for a "network for life" for every child, not just a family for life for some fortunate children.

In assessing the reality of permanence in a given case, we might ask whether the child has sustained access to people who will feel a sense of obligation to the child? And whether there are such people with whom the child has an actual or potential mutual commitment based on shared affection or complementary social or cultural ties? Whether there are people who can work alongside the primary carers without undermining their position or competing with them? And whether there are already people who provide a brief haven from storms that may blow up in the relationship between the young person and the carer?

I am thinking here not of some new corps of volunteers specially recruited and assigned; rather, of the kind of people who may naturally belong to young people's natural networks: siblings, aunts, grandparents, work colleagues, friends or the family of friends, people who belong to the same faith community, people who are members of the same sports club, or people who have taken on an informal mentoring role in the young person's life.

Good planning is focused not only on this placement, nor only on securing the desired permanent placement. It is also, I am suggesting, about cultivating ties to a set of network members, any one or more of whom may step in or be accessible where required, while the young person is under 18, or in young adulthood. Good planning is about identifying possible (what we might call) "guarantors"—people who may display and honour a commitment to the young person in adolescence—or later life—as required. These "guarantors" would be people to whom the young person feels a connection—one that makes an approach for, or an offer of, help or support seem natural and unobtrusive. The term "guarantor" is chosen deliberately. These "guarantors" could play a dual role in helping to protect the young person from the "endless tundra of loneliness" that might otherwise be his or her fate. They could serve as points of connection; and they could also serve as conduits through which the young person could tap into other parts of his or her social network. They can help the young person to stay connected to other parts of his or her social and cultural networks.

Importantly, their commitment to the young person arises not from a professional or formal role from which the person, realistically, may exit, or the mandate for which may run out. Long term, the young person may be guaranteed more from a commitment that arises from emotional or cultural ties rather than one that flows from bureaucratic roles or procedures. This is not to criticize or dismiss what professionals bring; it is merely recognizing the reality of the inevitable—and appropriate—limitations of their engagement. The professionals' role, I would propose, is to cultivate the "guarantors," not to displace them.

Research on social support yields up a key insight that a perception that support will be available when required is crucial to the sense of being supported, quite apart from the issue of using enacted support when actually required. All of this leads to the conclusion that valuing and cultivating a "social network" of concerned adults for each young person is important. Where are such adults to be found? Perhaps in the nuclear or extended family of origin (older siblings grandparents, aunts), in school, in the neighbourhood of origin, in families of friends. It is important that decisions made at critical junctures not have the effect of physically or morally excluding such network members from a potential role. We need to think *both/and* rather than *either/or* in our search for appropriate adults to play caring and supportive roles in a young person's life. We also need to think long term, not just about this placement, or what gets us through to 18, or what gets us through the early years of after-care. If we are truly concerned with the quality and impact of the care experience, we must be looking at the pathways of development and support for young people from the care system as they grow into middle adulthood.

Life in care as living between two worlds

How we think about the two worlds of the child in care is very central to our overall approach and I want to explore this issue a little by beginning with another story.

When I was a young boy, my parents brought me on holidays a number of times to the north coast of Ireland. I have many good memories of those times. A wonderful television documentary I saw in the weeks before writing this paper brought some of those memories back to me. The program[8] was about the story of the Morrelli family who have long run a very successful ice cream business in Northern Ireland. I had enjoyed their ice cream on many occasions on those childhood holidays. The Morrellis were economic migrants who had moved from Italy in the early 1900s. The family's story of migration is one that will be familiar to many readers.

The main figure of the television story was Angelo Morrelli, who in the program was a very fit 95 years of age. Having built up an ice cream empire, originally founded in 1911, he has now retired to his home town of Cassalattico in Italy. The documentary brought home the very strong ties between life in Italy and Ireland for this family. And one of Angelo's sons made clear that although he had lived most of his life in Ireland, he would still cheer for Italy whenever they might be playing an Irish team. You may reasonably be wondering how this story of Italy, ice cream and Ireland relates to my theme.

The family is certainly an excellent example of resilience in how this extended family transcended economic adversity in their home community by emigrating to Northern Ireland and by adapting so well to the opportunities life presented them. But it also illustrates wonderfully the possibility of living between two worlds, of how (at least some) exiles may resolve their dilemma of where they belong. Indeed, another man of Italian descent in Northern Ireland, Leo D'Agostino, has described this pattern of episodic migration between two worlds by using the Italian verb for commuting: *fare il pendolare*.[9] The cultural riches of these Italians living between two worlds certainly reinforces for me the idea that it may be enriching for our children in care to be allowed to live (in some senses) in two worlds—in both of which we hope they can have a strong sense of belonging. It is clear that the Morrelli family members used both worlds—Italy and Ireland—to draw on the social and cultural support and consolation that they needed at different stages of life. They were able to draw emotional and practical support from both worlds. This living between two worlds may be very testing at times, but it may also be enriching especially if there are nurturing sources within both worlds.

What is very impressive about the stories of these particular Italian migrants is their deep sense of past and of belonging to that past. For them the past seems to be a well from which they can draw. What is also striking is how frequently in the history of child welfare policy one sees attempts to erase the past. One thinks of the treatment of First Nation children forcibly removed from family and culture—so vividly illustrated in the wonderful Australian film, *Rabbit-Proof Fence*,[10] or of the stories of transportation of orphans from Britain to Australia,[11] Canada and elsewhere. But these practices are not fully consigned to the past. In Ireland, we now see comparable attempts by German child welfare agencies that place German young people with German immigrants in what must be to the German youngster the isolated and alien world of remote rural Western Ireland.

We must be careful to ensure that placement planning today does not entail unnecessary severing of positive threads from a child's past networks. Positive threads are hard to weave. Let us not cut them lightly. I say to my students that they should imagine meeting the child with whom they are dealing, grown to adulthood and imagine themselves justifying the choices they made or recommended for that child, choices that might have meant or led on to cutting ties with siblings, relatives, schools or other key anchor points in a child's life. I think that stance may humble us somewhat and temper any idea that we have—or know—the right answer at all times.

In the way we work with young people in care, I suggest that we need to have good tolerance for ambivalence in the child's relationships in, and between, the two worlds. We must try to appreciate that such ambivalence is almost bound to be the "natural state" for children in care. In some senses, children in care risk a *double exile*; ultimately, they may face a future in which they feel no sense of belonging to either world. We should be alert to this stark and real risk. We should avoid working with children in such a way that we force them to make a choice, or force a choice on them, between these two worlds. Just as exiles reach a range of positions between their two worlds, so should we leave children and young people in care the space to take up their own particular positions between the worlds of home and care at different points in their unfolding lives.

Our task must be to avoid closing down options for later choices.

Restricting contact with troubling parents for a younger child may be a justifiable position at one stage in a child's development. But I would suggest that it should not be at the price of eliminating the possibility of a thread of connection with those parents (or other relatives) that can be re-activated should the child wish this at a later stage. Children's preferences and priorities evolve with their development. Choices made at one point should not, ideally, compromise options at another.

The child has brought his or her past in some sense into the present and will merge both while bringing them to his or her future. In a sense, the caring task involves helping the child deal with the past, cope with the present and prepare for the future. Care is about much more than what is going on in the here and now, important, of course, though that is. Carers have to be custodians of the long-term interests and of the long-term connections of the children they serve.

Conclusion

In making the difficult translation from principles to practice, we should be searching for strengths or anchor points around which to build our efforts. In one case, a young person's interest or promise in education may influence our choice. In another case, a strong rapport with an older sibling; in another case a flair for music or sport; in another mentoring by a teacher; in another the tenacious concern of an older relative. It is likely that *combinations* of positive points will be more likely to deliver a good outcome. We should strive to assemble such combinations of potentially positive influences. This claim is supported by the evidence on prevention strategies that seems to demonstrate that *multiple* different types of interventions *together* are key to prevention efforts.

Children in care present complex and diverse needs reflecting their infinitely varied individual histories and circumstances. It is not unreasonable therefore to expect that responses to their needs will need to mirror that diversity and complexity. In devising strategies we need to be thinking *both/and* not *either/or*.

In assessing the quality of our efforts at providing care now or at building permanence, we should be thinking in terms of the legacy that we leave the young person to bring into and through adulthood. I suggest that most young people would hope that the legacy includes a pathway into a stable relationship, a stable job, and a stable social network—in other words, a pathway that offers access to reliable social support. And crucially they would hope for guarantees of connections to people with a partisan commitment to the young person, whether born of kinship ties or otherwise.

In marshalling the resources to respond to these needs, we should be careful to be as inclusive of potential resources as possible. In striving to promote resilience, we should not think of it as some fixed trait or as some magic bullet with guaranteed and pervasive qualities. Life is not that simple, much as we might wish it to be. Promoting resilience seems more about releasing positive energy and processes in the different contexts of a young person's life. In relation to young people in care, any potential resilience is likely to be enhanced by:

- a sense of secure base/confiding relationships;
- positive school experiences (academic and non-academic);
- social support;
- "childhood industry" and a general sense of competence; and
- constructive appraisal of self and circumstances.

If we look at some of the stories of adults and young people who have come through the care system and who have done well, it is clear there are many and varied pathways for doing well. There are many launching pads for trajectories of positive development. There are many different factors that may lead on to good outcomes. We certainly need to search for lessons that are common across successful cases. But we need to do so in appreciation of diversity rather than dogma. We also need to be cautious about over-reliance on a single route to permanence (e.g., adoption from public care); or about too narrow an interpretation of what we mean by permanence (e.g., engineering primary attachments to new carers); or too dogmatic a view about what leads to permanence (e.g., a strict compliance to a singular policy). We also need to avoid confusing placement outcome with outcomes for the child or young person. There are *many pathways to permanence*, and in a sense many places that can be called "permanence."

To quote again that mother making a good job of rearing her teenage boy in the unforgiving and violent streets of inner-city Philadelphia, "You have to be flexible, because life is flexible."

Given how difficult it is to engineer new connections for children in care that prove effective and sustainable, our approach to permanence building should be to draw on as wide a repertoire of resources as possible. We should be striving to paint the future from a broad palette of existing and new possibilities. Our goal should be to maximize the range of social and emotional assets the young person can call upon.

Our solemn privilege and duty is to act as custodians of the long-term interests of the child in care. I suggest that we can best do this by sustaining and building social connections for each child in the two worlds of which they are part.

References

Brodsky, A. (1999). "Making It": The components and process of resilience among urban, African-American, single mothers. *American Journal of Orthopsychiatry*, 69, 148–160.

Clausen, J. (1995). Gender, contexts and turning points in adult lives. In P. Moen, G. Elder, and K. Lüscher (Eds.), *Examining lives in context: Perspectives on the ecology of human development.* Washington, DC: American Psychological Association.

Eagle, R. (1994). The separation experience of children in long-term care— Theory, research, and implications for practice. *American Journal of Orthopsychiatry*, 64, 421–434.

Fearn, D. (2002). *Protective factors for a childhood in care in enriching education for children in care: Resilience, potential and attainment.* Report of conference held by Hertfordshire Council on November 8, 2002.

Furstenberg Jr., F. F., Cook, T. D., Eccles, J., & Elder Jr., G.H. (1999). *Managing to make it: Urban families and adolescent success.* Chicago: University of Chicago Press.

Gaita, R. (1999). *Romulus, my father.* London: Headline Review.

Gilligan, R. (2001). *Promoting resilience in children in out-of-home care.* London: British Agencies for Adoption and Fostering.

Maunders, D., Liddell, M., Liddell, M., & Green, S. (1999). *Young people leaving care and protection.* Hobart, Tasmania: Australian Clearinghouse for Youth Studies.

Romans, S., Martin, J., Anderson, J., O'Shea, M., & Mullen, P. (1995). Factors that mediate between child sexual abuse and adult psychological outcome. *Psychological Medicine*, 25, 127–142.

Rutter, M. (2000). Resilience reconsidered: Conceptual considerations, empirical findings, and policy implications. In J. P. Shonkoff and S. J. Meisels (Eds.), *Handbook of early childhood intervention* (2nd ed.). Cambridge: Cambridge University Press.

Simmons, R., & Blyth, D. (1996). Cited in K. Thiede Call, Adolescent work as an "arena of comfort" under conditions of family discomfort. In J. Mortimer & M. Finch (Eds.), *Adolescents, work, and family: An intergenerational developmental analysis.* Thousand Oaks: SAGE Publications.

Vaillant, G. E., & Vaillant, C. O. (1981). Natural history of male psychological health, X: Work as a predictor of positive mental health. *American Journal of Psychiatry, 138*, 1433–1440.

Vincent, J. (1998). A life in the day of Jemp Vincent. *The Sunday Times Magazine*, 28 November, 118.

1 Sonya in *Afterplay* by Brian Friel

2 I am grateful to a workshop participant who shared this story.

3 From Raymond Carver. (1996). *All of Us: Collected Poems.* London: Harville Press.

4 From the poem "Advent" by Patrick Kavanagh in The Complete Poems, p. 124–5.

5 Raimond Gaita is Professor of Moral Philosophy at King's College London and Foundation Professor of Philosophy at Australian Catholic University.

6 Debra Fearn, Senior Lecturer, University of Hertfordshire. Protective Factors for a Childhood in Care in Enriching Education for Children in Care – Resilience, Potential and Attainment. Report of conference held on November 8, 2002.

7 We also know that multiple social roles help to improve physical and mental health more generally.

8 http://www.bbc.co.uk/legacies/immig_emig/northern_ireland/ni_4/article_2.shtml

9 http://www.bbc.co.uk/legacies/immig_emig/northern_ireland/ni_4/article_3.shtml

10 For an outline of the true story on which the film is based, see Brian Pendreigh's review *Leaping The Fence Of Australia's Past* at www.iofilm.co.uk/feats/interviews/r/rabbit_proof_fence_2002.shtml

11 See for example Buti, A. (2002). "British Child Migration to Australia: History, Senate Inquiry and Responsibilities" Murdoch University Electronic Journal of Law Vol. 9, No. 4, December www.murdoch.edu.au/elaw/issues/v9n4/buti94_text.html and Bean, P. and Melville, J. (1990). Lost Children of the Empire: The Untold Story of Britain's Child Migrants. London: HarperCollins Publishers.

CHAPTER 3

Resilience theory and its relevance for child welfare practice

Ross A. Klein, Kathleen Kufeldt, and Scott Rideout

Introduction

Resilience is an increasingly popular concept, though not always well understood. Like other concepts that have influenced child welfare practice (e.g., permanency planning), there tends to be slippage between its real meaning and its application to practice. The degree to which resilience is understood and applied in practice will ultimately be determined by its usefulness. This chapter examines the resilience literature and links resilience to the *Looking After Children* (LAC) Assessment and Action Records (AARs). It demonstrates the value of the AAR in monitoring and promoting the resilient development of children in foster care.

Growing up in foster care

Children growing up in foster care face many challenges and risks in their lives. They typically lived in an unhealthy home environment prior to placement—many lacking protection, affection, encouragement and intimate contact typically offered in a stable family environment; some were further traumatized by maltreatment at home. After entering care, they must deal with the social isolation resulting from being moved to a new placement and with the inherent instability of the foster care system. Children in foster care typically experience frequent moves to new foster homes, changes of worker and school transfers. Each contributes to poor adult outcomes for these children.

Research has documented the plight of foster children well. They are at an increased risk of experiencing school failure (Altshuler, 1997; Sawyer & Dubowitz, 1994), becoming involved in the criminal justice system (*It's My Life*, 2001), experiencing periods of homelessness after leaving care (Kufeldt & Burrows, 1994; Kufeldt & Nimmo, 1987), and to experience physical, developmental and mental health problems (Child Welfare League of America, 2000; Dicker, Gordon & Knitzer, 2001).

Nevertheless, it would be a mistake to conclude that all children entering foster care will experience poor outcomes. The majority of foster children do in fact succeed while in care (CWLA, 2000; Kufeldt, 2003). Many children are able to overcome early adversity and develop into well-adjusted adults. The important question to ask is, "What factors or experiences enable some graduates of foster care to thrive while others do not?" The literature on resilience suggests some answers.

The concept of resilience

Resilience has been defined as the positive adaptation of an individual within the context of significant adversity (Luthar, Cicchetti, & Becker, 2000). Resilient children and adults have effective coping tools in their handling of stressful events. Coping tools provide the ability to deal with stressful events without becoming overwhelmed (Jenkins & Keating, 1998). Simply put, resilience is the successful adaptation of an individual despite adversity. It has two requirements (Masten & Coatsworth, 1998): there must be a significant threat, adversity or trauma; and an individual must be able to overcome these threats or crises through positive adaptation. Resilience can be illustrated through two related concepts: risk factors and protective factors.

Risk factors

Risk factors are the personal and environmental factors that act as barriers to achieving optimal health and well-being (Ungar, 2004). They can be internal (i.e., those existing within the individual) or external (i.e., those occurring within a social context such as in the family, school or community) (Christle, Harley, Nelson, & Jones, 2001).

The presence of risk factors does not inevitably lead to the development of problems. In fact, only one third of at-risk children actually experience a negative outcome (Newman & Blackburn, 2002). Research suggests the number of risk factors has a greater influence on a child's outcome than the type of risk factors. While the likelihood of behavioural problems increases proportionately to the number of risk factors experienced (Landy & Tam, 1988; Nollan, Arthur, Pecora, Hawkins, & Dillon, 2000), no single or combination of risk factors accounts for more than 30% of any problem behaviour (Ketchum, 2000). Regardless, many risks confronted early in life have their effect years later. Children exposed to multiple risks who show problems early in their lives may continue to show problems years later (Katz, 1997).

Protective factors

Protective factors reduce the risk of harm. They are conditions that can improve resistance to risk factors and contribute to successful outcomes, adaptation and child resilience (Landy & Tam, 1998). Protective factors can also be classified as internal or external (Christle et al., 2001).

Protective factors, like risk factors, have an additive effect—more means greater protection from poor outcomes. Protective factors help the child cope with risk factors in four ways (Newman, 2004; Rutter, 1990):

- altering the child's perception of the risk or reducing involvement or exposure to the risk;

- reducing the effects of negative chain reactions where one risk factor increases the possibility that others will be experienced—for example, a student who drops out of school is at increased risk of becoming unemployed. A protective factor, such as a caring teacher, can prevent a child from quitting school and thereby break the negative chain reaction;

- helping the child establish and improve self-esteem and self-efficacy; and

- creating opportunities for change.

Risk and protective factors reside in social situations such as family, in school and in their community. Table 1 provides an overview of common risk and protective factors present in the individual, family, school and community.

Individual characteristics of the resilient child

It is instructive to consider common personal characteristics shared by resilient people, though personal characteristics are not necessarily deterministic. One can possess resilience-promoting characteristics and yet not succeed in overcoming adversity (Gordon Rouse, Longo, & Trickett, 1999).

Several key characteristics are found in the lives of resilient children (Berliner & Benard, 1995; Masten & Reed, 2002). First, they are socially competent—they are able to establish and sustain caring relationships and to maintain a sense of humour despite the hardships in their lives. Second, resilient children are resourceful. They think critically and creatively about the problems in their lives in an attempt to develop possible solutions. They know when to turn to others for help and when they need assistance with a problem. Third, resilient children are autonomous. They have the ability to act independently and exert control over their environment. They know that they are masters of their own fate and do not have to accept the adversity in their lives. Finally, resilient children have a sense of purpose in their lives and a positive outlook for their future.

Table 1

Examples of Common Risk and Protective Factors		
	Risk Factors	**Protective Factors**
Individual	• Extreme prematurity or low birth weight • Pre-natal exposure to drugs/alcohol • Chronic medical conditions and repeated illnesses • Very difficult temperament • Behaviour problems • Learning disability • Peers who use alcohol/drugs • Early involvement in anti-social behaviours	• Sense of humour • Self-reliant • Strong self-image • Internal locus of control • Sense of purpose • Social competence • Problem-solving skills • Autonomy and self-efficacy • Sense of purpose and future
Family	• Highly critical or inconsistent parenting • An abusive or conflict ridden family. • Single-parent family • One or both parents diagnosed with a mental illness • Presence of alcohol or drug abuse • Low parental monitoring of the child's activities • Poor family management, discipline, and problem-solving styles	• Non-authoritarian and child-centred parenting • Positive attitudes towards the child's education • Opportunity to establish a close bond with at least one person • Establishing high but achievable expectations for their child's behaviour • Parental encouragement of children's participation in decision making
School	• Overcrowding • A high student/teacher ratio • Insufficient or inappropriate curriculum • Weak and inconsistent adult leadership • The presence of high demands and expectations for student performance without appropriate support systems	• Caring and supportive teachers • High but realistic expectations and the support needed to meet those expectations • Compassion and respect • Opportunity for involvement and participation.
Community	• Poverty • High levels of neighbourhood disorganization • High mobility rates • Few adults to monitor children's behaviour • High levels of drug and gang activity	• Caring and support • High expectations • Opportunities for meaningful participation

(Adapted from Benard, 1991; Christle et al., 2001; Ketchum, 2000; Landy & Tam, 1998; Newman & Blackburn, 2002)

Risk and protective factors in context

Three environments play a role in determining a child's developmental outcome: family, school and community. Since a child is dependent on family for support and guidance, it is not surprising that family characteristics can have a profound impact on development. Children and young people also spend a large proportion of time in school. It is here they learn new skills and develop relationships with both teachers and other classmates. Students learn how to respond to authority and experience clear rules, consequences and expectations. The school may be one of the few sources of a stable and predictive environment in the child's life. With children spending so much time in school, it is not surprising that the school environment has a great impact on their development. Finally, the family and school environments do not exist in isolation. The larger community can directly influence both. Each of these environments has both risk and protective factors associated with it.

External risk factors

There are three common risk factors in the family context (Ketchum, 2000). Parenting skills, styles and abilities is the first. Highly critical or inconsistent parenting is one of the most frequently identified predictors of problem behaviours in children. Parents with little time for their children and an abusive or conflict-ridden family are the other two risk factors. The latter is a stronger predictor of delinquency than is family structure (i.e., divorce or single-parent family).

School risk factors include overcrowding, high student/teacher ratio, insufficient or inappropriate curriculum, and weak and inconsistent adult leadership (Christle et al., 2001). The presence of high demands and expectations for student performance without appropriate support systems creates risks for students because some students fall through the cracks (Ketchum, 2000). Others become alienated from school. These youth are more likely to become involved in alcohol and drugs, delinquency, teen pregnancy, school failure, and depression and suicide.

Community risk factors include high levels of neighbourhood disorganization, high mobility rates, few adults to monitor children's behaviour, and high levels of drug and gang activity in the neighbourhood (Christle et al., 2001). However, the greatest risk factor for negative outcomes is poverty (Benard, 1991). Poverty is characterized by the lack of access to the basic resources that promote healthy development, including health care, childcare, housing, education, job training, employment and recreation. While poverty alone does not guarantee negative outcomes, it increases the risk.

External protective factors

Three resilience promoting protective factors can also be found in family, school and community. First is the importance of a caring and supportive relationship with at least one person (Masten & Reed, 2002). This person can be a parent, teacher, mentor or other adult who is interested and involved with the child. A close bond with at least one person has been repeatedly demonstrated as a powerful protective factor (Ketchum, 2000; Newman & Blackburn, 2002). As the number of positive relationships or experiences increases, a child's chances for overcoming adversity also increase. But even one positive relationship can make a major difference in the life of a child (Berliner & Benard, 1995).

The second protective factor is related to having high expectations for the child. Adults must consistently communicate clear and high expectations to children and provide the support and assistance needed to achieve them. Relationships that convey high expectations help children learn to believe in themselves and in their future. This enhances critical resilience-promoting traits: self-esteem, self-efficacy, autonomy and optimism (Benard, 1995).

The final protective factor is ensuring opportunities to participate in and contribute meaningfully to the social environment (Benard, 1991). Children are shown that their opinions are valued, thereby further promoting their self-esteem. Resilient children are provided with many opportunities to participate and contribute in meaningful ways within their family and are acknowledged as valued participants in the life of the family. Academic clubs and social organizations sponsored and supported by the school provide meaningful participation for youth, making it less likely they will fail or fall into deviant behaviour patterns. Communities may also provide youth with opportunities to participate in the life of the community.

The role of mentors as protective factors

Children require the presence of at least one caring person who can provide support for healthy development and learning, engender trust and love, and convey compassion, understanding, respect and interest (Laursen & Birmingham, 2003). Children with a significant attachment or bond face challenges more productively and are more likely to experience success (White-Hood, 1990). This attachment is often provided by a parent, but can also be with a mentor. A mentor is a person who forms a special, nurturing bond with another, usually younger individual. Through this bond, the mentor transfers valuable knowledge, wisdom and life lessons that leave a lasting imprint. For youth, this relationship can be a powerful force in helping them make the transition to adulthood (Katz, 1997).

Mentors are a critical support for children at risk as a result of poverty, trauma, substance abuse or other life events. The value of a mentor is reflected in how youth who have overcome major hardships in their lives often speak of a very special person who was there to help. The important role a mentor can have in an individual's life is demonstrated in Grossman and Tierney's (1998) study examining whether mentoring relationships had the potential to deter some of the negative effects that a high-risk environment can have on teenagers. The mentoring relationships were provided through the Big Brothers Big Sisters program. The study found that teens with a mentor showed improvements in school performance, attendance, family relationships and peer relations. They were less likely to use drugs or alcohol or resort to violent behaviour. Like families, friends and peers, and schools, mentors can promote resilience by providing care and support, high and realistic expectations, and meaningful social participation.

Resilience and foster children

Silva-Wayne's (1995) innovative study of resilient foster children echoes much of the literature on resilience: successful graduates of care had extensive use of role models; affiliation with one or more groups (school groups, clubs, etc.); experiences which raised self-esteem; exposure to opportunities; and use of protective thinking.

Gilligan (2000) offers guidance to foster parents on how they can help children in their care to become resilient. His suggestions are consistent with research. Three areas can serve as a source of protective factors: a sense of a secure base in a foster home, a strengthened social network, and a high level of self-esteem. Individually or together, these may serve as valuable protective factors that can offset the risk factors in the child's life and help them to overcome the negative effects related to them.

Foster families can provide this secure base through attachments provided for the child. These attachments, especially if stable, are important because they enable the child to learn through experience that people and the world are trustworthy and reliable. For a toddler, the sense of a secure base in the world is developed and sustained by reliable care from one or more key caregivers; it helps the toddler (or older child) feel safe in exploring the world and in developing relationships.

In addition to primary attachments with a few key people, emotionally meaningful attachments of lesser intensity can also be formed, particularly as the child ages. These relationships vary by degree of significance to the child (Trinke & Batholomew, 1997) but together are key parts of the growing child's social network. Primary attachments are strengthened by the presence of strong relationships with extended family members, teachers, and other interested adults in the child's life.

The process of achieving a secure base can be difficult for foster children. Traditional primary attachments may be deficient, thereby making the hierarchy of attachment relationships more valuable and significant. Relationships with people lower on the attachment hierarchy may take on greater meaning for these young people. The relationship a child has with his/her teacher or peers, for example, may hold more significance than the relationship with foster parents or birth parents. Because many foster children frequently change placements, attachment to foster parents is undermined and other relationships take on greater significance. These other (ideally long-term) relationships provide a strengthened social network and help foster resilience.

Self-esteem is also important for resilience; it is a protective factor for someone facing adversity. Positive self-esteem provides a cushion and helps a child cope with negative experiences. Because self-esteem comes in part through social relationships, even one positive relationship or experience in childhood can do much to counter the harm of negative relationships or experiences. Not surprisingly, it appears that success in a valued endeavour may do much to combat a sense of failure in other areas of a child's life. Fostering self-esteem has positive by-products.

The discussion thus far has focused on resilience. We have discussed what constitutes resilience and have explored ways in which resilience can be promoted by caregivers and foster families. We now shift attention to how a model for direct intervention—Looking After Children—can contribute to growing resilience in children and families.

The Looking After Children model

If foster care is truly going to succeed, it must go beyond providing only the basic necessities of life. It must provide the same support and guidance as the typical family. In order to accomplish such a feat, the characteristics that define an effective family must be clearly defined and identified. Looking After Children (LAC) does this by identifying the types of life experiences and life conditions that parents normally provide in order that their children develop and achieve success (Lemay & Biro-Schad, 1999).

Developed in the UK, LAC was a response to growing concern about the progress of children looked after by local authorities. The value of substitute care was debated: was the act of taking children into care a better choice than allowing them to remain with birth families? There was, however, little evidence to inform the debate about the effectiveness of particular courses of action and the outcomes for children (Jones, 2003). The void led the Department of Health to establish a working party of professionals in 1987 to examine the outcomes experienced by children in care and to develop a tool that would measure these outcomes. Their work concluded with the publication of *Looking After Children: Assessing Outcomes in Child Care* (Parker, Ward, Jackson, Aldgate, & Wedge, 1991). The tool was designed as an assessment, case planning and review system. Its intent was to promote positive development outcomes among children and young people who are required to live away from their biological families. It was designed as a practice tool, not as a research tool.

There were three main principles that guided the assessment of outcomes and the development of outcome measures in LAC (Parker et al., 1991). First, the LAC protocol assumed children in care are entitled to the same standards of care as children who are cared for by caring, loving parents in the community. When a child welfare agency removes children from their families, it can be seen as taking on the responsibility for parenting them and the parenting responsibilities of child welfare should reflect these norms and behaviours. Second, the LAC framework depended on a partnership including all key people involved in the child's life: biological family, foster family, social workers and other professionals. The team's ultimate goal is to ensure all aspects of the child's needs are met. Finally, knowledge of child welfare outcomes and how to improve them requires a careful assessment of the intervention results in relation to the principles of child development (Vachon, Nadeau, Simard, & Kufeldt, 2000).

A key component of the LAC approach is the Action and Assessment Records (AARs). These are age-specific forms that assess the youth's status in seven developmental dimensions: health, education, identity, family and social relationships, social presentation, emotional and behavioural development, and self-care skills. These assessment tools reflect the simple premise that good parenting will contribute to good outcomes. The information collected by the AARs provides a snapshot of the child at that point in time. They assess what has been done with the child thus far, the current and future needs of the child, and goals remaining to be accomplished.

One of the problems faced by children in care is the number of people responsible for ensuring that their needs are met. In addition to birth parents, there are social workers, foster parents, legal officials and others. This increased number of people is further complicated with changes in social workers, schools and foster parents—increasing the potential for needs to go unmet and contributing to one of the highest risk factors for poor outcomes (Parker, Ward, Jackson, Aldgate, & Wedge, 1991). The AAR helps ensure this does not occur.

The AARs were designed to improve the quality of parenting. All important information is maintained in one form. This allows those involved in the child's life to see how the child is doing, what services he or she has received, and importantly, what still remains to be done. For example, one of the most basic means of promoting children's physical health is by ensuring that they receive immunizations against common childhood diseases. To make sure these are not missed through ignorance of medical history, the Assessment and Action Record's health dimension records all immunizations and other significant health issues. If immunizations are due, then a plan is recorded to ensure it is done. This ideally should prevent children's needs from "falling through the cracks."

The process of completing the AAR explicitly involves young people and thereby empowers them in their own care. The AAR is completed in a personal meeting of the social worker, youth, and foster carers. It is not a quick checklist, but a vehicle for open discussion. Youth are asked questions and have opportunities to elaborate. For example, one question asks how much contact they have with their families. They are also asked if they feel that the amount of contact is right for them and what, if anything, could be done to change this. Youth have the opportunity to express their opinions and feel that their voices are being heard, and they have a sense of control over decisions affecting their lives. The process also develops deeper and stronger relationships between all involved.

The Assessment and Action Record: A tool for monitoring resilience

The discussion so far has dealt with resilience and the LAC model. The following sections will demonstrate how the AAR can be used as a tool not only to assess outcomes, but also to monitor and promote resilience. It will provide examples of how its use can be related to resilience.

The family environment

The information collected by the family and social relationships dimension section of the AAR focuses squarely on characteristics related to resilience. For example, one area of focus is the personal bond between the caregiver and child and their level of trust. This is an important area for assessment given what we know about the value to the foster child of a close bond and the way that this contributes to both resilience and positive outcomes for the child. The AAR looks not just at the relationship with the primary caregiver, but at relationships between the child and other family members. It records both the number of caregivers and other family members a child lives with and the quality of these relationships. Assessment of relationship quality is achieved by ascertaining the level of physical affection shown to the children. They are asked about the frequency with which physical affection is shown and whether the frequency feels right to them. Relationship quality is further assessed by asking whether they believe their foster family seems interested in the things they do and if they receive praise from them. These are important factors in acquisition of resilience and by assessing them the social worker is able to identify both strengths and deficiencies in the foster family-foster child relationship.

Given the importance of stable relationships to the development of close bonds and feelings of trust, the AAR is concerned with the frequency with which foster placements change and the impact this has on the child in care. Bonding and trust develop slowly, but can be undermined by moves from one foster care placement to another.

Support systems

Another key characteristic of resilient families and individuals is having a support network. These can include extended family, close friends, classmates, teachers and community groups. The defining quality is that the child has someone to turn to in times of need and crisis. These sources of social support may provide real help and advice, or they may simply act as a sounding board. In any case, the child is reassured that he or she is not alone in the world and that someone is available with whom he or she can feel comfortable.

The AAR includes questions that identify and assess sources of support a child may have. For example, children are asked how many members of their family they can name and how often they have contact with them. There are several questions within the "Family and Social Relationship Dimension" that provide information on the presence of a support network. They are asked whether they have someone in their lives, other than their parents or carers, to whom they could turn in times of crisis. If no one is available to them, they are asked if they would like to be in touch with someone who could give them support if needed. In addition, they are asked about the friends they have, whether they are long or short-term in nature, and how often they see them outside of school. Taken together, these questions assess the child's social supports, and give insight into the foundation being built toward resilience.

The school and resilience

School may be one of the few places where children in care can experience stability and predictability. If things are not going well at home, school can act as an escape and provide a safe environment in which to spend time with classmates and other adults. School also teaches social skills and problem-solving skills, and provides children with the chance to succeed at meaningful tasks. For some children, school may be the only place where they receive praise for doing a task well, which is an essential ingredient in building self-esteem. Each of these skills and experiences promotes resilience.

The Education Dimension of the AAR concentrates on these skills and experiences by assessing the child's school experiences. On the risk side, the AAR asks children to report on the number of times they have changed schools, the number of times they have been absent from school, and whether or not they have ever been suspended or expelled from school. Obviously, children do not benefit from school if they are not attending. Given the importance of the school environment to the acquisition of resilience, the AAR identifies deficiencies so they can be addressed. Knowing the reasons for unauthorized absences and suspensions can help a social worker identify problems that may be preventing the child from receiving the benefits of opportunities that are available.

The Education Dimension also focuses on the practical aspect of the school experience and the degree to which protective forces are at work. Children are asked whether they have someone to provide help and support with their schoolwork, whether they have a satisfactory place to complete homework and school assignments, and if there is someone who is in contact with the school to monitor their performance and show an interest in their schooling. They are also asked about their participation in extracurricular activities or in other structured group activities during school hours or after school. Schools increase a student's self-concept by rewarding success at meaningful tasks, and by giving specific feedback that delineates how the child's abilities and characteristics contributed to the success (Gordon Rouse, Longo, & Trickett, 1999).

Individual participation in decision making

The AAR is more than just an assessment tool that provides direction for intervention by identifying the risks and protective factors related to resilience. It is also a tool that gives the child an active role in decision making. This involvement positively affects self-esteem and provides youth a sense of control over their lives—two factors that help to build individual resilience. There are other benefits that accrue with the child's participation in decisions related to his or her care and placement.

There is some evidence that when children and young people in care have some choice about placements, placements tend to be more stable (Cashmore, 2002). This is probably because planning and decision-making processes that take the children's views into account are likely to be both more appropriate and more acceptable to them.

Youth participation is also important because children learn by example. Participating in decision making with support and guidance is a vital part of socialization of children and young people to prepare them for future independence and autonomy.

Gilligan (2000) offers other reasons why it is important to involve children in care in decisions that affect their lives. First are practical reasons for listening to the child. Plans and decisions are likely to be better informed and to stick if the child feels heard and has his or her views genuinely considered. Many children feel resentful when decisions are imposed on them; children placed in out-of-home placements against their will may be so resistant as to cause the placement to break down (Cashmore, 2002). Second, there are therapeutic reasons for involving and listening to the child. It is good for the child's recovery from adversity and for self-esteem and self-efficacy to be consulted and involved in decision-making process. Third, there are ethical reasons. Involvement helps to reduce the power imbalance between adults and the child and the risks of harm that may flow from that. Fourth, there are philosophical reasons. Consistency requires that if one values a child's welfare and interests, then one should also value the child's views and voice. Next, there are reasons related to good practice in management terms. Any service is likely to function better if to some degree at least it is accountable to end users. Finally, there are legal reasons. Heeding the voice of children is a requirement of the *UN Convention on the Rights of the Child* and of many child welfare statutes.

Conclusion

Children who come to the attention of child welfare agencies have already faced many risk factors that could easily cause problems later on in life. By intervening in their lives, it is expected that some good will come from it. All these children have the potential to overcome the adversities in their lives. Fortunately, resilience is not an innate characteristic. Rather, as Masten

(2001 and in this volume) reminds us, resilience does not come from some rare quality or trait. It appears to be a common phenomenon that comes from the everyday magic of ordinary, normative human resources that exist in the child's mind, brain and body as well as in the family and community. Children who succeed in life have adults who care for them, brains that are developing normally, and the ability to manage their own attention, emotions and behaviour (Masten & Coatsworth, 1998).

Windfield (1994) identifies three characteristics of fostering resilience. First, it is a process that is long term and developmental in nature. Secondly, resilience develops over a long time. It is dependent upon the presence of positive interventions by a significant individual, school or organization at critical life points in order to offset the accompanying risks and vulnerabilities. Finally, the process of fostering resilience nurtures protective processes so that children can succeed.

A resilience approach to working with youth is based on the assumption that by meeting a youth's developmental needs for safety, belonging, respect, accomplishment, power and meaning, adults are promoting positive youth development. This will have the additional effect of preventing problems associated with poor outcomes, such as substance abuse, teen pregnancy, delinquency and school failure. A resilience approach also places the focus on the positives in the child's life rather than emphasizing the negatives. A caring relationship experienced by a youth that conveys high expectations and provides opportunities for ongoing participation and contribution in natural settings has been found to promote positive youth development (Benard, 1999). The Assessment and Action Record is designed to record and monitor whether or not a youth's developmental needs are being met. If they are not, then steps are set out in order to ensure they will be. It reports on whether there are significant people in their lives to whom they can turn in times of need. The Assessment and Action Record has the potential to provide the basis for good practice that fosters resilience. In our own research, we have also found that its use can also contribute to resilience for workers and foster parents, thus reducing the potential for crises and placement breakdown. This is a win-win situation for everybody.

Authors' Note

The authors wish to acknowledge support from the Social Sciences and Humanities Research Council of Canada for this project.

References

Altshuler, S. J. (1997). A reveille for school social workers: Children in foster care need our help. *Social Work in Education, 19,* 121–127.

Benard, B. (1991). *Fostering resiliency in kids: Protective factors in the family, school and community.* Portland, OR: Western Regional Center for Drug-Free Schools and Communities.

Benard, B. (1995). *Fostering resilience in children.* (ERIC Digest No. EDOPS959). Retrieved March 11, 2004, from the World Wide Web: http://ericfacility.net/databases/ERIC_Digests/ed386327.html

Benard, B. (1999). Mentoring: New study shows the power of relationship to make a difference. In N. Henderson, B. Benard & N. Sharp-Light (Eds.). *Resiliency in action: Practical ideas for overcoming risks and building strengths in youth, families and communities* (pp. 93–99). San Diego, CA: Resiliency in Action, Inc.

Berliner, B., & Benard, B. (1995). *More than a message of hope: A district-level policy maker's guide to understanding resiliency.* Portland, OR: Western Regional Center for Drug-Free Schools and Communities. ERIC Documentation Reproduction Service No. ED 387946.

Cashmore, J. (2002). Promoting the participation of children and young people in care. *Child Abuse and Neglect, 26,* 837–847.

Child Welfare League of America. (2000). *Fact sheet: The health of children in out-of-home care.* Retrieved October 1, 2003, from the World Wide Web: http://www.cwla.org/programs/health/healthcarecwfact.htm

Christle, C. A., Harley, D. A., Nelson, C. M., & Jones, K. (2001). *Promoting resilience in children: What parents can do—Information for families.* Centre for Effective Collaboration and Practice. Retrieved February 19, 2004, from the World Wide Web: http://cecp.air.org/familybriefs/docs/Resiliency1.pdf

Dicker, S., Gordon, E., & Knitzer, J. (2001). *Improving the odds for the healthy development of young children in foster care.* New York, NY: National Center for Children in Poverty. Retrieved March 24, 2004, from the World Wide Web: http://www.nccp.org/media/pew02b_text.pdf

Gilligan, R. (2000). Promoting resilience in children in foster care. In G. Kelly & R. Gilligan (Eds.), *Issues in foster care: Policy, practice and research* (pp. 107–126). London, England: Jessica Kingsley Publishers.

Gordon Rouse, K. A., Longo, N., & Trickett, M. (1999). *Fostering resilience in children—Bulletin 875–99*. The Ohio State University Bulletin. Retrieved March 10, 2004 from the World Wide Web: http://ohioline.osu.edu/b875/index.html

Grossman, J. B., & Tierney, J. P. (1998). Does mentoring work? An impact study of the Big Brothers Big Sisters program. *Evaluation Review, 22,* 403–426.

It's my life: Summary of a framework for youth transitioning from foster care to successful adulthood (2001). Seattle, WA: Casey Family Programs. Retrieved August 15, 2003, from the World Wide Web: http://www.casey.org/Resources/Publications/ItsMyLife.htm

Jenkins, J., & Keating, D. (1998). *Risk and resilience in six- and ten-year-old children.* Hull, Quebec: Applied Research Branch, Human Resources Development Canada.

Jones, H. (2003). The relationship between research, policy, and practice in delivering an outcome-led child welfare service. In K. Kufeldt and B. McKenzie (Eds.). *Child welfare: Connecting research, policy and practice* (pp. 367–376). Waterloo, ON: Wilfrid Laurier University Press.

Katz, M. (1997). Overcoming childhood adversities: Lessons learned from those who have "beat the odds." *Intervention in School and Clinic, 32,* 205–210.

Ketchum, S. (2000). *Risk and protective factor summary.* Arizona Prevention Resource Center. Retrieved March 10, 2004, from the World Wide Web: www.azprevention.org/Prevention_In_Practice/What_Works/What_Works_Risk_summary.htm

Kufeldt, K. (2003). Graduates of guardianship care: Outcomes in early adulthood. In K. Kufeldt & B. McKenzie (Eds.). *Child welfare: Connecting research, policy and practice* (pp. 209–216). Waterloo, ON: Wilfrid Laurier University Press.

Kufeldt, K., & Burrows, B. (1994). *Issues affecting policies and services for homeless youth.* Report to National Welfare Grants. Calgary: University of Calgary.

Kufeldt, K., & Nimmo, M. (1987). Youth on the street: Abuse and neglect in the eighties. *Child Abuse and Neglect, 11,* 531–543.

Landy, S., & Tam, K. K. (1998). *Understanding the contribution of multiple risk factors on child development at various ages.* Hull, Quebec: Applied Research Branch, Human Resources and Development.

Laursen, E. K., & Birmingham, S. M. (2003). Caring relationships as a protective factor for at-risk youth: An ethnographic study. *Families in Society, 84,* 240–246.

Lemay, R., & Biro-Schad, C. (1999). Looking after children: Good partnership, good outcomes. *OACAS Journal, 43(2),* 31–34.

Luthar, S. S., Cicchetti, D., & Becker, B. (2000). The construct of resilience: A critical evaluation and guidelines for future work. *Child Development, 7,* 543–562.

Masten, A. S. (2001). Ordinary magic: Resilience processes in development. *American Psychologist, 56,* 227–238.

Masten, A. S., & Coatsworth, J. D. (1998). The development of competence in favourable and unfavourable environments: Lessons from research on successful children. *American Psychologist, 5,* 205–220.

Masten, A. S., & Reed, M. J. (2002). Resilience in development. In C. R. Snyder and S. J. Lopez (Eds.), *Handbook of positive psychology* (pp. 74–88). Oxford, NY: Oxford University Press.

Newman, T. (2004). *What works in building resilience?* Ilford, Essex, England: Barnardo's.

Newman, T., & Blackburn, S. (2002). *Interchange 78 – Transitions in the lives of children and young people: Resilience factors.* Edinburgh: Scottish Executive Education Department. Retrieved August 25, 2003, from the World Wide Web: http://www.scotland.gov.uk/library5/education/ic78.pdf

Nollan, K. A., Arthur, M., Pecora, P. J., Hawkins, J. D., & Dillon, D. (2000). *Relationships between risk factors, protective factors and outcomes among youth in long-term foster care.* Paper presented in poster format at the biennial meetings of the Society for Research in Child Development, April 15–18, Albuquerque, New Mexico.

Parker, R., Ward, C., Jackson, S., Aldgate, J., & Wedge, P. (Eds.) (1991). *Looking After Children: Assessing outcomes in child care.* London: Her Majesty's Stationery Office.

Rutter, M. (1990). Psychosocial resilience and protective mechanisms. In J. Rolf, A.S. Masten, D. Cicchetti, K.H. Nuechterlein, and S. Weintraub (Eds.), *Risk and protective factors in the development of psychopathology* (pp. 181–214). Cambridge, England: Cambridge University Press.

Sawyer, R. J., & Dubowitz, H. (1994). School performance of children in kinship care. *Child Abuse and Neglect, 18,* 587–597.

Silva-Wayne, S. (1995). Contributions to resilience in children and youth: What successful child welfare graduates say. In J. Hudson & B. Galaway (Eds.). *Child welfare in Canada: Research and policy implications* (pp. 308–323). Toronto, ON: Thompson Educational Publishing.

Trinke, S., & Batholomew, K. (1997). Hierarchies of attachment relationships in young adulthood. *Journal of Social and Personal Relationships, 14,* 603–625.

Ungar, M. (2004). *Nurturing hidden resilience in troubled youth.* Toronto, ON: University of Toronto Press.

Vachon, J., Nadeau, F., Simard, M., & Kufeldt, K. (2000). Looking after children in Quebec. *Canada's Children, 7*(1), 7–10

White-Hood, M. (1990). Taking up the mentoring challenge. *Educational Leadership, 5,* 76–78.

Windfield, L. F. (1994). *NCREL monograph: Developing resilience in urban youth.* North Central Regional Educational Library. Retrieved March 10, 2004, from the World Wide Web: http://www.ncrel.org/sdrs/areas/issues/educatrs/leadrshp/le0win.htm

CHAPTER 4

Identity formation and cultural resilience in Aboriginal communities

Christopher E. Lalonde

Introduction

The program of research in which my colleagues[1] and I have been engaged, and which I will describe in the pages that follow, was not intended to be about resilience. Nor was it meant to be about children in care. It began with studies of identity formation, moved on to encompass studies of youth suicide, and has increasingly come to focus on youth suicide in Aboriginal[2] cultures. Having admitted to all of that at the outset, the reader might feel in need of reassurance that this chapter actually belongs in the current volume. First, I really do have data to report on children in care. Second, the research in which we have been engaged—while not expressly about resilience in the usual sense—actually addresses issues of resilience at a cultural rather than individual level.

Getting from here to there—that is, from our work on identity formation and Aboriginal suicide to our data on children in care—will demand stretching the concept of resilience to try to explain not individual coping in the face of adversity, but the ability of whole cultural groups to foster healthy youth development. There are some who harbour strong doubts about the value of the concept of resilience, however, and it is best to put these doubts on the table before we begin tugging at the concept and testing its elasticity for the job at hand.

The concept of resilience has, of late, found itself living in an increasingly rough neighbourhood. The early excitement—prompted by the work of Garmezy (1970) and Werner and her colleagues (1971)—about the prospect of identifying and studying those "resilient individuals who have defied others' expectations and survived or surmounted daunting and seemingly overwhelming dangers, obstacles and problems" (Leshner, 1999, p. 2), seems to have lapsed somewhat. As Luthar, Cicchetti and Becker (2000) put it, there are "growing concerns about the rigor of theory and research in the area, misgivings which have sometimes culminated in assertions that overall, this is a construct of dubious scientific value" (p. 543).

Liddle (1994), for example, asks: "Does resilience qualify as an organizing concept with sufficient logical and emotional resonance to yield systematic theoretical and research inquiry that will make a lasting contribution?" (p. 167) For Tarter and Vanyukov (1999), the answer is clear: "based on both theoretical and practical considerations ...it is becoming increasingly evident that this construct not only lacks denotative meaning but has obscured thinking about the etiology and prevention of psychopathology, behavior disorder, and substance abuse" (pp. 100). If Tarter and Vanyukov pull no punches, for Bartelt (1994), the gloves are off:

> "Frankly, I feel that we are imbuing resilience with the same overarching powers that early chemists attributed to phlogiston, the mystical substance that was ostensibly released during combustion and, being contained within the object being consumed enabled it to successfully burn. Resilience, as a psychological trait, is seen as a component of the self that enables success in the face of adversity, and may either be consumed or, paradoxically, reinforced by adversity.
>
> In short, I make the case that resilience, as a concept is difficult, if not impossible to empirically specify, and is too easily conflated with measures of situational success or failure. It suffers from its roots in subjective interpretations of biographical events, and it is too closely dependent on observer-imputed stresses and resources for dealing with stressors" (pp. 98–99).

If resilience really does live in what is quickly becoming the dodgy part of town, we might all wonder, along with Tolan who asks in the title of his 1996 article, "How resilient is the concept of resilience?" Taking the two-part definition provided Luthar, Cicchetti and Becker (2000), it meets the test of being exposed to "significant threat or adversity" (p. 543). The open question is whether it can go on to achieve "positive adaptation despite major assaults on the developmental process" (Luthar, Cicchetti & Becker, 2000, p. 543). Perhaps I am predisposed to root for the underdog, but I believe the concept of resilience will, to use Garmezy's words, "manifest competence despite exposure to significant stressors" (Rolf, 1999, p. 7). There is much to do, of course, to improve the neighbourhood (if I have not pushed this metaphor too far already), and the work needs to begin with an examination of what might be called "the trait trap."

A common criticism of research on resilience is that it aims to identify those "at-risk" children who, when their peers are falling by the wayside, are seen to have "the right stuff" to shoulder the weight of adversity, if not with a smile, then at least without buckling to the pavement. The search for such "resilient children" who remain standing in the most crippling of environments fosters the mistaken and dangerous notion that resilience is a characteristic located somewhere within the child. This view of resilience as a trait was understandable given that early research reports referred to "invulnerability" (Anthony, 1974), or "stress resistance" (Garmezy, 1985), or "hardiness"—all of which have been taken to mean that some children "possess the phenotype of high resilience" (Tarter & Vanyukov, 1999, p. 87). This "trait trap" view is mistaken because even those researchers who were "first on the block" understood resilience to be a process rather than a trait (e.g., Werner & Smith, 1982; Werner, 1984), and whole armies of researchers have worked to establish the fact that resilience is not a feature of children, but a process that involves interactions between attributes of children, their families, neighbourhoods, and wider social and cultural environments. And it is dangerous because traits are rarely taken to be malleable, and if resilience can only be identified but not fostered (you either "have what it takes" to overcome adversity or you don't), and if risk factors are ubiquitous and inevitable (poverty will be with us until the meek inherit the earth), then we are left with little in the way of real motivation or useful tools to design prevention and intervention strategies for children facing adversity.

For those interested in the welfare of whole populations of children who are, almost by definition, taken to be "at-risk of adversity"—children growing up in care, Aboriginal children—the shackling effect of this narrow view of resilience is simply intolerable.

And here is where I want to begin—at the interface of child and culture and with our own attempts to better understand the interplay of risk and protective factors in development. My purpose will be to frame our research in a way that speaks to the issue of resilience in indigenous communities in Canada. I scrupulously avoided the phrase "resilient indigenous communities" both to steer myself clear of the trait trap that I have just warned against, and also to emphasize the point that, just as it is dangerous to imagine that resilience is a feature of children, so too, it would be ill-advised to use a phrase that implies that only some indigenous communities are resilient. Still, I will be presenting results from an ongoing program of research that shows that within the "context of significant adversity" that faces all Aboriginal communities in Canada, differences between communities regularly appear in what resilience researchers would call "positive adaptation."

Some communities seem to be "adapting to" or overcoming adversity better than others. As our data show, some First Nations communities have exceedingly high rates of youth suicide, for example, while in others suicide is entirely absent. Some communities have no children and youth living in care, whereas in others, almost 1 in 10 children is placed in care each year. It would be tempting to label some of these communities "resilient" or to talk of differences in "levels of resilience." That is, we have what appear to be similar levels of risk or adversity but large differences in outcome—the same phenomenon that continues to fuel research on resilience in child development—but expressed here at a cultural or community level.

If this is the same phenomenon, and if the detractors are correct, then we have every right to wonder whether the embattled concept of resilience is up to the task of explaining variability in rates of youth suicide or in rates of children in care across diverse groups of Aboriginal communities. In other words, can a concept developed for explaining individual differences be made to work at the level of whole cultural communities? And if resilience can be bumped upstairs to this higher level of analysis, can it be done in ways that avoid the trait trap—ways that resist the application of global judgments about whether a particular community is or is not resilient? Of course, I believe that it can, and if the task of stretching the concept is done carefully enough, I believe there is some potential theoretical clarity to be gained that can better capture the influence of culture on youth development. The sort of care that will be required comes in two forms.

First, I will need to be careful to avoid what is sometimes called "the psychologist's fallacy"—a kind of category error in which one applies psychological causes and explanations to every event in sight. My attempt to use the psychological concept of "resilience" at a sociological or cultural level, if not executed properly, threatens to become just this sort of embarrassing error.

The second kind of caution concerns, not the folly of *attempting* to use resilience in this way, but the dangers of actually *succeeding*. If the similarities between individual resilience and cultural resilience are more than just analogous, then (theoretically at least) all of the promise and all of the problems that have attended the history of resilience research will be seen to apply more or less directly to the study of entire cultures. The most pointed dangers—but also the most promising benefits—will come from applying the lessons of research on resilience in children to intervention efforts meant to minimize the effect of risk factors and maximize the effect of protective factors for whole cultural groups. In the current case, our work has identified a set of cultural or community practices and forms of indigenous knowledge that are associated with "better" youth outcomes. These findings threaten to set in motion a well-intentioned, but potentially disastrous, application of the standard "knowledge transfer" model.

What I have in mind here is a variation on the "trait trap" that would see these findings taken as licence to begin a strip-mining operation bent on extracting some set of cultural "best practices" from beneath the feet of "resilient" communities for processing at some central plant and eventual export to those poor "non-resilient" communities. That may seem a harsh characterization. Nevertheless, in the context of research and policy as it has been applied "to" indigenous communities in Canada and elsewhere, it is a well-founded fear.

Although these extensive introductory remarks—largely a list of doubts and dangers—are a necessary part of mapping out the terrain, they have done little to point the route ahead. Belatedly, then, here is how I plan to proceed.

Part I begins with a set of definitions common to research on resilience in childhood, and an attempt to show that the situation of contemporary Aboriginal cultures in Canada meets what will amount to the twin conditions of risk and competence that constitute the concept of resilience. This will be accomplished in two steps: (i) the first examines the level of risk faced by Aboriginal and non-Aboriginal persons in Canada—and works to establish the fact that a higher burden of risk is borne by the Aboriginal population; (ii) the second step will focus on outcome rather than risk and, as noted above, will include the presentation of data on rates of youth suicide that illustrate wide variability in community-level "adaptation" or "success" within a shared climate of heightened risk.

Having established at least a *prima facie* case for using the notion of resilience at this higher level of abstraction, I will go on in Part II to describe how our studies of individual identity formation have led us to use measures of cultural identity as the key to understanding variability in suicide rates and the issues surrounding children in care within First Nations communities. This will, again, be accomplished in two steps.

Step one will open with a brief discussion of the concept of "self-continuity." It will be devoted to making the point that acquiring a working sense of one's own personal persistence in time (in other words, an understanding that, despite all the changes that life and time has in store, you can claim confident ownership of your own past and feel a strong commitment to your own future) is a crucial part of the identity formation process. In fact, as I will go on to show, failures in the process of constructing or maintaining this sense of self-continuity are strongly associated with the risk of suicide.

Step two—and this is the tricky part where the threat of committing the psychologist's fallacy looms large—will concern the "levels of analysis" problem that arises whenever one attempts to use a concept developed at one level of analysis (in this case, at the level of individual persons) to explain phenomena at some higher level (communities, or cultures). The case I will present involves drawing parallels between the continuity of persons and the continuity of cultures. The essential argument is this: In our day-to-day experience, both selves and cultures are commonly understood to both change and yet remain the same. We experience ourselves and others as temporally stable or continuous, yet we also expect people to change—and often strive to bring about change in ourselves and others. In much the same fashion, we understand that cultures must change and yet, if they are to survive pressures of assimilation, or colonization, or conquest, must somehow remain "the same." Both persons and cultures, then, are obliged to find some procedural means of preserving identity (personal identity and cultural identity) across time and through change. Just as threats to personal continuity are associated with individual acts of suicide, our research has shown that threats to cultural continuity are associated with rates of suicide within cultural communities. More importantly, efforts to promote culture are associated with increased resilience as evidenced by data that will be presented on the relation between rates of children in care and rates of youth suicide.

The point to be made in all of this is that, if one is as careful as I will try to be, one can sometimes commit the psychologist's fallacy and get away with it. The concept of resilience *can* be applied at a group level. But more than that, the conclusion toward which I will work is that the process of creating and maintaining a strong sense of collective cultural identity not only promotes the continuity or resilience of the culture itself, but also acts to support and protect young persons in their efforts to build a commitment to their own future that is able to withstand and overcome periods of adversity.

Part I: Applying definitions of resilience to Aboriginal communities

In everyday usage, the term "resilient" can apply to almost anything. Militias and markets can be said to "recover quickly after a setback," and everything from contortionists to camisoles can "spring back quickly into shape after being bent, stretched or deformed." In the social sciences, however, a more precise meaning is intended. Here the term is reserved for those cases (i.e., children) in which exposure to risk or adversity fails to produce the usual or expected degree of negative effect, or the magnitude of recovery is greater than anticipated. In studies of child development, one can refer to a general hardiness in response to adversity—"manifest competence despite exposure to significant stressors" (Rolf, 1999, p. 7)—or to a more distributed and "dynamic process encompassing positive adaptation within the context of significant adversity" (Luthar, Cicchetti, & Becker, 2000, p. 543). Common language and scientific definitions of resilience both refer to a relation between risk and outcome but differ in the way this relation is characterized. In social science, risk is typically defined as that which commonly produces (or is statistically associated with) a negative outcome. Poverty, abuse, illness, etc. are all said to be risk factors in childhood because the population of children exposed to these factors is known to have a lower average score on some outcome measure than the average score for the population of children who were spared such adversities. The term "resilient" is used to describe any at-risk child who exhibits an outcome score that is higher than expected. Just how high one needs to score is a matter of serious scholarly debate. The score can be measured statistically relative to one's at-risk peers (e.g., scoring somewhere above the at-risk mean = resilient), or to scores in the non-risk group (scoring within the non-risk range = resilient), or to the total population (scoring in the top 10% = resilient). Masten, Best and Garmezy (1990), for example, refer to three forms of resilience: (1) positive outcome despite adversity; (2) sustained competence under stress; and (3) successful recovery from trauma. Resilience can also be measured by the presence or absence of certain conditions—at-risk children can be judged resilient if they graduate high school (presence of positive outcome) or if they fail to develop a mental illness (absence of negative outcome).

My purpose in rehearsing all of this is to highlight the key elements of the concept of resilience as it is commonly employed and to point out the fact that risk and outcome are often conflated. To determine whether the concept can be applied to the Aboriginal population, we will need to show that there is a special burden of risk or adversity within this population. This much is relatively straightforward. In a history that is shared with aboriginal people across the Americas, following contact with Europeans, the Aboriginal peoples of Canada have endured a series of sustained assaults upon their cultures. Communities have been forcibly relocated, access to resources and lands has been blocked, and traditional ways of living have been rendered all but impossible to sustain. In Canada, this history has included the official prohibition of religious practices and traditional forms of government, as well as the systematic removal of children from their parents care to be "educated" in residential schools. Such policies (as the Canadian government now admits) were "intended to remove Aboriginal people from their homelands, suppress Aboriginal nations and their governments, undermine Aboriginal cultures, [and] stifle Aboriginal identity" (*Report of the Royal Commission on Aboriginal Peoples*, 1996). And these policies were undeniably effective: Aboriginal groups continue to struggle to maintain the "matrix of stories, beliefs and values that holds a society together, allows individuals to make sense of their lives and sustains them through the trouble and strife of mortal existence" (Eckersley & Dear, 2002, p. 1592). While no one, perhaps, needs to be especially reminded of this shameful history of "colonial entrapment" (Carsten, 2000), the point of my recounting it is that the difficulties faced by contemporary Aboriginal communities need to be understood within this historical context. The legacy of these policies can be found on any number of indicators of risk status—from infant mortality, injury and disease rates, to life expectancy, school performance and drop out rates, and almost any measure of health, economic or social disadvantage one cares to choose.

For our present purpose, however, establishing a higher burden of risk satisfies only the first part of the preconditions for cultural resilience. If it were the case that rates of ill health or social disadvantage were uniformly high in each and every Aboriginal community or group, then there would be no hope for demonstrating resilience. That is, where risk and outcome are conflated, one needs to demonstrate that risk and outcome vary not by individual, but across communities.

Because resilience requires a positive outcome amid a climate of increased risk, we need to locate a community, or a set of communities, that have somehow managed to "beat the odds." The odds to beat that form the focus for this example will be rates of youth suicide.

Since 1987, we have been monitoring the suicide rates within all of the 196 First Nations communities located in British Columbia. These monitoring efforts reveal two clear trends. First, the rate of suicide for First Nations youth is much higher than for non-Native youth. By our calculations, the risk of suicide (i.e., the burden of risk) is 5 to 20 times higher for First Nations youth as a group. Second, within this climate of increased risk, there is, however, huge variability in the rates of suicide at the level of communities. This might be expected given that suicide is a rare event, and that many of these communities have small populations. For that reason, it is important to measure suicide rates over larger populations and for long periods of time. To date, we have data covering the years 1987 to 2000. With the names of particular First Nations communities (or bands) removed, the rates of youth suicide for this time period are displayed in Figure 1 below.

While it might be natural for the eye to linger on those especially sharp spikes in Figure 1 (on those communities that exhibit tragically high rates of youth suicide), it should be noted that the line also touches the axis at the zero point. That is, there are communities with youth suicides of zero. To highlight the importance of this phenomenon, the same data are sorted in Figure 2 from lowest to highest. As can be clearly seen in this figure, more than half of all communities suffered no youth suicides during the 14-year study window. By this reckoning, the heaviest burden of risk is borne by a tiny fraction of the communities.

Figure 1. Youth suicide rate by band (1987–2000)

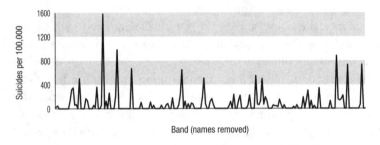

Band (names removed)

Figure 2. Youth suicide rate by band (1987–2000)

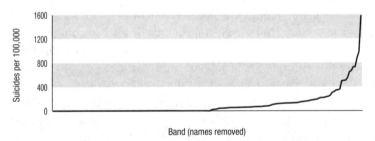

Band (names removed)

It might be the case that these differences in community level rates of suicide, while dramatic and apparently stable across time, are nonetheless essentially random. That is, even though the differences between communities persist, there is nothing that would help us distinguish high-suicide communities from their low-suicide neighbours. But our work has shown that there are ways of making sense of this variability and indeed of predicting which communities will have the lowest (or highest) rates, not just of suicide, but of other good and bad youth outcomes. The business of explaining why some communities manage to thrive in an environment of general adversity—why some communities are "resilient"—is taken up in the section to follow.

Part II: Personal persistence and cultural resilience

For more than a decade, my research colleagues and I have been struggling to understand how it is that young persons—first of different ages (Chandler, Boyes, Ball, & Hala, 1987), and then of different mental health statuses (Chandler & Ball, 1990; Lalonde & Ferris, 2005), and, most recently, of different cultures (Chandler, Lalonde, Sokol, & Hallett, 2003; Lalonde & Chandler, 2004)—comprehend their own personal persistence differently in the face of inevitable developmental and social change. The problem—the paradox—of personal persistence arises from the fact that our ordinary understanding of the concept of "person" or "self" contains two fundamentally contradictory features: selves "embody both change *and* permanence simultaneously" (Fraisse, 1963, p. 10). On the one hand, we understand that persons change—often dramatically so—yet, on the other, persons must somehow persist as continuous or numerically identical individuals, and be understood, as Locke (1694/1956) famously put it, "as the same thinking thing in different times and places." If persons were not understood to persist in this way, then the concept of self would be stripped of its usual meaning. Routine matters of everyday life—such as identifying individual persons at different moments in time—would become impossible, and any hope of maintaining a legal and moral order would collapse if persons could not be held responsible for their own past actions or compelled to follow through on future promises. A conception of the self that did not encompass personal persistence, or that failed otherwise failed to meet Flanagan's "one self to a customer rule" (1996, p. 65), would be unrecognizable as an instance of what we ordinarily take selves to be (Cassirer, 1923).

Though persistence or continuity is foundational to any workable definition of self, we are not born with arguments at the ready concerning how we ourselves (or anyone else) ought to be understood to change and yet remain "the same" person. It seemed clear enough to us at least, that there is a developmental story to be told here—a story about how young persons come to defend notions of their own continuity in the face of inevitable change. Before going on to briefly outline some of the findings of our own research on this topic, however, a few words need to be said about how it is that adolescents can be prompted to seriously consider matters of self-continuity and to offer up their own best solutions to the paradox of sameness in change.

What does *not* work (or more rightly did not work for us) is to ask young people outright how it is that they should be understood to persist through time. The more roundabout and more productive method of engaging adolescents with the problem is to begin by asking them to discuss instances of particularly dramatic personal change in the lives of fictional story characters. We managed this by presenting them with various "Classic Comic Books" (e.g., Victor Hugo's *Les Miserables* and Charles Dickens' *A Christmas Carol*) that depict examples of persistent identity in the face of personal change, and then pressed them for their own reasons for believing that, despite dramatic transformations, Jean Valjean or Ebeneezer Scrooge still deserve to be counted as the self-same continuous and numerically identical person. We followed this by asking them to describe themselves at some time in the past (typically 5 to 10 years in the past, depending on the age of the participant), and then to describe themselves in the present. Drawing out their thoughts on continuity in their own life involved pointing out the contrasts between these two self-descriptions and repeatedly asking them how such different descriptions could apply to the same person. In following these procedures with upwards of 600 young persons, we have found that even the youngest of typically developing adolescents can be counted on to engage the problem of personal persistence with serious attention and to work hard to construct what they take to be convincing arguments in favor of self-continuity.

Before recounting some of the details of our findings, it is important to consider the fact that, although we must each find *some* means of understanding our own persistence in time, there is no reason to suppose that everyone would arrive at precisely the *same* solution strategy. Developmental psychologists, for example, have every right to suspect that persons of different ages would process this problem differently. We might even predict that something like a developmental sequence of solution strategies would emerge. In some similar (though perhaps less clear-cut) fashion, cultural psychologists or anthropologists might predict that even if the problem of self-continuity turned out be one of those rare universals of human development, the procedural means for accomplishing personal persistence might still be free to vary considerably from one culture to the next. As it happens, both groups turn out to be right.

In brief, what we have found is that, as young persons themselves become more complex, so too do the arguments they offer up. In late childhood, for example, most employ simple physicalistic arguments concerning aspects of themselves that have managed to withstand the ravages of time: "My name/appearance/fingerprints are still the same." By the end of their teen years, the form of their reasoning has typically become almost excruciatingly abstract: "I am the ship that sails through the troubled waters of my life." Changes in the sophistication of their reasoning are associated (as every developmentalist has a right to expect) with increasing age and level of cognitive development. Between the ages of 12 and 18, our research suggests, the average young person can be expected to step through a series of up to five different and increasingly complicated ways of warranting his or her own persistence in time.

In addition, cutting across the different levels of reasoning, we have identified two general strategies for approaching this problem that appear to be associated with participants' cultural background. One of these aims to preserve continuity through time by denying that real change has taken place and by seeking sameness in those features or aspects of the self that have managed to endure despite surface change in other quarters. These "essentialist" strategies range from simple claims about physical features remaining the same (my eye colour, my birthmark) to increasingly abstract notions of personality traits and enduring souls. Though such claims can be made at different levels of abstraction, they all share in the idea that beneath a changing surface, more enduring aspects of self can remain untouched by time and change. The second strategy is more "narrative" and fully abandons the idea that change can be denied. Instead, these "narrative" accounts find continuity by creating an easy-to-follow story that stitches together the various and changing parts of their life. Of course, some of these stories are more sophisticated than others. Young adolescents, for example, typically offer a simple chronology of events that rarely amounts to anything like a real plot. Older adolescents can express the more poetic conviction that the only real "plot" to one's life is that of an endless series of attempts to interpretively reread the past in light of the present.

Understanding why some adolescents choose the Essentialist approach and others are more Narrative turns out to depend on matters of culture. Some 80% of the culturally mainstream Canadian youth we have tested employ an Essentialist view of personal persistence. Among Aboriginal youth, more than 70% are Narrative in their view. This dissimilarity results from certain deep-seated differences between Euro-American and Aboriginal cultural and intellectual traditions. Where contemporary Western culture routinely sees truth as hidden beneath an obscuring surface and where hidden essences need to be separated from mere appearances, Aboriginal cultures see a need for interpretation and the creation of meaning. Polkinghorne (1988) contrasts these views as "metaphysics of substance" and "metaphysics of potentiality and actuality." What adolescents drawn from these groups have to say about personal persistence largely reflects these contrasting cultural traditions.

In arguing that continuity or persistence constitutes what it means to be a person, I noted that without it, no one could be held accountable for his or her own past actions or be obliged to carry through on future commitments. Without this, no society could hope to maintain law and order and good government. But on an individual level, what would it mean to somehow fail or falter in the process of developing a persistent identity? What would it mean to lose a sense of personal persistence? If you had no way to weave together your own remembered past with any anticipated future, what would give you any sense of enduring identity worth caring about? If we are invested in our own well-being precisely because we understand that we persist, or, if Flanagan is right that, "As beings in time, we are navigators. We care how our lives go" (1996, p. 67), then without a sense of self-continuity, what would stop anyone from acting on those transient thoughts of self-destruction that occasionally haunt us all?

All of this would suggest that the costs of failures in personal persistence can be measured in individual acts of suicide. And this is precisely what we have found in our studies. Of the nearly 600 individual young people we have tested to date, the only ones who come up empty-handed when asked to defend notions of persistence in themselves and others are patients in psychiatric settings whom we know to have been actively suicidal at the time of the interview. Unlike all of our other participants—and unlike their non-suicidal ward-mates—those who are without a working sense of self-continuity are marked by being suicidal. Read in the opposite direction, roughly 85% of suicidal participants utterly fail to produce reasons for personal persistence.

As compelling as such data may be, we are not, of course, free to conclude that losing a sense of self-continuity *causes* one to become suicidal. Other explanations are possible. But the kernel idea that we have been exploring is that the same natural developmental process that drives young persons forward through a series of different solutions to the paradox of their own persistence also works to create the possibility of awkward transitions between earlier and later ways of framing this problem. Thus, it threatens to leave them, if only temporarily, in the dangerous position of having no working conception of their own enduring identity and no ready care and concern for their own future. One of the special merits of this approach, at least in our own view, is that it provides the basis for a developmental account of why it is that adolescence should prove to be the fraction of the lifespan with the highest attendant risk of suicide. If the usual course of development can be seen to put adolescents at higher risk of suicide, then what would explain the fact that Canadian Aboriginal youth suffer rates of suicide that are 5 to 10 times higher than the already elevated rates of the their non-Aboriginal peers (Chandler & Lalonde, 1998)? Two possibilities immediately present themselves. First, it might be that the usual constellation of socio-economic and psychological risk factors (inadequate income, education, housing, health care, etc.) simply cluster more tightly around Aboriginal communities. That much is true enough of many Canadian Aboriginal groups—but is not especially true of those communities in Figure 2 above that are marked by high suicide rates. Alternately, and in keeping with my earlier claim that Aboriginal youth tend to take a different approach to the problem of personal persistence, it might be that their pre-ferred Narrative strategies are somehow inherently defective and fail to ade-quately sustain self-continuity, or otherwise operate to more often put them in harm's way. There is nothing in our data to suggest that a Narrative approach is any less effective than its Essentialist counterpart in actually solving the problem of personal persistence. Both yield solutions that pre-serve a sense of connection to one's past and present, and a reasoned com-mitment to one's future. In fact, it is only among those who have entirely lost the thread of their own continuity that we find increased suicide risk. If one can mount an argument of any kind—whether Essentialist or Narrative, simple or complex, one is insulated from risk.

To understand why suicide risk seems to be so unevenly distributed across communities, we need to look more carefully at the relation between personal and cultural continuity. Our claim is that just as the loss of per-sonal continuity puts individual young persons at risk, the loss of cultural continuity puts whole cultural groups at risk. Given the history of Aboriginal peoples in Canada, no one could seriously doubt that the conti-nuity of Aboriginal culture has been compromised. Indeed, this is part of the climate of adversity argument outlined in Part I. Still, although all Aboriginal cultures have suffered and had much of their culture stolen from them, they have not all responded to these assaults in identical ways. Some communities have been able to rebuild or rehabilitate a connection to their own cultural past with more success than others. Perhaps differ-ences in suicide rates between communities are associated with differing levels of success in their struggles to resist the sustained history of accultur-ative practices that threaten their very cultural existence.

To test this idea, we needed some way to measure the extent to which these communities have taken active steps to preserve and promote their own cultural heritage and to regain control over various aspects of their communal life. Our measures of cultural continuity include efforts to regain legal title to traditional lands and to re-establish forms of self-government, to reassert control over education and the provision of health care, fire, and policing services, as well as steps to erect facilities within the community devoted to traditional cultural events and practices. More recently, we have added measures of the participation of women in government, and control over the provision of child and family services. Though this handful of items might not be among the first to leap to mind when searching for indexes of cultural continuity, they do reliably capture concrete steps that communities can take to wrestle control of their lives from the hands of government overseers, and to reintroduce their own culture into their children's schools and their own communal spaces. The balance of my remarks will (as promised) focus on the relation that these measures of cultural continuity have with rates of youth suicide and the number of children in care.

What we have consistently observed, using suicide data that now cover a 14-year period, is that success on each one of these measures is associated with a decrease in the rate of youth suicide. For example, within Aboriginal communities that succeed in their efforts to restore systems of self-government, the relative risk of suicide among youth is 85% lower than in communities that have not. The risk is 52% lower within communities that control education—and the list goes on like this for each one of our measures. More important than the effect of these single variables, however, is the cumulative effect of such successes. When one counts the number of factors present in each community and then calculates the suicide rates separately for those communities with 0, 1, 2 ... etc. factors present, a clear step-wise pattern emerges. When none of these marker variables is present, the youth suicide rate is 10 times the provincial average; when all six are present, the rate falls to zero (see Figure 3 below). As this figure clearly shows, investing in activities that further cultural goals pays dividends in dramatically lower rates of youth suicide within these communities.

Figure 3. Youth suicide rate by number of factors present

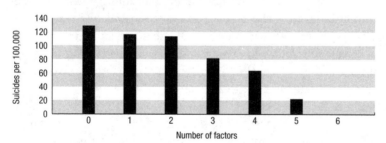

This same relation between cultural continuity and youth suicide holds when one examines the level of control that communities exert over the provision of child and family services. As with suicide, a disproportionate number of children in care are Aboriginal. Just as with suicide rates, there is wide variability from one community to the next in the number of children in care. And, just as we have seen with suicide, this variability is not random but instead attaches itself to community efforts to promote culture and regain control of services. As part of a continued "devolution" of power, provincial agencies are in the process of returning control of these services to First Nations communities. Some First Nations are farther along in this process than others. Within those communities that have assumed control and implemented plans for their children in care, the youth suicide rate is 25% lower than in communities that still lack control over children and family services. Although when one casts an eye across the whole of the province, there is no direct relation between youth suicide and the number of children in care (see Figure 4, $r = .115$), a closer inspection of the data reveals that, within the group of communities that experience no youth suicide, the number of children in care is 25% lower.

Figure 4. Youth suicide rate by number of children in care

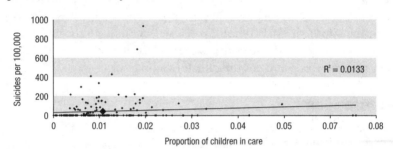

Resilience implies transcendence. While there is perhaps no happy ending to be found in the story told by these data, there is hope. Within a population that suffers the highest rate of suicide in any culturally identifiable group in the world (Kirmayer, 1994), and that even after the "60s scoop" continues to see a disproportionate number of children taken into care, there is evidence of resilience. The surprising outcomes—the transcendence—is not found in the single "hardy" or "invulnerable" child who manages to rise above adversity, but in the existence of whole communities that demonstrate the power of culture as a protective factor. When communities succeed in promoting their cultural heritage and in securing control of their own collective future—in claiming ownership over their past and future—the positive effects reverberate across many measures of youth health and well-being. Suicide rates fall, fewer children are taken into care, school completion rates rise, and rates of intentional and unintentional injury decrease.

In contrast to the critics, this cultural resilience is not simply a "situational success or failure" (Bartelt, 1994). The association between community efforts and outcome shows that instances of success are not random. And rather than working to "obscure thinking about the etiology and prevention" (Tarter & Vanyukov, 1999), the success that these communities have achieved has clear implications for policy makers and service providers. The most important implication follows from the source of the success: the First Nations themselves. If there is any take-home message to be found in our research efforts, it is that some communities have evidently already found solutions to the problems faced by Aboriginal youth. As we have argued elsewhere (Chandler & Lalonde, 2004), the parachuting of solution strategies into Aboriginal communities from far-off university campuses or government offices is not just disrespectful but also bound to fail. What is needed instead of the usual top-down forms of "knowledge transfer" is some way to facilitate lateral "knowledge exchange" and the cross-community sharing of those forms of indigenous knowledge that have already proven their worth in First Nations communities. If the concept of resilience can be stretched to apply to First Nations, as I believe that it can, then the best chances for success lie in the efforts of First Nations to reassert cultural sovereignty and to expand the indigenous knowledge base that has allowed them to adapt to and, in some cases, overcome the climate of adversity.

References

Anthony, E. J. (1974). Introduction: The syndrome of the psychologically vulnerable child. In E. J. Anthony & C. Koupernik (Eds.). *The child in his family: Children at psychiatric risk* (vol. 3, pp. 3–10). New York: Wiley.

Bartelt, D. W. (1994). On resilience: Questions of validity. In M. C. Wang & E. W. Gordon (Eds.), *Educational resilience in inner-city America* (pp. 97–108). Hillsdale, NJ: Erlbaum.

Carsten, J. (2000). *Cultures of relatedness: New approaches to the study of kinship*. Cambridge, UK: Cambridge University Press.

Cassirer, E. (1923). *Substance and function*. Chicago: The Open Court Publishing Company.

Chandler, M. J., & Ball, L. (1990). Continuity and commitment: A developmental analysis of the identity formation process in suicidal and non-suicidal youth. In H. Bosma & S. Jackson (Eds.), *Coping and self-concept in adolescence* (pp. 149–166). New York: Springer-Verlag.

Chandler, M. J., & Lalonde, C. E. (1998). Cultural continuity as a hedge against suicide in Canada's First Nations. *Transcultural Psychiatry, 35,* 193–211.

Chandler, M. J., & Lalonde, C. E. (2004). Transferring whose knowledge? Exchanging whose best practices? On knowing about Indigenous knowledge and Aboriginal suicide. In J. White, P. Maxim, and D. Beavon (Eds.), *Aboriginal policy research: Setting the agenda for change, Vol. 2.* Thompson: Toronto ON.

Chandler, M. J., Boyes, M., Ball, S., & Hala, S. (1987). The conservation of selfhood: Children's changing conceptions of self-continuity. In T. Honess and K. Yardley (Eds.), *Self and identity: Perspectives across the life-span* (pp. 108–120). London: Routledge & Kegan Paul.

Chandler, M. J., Lalonde, C. E., Sokol, B., & Hallett, D. (2003). Personal persistence, identity development, and suicide: A study of Native and non-Native North American adolescents. *Monographs of the Society for Research in Child Development, Serial No. 273, Vol. 68, No. 2.*

Eckersley R., & Dear, K. (2002). Cultural correlates of youth suicide. *Social Science & Medicine, 55,* 1891–1904.

Flanagan, O. (1996). *Self expressions: Mind, morals and the meaning of life.* New York: Oxford University Press.

Fraisse, P. (1963). *The psychology of time.* New York: Harper & Row.

Garmezy, N. (1970). Process and reactive schizophrenia: Some conceptions and issues. *Schizophrenia Bulletin, 2,* 30–74.

Garmezy, N. (1985). The NIMH-Israeli high-risk study: Commendation, comments, and cautions. *Schizophrenia Bulletin, 11,* 349–353.

Kaplan, H. B. (1999). Toward an understanding of resilience: A critical review of definitions and models. In M. Glantz and J. Johnson (Eds.), *Resilience and development: Positive life adaptations* (pp. 17–84). New York: Klewar Academic/Plenum Publishers.

Kirmayer, L. (1994). Suicide among Canadian Aboriginal peoples. *Transcultural Psychiatric Research Review, 31,* 3–57.

Lalonde, C. E., & Ferris, J. M. (2005). *Reasoning about self-continuity and self-unity among psychiatrically ill adolescents.* Unpublished manuscript, University of Victoria, Victoria.

Lalonde, C. E., & Chandler, M. J., (2004). Culture, selves, and time: Theories of personal persistence in Native and non-Native Youth. In C. Lightfoot, C. Lalonde and M. Chandler (Eds.), *Changing conceptions of psychological life (pp. 207–229).* Mahwah, NJ: Laurence Erlbaum & Associates.

Leshner, A. (1999). Introduction. *Resilience and development: Positive life adaptations* (pp. 1–5). New York: Klewar Academic/Plenum Publishers.

Liddle, H. A. (1994). Contextualizing resilience. In M. Wang & E. Gordon (Eds.), *Educational resilience in inner-city America* (pp. 167–177). Hillsdale, NJ: Erlbaum.

Locke, J. (1694/1956). *Essay concerning human understanding.* Oxford: Clarendon Press.

Luthar, S. S., Cicchetti, D., & Becker, B. (2000). The construct of resilience: A critical evaluation and guidelines for future work. *Child Development, 71,* 543–562.

Masten, A., Best, K., & Garmezy, N. (1990). Resilience and development: Contributions from the study of children who overcame adversity. *Development and Psychopathology. 2,* 425–444.

Polkinghorne, C. (1988). *Narrative knowing and the human sciences.* Albany, NY: SUNY Press.

Rauh, H. (1989). The meaning of risk and protective factors in infancy. *European Journal of Psychology of Education IV, 2,* 161–173.

Report of the Royal Commission on Aboriginal Peoples. (1996). Hull, Quebec, Canada: Canada Communications Group Publishing.

Rolf, J. (1999). Resilience: An interview with Norman Garmezy. In M. Glantz and J. Johnson (Eds.), *Resilience and development: Positive life adaptations* (pp. 5–17). New York: Klewar Academic/Plenum Publishers.

Tarter, R.E., & Vanyukov, M. (1999). Re-visiting the validity of the construct of resilience. In M. Glantz and J. Johnson (Eds.), *Resilience and development: Positive life adaptations* (pp. 85–100). New York: Klewar Academic/Plenum Publishers.

Tolan, P. T. (1996). How resilient is the concept of resilience? *The Community Psychologist, 29,* 12–15.

Werner, E. E. (1984). Resilient children. *Young Children, 1,* 68–72.

Werner, E. E., & Smith, R. (1982). *Vulnerable but invincible: A study of resilient children.* New York: McGraw-Hill.

Werner, E. E., Bierman, J. M., & French, F. E. (1971). *The children of Kauai Honolulu.* Honolulu, HA: University of Hawaii Press.

1   The program of research described in this chapter has a long history and has included a shifting set of contributors all of whom are (or were) graduate students working with Michael Chandler at the University of British Columbia. These include: Lorraine Ball, Michael Boyes, Suzanne Hala, Darcy Hallett, Bryan Sokol and me.

2   The term "aboriginal" refers to indigenous people in general, while "Aboriginal" is meant to reference specific groups within Canada. The Aboriginal peoples of Canada consist of three distinct groups: First Nations, Inuit and Métis. The First Nations were once termed "Indian." The Inuit were formerly referred to as "Eskimos." The Métis trace their origins to marriages between the First Nations and European settlers.

CHAPTER 5

Resilient society or resilient children? A comparison of child welfare service orientations in Sweden and Ontario, Canada

Evelyn G. Khoo, Lennart Nygren, and Ulf Hyvönen

Introduction

Resilience may be thought of as the ability to bounce back from adversity. While all of us may, in fact be vulnerable to stressful life situations, it has become common knowledge that some children experience good developmental or life outcomes (in school, in the community or personally) despite having been placed in high-risk situations or having experienced severe difficulties. Are only some children who face difficult life circumstances resilient, or is resilience open and available to all (Place, Reynolds, Cousins, & O'Neill, 2002)? If only some children are resilient, the task of research is to identify strengths and strategies common to survivors of adversity. If it is available to all, we must begin to look at the child's social world for sources of resilience (Sagy & Dotan, 1999).

We explore two orientations to the protection and care of children— Swedish child welfare and Canadian child protection (Khoo, 2004)—and ask what influence each of these orientations has had on conceptualizations of resilience in childhood. We define an orientation as an enduring and targeted social service structure (including service context and service features) coupled to specific forms of social intervention (activities and decision-making processes engaged in by social or case workers). Previous research has shown that the concepts of child welfare and child protection have a measurable effect on social work practice and outcomes for families (Jack, 1997). We suggest that differing conceptions of a number of normative principles found in these orientations to the protection and care of children are linked to understandings of resilience and reflect something about the very different contexts in which services are provided. We begin an examination of these conceptions by comparing the key principles of *need*, *risk* and a *child's best interests* to illuminate how seemingly universal principles are transformed by and through context. We will then show how the contextually limiting aspects of these principles distinguish explanations of resilience in Sweden and Canada. Putting resilience in context will help us to understand the implications of different orientations on policies and practices aimed at promoting children's resilience. We conclude with a discussion of the possible implications of these different orientations to the implementation of the Looking After Children approach in each country.

Within these two structurally and organizationally complex countries, we have developed a typology reflecting their different structural and intervention orientations. We recognize the problems inherent in *trying to fit countries* or welfare systems *into typologies*—orientations can change; typologies risk oversimplification. Nevertheless, there are sufficient differences in the two countries to be able to talk about Sweden representing a general child welfare orientation and Canada (and specifically, for purposes of this paper, Ontario) as having a predominantly child-protection orientation.

"Child welfare" is a term sometimes used to describe the broad scope of involvement by the state and its authorized professionals in assisting children and their families—both in cases of abuse and neglect and when families and children are found to be in need. This reflects the notion that child welfare is a broader term than child protection. The latter term delimits specific services for children in need of protection from abuse and neglect and is a term more often used in the Canadian context.

To contextualize our theorizing of resilience in these different orientations, we briefly highlight some of the main points that distinguish Swedish child welfare from Canadian child protection. Our research thus far has focused primarily on the front-end of service delivery—at the time a referral or report is received by an agency and during the assessment/investigation phase. Yet we have also found interesting points of comparison at the back-end (ongoing services, particularly placement of children in out-of-home care).

To begin, Swedish child welfare is one arm of a comparatively strong social democratic welfare state. Here, unified social and family policies are grounded in an ideology of social justice wherein all citizens are equal and entitled to decent living conditions and the chance to live a fulfilling life regardless of age, sexual orientation, ability, or ethnic origin. Family policy has emphasized a woman's right to employment and children's rights to a secure upbringing and care. Redistributive welfare policy is supposed to balance wealth and make sure that all citizens have at least a minimally acceptable standard of living. Child benefits are universal. Child care is almost fully subsidized. Further, allowances for parents to stay at home with their children during the early years are very generous. These features (and others) underscore the ways in which Sweden promotes a robust and caring society.

Our research (Khoo, Hyvönen, & Nygren, 2002 and 2003) has shown that Swedish and Canadian social workers have different states of readiness to intervene in families. Swedish social workers appear to have a greater readiness to intervene in families and have more resources available to support family members, promote welfare and prevent harm. When concerns surface regarding the well-being of a child or youth, Swedish welfare emphasizes assessment and family preservation while upholding the ideal of working in solidarity with parents. Without standardized risk assessment tools, interventions are heavily reliant on the expertise of social workers, who have a higher status than their Ontario child protection counterparts. A weakness in the system lies in its lack of local or national information management systems (SoS-rapport, 1998) that document the reporting or incidence of abuse allegations or substantiation.

Child protection in Ontario, Canada, is strongly tied to principles of residualism. In the residual Canadian welfare state, the emphasis is on individual freedom and limited state intervention. Family allowances and income maintenance services are income-tested. Services to support working parents (e.g., day care) are not a right of citizenship. Pathology lies in individual behaviour. Therefore, social work's role in residual welfare is to control individual behaviour, often by calling on due process and the rule of law. Evidence from our research in Ontario showed that research participants found the Ontario Risk Assessment Model (ORAM) to be a helpful aid to clarify roles and to decide how services will be offered. In talking about the work they do, social workers there made strong connections between working within the parameters of child protection legislation and using risk assessment tools and other standard procedures in their everyday work. In this context, Canadian social workers appear to have less professional autonomy than their Swedish counterparts. However, child protection workers in Ontario, Canada, may more consistently identify abused and neglected children.

In both contexts, social workers must investigate a client's needs, decide what measures must be taken, and then act upon the decision. They must: obtain background information; consider whether to provide services on a compulsory or voluntary basis; consider the interests of children; and use some sort of analysis in developing a social work plan. The differences lie, more significantly, in the relationship between the service structures and interventions carried out. For example, both countries have similar definitions of child abuse, yet family preservation frames Swedish child welfare and stands in stark contrast to the permanency ideal in Canadian child protection. Additionally, through one view offered in a focus group in Ontario, Canada, we can see the significance of differences between child welfare and child protection—differences bound by both place and time:

> We're no longer in the child welfare business. Child welfare is a term of the 1980s. It's an 80s philosophy. And the 90s pretty much pounded the word "child welfare" into oblivion. So, now it's the child protection business.

The normative principles of need, risk, and a child's best interests

Media headlines cry out about a little boy who was beaten to death in his home. He was only six months old. An 11-year-old girl was repeatedly molested by her foster father. These cases are neither isolated nor a long-buried history. They occurred in Canada and Sweden in the late 1990s. As the media would have it, both countries are rife with problems, leaving children hostage to abuse in substitute care or languishing at home because of individual social worker or systemic incompetence. Mounting pressure, not only from the media but also from official public inquiries, has led to changes in both countries in recent years. A strong theme in these changes is that child welfare services must be provided for the best interests of children, not their parents, the family system, or the social workers providing services.

As a general concept, the "best interests" principle emphasizes a notion that, in matters concerning a child, the best possible solution should be sought in individual cases (Faulconer, 1994). Vague definitions such as this leave open the possibility of wide variations in applications of the principle based on value judgments rooted in culture, social policy, and ideology. Therefore, there may be significant differences in the application of the best interest principle in different countries and in different policy contexts, child welfare being a critical field wherein the policy is applied.

Below, we compare adaptations of the principle to Swedish child welfare and Canadian child protection; examine how *need* and *risk* connect to the *best interests* principle; and analyze the impact generated by various tensions between these principles. We use the comparative method to tease out a critical understanding of the similarities and differences in welfare approaches (Pringle, 1998). The methodology is particularly appropriate because comparisons of superficially common principles may reveal significant differences in how principles are put into practice.

A number of important choices were made to limit the amount of material to be compared. The first concerns situations in which the principle is applied. Given our interest in a social work perspective, we bring together data from previous work in comparing local child welfare agencies and placing them in a broader structural context. Details of the methodology can be found in Khoo (2004) and Khoo, Hyvönen, and Nygren (2002 and 2003). We also bring in findings from an examination of legal texts focusing on the position and application of specific references to a child's best interests. The texts we examined were the following: the *Child and Family Services Act*, Ontario (2001, 1984); Sweden's *Socialtjänstlagen* [Social Service Act] (SoL) and *Lagen med särskilda bestämmelser om vård av unga* [Care of Young People Act] (LVU). We do not claim a complete knowledge of current and past legislation. Rather, we examine these documents to assemble information about ideal arrangements reflected in law, such as the position of a child's best interests relative to the principles of need and risk. Other sources are also used to complete the puzzle of the interplay between child welfare and child protection orientations and their contributions to the normative principles and the notion of childhood resilience.

Tension between principles

In child welfare, principles such as the best interests of the child are inconsequential until they are picked up by people such as lawyers, judges and social workers who know that they are supposed to act upon them in ways that are considered appropriate to the context in which they find their purpose. In the following, we present two examples of social workers giving expression to the context-dependent meaning of a child's best interests.

> **Swedish Social Worker:** I feel that we have this in the back of our heads…how damaging it is to separate children from their families. I think this is difficult. We get hung up sometimes, I think. I can sometimes feel that we don't really see to children's best interests. It's more about the parents…to try every single possibility to try to keep the child at home. And that's actually the purpose of the law. Everything should take place in cooperation and mutual understanding…even if we have a child focus more now than when I started working.

> **Canadian Social Worker:** We already made the psychological shift. I think the legislation was [pause] family preservation guided practice. And we know that preserving the family is not always in some of these

children's best interests...The child is your client, your primary focus...
But, as much as the child is our client, we also make those decisions for
them. And, so you know, kids love their parents no matter what...so
we have to battle it out with that child because what they think they
want, we think is not in their best interests.

These examples provide striking examples of a tension between different
principles played out in the minds of social workers but also reflecting a difference in the balance created between different principles at work in Sweden
and Canada. After all, social work, as a value-committed profession, is shaped
by a meeting between politics and science (Kilty & Meenaghan, 1995).
However, the use of politics and science is selective and results in certain questions being viewed in a value-laden way. This is especially true in Swedish
child welfare and Canadian child protection where the value-laden principles
of need and risk are instrumental in shaping the equally value-laden principle
of best interests. Moreover, trying to create a balance between sometimes
competing principles can explain much of the tension experienced in social
work practice (Trocmé, Mertins-Kirkwood, MacFadden, Alaggia, &
Goodman, 1999) in different contexts. However, inasmuch as Sweden and
Canada have different orientations to the welfare and protection of children,
we would anticipate that these tensions arise from different sources.

How is it, then, that assessing the best interests of children has proven to
be such a difficult task? Social workers in Sweden seemingly try to balance
the needs of children with family preservation, all the while worried about
the risks posed by the different choices they make. Meanwhile, Canadian
social workers seem to be firmly fixed on the best interests of children, but
can still end up clashing with the very children they are dedicated to protecting. In both contexts, social workers are engaged in a professional practice wherein the best interests of children are constructed within the very
different perspectives of child welfare and child protection. That is, the orientations of child welfare and child protection can each be understood as a
way of structuring, organizing and delivering social work services to particular groups of people. These services are then instrumentalized through
the use of texts (policy, legal and professional) that seek to codify the mean-
ings of need, risk and a child's best interests.

The best interests of the child

As a socio-legal principle, the best interests of the child has found its way
into the legislative contexts of Swedish child welfare and Canadian child
protection. The legal contexts of these orientations leave open the possibil-

ity of interpreting what is meant by best interests, although legal definitions tend to be tied to discourses of "child welfare science" (King & Piper,
1995). They are predicated on psycho-legal notions of physical well-being,
proper moral upbringing, and psychological needs (White, 1998) and are
put in relationship to notions of risk, security (safety) and need. Therefore,
in comparing different child welfare orientations, the best interests of a
child must be examined from the perspective of the policy context in which
the principle is found and of the statutory rules that give effect to it because
these both condition how social workers engage with it in their daily work.
That is, how the best interests of children are identified and presented in
the socio-legal context may facilitate or impede the actual recognition of a
child's interests or needs.

Swedish legislation

In the legal context of Swedish child welfare, the *Social Services Act* (SoL)
(Socialtjänstlag, 2001) and the *Compulsory Care of Young Persons Act* (LVU)
(Socialstyrelsen, 1997) both make direct reference to the best interests of
the child. The SoL is a law framing the delivery of a wide range of social
services from needs-tested economic aid to care services for the elderly,
people with disabilities, and individuals or families. In the last group we
can find the equivalent of child welfare services. The law is targeted toward
certain populations and needs, setting broad goals and standards of care
that citizens have a right to expect of the state. The LVU is specifically
aimed at setting socio-legal standards for children and youth who are
looked after by the state on a compulsory basis.

In the SoL (2001:453) we can clearly see the ideological positioning of
the best interest principle in relation to other principles that fall outside of
the area of child welfare. The portal paragraph of the law (1 kap. 1 §
Socialtjänstens mål [Social Services Goal]) states that social services shall be
provided on the basis of: "…democracy and solidarity and for the purposes of promoting economic and social security, equality of living conditions,
and active participation in society."

Particular mention of the best interests principle does not come until
the second portal paragraph: "In measures regarding children, particular
attention shall be paid to what the best interests of the child demand."

The law further states that Social Services will work to ensure that children grow up in secure and good conditions. Services are to be provided in
cooperation with the home, to promote a holistic approach to the physical
and social personal development of children with particular attention paid

to children who have shown signs or risk of an unfavourable development.

Thus, while the best interests of the child is a main consideration in the SoL, the law's emphasis on solidarity and on the right of the state to intervene to ensure that children are brought up in adequate living conditions suggests that the best interests principle is contributory to the broader purpose of the social services in fostering a civil society. Further, ensuring the best interests of children is perhaps another way of upholding democracy and solidarity in the social services.

The LVU law states the conditions wherein the state may take a child into care without parental consent and states the social services obligations in providing care to children in compulsory care. Within the context of this law, the best interests of the young person are to be the overriding factor in decisions taken, and the young person's wishes should be taken into account based on his or her age and level of maturity. However, it has been the state's position that it is always in children's best interests to return home eventually to their biological parents. Only in June 2003 did the state begin to implement measures allowing a transfer of custody of children in long-term care to their foster parents (Socialstyrelsen, 2003). This change may signal an ideological departure away the state's previous position toward a model of permanency planning, though changes are aimed at a small minority of children in care.

Ontario legislation

The best interests principle has a considerable history in the Canadian content. In the case of Ontario, the best interests of the child assumed a prominent position in child welfare legislation with the *Child and Family Services Act* (CFSA) (1984). At that time, the principle was put into direct tension with other principles of least intrusiveness and protection. The least intrusiveness principle was based on the notion that even when a family failed in its responsibilities, the state should intervene in the least intrusive manner to secure the safety of a child. Protection then referred to the functions of the authorities to investigate, assess risk, and remove a child if there were legally defined grounds to believe a child may have been harmed or was at significant risk of being harmed.

Since then, the amended act has sought to strengthen the best interests principle, directly in connection to a strengthening of the protective function of the law, and making secondary the autonomy and integrity of the family unit and notions of mutual support for families. The paramount purpose of the Act (*Child and Family Services Act*, R.S.O. 1990, c. C-11 Amended November 30, 2001.) is: "…to promote the best interests, protection and well-being of children."

The paramount importance of these fused principles means a dramatic shift toward protectionism as the defining element of a child's best interests. Protection now refers to the functions of the authorities to investigate, assess risk and remove a child if there are legally defined grounds to believe a child may have been harmed or there *is a risk that the child is likely to* suffer harm [our emphasis]. The other purposes of the CFSA come into play only if they are consistent with the paramount purposes of the act. Therefore, amongst other aspects, the integrity of the family and least intrusive approaches to service delivery are secondary to the paramount purpose of the law.

The CFSA is quite specific about the criteria that should go into making a determination in the best interests of the child. It mentions no fewer than 14 criteria to take into consideration including: the child's physical, mental and emotional level of development and special needs; the child's religious and cultural background; and the child's need for a positive relationship and continuity of care with a parent or family by blood or through adoption. Here a judge must consider a Children's Aid Society's plan of care (including adoption) over a parent's plan. Consideration must be made of the child's views and wishes, if reasonably ascertainable. Moreover, judgements must be made expeditiously and take into account concerns about risk to the child.

Although the Act says that its purpose is to promote the best interests of children, in fact, it is only children identified by the legal system as "in need of protection" whose interests are identified. As we will discuss in the sections below, the construction of need in Canadian child protection diverges sharply from that of Swedish child welfare. These constructions establish when and on what bases a child's best interests will be given voice.

Need in the contexts of child welfare and child protection

The principle of need is used alongside of the best interests principle when considering a threshold for intervention and then in determining what to do with a child who comes into contact with child welfare authorities. The decision unfolds thusly: (1) a decision has to be made about a need for intervention, and then (2) that a particular plan would be in that child's best interests, considering (a) certain *ideals* or *prima facie* duties about what constitutes adequate parenting, the role of the stated, professional responsibility, danger to a child, good care, good parenting and so on; and (b) then turning to a *standard of reasonableness* (Kopelman, 1997).

In child welfare generally, the threshold for intervention may or may not be explicitly stated in legislation. However, as a gatekeeping process (Swift, 1995), social workers must determine whether a need exists and whether a child's best interests would be served by the actions of a child welfare agency. To override parental authority, the social workers must present a convincing case that intervention is needed. However, the threshold for intervention varies over time and place.

Need in the context of Swedish child welfare

In Sweden, need must be understood from the perspective of its cradle-to-grave welfare system. In Swedish child welfare, all children in need are to be served; efforts emphasize prevention; abuse and neglect are not typical preconditions for beginning child welfare services (corporal punishment of children is illegal); measures are supposed to be offered on a voluntary basis wherever possible; and parents rarely lose custody of their children (Hessle & Vinnerljung, 1999). However, broad local autonomy and the openness of Social Services law to interpretation have produced conditions for wide variations in the provision of child welfare services (Östberg, Wåhlander, & Milton, 2000). Also, while the removal of children has been an option pursued with reluctance—occurring most often among poor families (now more than ever migrant/refugee)—rates are not all that low (8 children/ youth per 1000; Vogt Grinde, 2003), and they signal trends toward the use of more compulsory care and an increasing consideration of long-term/permanent placement and change of custody for certain children.

Swedish child welfare is strongly solidaristic rather than individualistic. The implications of social solidarity are that social care services for children are often universal, generally aimed at reform rather than correction (of parents) and designed to promote the well-being of children. Social services, however, do have an element of social control as social workers must gatekeep and have relatively coercive powers in certain situations such as when parents abuse alcohol or drugs. Nevertheless, need is de-pathologized to a greater extent in the sense that there is a common belief that all citizens may at some point find themselves in need and that the state should be a major player in seeing that various needs are met.

In a country where control over everyday decision-making is highly decentralized, social workers rely on the assessment process (rather than forensic evidence) to produce cumulative information with which to assess need of assistance rather than need of protection. An emphasis on solidarity rather than on procedures is reflected in a different set of questions asked by social workers in Swedish child welfare.

- How is the child?
- Are the child's needs being met, and by whom?
- Can Social Services be of some help and be the source of some kind of measures?

In Sweden, the benchmark for intervention is need. The law and practice relating to child welfare emphasizes a broad concern for children's growth, development and well-being within the context of stable family relationships. It is presumed that it is in every child's best interests to be cared for in the family of origin (though there seems to be a retreat from this position in regard to children in long-term care). Thus, this presumption that care in the home is the best has led social workers to accommodate a principle of partnership with parents over a child focus or child perspective, which have often been mentioned as missing in Swedish child welfare (Rasmusson, Hyvönen, & Mellberg, 2004).

Need in the context of Canadian child protection

The Canadian child protection system (Swift, 1997) is located within a liberal, Anglo-American social welfare regime typology (Esping-Andersen, 1990) lying somewhere between the ambitious, social democratic model of Sweden and the barren model that characterizes the United States (Lightman & Riches, 2000). With regard to child abuse, Canada developed more along the lines of the UK and USA with organizations dealing with it at the start of the 20th century. The Canadian system is residual, with only the most vulnerable served by child protection agencies in which work processes are increasingly standardized and carried out by suitably trained child protection workers. In contrast to Swedish child welfare, the over-riding concern in child protection is to control risk via regulation and the proceduralization of work strategies.

In Canadian child protection, the threshold for state-sanctioned intervention has progressively been falling as social work has become highly formalized, regulated and textually-mediated through the use of eligibility, safety, and risk assessment tools within the ORAM (OACAS, 2000). In Ontario, the legislation has been amended to allow intervention when there is a risk that a child is likely to suffer harm. While the threshold for intervention has loosened, allegations of child maltreatment continue to elicit a strong protectionist response. The social workers to whom we spoke were very clear as to the kinds of questions that they had to answer in screening referral information.

- Is the child in need of protection?
- Are these children/is this child safe?

- In the future, if we were to walk away, would we be leaving this child at risk?

Thus, need in the Canadian system is strongly attached to the legal bases for protection. Need is first of all attached to the child's conditions. The child must be in need of protection to be served. Protection is regarded as the first threshold of intervention. That is, social workers must focus on the need of a child to be protected from abuse, harm, or the risk of harm. Even in terms of neglect, the standard to be applied is aimed at the protection of the child from a parent's failure to provide or to permit others to provide the care needed, such that this has resulted in harm.

Risk and a child's best interests

Risk and best interests are key principles in both countries, but these principles have become connected to social work practice in very different ways. In both countries, elucidation of risk, need and a child's best interests are made in relation to the particular needs and circumstances of individual children. When these principles are left as rather indeterminate concepts, social workers are able to decide creatively and flexibly based on a child's particular circumstances. But when risk is objectified or codified, decision making around these principles is increasingly tied to the specific legal context and texts wherein the concept has been defined.

Risk in Swedish child welfare

Although the emphasis in Swedish child welfare is on understanding acts or circumstances producing psychosocial difficulties experienced by families, risk assessment also has a place there in spite of the fact that there is no wide use of systematic or standardized risk assessment tools (Lagerberg & Sundelin, 2000). Given the different emphasis of Swedish child welfare, there is understandably a different notion of what constitutes risk, how to look for it, and what to do about it.

There is agreement between Swedish and Canadian social workers that risk factors associated with child physical abuse and neglect include: alcohol or substance abuse, violence in the home, a protective parent, extended family, age of the child, previous history, child behaviour, socio-economic factors, and mental health issues. However, in Sweden, conflict between parents over the custody of children following divorce would also pose sufficient risk to consider the child to be in need of assistance. At the same time, children have more clearly defined rights to satisfactory life conditions and not to be subjected to "physical punishment or other degradation" (Socialstyrelsen, 1997). This broader approach to defining risk means a greater willingness of the state to intervene in the private realm of the family.

The assessment-driven nature of Swedish child welfare means that social workers there spend more time (policy allows a four-month assessment period) looking for risk and identifying the needs of a child and family. Given Sweden's broad-based social services, there is a wider variety of services available to assist children in need. Intervention may begin earlier, with more preventive services, and services available to deal with problems as they arise—including contacting families and the placement of whole families together in out-of-home care for assessment and treatment. When things do go wrong, the government's policy is to de-stigmatize social services, making them accessible based on mutual consent, and wherever possible, seeing to the child's best interests within that child's family. This partially explains why in Sweden only 25% of children in care are there under a court order; why care is considered a temporary measure; and why parents rarely lose custody of their children (Nordin, 2003) even when (from a perspective of protection) it might be seen to be in a child's best interests.

Despite many differences between Ontario and Sweden, similar proportions of children and youth are placed in out-of-home care (Table 1). The similarity in numbers does not, however, contradict our proposition that these orientations matter to how we serve children in care. Compulsory care is more frequently used in Ontario both because the orientation drives placement in a compulsory direction and because, as we can see from other research (Whitehead, Chiodo, Leschied, & Hurley, 2004), the grounds for care are becoming increasingly serious—Canadian society has "harder" cases with more serious problems resulting in the need for children to come into state care under court protection orders. Swedish social workers can place children on a "voluntary" basis in situations where compulsion may be required in Canada. Given the lack of standardized practices, more Swedish children come into care under "looser" legal conditions than in Canada— meaning that the authority of individual Swedish social workers is somehow stronger. These hypotheses require further investigation and testing against antithetical propositions. Perhaps similar placement rates reflect a considerable overlap between child welfare typologies, stemming from the residual nature of all child welfare systems (Hessle & Vinnerljung, 1999), or maybe we use placements as a reified solution to wider problems (White, 1998). We would argue, however, that the grounds for the placements are more significant and illustrative of differences between the two orientations than are the numbers of children placed (Figure 1).

Table 1. Comparable statistics (Child Welfare Services; 2003)

Measure	Ontario/Canada	Sweden
	Number of children and youth (proportion of child population)	
Out-of-home care	18,126 (7.8 per 1,000)	14,911 (7.62 per 1,000)
Open child welfare cases (non-placement)	6,503	28,600
Protection	26,959	Unknown

Sources: OACAS (2004)
        Socialstyrelsen (2004)

Figure 1. Total children in care by status (2003)
        Number of children in care on 1 day in Sweden (November 1, 2003)
        and Ontario (March 31, 2003)

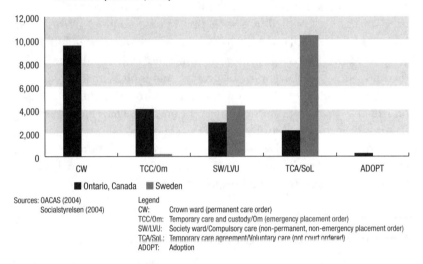

Sources: OACAS (2004)
        Socialstyrelsen (2004)

Legend
CW: Crown ward (permanent care order)
TCC/Om: Temporary care and custody/Om (emergency placement order)
SW/LVU: Society ward/Compulsory care (non-permanent, non-emergency placement order)
TCA/SoL: Temporary care agreement/Voluntary care (not court ordered)
ADOPT: Adoption

Risk in Canadian child protection

In Canada, where risk has had a long hold over need, a child's best interests are considered best served through an elimination of risk obtained by protection interventions that more often translate into the permanent removal of a child from the parental home. Assessment of risk and dangerousness has become a key role for social workers in Canadian child protection where decisions are carried out in an increasingly legalized context characterized by concern about risk (Longlade, 1999).

Risk assessment aspires to give social workers a way of generalizing needs for welfare and safety. All the same, risk has also come to mean a concern about liability. It is not just the child who is at risk but the social worker as well because the disputable nature of trying to make risk measurable has opened up social work practice to the dangers of blame, accusation and error. This atmosphere of scrutiny and accountability is acutely felt by social workers in child protection (Kanani, Regehr, & Bernstein, 2002). This has been noted in the Canadian court system as well as by researchers in other child protection systems (Parton, 1998). Social workers face criticism for making decisions not to take action when there is a claim (in clear hindsight) that dangers were evident. They are also damned for making a case for intervention based on "not serious enough" allegations.

Thus, in the Canadian context, child protection and risk have, in a sense, joined forces, making permanency planning the most obvious "winner" in the contest of deciding a child's best interests. The use of risk assessment tools has begun to erode social work and replace it with a technician's practice, but has not resulted in a reduction in case numbers (Whitehead, Leschied, Chiodo, & Hurley, 2004). Child welfare referrals end up being weighed according to child protection principles, which tend to be legalistic. And, while the sharpening of professional tools to manage risk has meant greater consistency in how decisions are made about the grounds on which to provide protection interventions, there have been alarming failures to see to the best interests of the child through prevention. The result: dramatic rises in caseloads, huge increases in the numbers of cases involving neglect and emotional abuse, and a cross-generational cycle of family involvement with child protection authorities (Whitehead et al., 2004).

Resilient society—resilient children

The orientations of child welfare and child protection both impose limits on applications of the best interests of children, requiring social workers to weigh best interests against need and risk, but in different ways (Table 2). In Canadian child protection, best interests are paramount but intimately connected to "need of protection" and risk assessment. In Sweden, the fulfilment of children's needs is identified as the ideal way to secure the best interests of children. Social workers in this context have a greater latitude to address children's best interests where the mind-set seems to be one of seeing to broad needs in a positive sense aimed at ensuring equality and improving community.

How then can we understand the notion of resilience within the landscapes of Swedish child welfare and Canadian child protection? Simply put, Sweden concerns itself more with the development and preservation of a resilient society, whereas Canada seeks to enhance resilience in individual children.

Table 2. Key principles and their parameters in Canadian child protection and Swedish child welfare

	Canada	Sweden
Best interests	Paramount	Contributory
Need	Connected to protection	Broadly defined, diversified to whole child population.
Risk	Focused on avoidance using standardized tools	Accepted but contributory to ideals of equality, solidarity and right to a good life

How far has Sweden been able to go in promoting resilience in its society? The country's aggressive laws and policy have resulted in the development of a broad social service system that responds to and assesses children's situations and protects them individually from discrimination and harm. Children have statutory respect in family decision making (Parent's Code) and have a right to be free from corporal or degrading punishment. The emphasis there is on actively preventing harm before it occurs by refusing to allow or benignly accept certain kinds of violence in the home under the guise of "deserved punishment." In this sense, Sweden may be among the least violent of societies and certainly stands apart from Canada, where the *Criminal Code* (Section 43) states that, "Every school-teacher, parent or person standing in the place of a parent is justified in using force by way of correction toward a pupil or child, as the case may be, who is under his care, if the force does not exceed what is reasonable under the circumstances." Although systemic variation is a significant weakness in the Swedish system because each of Sweden's 290 municipalities must organize and implement social services and decide the degree of specialization of child welfare services (Pringle, 1998), it can still be argued that Swedish children are less vulnerable than Canadian children.

In Canada's child protection system, children in need and prevention measures are low priorities. Without ensuring that sufficient supports are available for parents (especially high-risk parents) to prevent abuse or neglect (not just the speedy removal of children when necessary), the best interests of marginalized children will never be fully served. The current state of child protection in Canada reflects an uneven commitment to the implementation of best interests as a child-centred and child's rights principle.

Lindström (2001) reminds us that although knowledge of resilience factors can assist some young people in overcoming adversity, changing fundamental social inequalities may be more important if we want to produce a more civil society. In addressing one of the roots causes of violence against children—namely, poverty and structural inequality—we would argue that Sweden has gone much farther than Canada in upholding all children's best interests, thereby avoiding the characteristic failures of the child protection model where searching for the best risk avoidance tools has resulted in an "endless game akin to chasing our tail" (Anglin, 2002).

Research has broadly shown that the problem of child abuse and neglect has not been eradicated through existing state efforts. It has even been suggested that increasing numbers of children are being maltreated. Certainly, a significant number of youth and adults report they were abused children (Meyerson, Long, Miranda, & Marx, 2002). Other studies suggest that more children are coming into the care of the state and that these children, more so than in recent decades, bear with them a legacy of greater deprivation, often reflected in more difficult behaviours (Mallucio, Canali, and Vecchiato, 2002). Others have even suggested that the state should remove itself from the child welfare business (Epstein, 1997).

As a consequence, the question becomes whether and to what degree we should direct our efforts toward identifying and developing coping resources for young people versus eradicating the causes of social vulnerability. While we certainly would not wish to thwart efforts to strengthen childhood resilience, let us not forget the obvious benefits of primary prevention targeted at the factors shown to have the capacity to lead to abuse or neglect. Preventive efforts that address poverty, unemployment, lone-parenthood, and a lack of social networks and health care remain imperative to building resilience in communities and in the people who are an integral part of them. Yet, the broad goals of promoting resilient society and resilient children are probably more complementary than competitive because we know that, even in a resilient welfare state like Sweden, some children will face adversity. One way that Sweden and Canada have both sought to (at least indirectly) promote resilience in some children is through the implementation of the Looking After Children initiative (Kufeldt & McKenzie, 2003; Socialstyrelsen, 2001; Ward, 1995).

Reflections on Looking After Children

Looking After Children is attracting international attention, offering a standardized framework and tools to guide and measure interventions of individuals and organizations responsible for looking after children in contact with the child welfare system (Ward, 1995). In Sweden, this approach is called "Barns behov i centrum" (The child's needs in the centre) (BBIC) (Socialstyrelsen, 2001). The BBIC project has been ongoing in seven municipalities since 1999. Currently, it is being implemented variably— sometimes with children in care, at other times with children and their parents receiving community-based services. The Canadian version of the

Looking After Children system was "imported" in 1996 and has undergone progressive piloting and revision since then. To date, there are still variations from jurisdiction to jurisdiction in the headway made in its implementation. (See: http://www.cwlc.ca/pdfs/canLACnewsspring02.pdf).

With LAC licensed by the UK Department of Health, some limits are placed on international adaptations. Nevertheless, some differences are already beginning to emerge. For example, the main LAC tool in Ontario, Canada, is the Assessment and Action Record (AAR). The AARs are already showing usefulness as a tool for measuring resilient outcomes for children in care (Flynn, Ghazal, Legault, Vandermeulen, & Petrick, 2004) and are promoted for their practice, management and policy functions. The Swedish BBIC project is promoted as a quality assurance model wherein child welfare investigation, as well as planning and follow-up of care services, can be improved while at the same time strengthening children's rights (Socialstyrelsen, 2001). AARs comprise a minority of the BBIC materials.

One question is whether and to what extent the LAC approach has been incorporated into or replaced existing child welfare service features. Another important question for future investigations is: How do the Swedish BBIC and Canadian versions of LAC compare with each other? What common ground do they share? How do they differ? And, finally what kind of an impact has context had on the shaping and implementation of LAC?

Researchers and policy makers share an interest in finding ways to transfer knowledge critically across national boundaries through developing best practices, improving outcomes, building evidence-based social work, protecting children from harm, and recognizing children's rights. LAC represents a major new direction that aims to cover many of these goals. A next step in LAC evaluations ought to include culturally relevant analyses to further our understanding of what works and why so that we can improve child welfare policy and program development, thereby ensuring better outcomes for children in need of state help and care.

Authors' note

We gratefully acknowledge the financial support for research received from the Swedish Council for Working Life and Social Research. We also thank the social workers in Sweden and the province of Ontario who participated in the research.

References

Anglin, J. P. (2002). Risk, well-being, and paramountcy in child protection: The need for transformation. *Child and Youth Care Forum, 3*, 233–255.

Child and Family Services Act (Ontario), (2001, 1984), R.S.O. 1990, CHAPTER C.11.

Epstein, W. M. (1997). Social science, child welfare, and family preservation: A failure of rationality in public policy. *Children and Youth Services Review, 19*, 41–60.

Esping-Andersen, G. (1990). *The three worlds of welfare capitalism.* Oxford, U.K.: Blackwell.

Faulconer, L. (1994). In the best interests of children? *Family Relations, 43*, 261–264.

Flynn, R. J., Ghazal, H., Legault, L., Vandermeulen, G., & Petrick, S. (2004). Use of population measures and norms to identify resilient outcomes in young people in care: An exploratory study. *Child and Family Social Work, 9*, 65–79.

Hessle, S., & Vinnerljung, B. (1999). *Child welfare in Sweden: An overview.* Stockholm: Stockholm Studies in Social Work (vol. 15).

Jack, G. (1997). Discourses of child protection and child welfare. *British Journal of Social Work, 27*, 659–678.

Kanani, K., Regehr, C., & Bernstein, M. M. (2002). Liability considerations in child welfare: Lessons from Canada. *Child Abuse and Neglect 26*, 1029–1043.

Khoo, E. G., Hyvönen, U., & Nygren, L. (2002). Child welfare or child protection. Uncovering Swedish and Canadian orientations to social intervention in child maltreatment. *Qualitative Social Work, 1*, 451–471.

Khoo, E. G., Hyvönen, U., & Nygren, L. (2003). Gatekeeping in child welfare: A comparative study of intake decision making by social workers in Canada and Sweden. *Child Welfare, 82*, 507–525.

Khoo, E. G. (2004). *Protecting our children: A comparative study of the dynamics of structure, intervention and their interplay in Swedish child welfare and Canadian child protection.* Umeå University (Ph.D. Dissertation, Umeå University Studies in Social Work, N. 39). Umeå, Sweden.

Kilty, K. M., & Meenaghan, T. M. (1995). Social work and the convergence of politics and science. *Social Work, 40*, 445–453.

King, M., & Piper, C. (1995). *How the law thinks about children* (2nd ed.). Aldershot, UK: Arena.

Kopelman, L. M. (1997). The best-interests standard as threshold, ideal, and standard of reasonableness. *Journal of Medicine and Philosophy, 22,* 271–289.

Kufeldt, K., & McKenzie, B. (Eds.). (2003). *Child welfare: Connecting research, policy and practice.* Waterloo: Wilfrid Laurier University Press.

Lagerberg, D., & Sundelin, C. (2000). *Risk och prognos i socialt arbete med barn. Forskningsmetoder och resultat [Risk and prognosis in social work with children: Research methods and results].* Stockholm: The Authors, Centrum för utvärdering av socialt arbete and Gothia.

Lightman, E. S., & Riches, G. (2000). From modest rights to commodification in Canada's welfare state. *European Journal of Social Work, 3,* 179–190.

Lindström, B. (2001). The meaning of resilience. *International Journal of Adolescent Medicine and Health, 13,* 7–12.

Longlade, P. (1999). Evaluating child homicide inquests as a learning process: A social constructionist analysis of a Canadian experience. *Child and Youth Services Review, 21,* 295–310.

Mallucio, A. N., Canali, C., & Vecchiato, T. (Eds.). (2002). Assessing outcomes in child and family services. *Comparative design and policy issues.* New York: Aldine de Gruyter.

Meyerson, L. A., Long, P. J., Miranda, R. J., & Marx, B. P. (2002). The influence of childhood sexual abuse, physical abuse, family environment, and gender on the psychological adjustment of adolescents. *Child Abuse and Neglect, 26,* 387–405.

Nordin, H. (2003). *Permanenta eller tillfälliga placeringar? Om lag och verklighet vid flyttningsförbudsbestämmelsens tillämpning [Permanent or temporary placements? On the law and reality in the application of court decisions on refusing reunification].* Stockholm University, Stockholm.

Ontario Association of Children's Aid Societies (OACAS). (2000). *Risk assessment model for child protection in Ontario: Eligibility spectrum, risk assessment model for child protection in Ontario.* Toronto, Canada: Ontario Ministry of Children, Family, and Community Services.

Oppenheim, E., & Bussiere, A. (1996). Adoption: Where do relatives stand? *Child Welfare, 75,* 471–488.

Östberg, F., Wåhlander, E., & Milton, P. (2000). *Barnavårdsutredningar i sex kommuner – en vinjettsudie [Child welfare investigations in six communities: A vignette study]* (No. 3). Stockholm: CUS-skrift 2000:3.

Otway, O. (1996). Social work with children and families. From child welfare to child protection. In N. Parton (Ed.), *Social theory, social change and social work* (pp. 154–171). London: Routledge.

Parton, N. (1998). Risk, advanced liberalism and child welfare: The need to rediscover uncertainty and ambiguity. *British Journal of Social Work, 28,* 5–27.

Place, M., Reynolds, J., Cousins, A., & O'Neill, S. (2002). Developing a resilience package for vulnerable children. *Child and Adolescent Mental Health, 7,* 162–167.

Pringle, K. (1998). *Children and social welfare in Europe.* Buckingham, U.K.: Open University Press.

Rasmusson, B., Hyvönen, U., & Mellberg, L. (2004). *Utvärderingsmöten i BBIC. En studie av barns delaktighet och medbestämmande. [Child's needs in the centre review meetings: A study of children's participation and joint decision-making].* Stockholm: Socialstyrelsen.

Sagy, S., & Dotan, N. (1999). Coping resources of maltreated children in the family: A salutogenic approach. *Child Abuse and Neglect, 25,* 1463–1480.

Socialtjänstlag 2001: 453 [Social Services Act 2001: 453].

Socialstyrelsen. (1997). *Tillämpningen av lagen (1990:52) med särskilda bestämmelser om vård av unga [Application of the law (1990:52) with particular regard to the care of youth].* Stockholm: Socialstyrelsens författningssamling.

Socialstyrelsen. (2001). *Barns behov i centrum. ett system för utredning, planering och uppföljning av barn i den sociala baravården [The child's needs in the centre: A system for investigating, planning and follow-up of children in the child welfare system].*Unpublished manuscript. Jag förstår inte. Tack.

Socialstyrelsen. (2003). *Meddelandeblad. Stärkt skydd för barn i utsatta situationer m.m. [Memo. Increased protection for children in vulnerable situations and more].*

SoS-rapport. (1998). *Anmälan, utredning, insats [Referral, investigation, measures]* (No. 4). Stockholm: Socialstyrelsen.

Swift, K. J. (1995). *Manufacturing bad mothers.* Toronto: University of Toronto Press.

Swift, K. J. (1997). Canada: Trends and issues in child welfare. In N. Gilbert (Ed.), *Combatting child abuse: International perspectives and trends* (pp. 38–71). London: Oxford University Press.

Trocmé, N., Mertins-Kirkwood, B., MacFadden, R., Alaggia, R., & Goodman, D. (1999). *Final report. Ontario risk assessment model. Phase 1: Implementation and training.* Toronto: Centre for Applied Social Research. Bell Canada Child Welfare Research Unit. Faculty of Social Work, University of Toronto.

Vogt Grinde, T. (2003). *Terskelen for barneverntiltak og beslutningprocessen ved bruk av tvang [Placement rates and decision making around the use of compulsion].* Paper presented at the meeting, Nordisk Barevern [Nordic Child Welfare], Reykyavik, Iceland.

Ward, H. (Ed.) (1995). *Looking After Children: Research into practice.* London: Department of Health.

White, S. (1998). Interdiscursivity and child welfare: The ascent and durability of psycho-legalism. *Sociological Review, 46,* 264–287.

Whitehead, P., Chiodo, D., Leschied, A., & Hurley, D. (2004). Referrals and admissions to Children's Aid Society: A test of four hypotheses. *Child and Youth Care Forum, 33,* 425–440.

Zeigert, K. A. (1987). Children's rights and the supportive function of law: The case of Sweden. *Journal of Comparative Family Studies, 18,* 157–174.

CHAPTER 6

Is permanence necessary for resilience? Advice for policy makers

Ivan Brown, Sophie Léveillé, and Pamela Gough

The Centre of Excellence for Child Welfare (CECW) sponsored a policy symposium in Ottawa, Ontario, on August 19, 2004. The focus of the symposium was the question: *Is permanence necessary for resilience?* This question emerged from discussions during the previous year at various activities and forums of the CECW on key current policy and practice issues. Child welfare policy and practice throughout Canada generally reflect the assumption that children are more resilient when they move quickly to a stable, permanent living environment. Yet, these assumptions are not strongly supported by the research available, and this suggests that sweeping policy generalizations are likely to be dangerous.

It was considered that expert discussion and clarification of the key symposium question would be beneficial to the field of child welfare. In addition, it was determined that, as a body whose mandate includes generating policy advice, the CECW should endeavour to solicit specific policy recommendations—or "best advice"—based on what we know at present.

The symposium took the form of a "town hall" meeting, where a moderator (the first author) called upon six expert panellists, as well as other experts in the symposium audience, to generate information about: what is meant by resilience and permanence; what research tells us about resilience and permanence; how current practices and policies in child welfare promote resilience through permanency planning; and what the lessons are for policy makers in Canada. The ideas that emerged from this symposium reflect what research, practice, and policy can inform us about the key question, from the perspective of those who attended the symposium.

The information contained in this chapter is that expressed by the panellists and members of the audience during the symposium discussion. The discussion was audiotaped and transcribed, and the chapter authors organized themes and specific information points. No particular attempt was made to relate the ideas generated at the symposium to current theoretical or evidence-based knowledge in the broader child welfare literature. Rather, readers are invited to weigh the content of this chapter against their own knowledge and experience, and to draw their own conclusions.

The panel comprised experts in child welfare, many of whom have multiple roles as academics, researchers, practice experts, and policy advisors. This expertise was based on experience in Canada, the United Kingdom, Ireland and Australia. The panelists were: Jim Barber (Faculty of Social Work, University of Toronto), Cindy Blackstock (First Nations Child & Family Caring Society of Canada), Bob Flynn (Centre for Research on Community Services, University of Ottawa), Robbie Gilligan (Children's Research Centre, Trinity College, Dublin), Helen Jones (Department for Education and Skills, UK), and Robin Laycock (Ministry of Children and Family Development, British Columbia).

Resilience

It was proposed by the symposium organizers that we begin by assuming that resilience in child welfare refers to children's functioning well, in spite of serious threats to their adaptation and development. This was considered by the expert panelists and symposium participants to be a good general description of the term.

What do we mean by resilience?

Three concepts that expand our understanding of the meaning of this general description are that resilience is:

- *Part of personal identity*. Resilience is part of the personal identity that children have with themselves—that part of their identity relating to their ability to deal with change over time in very dynamic and unexpected circumstances.

- *A personal resource*. Resilience is something that may "constantly flow" within a person, or be "tapped into" at certain points in a person's life. Either way, it is the personal strength to connect with intra-personal, inter-personal, societal, and cultural resources.

- *An exceptionally helpful personal quality*. Resilience is the magic that can occur within children that allows them to endure and excel under amazingly difficult circumstances. It is keeping faith. It is stepping from light into darkness and knowing that there will be something solid upon which to stand, or from which one may suddenly "learn to fly."

Part of this exceptional quality is to have, and act upon, curiosity. Curiosity leads to exploration, exploration is discovery, discovery results in pleasure, pleasure results in repetition, repetition results in mastery, mastery results in new skills, new skills leads to confidence, confidence contributes to self-esteem, self-esteem increases sense of security, and security results in more exploration. Bruce Perry, a specialist in children's mental health and consultant on child development, has written in this vein about the role of curiosity as the "fuel" of development in the cycle of learning (Perry, 2005).

Importance of understanding resilience in children

One way to promote resilience is to recognize and make use of the successful coping strategies already in place in a child. When children are introduced into the child welfare system, the primary focus is often on their having access to a childcare worker or a therapist, or moving them into care. Interventions of this type frequently overlook the fact that such children typically already have successfully used one or more resilience strategies within themselves and/or within their family. In addition, there may be within the child's environment a number of strategies and resources that encourage and help him or her to be resilient. It is important not to interrupt a child's successful ways of being resilient by introducing other methods and conditions that may not be as successful. This constitutes over-servicing.

A number of factors have been identified that foster resiliency in children. Box 1 describes some of these that emerge from the work of Ann Masten.

Ann Masten's research

Ann Masten, of the University of Minnesota, has identified several important factors that foster resilience in children. Masten has developed a list of "human protective factors" that have repeatedly been found to be associated with resilient children. The most important protective resource for development, according to Masten, is a strong relationship with a competent, caring, pro-social adult. The most important internal quality is normal cognitive development, which is best operationalized as good attention skills, average or better IQ scores, and "street smarts." Other factors include connections to positive role models, feelings of self-worth and self-efficacy, feelings of hope and meaningfulness in life, attractiveness to others, talents valued by self and others, faith and religious affiliations, socioeconomic advantages, good schools, and opportunities to learn or qualify for advancement in society (Masten, 1997, and chapter 1, this volume).

Permanence

What do we mean by permanence?

Permanence is a term that is used in a variety of ways within the field of child welfare. One model suggested by panelist Helen Jones, which helps us to understand and clarify this variety, views permanence as a 3-dimensional concept, comprising emotional, physical and legal elements (Department for Education and Skills, 2004). Emotional permanence is the attachment children feel for others. Physical permanence occurs when a child has a stable and continuous living arrangement, and legal permanence refers to a variety of legal orders, including adoption. Emlen, Lahti, Downs, McKay and Downs (1977) referred to the quality of permanence as including the following features: (1) the home is not guaranteed to last forever but is "intended to last indefinitely"; (2) "permanence means commitment and continuity in the child's relationships"; (3) the family is one in which the child has a real belonging and "definite legal status"; and (4) the child has "a respected social status" in contrast to the second-class status typical of temporary foster care (pp. 10–11). (See box on permanency planning.)

Permanency planning

Permanency planning in social work essentially embodies the following key features (Fein, Maluccio, Hamilton & Ward, 1983):

- A philosophy highlighting the value of rearing children in a family setting, preferably with their biological families;
- A theoretical framework stressing that stability and continuity of relationships promote children's growth and functioning;
- A program based on systematic planning within specified time frames for children placed (or at risk of placement) in foster care;
- A sense of mutual respect and a spirit of active collaboration among child welfare personnel, lawyers, judges, and others working with children and their parents.

Emotional permanence

Two aspects of emotional permanence are key to healthy child development:

A child's sense of belonging. Emotional permanence involves children's sense that they belong. Children, especially those in care, need to have somebody or a number of people to whom they are connected. Such connection occurs when a child knows he or she has significant connections, feels assured that those significant connections are ongoing, and looks forward to the future with them.

A child's stable personal identity. Emotional permanence also involves personal identity that is both vital and does not change significantly over time. Children need to have a strong internal, ongoing sense of who they are and how they fit into the world around them (see Lalonde, chapter 4, this volume).

Physical permanence

The term physical permanence has been used in different ways. One operational definition used by some is a stable living condition for 24 months. For other people, it has come to be associated with adoption. For yet others, especially child care agencies, permanence is the feeling that we have succeeded if a decision is made that the child can stay in the family home. There are many others. Any of these may be preferable, practical, or ideal, but no one option is always in the best interests of all children. For this reason, physical permanence must involve a *continuum of options* (Barber & Delfabbro, 2004), with reunification with the family or extended family at one end of the continuum, adoption at the other, and a number of possible options along the way, including transfer of custody and others.

Achieving physical permanence—being stable in one living environment—is a frequent objective of child welfare service organizations. More often than we would like, this is attained only after moving children from one place to another until a good "fit" is found. It is essential to find a good fit, and it appears not to be particularly harmful to children to move them—even many times—in the search of such a fit. In fact, physical and other types of permanency are not always well served in the long run by sticking doggedly to attempting to make one living placement work out (Barber & Delfabbro, 2004).

> Short-term foster care is not usually interpreted by children as permanence, because they know, despite the best efforts of foster parents, that their foster parents are not going to keep them forever.

Legal permanence

There are many ways to achieve legal permanence, but in general it refers to a permanent care-providing relationship between a child and one or more others. These others may be parents, other family members, or people who are unrelated. Legal permanence involves procedures and documentation that are recognized in law.

Transfer of custody is one such legal arrangement. It involves a child and an adult who is not the parent, and is separate from adoption. This came about because we have a number of children, sometimes adolescents, who do not want to be adopted, but still want to have a permanent legal relationship with an adult. It is also an attractive option for some Aboriginal cultures, especially where adoption as we think of it in Euro-centric terms is not a strong aspect of culture.

What is most important for an individual child?

Of emotional, physical and legal permanence, is one more basic than the others? Emotional attachment of some form appears to be essential. If children have a very strong emotional attachment, they can probably cope with some physical moves. However, this is not always the case. For some children, though, a legal order is important. Such children need to feel there is a legal commitment between themselves and their caregivers, and, perhaps, that they cannot be returned to the previously unhappy circumstances—a situation they may have experienced before. Thus, what is most important differs from one child to another.

Indeed, it might be said that permanence is a concept that *differs in meaning for individuals*. There is no one common meaning. For some children, the most important aspect of permanence may not be related to adults at all, but rather is their relationship with, for example, their pet dog. For others, permanence may, most importantly, be about their relationship with art, or their culture, or their ability to dance, or to be able to write or speak.

The meaning of permanence can change considerably for children (and adults) over time. What may be most important to children and to others one year may be quite different in previous or subsequent years. Thus, permanence is a *dynamic* concept within the lives of individuals.

Permanence is a concept that both includes and reflects the perspective of one's cultural community. For example, in Euro-Western societies, *adoption* has come to mean taking in children (on a permanent basis) who do not have another home. In Aboriginal societies, by contrast, it is more typical to adopt children and adults as a representation of the interconnection that we all share. Some aspects of permanence may be more or less important to individuals, then, because of the cultural "ways" that are used to deal with them, and the emphasis their culture places on them.

Because a number of factors influence what is important to individuals in permanence, it may sometimes seem to be an *elusive* concept. Making it seem even more elusive, individuals are constantly changing throughout their lives, and the environments around them are constantly changing as well. All this may make it seem that permanence does not actually exist anywhere in the world, for anyone. In a sense, this is true. Life is not permanent. But many aspects of life are both stable and positive over long periods of time, at different times in people's lives. What we strive for in child welfare when we look for permanence in a child's life is a number of overlapping aspects of life, stable and positive over long periods of time.

How do we reduce loneliness and isolation in adulthood for people who lived in foster care, if we consider that placement stability does not necessarily include emotional well-being? We need to work with attachments to make sure they are sustained into adulthood. The key to promoting permanence lies in fostering these attachments.

Who makes permanence decisions?

There is probably no one set of policies that can set out specifically how to make decisions about permanence. Instead, we have to rely on the clinical judgments of child welfare workers who know the children, know their families and communities, and who are able to make sound assessments about which of several options is going to work best in the life of the child. Although checklists and other assessment tools are very useful supports, it is probably not possible to develop an assessment tool that accurately informs social workers about the precise conditions that would lead to a child, for instance, returning to live with the family or to become a candidate for adoption. No matter to what degree such tools are used, ultimately, a clinical decision needs to be made.

In making such decisions, child welfare workers need to listen to children's views about which of several connections and options in their lives are best for them in the long run. Children who are being maltreated are not always able to make accurate judgments, however, and they may need to be assisted to move to different living circumstances, even temporarily, in order to form an opinion about which situation they consider best for them. Unique, child-centred decisions are required to serve the best interests of individual children.

Whether children are 4 or 14 years old, when they have something to say about the way the placement is, then they benefit from it.

The child welfare system itself, though, often acts as a barrier to unique and child-centred decision making and problem solving that are in the best interests of individual children. Disability services, for example, have stressed the importance of person-centred solutions for a number of years. Disability policy is based on the simple notion that each human being is unique, and that, in carrying out individual support, service workers have to pick from a menu of different kinds of services in order to respond to the uniqueness of that person. Policy in the field of social work has been reluctant to move in this direction to date. Rather, our field has tended to rely on programs with rather narrow mandates and types of solutions to problems. With regard to making permanence decisions that are best for the child, it would be instructive for our field to examine what other closely related fields are doing, to consider more carefully what is known about child development, and to critically examine the types of programs and services we currently have in place.

> When developing both policy and practice, we need to look at our plans through the eyes of children, and develop them on a child's timeline rather than an adult's timeline.

How to achieve permanence

There are many pathways to permanence. Two of the most important ways are a child's relationship with his or her family members, and a child's relationship with people other than his or her family members, including those formed while engaged in social and community activities, and in school. Within these environments outside the family, there may be adults in a young person's life for whom there is an attachment, or bond, that is going to sustain him or her to adulthood and beyond.

Working with families to achieve permanence

We know from the data gathered by Looking After Children that most children go back to their families of origin when they leave care (Bullock, Little, & Millham, 1993). The reality of most children in care is that, when they reach the age of 16 or 18, their connection with their foster family, even if it has been "stable" over time, is virtually wiped out when their placement comes to an end. There are two problems here. First, we have done little or no work at a practice level, and have no policy in place, to support an ongoing relationship between the youth and the foster family. Because of this, valuable emotional attachments and pseudo-family connections are usually lost. Second, even though the child may have been in care for 10 or 15 years, we typically have done little or no work with their natural families to help change their patterns of interaction. We have done no work to build resilience in these families, so the youths leaving foster care go right back into the environment that we felt was not safe in the first place and start another generation. For this reason, we need to start looking at the work we do with families of origin.

A word of caution, though, is in order: decisions to work with families in this way should be made on a child-by-child basis. Sometimes it is good for a child to separate from the family, to disengage, or pull back from an abusive family. Many children leave their families because their parents have mental health or other issues that prevent them from carrying out their family functions in a positive way. In such cases, working with the family of origin may not be fruitful, but assisting the youth to have ongoing connection to the foster family and other families may be helpful to his or her healthy adjustment.

Still, there are many good reasons to work with families, with the possible exception of trying to preserve a relationship that is not good, has little hope of being good, and can cause harm. Sometimes a child or youth needs to come together with the rest of the family in order to resolve underlying conflicts, or to help the child learn about aspects of healthy relationships. Resolution of conflict or learning about healthy relationships does not typically occur on its own in the family environment; rather, it is likely that professional support will be required. Support is also sometimes needed to nurture the good aspects of a child's relationship with his or her family members, as these aspects may otherwise go unrecognized or remain neglected by either the child or the family members. For some children, such processes take place by living full time with their families, but for others periodic stays or visits may be more beneficial to developing positive connections that lead to a sense of permanence.

If longer-term placement is required for the child outside the family home, it may be very helpful for child welfare workers to encourage all those involved in the child's life to see themselves as part of an extended family, or at least as part of a cooperative, extended network. Here, we consider all the adults who have some connection with the child as working together as an "extended family"—some with more responsibility for daily care than others, but all concerned with the welfare of the child. In this role as extended family members, such people can offer support and practical help to a child to maintain positive relationships with his or her family. This process can be helpful for the child because it gives a sense of permanence to the personal connections in his or her life.

> We should be working with the family of origin whenever possible if it does not add to the burden of the child.

Encourage children to form significant relationships and connections with others

Although ideally speaking, a child's relationship with his or her family members is usually the most important pathway to permanence, this is not always possible or in the best interests of the child. In these cases, a child's relationships with people outside the family may be all the more important. Relationships such as those formed while engaged in social and community activities and in school can also be important pathways to permanence because they act as emotional attachments, ensure safe environments, and offer opportunities for growth and healthy development (see Flynn, Beaulac, & Vinograd, chapter 13, this volume).

There are almost always many opportunities for children to make such connections in their own communities. For example, children can become a member of a sports team, an arts centre, or a neighbourhood committee. In many cases, though, it is helpful for child care workers to help children and youth who are in care make these connections.

The roles children play in school, whether social or academic, are also important in fostering permanence. It is striking how often children who do well in care, who persevere despite difficulties in their care experience or pre-care experience, have had success in roles played at school (Gilligan, 2004, and chapter 2, this volume). Changing schools can often have very damaging effects on children in care. This suggests that an important factor to consider in decision-making concerning permanence is whether or not a change in a child's living arrangement would cause a school change that would take away important relationships and sources of strength for the child.

> Relationships that children in care form while engaged in school and community activities can be very important. They may not be primary attachment relationships, but they get children through certain stages, because they are safe places that help build the child's sense of identity and sense of connection.

The inter-relationship between permanence and resilience

A question that arises from the above discussion is this: Does permanence create resilience, or does resilience create permanence? If it is the former, the assumption is that when children experience permanence, including placement stability and consistent care, they have a supportive context within which resilience can blossom. If it is the latter, on the other hand, the assumption is that children who already possess characteristics that contribute to resilience are more likely that those who do not have such characteristics to experience permanence, because they are more likely to take the risk of attaching again, and have more developed skills for managing adversity. Both positions have merit, and thus it seems reasonable to take the view that permanence and resilience have a "chicken and egg" or reciprocal relationship. Each develops from the other in a cyclical fashion. There seems little doubt that:

- Children who are resilient typically experience greater degrees of permanence.

- Permanence is one of several important factors that foster further resilience.

Factors Associated with permanence and resilience in children in care

A number of factors appear to be associated with the reciprocal development of permanence and resilience in children in care:

1. *The importance of caregiver attitudes.* The attitudes of caregivers toward the permanence of the placement seem to be related to some resilience measures of children in care. Research undertaken to date suggests that the caregiver's attitude toward the placement is predictive of children's psychological well-being, whereas the actual placement permanence may not be. Over 20 years ago, Lahti (1982) found that the best predictor of child well-being was the carer's perception of placement permanence. Irrespective of where the child was placed, the degree to which the child was seen by the carer to be part of the placement family accounted for more of the variance in child well-being than any other factor. Barber and Delfabbro (2004) pointed out that Lahti's results, which found no association between number of previous placements and child well-being, or between length of time in temporary foster care and well-being, may actually imply that the attitudes and perceptions of caregivers are more important than the stability of the placement itself. In analyses of data from the Ontario Looking After Children project that he had carried out in preparation for the policy forum, Flynn similarly found a modest positive relationship between the foster parent's belief that the placement was permanent and the children's perception of well-being. As a result of these findings, the panelists suggested that, under some conditions, the attitude of the caregiver toward the child may be more important to the child's well-being than the stability of the placement.

2. *Lack of religious observance.* Children in placements with caregivers who do not place a high premium on religious observance tend to do better for reasons that are not fully understood (Barber & Delfabrro, 2004).

3. *Flexible caregiver expectations in relation to school performance.* We know that children with caregivers who are very flexible in relation to their performance at school, do better (Barber & Delfabrro, 2004).

4. *Caregiver previous experience as a recipient of child welfare.* We know, too, that children with caregivers who have had some childhood experiences of child welfare also do better (Barber & Delfabrro, 2004).

What we do not know, however, and what is often speculated about, is whether permanence experienced by children while they are in care is going to produce resilient adults. Are measures of permanence positively related to measures of positive adjustment to adult life in 10, 15, or 20 years?

Matching policy and practice

Good policy does not necessarily lead to good practice, but good policy is often necessary as a context for good practice to flourish. Policy is sometimes set up for many reasons—social, political, legal and practical. As a consequence, policy in the field of child welfare, like that of other fields, sometimes even contradicts the practice values and objectives of professionals. This leads to difficulties because there is a mismatch between policy and practice objectives. One such problem that we see often is that there are often wide discrepancies between the outcomes that are set out in the care plans at the beginning of placement and those actually achieved. The problem is that a variety of policies get in the way of achieving the planned outcomes and it is not possible for them to be realized. There are many other examples of policy and practice not working in harmony. The question that arises from this for policy change is: What policy would improve the ability of practitioners to achieve their objectives more accurately?

Specific challenges in matching policy and practice

The panelists identified a number of specific current concerns or challenges that are highly pertinent to policy change that would support and enhance practice:

1. *Operationalizing the concepts of permanence and resilience.* Perhaps one of the most problematic challenges facing policy makers is the operationalization of the concepts of permanence and resilience when their respective elements are so hard to define. One panelist described the challenge as finding the best overall perspective without losing the value of detail and individual characteristics:

> Operationalizing the concept of permanence reminds me a bit of that poem *The Six Blind Men of Hindustan*, in which the six men are all standing around an elephant trying to describe what the elephant is and, of course, because they are blind, they do not have the sense of sight to rely upon. They decided that an elephant can be like a snake if you touch its trunk, or it can be like a tree it you hug its leg.

2. *Over-generalizing complex risks.* Another important concern is that policy in the child welfare field tends to be driven by generalizations surrounding the risks posed to children in care, and simple solutions are designed to reduce these complex risks. Policy design is based on the assumption that all children in care are exposed to the same risks, and would benefit from the same risk reduction strategies. Because of this design philosophy, policies tend to be very prescriptive, and dictate a tick box approach to practice (e.g., the child is experiencing X, Y, and Z and therefore adoption is the answer).

3. *Arbitrary benchmarks derived from policy.* One other concern raised by inflexible policy design is that policy dictates the use of arbitrary standards, or benchmarks, that agencies must reach in relation to permanence, or else they run the risk of having their funding affected. The effect of this policy is to elevate permanence to the level of an *end*, as opposed to a *means to an end*, which is the child's well-being and development. The challenge, therefore, is to design policy so that it enhances permanence and resilience rather than enhancing placement stability.

4. *Caregiver quality and attitudes to placement.* Another important policy challenge facing the child welfare system is the quality of caregivers to whom the system has access. Given that, as we have seen, the attitudes of caregivers toward children in their care is important to a child's sense of well-being, it is of fundamental importance that the system attract caregivers with positive attitudes towards children's placements. However, as one symposium partic-

ipant put it, "The reality is that we are just so bereft of caregivers, that we'll take anyone who's warm and vertical as a foster care parent. We want to make sure that we select on the basis of certain attributes, attitude toward the placement being one of them, but our reality is that we have such a desperate shortage of foster parents that we cannot afford to be that choosy."

Ideas for addressing these concerns

The panelists formed a consensus that policy should support pursuing an individualized approach to care, fostering resilience, and expanding the range of supports we provide for children. More specifically:

1. Policy design should set the stage for an individualized approach to permanence. There are no simple solutions to the challenges faced by children in care. Policy must be flexible enough to allow system workers to create individual permanency enhancement strategy plans for children in their care. No one permanency option (i.e., adoption) should be the desired result for every child. *Policy should allow for the consideration of a whole spectrum of options, with some being better than others for particular children in care.*

2. We should target as service goals resilience in children and families. The child welfare system is currently not always the best judge of resilience in children, and needs to develop ways to assess this more accurately, so that action can be taken with individual children that is most beneficial to them. Policy should provide that, if possible and with the proper supports, children remain in the family of origin, although this is not always possible or even desirable. But families often need direct help to become resilient. This might be accomplished by using resources currently in the system, redirected toward building family competence. If this can be achieved, over the long term many children may experience better quality of life and more stability.

3. We should provide broader community-based options to placing children in care. In situations where remaining with the birth family is not a viable option for a child, policy should provide options so that children do not necessarily have to placed in care. Rather, policy should make it easy to establish living arrangements with people with whom the child has an existing relationship, and these new caregivers should be supported just as foster parents are supported. The way the

system is now, social workers have to make their way through a heavy burden of cumbersome paperwork, which has made this option a very difficult one for social workers to exercise for a child. The child welfare system in British Columbia can serve as a model to other Canadian jurisdictions in this regard. It has operationalized the "kith and kin" concept, which gives social workers the option to place children who require removal from the home with a neighbour or a relative, or somebody with whom that child has an established relationship. Policy should stress the importance, especially for members of the Aboriginal community and other cultural groups, of finding solutions concerning permanence at the community level. Policy, in many cases, must empower a community in the solution-making process (see Lalonde, chapter 4, this volume).

4. We should support existing and new connections for children in care. When the most viable option for a child is to be removed from the home and placed in care, policy should provide support to encourage and enhance any existing connections that are meaningful for a child, and remove any barriers to fostering these connections. To accomplish this, it is essential that policy and practice methods be reviewed and revised periodically.

Policy should also find ways to encourage a continued relationship between the child and his or her birth family, so long as this is not detrimental to the child. For example, we could use caregivers creatively to work with the child's family so that children do not lose their family contact. However, policy should also reflect the fact that decisions to work with families should be made on a child-by-child basis, as it may well be in the best interests of the child to disengage or pull back from an abusive family. Policy should also encourage foster children in care to form new connections and relationships by engaging in new social and community roles, and it should seek to enhance a child's existing social resource base, so long as it is beneficial to the child.

5. We should periodically re-evaluate home situations for children in care. When the most viable option for a child is to be removed from the home, policy should provide for periodic re-evaluations of the safety and stability of the birth family, as it may be possible for the child to return home, with adequate supports. When carrying out such re-evaluation, it is important to remember that risk changes with age. For example, risk to a child in his or her family at age two

is very different from the risk to that child at age 12. Policy should reflect this reality.

6. We should provide some time for placement instability. Another important suggestion for policy change in the child welfare system is that it not seek instant placement stability for every child in care. Rather than having time lines "carved in stone," they should be set in accordance with the child's comfort level. Policy could be designed to provide for some placement instability for awhile, in order to allow children to feel out their current living arrangement.

Key advice to policy makers

The expert panelists at the symposium were asked to summarize their views by offering key policy advice to policy makers concerning permanence and resilience in child welfare. The following advice was provided:

- Do not rush to permanence.

- Do not rush to adoption.

- Do not rush to extinguish parental rights.

- Do not be afraid to allow some degree of instability in the early to mid-term of a placement if something better comes along. Allow for some testing of the waters.

- Policy should reflect a commitment to furthering research and information gathering in a number of areas. One area in which long-term accumulation of information would be helpful is the extent to which permanence produces resilience in young adults. Another area in which more information would be useful is service effectiveness. Child welfare should get good information on the effectiveness of the services the system provides, particularly in relation to services for children in care, because they are the most expensive. If we find that the current ways that we are allocating our resources are not overly effective, we could be developing services that would support children in more beneficial ways.

> If we do not invest in following large numbers of young people for considerable amounts of time, all we can ever do is rely on our intuition and our experience, which are useful but faulty guides. We will never be able to examine permanence or stability in any rigorous way if we do not invest in long-term efforts to follow large numbers of people into foster care and then out of foster care, to about age 30.

- Policy should provide for the extension of child welfare services beyond the current age of 18 and, as mentioned, for the study of long-term outcomes. The range of services available, and the number of children in care to whom they are available, should be expanded.

- Resilience needs enhancement. The underlying philosophy of policy should move toward the idea that permanence is good for children in care, but only if it promotes resilience. Conversely, one way of promoting resilience for many children is through permanence, with the exceptions mentioned earlier. Another way, which should be reflected in policy, is the attitude of caregivers toward the placement. Hiring policy for caregivers should develop some very specific procedures for evaluating caregiver attitudes toward the placement and the child. Caregivers should be selected on the basis of their perceived attitude, as this is one attribute of care that is associated with better outcomes in children.

- Policy should find ways to operationalize the promoters of resilience identified by Masten (chapter 1, this volume), such as nurturant systems, cognitive development, development of faith or philosophy of life, and engagement in healthy social activities. As well, policy should enhance children's opportunities to improve their curiosity and to encourage their progress at every stage in the cycle of learning identified by Perry, including exploration, discovery, mastery of new skills, confidence, and self-esteem building. Policy could attempt to operationalize these resilience promoters by providing for programs offering children opportunities to engage in sports, creative music, arts, drama and others, and ensuring that all children in care have access to those opportunities, perhaps through targeted programs.

Further reading and more resources

The material in this chapter emerged from the discussion at a policy symposium, held August 19, 2004, and sponsored by the Centre of Excellence for Child Welfare. The opinions expressed here are those of the symposium participants and do not reflect the full range of knowledge that is available on permanence and resilience in child welfare. Readers are invited to consult the readings and resources listed under "References" and "Web resources," as well as the other chapters in the present volume, to explore this topic further.

References

Barber, J. G., & Delfabbro, P. H. (2004). Placement stability and the psychosocial well-being of children in foster care. *Research in Social Work Practice, 13*, 415–431.

Bullock, R., Little, M., & Millham, S. (1993). *Going home: The return of children separated from their families.* Dartmouth, UK: Aldershot.

Daniel, B. & Wassell, S. (2002a). *The early years: Assessing and promoting resilience in vulnerable children.* London: Jessica Kingsley Publishing.

Daniel, B. & Wassell, S. (2002b). *The school years: Assessing and promoting resilience in vulnerable children.* London: Jessica Kingsley Publishing.

Daniel, B. & Wassell, S. (2002c). *Adolescence: Assessing and promoting resilience in vulnerable children.* London: Jessica Kingsley Publishing.

Department for Education and Skills (2004). *Draft regulations and guidance for consultation: Care planning and special guardianship.* London, DFES.

Emlen, A., Lahti, J., Downs, G., McKay, A., & Downs, S. (1977). *Overcoming barriers to planning for children in foster care.* Portland, OR: Regional Research Institute for Human Services, Portland State University.

Fein, E., Maluccio, A. N., Hamilton, V. J., & Ward, D. E. (1983). After foster care: Outcomes of permanency planning for children. *Child Welfare, 62*, 485–562.

Gilligan, R. (1997). Beyond permanence? The importance of resilience in child placement practice and planning. *Adoption and Fostering, 21*, 12–20.

Gilligan, R. (2001). *Promoting resilience: A resource guide on working with children in the care system*. London: British Agencies for Adoption and Fostering.

Gilligan, R. (2004). Promoting resilience in child and family social work: Issues for social work practice, education and policy. *Social Work Education*, 23, 93–104.

Lahti, J. (1982). A follow-up study of foster children in permanent placements. *Social Service Review*, 56, 556–71.

Masten, A. (1997). *Resilience in children at-risk*. University of Minnesota Centre for Applied Research and Educational Improvement. Retrieved March 29, 2005, from http://education.umn.edu/carei/Reports/Rpractice/Spring97/resilience.htm

Masten, A. S., & Coatsworth, J. D. (1998). The development of competence in favorable and unfavorable environments. *American Psychologist*, 53, 205–220.

Newman, T. & Blackburn, S. (2002). *Transitions in the lives of children and young people: Resilience factors*. Edinburgh: Scottish Executive Education Department.

Perry, B. (2005). *Curiosity: The fuel of development*. Retrieved March 29, 2005, from http://teacher.scholastic.com/professional/bruceperry/curiosity.htm

Web resources: Resilience and permanence

The ResilienceNet Virtual Library is a collection of full-text publications related to the resilience of children and families in the face of adversities. Publications are mainly in English, with some in Spanish and Chinese: http://resilnet.uiuc.edu/library.html

Publications on resilience and other related topics by Robbie Gilligan of Trinity College, Dublin: http://www.tcd.ie/Social_Studies/gillpub1.htm

A framework of permanence for young people, developed by the National Resource Centre for Foster Care and Permanency Planning at the Hunter College School of Social Work, at the City University of New York: http://www.hunter.cuny.edu/socwork/nrcfcpp/downloads/permanency/Permanency_Framework.pdf

Part 2:

Resilience and Foster Care Research, Policy, and Practice

Foster care services for infants with prenatal substance exposure: Developing capacity in the caregiving environment

Lenora Marcellus

Introduction

Foster parents have historically cared for infants and children whose main issue was parental neglect. However, the characteristics of infants and children in care have changed dramatically in the past 30 years. A number of studies in the United States have found that for between one third and two thirds of children in foster care, parental substance use is a contributing factor to their need for alternative care (U.S. Department of Health and Human Services, 1999). Infants with prenatal exposure to drugs and/or alcohol are often parented within the environment of foster care. Supporting the care and nurturing of infants exposed prenatally to alcohol and/or drugs remains a major challenge to social workers, child and youth workers, health professionals and parents (natural, foster, and adoptive) (British Columbia Children's Commission, 1998).

Resilience in the infant population is particularly impacted by the caregiving environment. This article will describe resilience in terms of the population of infants with prenatal substance exposure and apply that knowledge to discussion of the development of support and education initiatives for foster family caregivers. The Safe Babies Project will be presented as an example of programming that supports development of resilience in the infant foster care population. The Safe Babies Project was initiated in Victoria, British Columbia, by the Ministry of Children and Family Development and the Vancouver Island Health Authority to respond to a need for improved education, training and support for foster caregivers who care for infants exposed prenatally to alcohol and drugs (Marcellus, 2004).

Resilience and infants

Resilience may be simply defined as the maintenance of positive adjustment under challenging life conditions (Health Canada, 1997). Historically, the concept of resilience emerged from the studies of individuals dealing with major and often devastating stresses and was sometimes considered a personal trait. Thinking has by now advanced to realize that resilience is more than simply a personal trait; it may be affected by one's experiences, personal genetics, surrounding environment and supports (Kaplan, 1999; Masten, 2001; Masten, chapter 1, this volume).

In many key theoretical discussions in the literature, resilience is conceptualized as an outcome of the dynamic interaction between two counter forces: protective processes and vulnerability processes. Protective processes (strengths and capacities) develop and act at several levels, within individuals, families, communities, and societies. Vulnerability processes (risks or adversities) also develop and act at several levels and can be operationally defined in diverse ways—most commonly as indicators of risk, such as socioeconomic status, life event stressors, health state, or environmental threat (Drummond & Marcellus, 2003).

Three protective processes are consistently identified within the literature in relation to infants at risk: the quality of parent (or surrogate)-child attachment relationships, cognition, and self-regulation (Kumpfer, 1999; Poulsen, 1993; Rouse, 1998). These three processes need to be considered from not only the developmental stage of the individual but also from a range of perspectives such as culture and environment. Infants and children will have different vulnerabilities and protective processes at different ages and points in development. The requirements to support or counter these processes will also most likely change over time and in relation to the environment in which the child is being raised. Rouse (1998) describes characteristics of resilient, or competent, infants as having an easy temperament, being socially responsive, and displaying features of self-regulation such as impulse control and gratification delay. Analysis of longitudinal resilience data finds that infants who were agreeable, friendly, relaxed, responsive, self-confident and sociable are more likely to be resilient in their adult years (Werner & Smith, 1992).

There has been a recent trend in research that confirms the importance of environmental variables in the long-term outcomes of children. Lester, Boukydis and Twomey (2000) have developed multiple-risk models for their study of outcomes in substance-exposed infants and children and have incorporated environmental conditions as protective factors. Ann Streissguth (1997), a leading U.S. FASD (Fetal Alcohol Spectrum Disorder) researcher, identifies a consistent caregiving environment in the first six years as one of the key factors in improved outcomes for children with FASD. Environmental factors such as competent caregiving and early relationships are increasingly presented as playing a major role in determining developmental outcomes for infants and children and playing a considerable role in enhancing healthy physical, emotional, and social development of infants (Committee on Early Childhood, Adoption, and Dependent Care, American Academy of Pediatrics, 2000; Heller, Smyke, & Boris, 2002; MCFD, 1998). Features of a protective environment for infants include consistent and responsive care within a trusting and loving relationship, by caregivers who are knowledgeable, competent, and supported in their work by communities, systems, and policies.

Vulnerability processes for infants with prenatal substance exposure in foster care are numerous. As a specific population of children in care, infants are at risk of development of a wide array of health issues specific to their developmental age. They are more vulnerable to the effects of malnutrition, physical abuse, and emotional deprivation than any other age group as these all have the potential to impede physical development and brain growth (Silver et al., 1999). Clyman, Harden and Little (2002) suggest that as many as 75% of young children in foster care placement need further developmental evaluation or have a developmental delay. Frequently noted health issues for infants include drug and alcohol exposure, risk of exposure to infectious diseases, failure to thrive, poor weight gain, prematurity, feeding problems, developmental delays, immunization delays, upper respiratory illnesses, and skin conditions (Silver et al., 1999).

From an attachment theory perspective, infants placed into foster care are also at risk for later difficulties for multiple reasons—they experience many disruptions in their relationships with primary caregivers, and they have histories of neglect, abuse, parental drug abuse, and/or family instability (Stovall & Dozier, 1998). As well, infants with prenatal substance exposure may have spent prolonged periods in a neonatal intensive care unit being cared for by multiple staff members, or they may have entered foster care from the home of the birth parents and may have experienced irregular and inconsistent daily care (Marcellus, 2004a). The behaviours and health and social issues that the infant brings to the interaction often may be considered challenging. Foster parents, professionals, and other caregivers report specific challenges in caring for infants with prenatal substance exposure on a daily basis, including irritability, inconsolability, difficulty with feeding, difficulty settling and being soothed, and sensitivity to change and stimulation.

Interventions to promote resilience may be designed to focus on both protective and vulnerability processes, at the level of the infant, the caregiver, the interaction, and/or the broader environment in which the interaction takes place. These multiple foci suggest that an ecological framework for project development would be most effective at meeting the multiple and multi-level needs of foster families caring for infants with special needs. An ecological framework is one that looks not only at the immediate level of interaction, such as that between the daily caregiver and the infant, but also at the larger levels of family, community, government systems, and policy (see Barber, chapter 25, this volume).

Foster care and infants

Foster care services were conceived in the early 1900s as an alternative to the prevailing use of institutional care for children whose parents were unable or unwilling to parent in a way that met the standards of the time. Foster care was originally intended to be a only a temporary measure of support for children while their biological families dealt with the social and economic issues that contributed to their parenting difficulties. However, as poverty and other social issues continue to increase in North American society, the number of children in foster care and the length of time during which they require services continue to increase (Mauro, 1999). There have also been increases in the number and intensity of health and emotional issues experienced by children in care. Many now entering foster care have been severely traumatized and have special medical, psychological, and social needs that traditional child welfare and foster care services were not designed to address (Rosenfeld et al., 1997). Research has consistently shown that children receiving foster care in general have an increased incidence of chronic medical conditions and a lack of general health care and developmental and mental health monitoring (Committee on Early Childhood, Adoption, and Dependent Care, American Academy of Pediatrics, 2002; Halfon, Mendonca, & Berkowitz, 1995; Kools & Kennedy, 2003). The Child Welfare League of America (1988) has coined the term "new morbidities" to reflect the health outcomes that result in children exposed to environmental factors such as poverty, violence, and substance use.

The intense developmental and health monitoring and daily care required by infants with prenatal substance exposure may lead to compromise of care through caregiver stress and multiple birth and foster family placement transitions within the first few years of life. The challenge for professionals working with foster parents of infants with prenatal substance exposure is to creatively devise ways to modify parenting strategies to the needs of infants with challenging behaviors, as well as to provide sufficient community support for both consistency and responsiveness to be maintained in the early caregiving environment.

Recent trends in the field of child welfare, including the shift to a greater population of infants in care, have underscored the importance of examining infants as a unique population (Wulczyn et al., 2002). The large body of knowledge on infant development offers one framework for the study of the child welfare experiences of infants in foster care. For example, with older children, the policies and guidelines focus on issues such as management of behavior and support of emotions. With infants, the developmental equivalent is to have the focus on the responsiveness of the caregiver to the needs of the infants and the ability of the caregiver to interpret the cues of the infant accurately.

Addressing the protective effect that support of foster parents may have on the health and well-being of infants will provide guidance for program enhancement. Although children in foster care spend more time with foster parents than with any other representatives of the health or child welfare system, foster parents often are the least prepared for, and the least supported in, their responsibilities. The challenge for child welfare and health professionals is to develop services that meet the needs of the primary clients (infants and their foster caregivers), address recent best practice research, meet policy requirements, and are flexible enough to adapt to a range of community situations. Few communities have developed programs related to education and support of foster parents caring for infants with prenatal substance-exposure despite the number of infants requiring specialized foster care (Burry, 1999; Zukoski, 1999).

Context for development of the Safe Babies Project

Several high-profile, tragic events involving high-risk infants in Victoria, British Columbia, prompted a provincial Children's Commission investigation and a Ministry of Children and Family Development (MCFD) review of high-risk infants and young children in foster care within the Capital Region. A key recommendation from both investigations was development of support and education services for drug and alcohol exposed infants, their parents and caregivers, and professionals. In June 1997, representatives from the Capital Health Region (now renamed the Vancouver Island Health Authority, VIHA) and MCFD met to discuss current services for substance-exposed infants and their families, and to raise issues surrounding practice in Victoria with this population. Drawing upon the varied experiences of the group (health care, child welfare, alcohol and drug services, infant development, foster care, and others), a pilot program was developed and initiated. The three primary goals of the program were to: (1) develop and implement a "best practice" intervention model; (2) provide education and support regarding the daily needs of the infants and their parents during the first year of life; and (3) recruit new foster homes to care for high-risk infants (Marcellus, 2000).

As it was hoped that the model would eventually be adapted to other regions of the province, the project was designed with several key development principles in mind. The education program that would be developed needed to be attainable and sustainable to ensure continuity. Training strategies also needed to be flexible enough to accommodate wide variations in geography, resources, and communities. Finally, recognition and development of local expertise was seen as being central to supporting sustainability of the project beyond the implementation phase.

Project development was guided by the community development model outlined in "Healthy Communities: The Process" (British Columbia Ministry of Health, 1996). Use of this model enabled the development of services that focused on the community as a whole, not just on one specific group of professionals or caregivers. The project recognized and built on existing strengths in the community. The model also provided for continual reassessment of progress throughout development and implementation of the project (Marcellus, 2004b).

Key project components

The overall mission for the project was to ensure that infants exposed to alcohol and drugs during pregnancy were cared for in a safe environment that supported optimal physical, cognitive, and emotional development. Five key components of the project were developed and implemented. These key components addressed needs at multiple levels, from that of the infant-caregiver relationship, through to inter-ministry policy development. Although not discussed in this article, additional components adapted in varying degrees by communities included designation of specialized social workers to manage infant placements, redesigned fee schedules, outreach seminars for related professionals such as family service agencies and pregnancy outreach programs, foster family recruitment criteria, and complex case management support.

Community education program

Education was a central element in this project. The major goal of the education program was to provide participants with the knowledge and skills they would require to begin caring for substance-exposed infants in their roles as family members, foster parents, or community professionals. To meet this goal, the education program was based on four key philosophies: (1) encouragement and support of a family training model (both adult partners were required to attend, and older children were invited); (2) respect for the knowledge and life experience in the group; (3) promotion of the use of local resources to ensure sustainability and development of local expertise; and (4) support of group discussion as an important teaching strategy (Marcellus, 2000).

A 10-session, 20-hour initial community education program was developed, based on results from a community consultation process that included a needs assessment, surveys and interviews of key stakeholders (particularly foster parents and social workers), and also on a review of the literature and existing programs across North America. Sessions were offered by community professionals as diverse as nurses, physicians, alcohol and drug counsellors, foster parents, birth parents, social workers, and infant development specialists. An outline of program topics is presented in Table 1. In addition to being attended by foster parents planning to specialize in fostering with an infant population, the program was also open to any community professionals, birth family members, respite caregivers, and interested potential adoptive parents.

Infant placement guidelines

An issue identified in many references is the incompatibility between the experience of frequent foster home placement changes for infants and the need for those infants to develop secure attachments (Morrison, Frank, Holland, & Kates, 1999; Stovall & Dozier, 1998; Wulczyn, Hislop, & Harden, 2002). Bishop et al. (2001) studied a sample of juvenile court records and reported that over half the infants in their study experienced multiple placements during their time within the child welfare system. A study by Stovall and Dozier (2000) of infants in foster care found that attachment with foster mothers took from two weeks to two months to stabilize in infants. One implication of these studies is that infants in foster care often may not be given the opportunity to develop an enduring relationship with a consistent caregiver.

Substance-exposed infants are often presented as a homogenous group, even though individually they present with a broad spectrum of possible effects, ranging from healthy term newborns with no apparent effects to high-risk births with significant effects (U.S. Department of Health and Human Services, 1993). This range in needs requires an approach to infant placement that focuses on "goodness-of-fit." A major challenge within the

Table 1. Summary of Safe Babies Project Education Program Content

Topic 1: Understanding the impact of substance abuse during pregnancy

Understanding the community experience emphasizes the need for specialized training and services. This class provides a broad overview of the issues for infants, families, and communities related to substance use during pregnancy. The overview will introduce key concepts to be addressed during the training. The first session also provides an opportunity for beginning the process of group building.

Key concepts: effective work between group members, promotion of learning, society's response to substance use during pregnancy, high-risk pregnancy, limitations of current information.

Topic 2: The effects of drugs and alcohol on the body

This class reviews basic knowledge of the effects of commonly abused substances on development of and function in the fetus, infant, child, adolescent and adult. Understanding the effects of drugs and alcohol provides a context for interpretation and effective support of behaviors.

Key concepts: fetal vulnerability, continuum of substance use, polydrug use, teratogen.

Topic 3: Partnership with birth families

This class will present information that will help professionals, foster, and adoptive families to develop the ability to work effectively with birth families and to maintain connection of the infant with the birth family. An opportunity is provided to learn from the personal experience of a birth mother, father, or other family members.

Key concepts: cycle of dependence, stages of change, harm reduction, barriers to treatment.

Topic 4: Withdrawal in the newborn

The purpose of this class is to describe the experience of withdrawal for the infant during the first few weeks and months of life and provide information about the medical, environmental, and social support of the infant and their family during this stage.

Key concepts: environmental support, infant cues, transition, self-calming.

Topic 5: Neurodevelopmental support of the infant

Development of an infant is influenced by the interaction between the infant, the caregiver, and the environment. Each infant is unique and requires individualized care to meet his or her own needs. This class will review early brain development, provide strategies to support development of successful interactions, and present information on available local support services.

Key concepts: early intervention, family-centred services, collaboration, self-regulation, resilience.

Topic 6: Health issues for the substance-exposed infant

The substance-exposed infant is at risk for not only withdrawal sequelae, but also for other health conditions related to maternal substance abuse and lifestyle issues. Caregivers must be aware of the implications of these conditions so that they are able to: (a) anticipate complications; (b) develop appropriate interventions; and (c) prepare themselves and their families.

Key concepts: health pattern.

Topic 7: Caring for substance-exposed infants: A foster parent's perspective

Infants in foster care present with a wide range of needs. Foster parents must work effectively with not only the infant, but also with his or her family, and numerous professionals. This class will provide caregivers and professionals with a review of the care of infants, the philosophy of self-care, and collaboration with families and professionals.

Key concepts: infant care, self-care, collaboration

Topic 8: Infant Cardiopulmonary Resuscitation (CPR)

Substance-exposed infants have a higher incidence of Sudden Infant Death Syndrome (SIDS) than the general infant population. They may also have other related health issues that place them at further risk of SIDS, including prematurity. Caregivers within the Safe Babies program are required to maintain current certification in infant CPR.

Key concepts: SIDS

Wrap-up

Summary activities are included at the end of the final class. The activities will provide an opportunity for participants to measure their learning, review resources, and continue to make connections with other caregivers and professionals.

foster system is to try to match an infant with challenging behaviors to a foster family with the skills and resources to manage his or her daily care needs. Poulsen (1993) suggests that infant vulnerability significantly decreases when there is a good fit between parental expectations and the child's characteristics and special needs. A key strategy to address this issue was the development of closer links between the hospital social workers who supported the discharge of infants from neonatal intensive care units, and the social workers in the community responsible for matching incoming children to foster homes. Other strategies included using homes with few or no other foster children for infants who were greatly affected by substance exposure; the foster parents would thereby have extended periods of time to devote to care of the infant. A critical outcome measurement for the Safe Babies Project was to reduce the number of placement moves experienced by infants. The project was very successful with this objective, and almost all infants remained in their original placement home until they returned to their birth family or were adopted. In addition, a number of the infants were adopted by their foster families who had cared for them since birth.

Interagency discharge guideline for infants going from hospital to home

While all infants discharged from hospital require coordinated care during the transition to the community, infants with prenatal substance exposure frequently present with a complex mix of medical and social needs that requires a comprehensive discharge plan (BCRCP, 1999). The goal of developing this guideline was to provide all members of the interdisciplinary team caring for substance-exposed infants with the information that facilitates discharge planning and ensures the safety and well-being of the infant and their family/caregiver in the community. The guideline was developed using an inter-agency consultation process and was adapted from key health and child welfare discharge recommendations (American Academy of Pediatrics, 2004; British Columbia Reproductive Care Program, 1999; U.S. Department of Health and Human Services, 1993). In addition, input for development was obtained from all professionals involved in some way with the support of infants with substance exposure and their families. Segments of the guidelines included readiness of the infant and family for discharge, a minimum length of stay in hospital, recommended laboratory studies, a discharge meeting requirement, and community follow-up. The regional director of child and youth services with the health region and the director of children's services for the region approved the final guideline.

Ongoing education programs

It is acknowledged that information and research in this field are changing rapidly. Participants were encouraged to continue to attend educational opportunities related to this topic to maintain a current knowledge base. To support this goal, the Safe Babies Project has sponsored monthly educational sessions on topics of interest generated by both foster families and by professionals. Some of the topics presented have included: an infectious disease update, nutrition for infants and toddlers, car seat safety, supporting transition to adoption, and infant massage. In addition, foster families are invited to refresher sessions at ongoing community education programs.

Teaching resources

During the early community consultation phase, many community professionals expressed the need for access to reliable, current, low-cost training materials. A range of training materials was developed and made accessible electronically through both e-mail and the MCFD intranet site. Materials included a facilitators' planning guide, a participants' manual, a parent daily care handbook, teaching pamphlets on substances, biannual newsletters, and strategies for community social workers. All materials were made available at no charge and were designed in such a way that they could be adapted to the needs of a range of communities. (These materials are all available electronically at no cost from the author.)

Foster parent support

A 1991 study done by the National Commission on Family Foster Care in the United States found that as many as 60% of foster parents withdrew from the program within the first 12 months, citing lack of agency responsiveness, communication and support as primary reasons for leaving. Similar to other reports on the current state of the foster care system, the 1997 Victoria Capital Region *Review of High-Risk Children in Foster Care* report found that foster care resources were stretched beyond their limit, with placement needs far outweighing available services: caregivers reported dealing with issues such as high turnover of social workers, placement of children with increasingly severe health and social issues, increased stress from working with birth families, insufficient relief, poor information flow, and a negative public image (Butler et al., 1997).

Foster parents have also stated that the care of the child is often the simple part, whereas the complex part of their work is the interaction with the child welfare system. Brown and Calder (2000), in their concept map of the needs of foster parents, identified good relationships with social workers and support from social services as two key concept clusters. In addition to support and communication, foster parents have identified the need for education, respite services, and a clear plan for follow-up as key components in preparing to care for an infant with special needs (Barton, 1998; Dozier, Higley, Albus, & Nutter, 2002; Soliday, McCluskey-Fawcett, & Meck, 1994). A recent stressor for foster families has been the current emphasis on reunification: foster parents are increasingly expected to provide support and training for the birth parents of the child in their care. Many of these families have complex social and emotional issues with which foster families do not feel comfortable or qualified to manage.

Depending on the needs of the community, a variety of foster parent support strategies were devised. One strategy that was particularly effective was creation of the caregiver advisor role. The caregiver advisor was an experienced foster parent who acted as a senior mentor for novice foster families. The advisor provided ongoing telephone or visiting support in relation to strategizing about effective care of the infant on a daily basis, and sponsored regular social events such as coffee mornings and Christmas celebrations for the foster families and their infants. The advisor also assisted child welfare staff with coordination of education sessions and development of training resources. Another effective strategy was creation of a nurse consultant position. The nurse consultant provided recommendations related to the health and care of the infant and liaised between the health and child welfare systems. The most important feature of both these positions was that they were available to hear the concerns of the foster families and to respect the experiences and realities of fostering. The result was improved retention and satisfaction of foster families (Marcellus, 2004b).

Development of respite services was also a key support strategy for foster families. In addition to recruiting full-time foster families, individuals and families were also recruited who were interested in providing respite services to the full-time families. When families completed the training, they were encouraged to identify and bring along neighbours, friends or family members who were interested in supporting them in their foster practice. One creative region recruited respite workers who were contracted to work full time, and then supported a core group of families. Over time, consistent respite workers became trusted caregivers by the families and their young foster children and key members of the Safe Babies foster family circles.

Evaluation

One key development principle for this project was sustainability. Following initiation of the pilot project in Victoria, MCFD extended funding to an additional five regions. Each region received project materials and the support of the nurse consultant and was encouraged to adapt the project principles to the specific needs of its own communities. A formal outcome evaluation was conducted at the end of the first year with positive results (Marcellus, 2004b). Results included a high education participation rate, a minimal number of critical incidents, a minimal number of infant placement moves, an increase in satisfaction from foster families and social workers, and improved communication between health and social services.

The Safe Babies Projects continue to exist in diverse forms and to varying degrees in each community. Some regions have continued targeted funding for resources such as caregiver advisors, foster parent support staff, and nurse consultants. The Vancouver Coastal Region was recently a finalist in the 2004 Province of British Columbia Innovation in Practice Awards. However, with government reorganizations and ongoing budget pressures, regions report that it is a struggle to maintain the same focused level of care. Some regions have had greater difficulty than others in continuing the momentum of project development within a complex practice environment with many internal and external pressures. As perinatal substance use remains a critical health issue in communities across Canada, it is important that specialized resources for infants within foster care remain a key element of planning and funding.

Summary

The increasing complexity and diversity of the needs of young infants and children entering foster care result in a requirement for more sophisticated expertise and a strengthened support system for foster parents. The Safe Babies Project includes education and support strategies that develop the knowledge, skills, and capacities of birth family members, foster families, professionals, and community members in providing the best care possible for infants and their families affected by prenatal substance use. This project has provided an opportunity to develop a shared language and knowledge base and promote consistency and currency in approaches and services throughout the community. As infants at risk have considerable potential to overcome or compensate for early stressors, the development of multi-level resilience-focused interventions has the potential to strengthen the protective effects of caregiving excellence within foster families.

References

AAP District II Task Force on Health Care for Children in Foster Care. (2004). *Fostering health: Health care for children and adolescents in foster care* (2nd ed.). New York: American Academy of Pediatrics.

Barton, S. (1998). Foster parents of cocaine-exposed infants. *Journal of Pediatric Nursing, 13,* 104–112.

Bishop, S., Murphy, J., Quinn, D., Lewis, P., Grace, M., & Jellinek, M. (2001). The youngest victims of child maltreatment: What happens to infants in a court sample? *Child Maltreatment, 6,* 243–249.

British Columbia Children's Commission. (1998). *The investigation of baby M.* Victoria, BC: Author.

British Columbia Ministry of Health. (1996). *Healthy communities: The process* (2nd ed.). Victoria, BC: Author.

British Columbia Reproductive Care Program. (1999). *Principles of perinatal care for substance-using women and their newborns.* Vancouver, BC: Author.

Brown, J., & Calder, P. (2000). Concept mapping the needs of foster parents. *Child Welfare, 79,* 729–746.

Burry, C. (1999). Evaluation of a training program for foster parents of infants with prenatal substance effects. *Child Welfare, 78,* 197–214.

Butler, V., Dane, B., Maxey, C., Moir-van-Iersel, C., & Pollard, R. (1997). *Review of high-risk children in care. Phase 1: Children 0–5 years.* Victoria, BC: British Columbia Ministry for Children and Families.

Child Welfare League of America. (1988). *Standards for health care services for children in out-of-home care.* Washington, DC: Author.

Clymen, R., Harden, B., & Little, C. (2002). Assessment, intervention, and research with infants in out-of-home placement. *Infant Mental Health Journal, 23,* 435–453.

Committee on Early Childhood, Adoption, and Dependent Care, American Academy of Pediatrics. (2002). Health of young children in foster care. *Pediatrics, 109,* 536–541.

Committee on Early Childhood, Adoption, and Dependant Care, American Academy of Pediatrics. (2000). Developmental issues for young children in foster care. *Pediatrics, 106,* 1145–1150.

Dozier, M., Higley, E., Albus, K., & Nutter, A. (2002). Intervening with foster infants' caregivers: Targeting three critical needs. *Infant Mental Health Journal, 23,* 541–554.

Drummond, J., & Marcellus, L. (2003). Resilience: An opportunity for nursing. *Neonatal, Paediatric and Child Health Nursing, 6,* 2–4.

Halfon, N., Mendonca, A., & Berkowitz, G. (1995). Health status of children in foster care: The experience of the Center for the Vulnerable Child. *Archives of Pediatric and Adolescent Medicine, 149,* 386–392.

Health Canada. (1997). *Resiliency: Relevance to Health Promotion—Detailed Analysis.* Accessed September 15, 2004, from: http://www.hc-sc.gc.ca/hppb/alcohol-otherdrugs/pube/resilncy/analysis.htm

Heller, S., Smyke, A., & Boris, N. (2002). Very young children and foster families: Clinical challenges and interventions. *Infant Mental Health Journal, 23,* 555–575.

Kaplan, H. (1999). Toward an understanding of resilience: A critical review of definitions and models. In M. Glantz & J. Johnson (Eds.), *Resilience and development: Positive life adaptations* (pp. 17–84). New York: Kluwer.

Kools, S., & Kennedy, C. (2003). Foster child health and development: Implications for primary care. *Pediatric Nursing, 29,* 39–46.

Kumpfer, K. (1999). Factors and processes contributing to resilience: The resilience framework. In M. Glantz & J. Johnson (Eds.), *Resilience and development: Positive life adaptations* (pp. 179–224). New York: Kluwer.

Lester, B., Boukydis, C., & Twomey, J. (2000). Maternal substance abuse and child outcome. In C. Zeanah (Ed.), *Handbook of infant mental health* (2nd ed.) (pp. 161–175). New York: Guilford Press.

Marcellus, L. (2000). The Safe Babies project. *Canadian Nurse, 96*(10), 22–26.

Marcellus, L. (2002). Care of substance-exposed infants: The current state of practice in Canadian hospitals. *Journal of Perinatal and Neonatal Nursing, 16(3),* 51–68.

Marcellus, L. (2004a). Foster parents who care for infants with prenatal drug exposure: Support during transition from NICU to home. *Neonatal Network, 23,* 33–41.

Marcellus, L. (2004b). Developmental evaluation of the Safe Babies Project: Application of the COECA model. *Issues in Comprehensive Pediatric Nursing, 27,* 107–119.

Masten, A. (2001). Ordinary magic: Resilience processes in development. *American Psychologist, 56,* 227–238.

Mauro, L. (1999). Child placement: Policies and issues. In J. Silver, B. Amster, & T. Haecker(Eds.), *Young children and foster care: A guide for professionals* (pp. 261–278). Baltimore, MD: Paul H. Brookes.

Morrison, J., Frank, S., Holland, C., & Kates, W. (1999). Emotional development and disorders in young children in the child welfare system. In J. Silver, B. Amster, & T. Haecker (Eds.), *Young children and foster care: A guide for professionals* (pp. 33–64). New York: Brookes.

National Commission on Family Foster Care. (1991). *A blueprint for fostering infants, children and youths in the 1990s.* Washington, DC: Child Welfare League of America.

Poulsen, M. (1993). Strategies for building resilience in infants and young children at risk. *Infants and Young Children, 6*(2), 29–40.

Rosenfeld, A., Pilowsky, D., Fine, P., Thorpe, M., Fein, E., Simms, M., et al. (1997). Foster care: An update. *Journal of the American Academy of Child and Adolescent Psychiatry, 36,* 448–457.

Rouse, K. (1998). Infant and toddler resilience. *Early Childhood Education Journal, 26,* 47–52.

Silver, J., Amster, B., & Haecker, T. (1999). *Young children and foster care: A guide for professionals.* New York: Brookes.

Silver, J., DiLorenzo, P., Zukoski, M., Ross, P., Amster, B., & Schlegel, D. (1999). Starting young: Improving the health and developmental outcomes of infants and toddlers in the child welfare system. *Child Welfare, 78,* 148–165.

Soliday, E., McCluskey-Fawcett, K., & Meck, N. (1994). Foster mothers' stress, coping, and social support in parenting drug-exposed and other at-risk toddlers. *Children's Health Care, 23,* 15–32.

Stovall, K., & Dozier, M. (1998). Infants in foster care: An attachment theory perspective. *Adoption Quarterly, 2,* 55–88.

Streissguth, A. (1997). *Fetal alcohol syndrome: A guide for families and communities.* Baltimore, MD: Paul H. Brookes Publishing.

Testa, M., & Rolock, N. (1999). Professional foster care: A future worth pursuing? *Child Welfare, 78,* 108–124.

United States Department of Health and Human Services, Center for Substance Abuse Treatment. (1993). *Treatment improvement protocol (TIP) series 5: Improving treatment for drug-exposed infants.* Rockville, MD: DHHS Publication No. CHSA 93-2011.

Werner, E., & Smith, R. (1992). *Overcoming the odds: High-risk children from birth to adulthood.* Ithaca, NY: Cornell University Press.

Wheway, D., Durnford, S., & Fey, H. (1997). *Foster parent issues and concerns: A paper detailing issues and concerns of foster parents in British Columbia.* Vancouver, BC: BC Federation of Foster Parent Associations.

Wulczyn, F., Hislop, K., & Harden B. (2002). The placement of infants in foster care. *Infant Mental Health Journal, 23,* 454–475.

Zukoski, M. (1999). Foster parent training. In J. Silver, B. Amster, & T. Haecker (Eds.), *Young children and foster care: A guide for professionals* (pp. 473–490). Baltimore, MD: Paul H. Brookes.

CHAPTER 8

Growing up in care: Resilience and care outcomes

Elizabeth Fernandez

Introduction

This chapter presents research into the pattern of outcomes achieved by children in out-of-home care in the spheres of family and social relationships, emotional and behavioural development and education. The overall aim of the research is to capture perceptions of children's established relationships with birth families and developing attachments with foster families, and to analyze perceived psychological functioning of the children over time while living in care. Designed as a five-year longitudinal study, the research explores children's conceptions of their experiences in addition to caseworkers', carers' and teachers' assessments. Selected data from the first three years of the study are presented in this chapter.

Research context

The issue of substitute care for children who cannot be cared for by their families of origin, the quality of that care, and its impact on children's development are highly significant for Australian Society. There was a continuing upward trend Australia-wide with the number of children on care and protection orders increasing from 15,718 at June 30, 1997, to 22,130 at June 2003. At June 2003, there were 4.6 children aged 0-17 years per 1000 in care with Care and Protection orders—a rise from 3.3 per 1000 in 1997 (AIHW, 2004).

The out-of-home care system has been subject to criticism in relation to protracted periods children spend in unplanned care, the instability they experience through multiple placements, their poor educational achievement and vocational prognosis. The phenomenon of children experiencing discontinuities and disruptions as a result of placement breakdown in care is documented (Berridge & Cleaver, 1987; Fernandez, 1999; Delfabbro et al., 2000) and is perceived to have costly repercussions for children and the community in terms of adult outcomes (Stein, 1994). Evidence of increasing emotional and behavioural problems among children and adolescents in long-term care has been found in a number of studies (Heath et al., 1994; McAuley, 1996; Flynn & Biro, 1998; Barber & Delfabbro, 2004; Farmer et al., 2004) with the rate of disturbance noted to be higher than in the general population. In the research of Fanshel, Finch and Grundy (1989), children who experienced multiple placement moves were described as having more behavioural and health problems and delayed educational attainment than peers who had more stable experiences. Studies undertaken point to the educational deficits children bring to care and which are exacerbated by the care experience (Aldgate, 1990; Heath et al., 1994; Jackson, 2001).

The level of contact maintained between children in long-term care and their birth families and its effect on placement outcomes have also received considerable research interest (Cleaver, 2000; Delfabbro et al., 2002; Pecora et al., 2000; Bullock et al., 1998; Milham et al., 1986; Thorpe, 1980; Fernandez, 1996). A significant association has been noted between parental visiting and various domains of child well-being (Cantos, Gries, & Slis, 1997). Higher levels of identification with birth parents have reinforced foster family attachment and self-esteem (Salahu-Din & Bollman, 1994). Research attention has also begun to move beyond the question of placement continuance and stability towards concern with long-term developmental outcomes. Parker et al. (1992) and Ward (1995) advocate the study of measurable developmental outcomes of children in care such as physical health, educational progress, family and social relationships, and emotional and social growth.

Resilience and out-of-home care

There has been developing support for resilience-led perspectives in child welfare practice to provide a balancing focus against the background of traditional deficit-based approaches and risk assessment models that have predominated (Walsh, 1998; Rutter, 1999; Gilligan, 2001, and chapter 2, this volume; Daniel & Wassell, 2002; Flynn et al., 2004). Concern about early intervention and prevention has redirected attention in the last three decades towards understanding vulnerability to risk (Garmezy, 1974) as well as protective factors that strengthen the resources of children and promote their resilience (Rutter, 1985; Masten, Best & Garmezy, 1990; Masten, chapter 1, this volume; Luthar & Zigler, 1991). Resilience is conceptualized as the process of, capacity for, or outcomes of successful adaptation despite challenging or threatening circumstances (Masten et al., 1990). Elucidating the concept of resilience further, Gilligan (1997) emphasises the "qualities which cushion a vulnerable child from the worst effects of adversity…and which helps a child or young person to cope, survive, and even thrive in the face of great hurt and disadvantage." Children's resilience is said to be enhanced when they have developed attachment to a caring parent/caregiver or supportive adult in their family or social world. Resilience is also nurtured and enhanced by support from friends, teachers, coaches and other mentors including caseworkers, given that development occurs across a range of contexts (Werner & Smith, 1992; Masten & Coatsworth, 1998; Masten, chapter 1, this volume; Gilligan, 2000). A life cycle perspective is important for understanding resilience. Werner and Smith's (1992) view that resilience can develop at anytime in the life cycle—that nothing is cast in stone—is supported by other researchers (Masten et al., 1990; Wyman, 1991).

Rutters' (1990) work on risk and protective factors affecting child development shows that although the effects of risk factors may be significant, cumulative protective factors may have disproportionate positive effects. This prompts optimism as to the valuable role that foster/adoptive carers can play in enhancing protective factors for children in order to promote an improved sense of self-esteem and self-efficacy. Optimal experiences through planned substitute care can provide the key elements of consistency, nurturance, and predictability to diminish the traumatic impact of children's early experiences, and promote resilience (Hughes, 1997; Gilligan, 2001).

Given that a significant proportion of fostered children enter care with a disadvantage that is often exacerbated by the experience of disrupted placements, the processes involved in optimizing developmental outcomes and enhancing resilience constitute an important area of research. To date, there has been very limited longitudinal research on children currently living in substitute care that elicits their perspectives (Wilson & Conroy, 1999). Research that views outcomes from different participants in the foster care process is also very limited. In this respect, this longitudinal study attempts to make a contribution to the field of out-of-home care research.

Methodology

The research involves a five-year longitudinal study using a prospective, repeated measures design with qualitative and quantitative methods (Menard, 1991). The nature of children and young people's needs, strengths and difficulties and caregivers responses to these are assessed at different stages of the care process: at four months after entry to care and at 18-month intervals thereafter. Personal interviews with children over eight years of age and caseworkers and foster carers of children of all ages are the main sources of data. Semi-structured interviews consisting of pre-coded and open-ended questions were used. Qualitative methods were chosen for understanding the process of interactions between service users and providers and evaluating intermediate and long-term outcomes. This included the grounded theory approach developed by Glaser and Strauss (1980) with its emphasis on "close up" observations of the natural world and identification of concepts that emerge from the data. The quantitative instruments incorporated items from the Assessment and Action Records that are part of the Looking After Children protocols. This case management system was adapted and implemented through a collaborative project between the author and Barnardos Australia. In order to provide some indication of the level of need of the study children, a range of standardized measures (for which general population normative data are available) are used in this study. This included the Achenbach Child Behaviour Checklist (Achenbach, 1991), with versions designed to be completed by carers and teachers, the Hare Self-Esteem Scale (Hare, 1985), and the Interpersonal Parent and Peer Attachment Inventory (Armsden & Greenberg, 1987).

About the children

The site of research is Barnardos Australia, a major child welfare provider receiving referrals from the state Department of Community Services. The sample included 59 children from 2-18 years placed in foster families in Sydney through the Barnardos Find a Family Program, a long-term foster care service. The sample included 29 boys and 30 girls. Their ages ranged from 2 to 15, with an average age of 8.8 years. The children were exclusively placed with foster families, with a single exception, which was a kin placement.

Prior to their placement with Barnardos long-term foster care program, 45% of children had been placed in care away from their birth family. Some children had 5 or more placements. The children had a median of 2 prior placements and an average of 1.9 placements. The number of foster family placements that children subsequently had with Barnardos varied. The median number of placements was 2 and the average was 2.4. The total number of placements, before and during Barnardos' care, ranged from a single child with only 1 placement to another child with 13 placements. Just under a third of the children had more than 5 placements in total. In more detail, this included 17% with 5 placements; 6% with 6 placements; 4% with 7; 2% with 8; 4% with 12; and the one child with 13 placements. The median number of total placements was 4 and the average was 4.3. The children had spent between 15 and 159 months in care in all placements, at an average of 71 months per child ($SD = 28$ months). Time in care was strongly related to number of placements ($r = .58, p = .000$), but neither time in care nor number of placements was affected by the child's age or sex or age at entry.

Placement stability was an important theme in children's accounts of their experience in care. Although many children wish to return to their birth family, they also desire a stable placement. From the qualitative analysis of children's perceptions, their anxiety about moving on was evident, as was their perception of their behaviour as a factor related to being able to stay. Children frequently internalized responsibility for breakdown or continuation of the placement:

> (SIGH) Well if I am very very, extremely good I might stay here and this might be my forever family but if um, if this isn't a good place I will have to move, which I don't want to. (female, 8 yrs.)

> Never chuck a temper tantrum 'cause it gets you kicked out. I've like been in 12 homes now. (male, 13yrs.)

While the children in this study seemed to be aware that their behaviour may be a reason for the carers to reject them, they also felt let down by a lack of openness around placement changes. The child below was told that his carers were no longer able to care for foster children; however, after the child moved on to another placement, he met the new children the couple had taken on. "But they told me a lie, cause they got some more kids...I was being naughty and they don't want me." (male, 9 yrs.)

Family and social relations

Children's cohesion with foster family

Children who come into care are vulnerable to disrupted attachments. There is a strong view that children who have experienced such disruptions need continuity and stability through alternative attachment figures. Consistent with attachment theory, the concept of resilience stresses the importance of relationships in enhancing children's sense of belonging and their secure base. The children were asked to describe and rate the level of cohesion they experienced with their current foster family. They were asked, "How well do you get along with the people you stay with?" They were asked about the cohesion with their foster mother, foster father and other children, and the responses were "very well," "quite well," "not very well," "badly" or "don't know."

The majority of children reported that they got on very well with their foster families. Because of the small number of children who did not get on well with their foster families, Table 1 includes an "other" category to include children who reported they did not get on well or did not know. In fact, only one child, a boy aged under 10.5 years, reported getting on "not very well" with his foster father. A small minority felt that they did not know how they got on with their foster father (16%) or foster mother (10%).

Table 1. Children's cohesion with foster family members at interview 1

	All	Boys	Girls	Age < 10.5	Age > 10.5
	(%)	(%)	(%)	(%)	(%)
Foster mother					
Very well	63	66	67	73	60
Quite well	27	17	28	20	27
Other	10	17	5	7	13
Foster father					
Very well	63	71	50	71	50
Quite well	21	21	20	21	20
Other	16	8	30	8	30
Other children					
Very well	70	63	86	75	64
Quite well	30	37	14	25	36
Other	0	0	0	0	0

Children expressed in many ways the cohesive relationship developed with their carers. Thy talked of their carers helping them with homework, keeping them safe, and, as expressed in the quotations below, making them feel part of the family:

> She, um, she'll spend lots of time on me and she's really nice, and...she helps me with things when I need help...she always has the right advice to tell me...'cause they treat me like I'm part of the family so I think I am. (female, 10 yrs.)

> He teaches me stuff, like he teaches me soccer and all that. Sometimes he goes down to the park and teaches me stuff like soccer...They take care of us, make sure we're safe as well...I give them a hug, sometimes in the day time, and before I go to bed. They give me hugs, but not kisses. I don't like kisses. (male, 11 yrs.)

Caseworker assessments of the child's cohesion with members of the foster family were almost always positive, most strongly with the foster mother, and least strongly with a foster sibling, or other child in the family. Caseworkers' cohesion ratings emphasize the key role that the child's relationship with his or her foster mother plays. At both interviews about two thirds of the children were perceived to get on very well with their foster mother, and only at Interview 2 did one child not get on well with the foster mother. Cohesion with the foster father, while almost always favourable, was perceived to be in the highest range (getting on "very well") for about 4 in 10 of the children at Interview 2, compared to 5 in 10 at the first interview. Similarly about 1 in 4 of the children was perceived to get on "very well" with foster siblings at Interview 2, compared to about 1 in 3 at Interview 1.

The caseworker ratings of cohesion were compared to the child's age, sex and history in care. Using correlational analyses, a range of important relationships emerged as statistically significant. First, at Interview 2, children who were older were less likely to be rated as getting on very well with either the foster father ($r = .41, p = .017$) or foster siblings ($r = -.36, p = .05$). Similarly, age at entry to care was negatively correlated with very good cohesion with foster siblings ($r = -.43, p = .017$). Finally, the total number of placements was negatively related to foster father cohesion ($r = .45, p = .009$), such that more placements were associated with poorer cohesion. Cohesion with the foster mother, however, remained independent of all these variables.

Contact with family of origin

There has been a long history of support for an "inclusive" approach that enables children to maintain connection with significant members of their birth family (Milham et al., 1986; Weinstein, 1960). Fratter et al. (1991) note that contact with birth parents can serve as a protective factor providing positive outcomes. This study explored children's experience of contact with birth parents and extended family.

Contact with members of their family of origin varied considerably according to the family member (see Figure 1). Just over one third of children (36%) saw their birth mother on a monthly basis and a further 36% saw her every three months. About half the children (52%) had no contact with their father while only one in five of the children saw their father monthly. Twenty-six children reported they had siblings, and they were the most frequently contacted family members, including 49% who saw a brother or sister at least monthly.

Figure 1. How often children report seeing members of their family of origin (%)

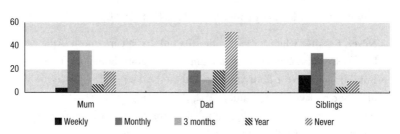

The qualitative analysis of the children's interviews provides an enriched expression of the connection many of the children have to their birth mother. In response to the question, "How do you feel when you see her (birth mother)?":

> "Happy...Mmm, I dunno, I just have this feeling...Mmm, nice, mmm happy, mmm that's about it." (male, 11 yrs.)

> "Um, the fact that I'm happy." (female, 11 yrs.)

One child's feelings about her mother were so private that she had made the interviewer promise not to put her nonverbal queues into words that could be heard on the tape recorder. (female, 8 yrs.)

When the interviewer asked one of children whether he was happy with the present arrangements, the child answered as if he were out of *Oliver Twist*. "More, please, just more." (male, 9 yrs.)

As part of the interview schedule, the children were given three hypothetical wishes. Many of their responses related to having their family back together. "Um, that I was rich. I was living with Mum. Um, play for Australia (rugby)." (male, 12 yrs.) "OK first...back with my mum...second...have all my things back together again...and third, have all the happiness..." (female, 11 yrs.)

The majority of children wanted more contact with their family of origin: most often their siblings (65%), but also their mother (56%) and the same proportion with their fathers (56%). A small minority desired either less contact or no contact at all, predominantly in relation to their fathers (16%).

In regard to the qualitative analysis of the children's interviews, data relating to the birth father were very thin. In reviewing responses to questions concerning access visits with their fathers, presented below, it can be seen that many of the children's fathers are not a large part of their day-to-day experience:

> Well I don't know my Dad. (male, 9 yrs.)

> I dunno. I never have any contact with him. (female, 11 yrs.)

> Never. Because when I was 12 months old, he left my mom. And I haven't seen him for a while. And I don't give a damn about it any more. But if he came to the door and knocked on the door, and I opened the door, and he says (child's name), I'd say, "Hey Dad, how you goin'?" and slam the door to him. Because I don't like him, not after what he did to me. But I only care about this dad now. (male, 13 yrs.)

Contact with extended family members, previous carers and caseworkers

The caseworkers provided additional information on the frequency of contact between the child and members of his or her extended family. Grandparents and maternal aunts were an occasional point of contact for some children, a few times a year. Approximately 4 children in 10 had ongoing contact of some description with their previous carers.

Sixty per cent of carers reported that the child had had the same case worker for the duration of their current placement. Visits were most frequently on a monthly basis, would last between two and three hours, and caseworkers "often" spent time alone with the children. One particular carer who had five siblings in her care observed the caseworker was able to give each child individual attention:

> She tries to have private time for each individual, or if they have problems and they need her, she is there. Because there are five of them, each week she will try to take one of them for a drink or ice cream, so they have got a one on one...

Some of the children had built strong ties with their case workers and looked forward to the time they spend together. This bond is acknowledged by the carer:

> I can see they get on very well. He is quite excited and at times he will ask, is (worker) coming this week? And he usually greets her with a hug and tells her of something exciting that happened.

Perceptions of schooling

There is a catalogue of research that highlights the disadvantage children in care experience in relation to their education (Aldgate et al., 1991; Jackson, 2001; Heath et al., 1994). The satisfaction of educational needs brings benefits to children in other domains of development (Weyts, 2004). Exploration of this area revealed some disquieting findings in that children had several unscheduled school changes.

Based on carer accounts, three quarters of the children had experienced at least one change in schooling since their separation from their birth family. More than half of the children had had three or more changes. Changing school not only interrupts a child's education, but also breaks the continuity of friendships. Some struggle to keep up with their peers and are conscious of the disruption caused by their many moves. The children's responses to the question, "How many times have you changed school since leaving the home of your birth mom and dad?" are informative:

> I don't know about three or four. It was pretty bad for my education. (male, 12 yrs.)

> I hate it….'Cause I love all my schools that I went to. (female, 8 yrs.)

> About 10 hundred times, 'cause I went to 10 hundred schools. (female, 8 yrs.)

> I think she's been to about 9 different schools and this is the longest year and a half that she's been in this school. I think that's the longest she's ever been in her life. (carer)

In 78% of cases, school age children changed schools when they moved into their current foster care placement. Just under a half of the carers (48%) felt that the child was performing very well at school, while the majority of the children were perceived to be coping moderately or well. Sixteen per cent, however, rated the child in their care as performing "not very well" at school. Noting the qualitative data, it can be seen that the carers, in many cases, take an active role in the children's education. Carers recognize that if they are going to give the child the best chance at a good future, they have to be proactive in the child's education:

> Well they're just so far behind in their learning, they could barely read or write when they come here…even now it's "how do you spell child" so they're way, way behind but with the extra support they've really come on well. (carer)

> I think my biggest challenge is giving him a reasonable education. That is our biggest concern for him…childhood years, like he is really behind…I think you have to give him a fair go, give him an education, I think that is very important to me. (carer)

Friendship networks

Resilience enhancing factors are inherent in supportive contexts and relationships, including friendships. Friends offer support and buffer the effects of stress. The carers' perceptions about the child's ability to initiate and maintain friendships suggests the child easily made friends in 60% of cases but was considered to have difficulties in 29% of cases. Carers reported most often that children had a broad friendship network including "a few" or "many friends" (39.6%). In total, 61% of girls had a few or many friends and 42% of boys. There were 10 carers who reported that the child had only one or no friends, and this included 7 boys and 3 girls. In subsequent interviews, the carers perceived that in 58.3% of cases the child had improved in his or her friendship domains in the previous 18 months.

The importance of friends in the children's lives is a pervasive theme in the data. From the qualitative analysis of the time-two child interviews, it is clear the children have been able to maintain long-term relationships with their friends. Furthermore, the children were keen to express how many friends they have and for how long they have had them. When discussing friends, there is a brief window where we leave the world of foster care and enter the child's world. The conversations around friends express a sense of control they have over their lives. In making friends, the children have a choice of who they want to be with and who they don't:

> I've got friends since primary school and from my old school. I can still call them and it would be fine. Just say "Hi how are you, what's happening?" We just talk about everything and sometimes we meet up and sometimes we don't. We still keep in contact. (female, 16 yrs.)

However, from the qualitative data from carers, the challenges and perceived dynamics for a foster child in making friends are evident:

> …when she first came to us she finds it really, really easy to play with children that are younger, or older…her own age group she's found it really difficult to relate to and I think again that comes from "Why bother, I'm going to be moving, why should I have a relationship with you?"…But she's now made another friend further down, and she does have friends at school, that you would call friends not just an acquaintance.

Children's experience of negative and positive events

Gilligan (2001) stresses the importance of multiple roles for children and young people to give them the opportunity to achieve and be acknowledged, and to foster their talents. The children's experience of adversity and risk factors were highlighted by carers in addition to their positive attainments. Carers were asked their knowledge of significant events that the children had experienced. The range of events included experiences where the child had been a victim of emotional, physical or sexual abuse, through to their own behaviour, and events affecting their well-being and future, including parental divorce or death.

Table 2. Critical or crisis events affecting the child

Incident	%	Incident	%
emotional abuse	31.4	accident	15.7
experience of violence	29.4	loss of sibling/foster sibling	15.4
experience of bullying	29.4	running away	13.7
physical abuse	21.6	none	11.8
stealing	21.6	death of significant other	9.6
sexual abuse	17.6	divorce/separation of parents/caregivers	7.7
placement breakdown	17.3	court involvement (charges)	7.7
expelled/quit school	17.6	death of parent	5.8
serious illness/disability	17.6	pregnancy/abortion	1.9
		other	19.6

The most frequently reported critical or crisis events reported included the experiences of bullying, emotional abuse and violence or physical abuse (Table 2). Children's cumulative number of events ranged from 0 to 14, with the average being 3. Only eight of the children were free of any of these negative events. The carers were also asked to reflect on potentially positive events which the child had experienced. The most frequently endorsed was a stable foster placement and the bond with the current caregiver. Nevertheless, the majority also experienced events such as vacations, having a pet, and achievements in a range of domains (Table 3).

Table 3. Positive events and changes experienced by the child in the previous 18 months

	%		%
stable foster placement	86.8	healing—emotional, psychological	48.1
trips, vacations	84.6	bond with birth parent	44.2
bond with present caregiver	73.1	developmental achievements	44.2
educational achievements	63.5	recreational/creative activities	39.6
having a pet	61.5	significant other attachment	38.5
sports or athletic achievements	60.4	bond with previous caregiver	28.8
friendships	57.7	move to adoption/permanency	28.3
better health	50.0	reconnecting with culture	13.5
visiting siblings, birth parents, extended family	48.1	job/employment	5.8
participation in family events	48.1	other	17.3

All children experienced multiple positive events in the previous 18 months, with a third having more than 10 of these events (Table 3). The median number of positive events was 10 and the average was 10.6.

Children's emotional and behavioural development

The Looking After Children Assessment and Action Records: Children and caseworker ratings

Increasing attention is being paid to emotional health and behavioural development of children in care. This is a particularly vulnerable dimension for children. Previous studies have identified a high level of emotional and behavioural concerns affecting children in care (Ward, 1995; Barber & Delfabbro, 2004). A core part of the children's interview schedule included the children's 30-item self-assessment of their feelings and interpersonal skills from the Looking After Children (LAC) Assessment and Action Records (Parker et al., 1992), revised recently by Quinton and Murray (2002). The LAC includes child and carer versions. It can be analyzed using six subscales or one total scale, the subscales showing good validity and in most cases adequate reliability. In this study, the data from the 30 items were examined in two ways. First, the data were scored using the LAC subscales developed by Quinton and Murray (2002). This enabled description using the areas covered by six subscales and comparisons with normative data from 100 children in UK care (Table 4). This analysis is complemented by the children's caseworkers' ratings of the 30 items. Second, the data were scored more conservatively, noting only the presence or absence of each feeling or behaviour to allow description of individual items and a sum of problematic items for each child in three areas: relationship building skills, anxiety symptoms, and concentration/behavioural difficulties.

The children and their caseworkers were asked about 30 feelings or behaviours. Items were both negatively and positively phrased. Both children and caseworkers were asked independently to rate the extent to which the child behaved in relation to each item using a four-point scale ("a lot like me/the child," "quite like me/the child," "a bit like me/the child," or "not at all like me/the child"). Caseworkers' training in the LAC enabled consistency in rating. The (LAC) rating scale yields six subscales:

- Emotional problems   Fears, unhappiness, depression
- Conduct problems   Fighting, destructiveness, stealing
- Overactivity   Restlessness, failure to settle to tasks, poor concentration
- Peer relationships   Popular, finds it hard to mix, shares, lets others join in
- Pro-social disposition   Positive behaviour toward others

- Carers   Trusts and confides, goes for reassurance, likes affection

A higher score is always used to indicate more problems—except with the pro-social subscale, which is positively scored (a higher score meaning better functioning).

The scores reported for each of the subscales in Table 4 are within the same range or greater than those reported by Quinton and Murray (2002), based on 100 children aged 10-18 in the UK. There were no significant relationships between any of the LAC scores by either gender or age.

Table 4. Children's scores on LAC subscales and normative data from a comparable group of 100 children in care (UK)

Subscale	Mean	SD	UK Mean	SD
Emotional	7.2	5.1	3.8	3.4
Conduct	4.1	2.9	3.4	2.7
Overactivity	5.5	2.4	4.7	2.9
Peer relationships	3.3	2.3	2.9	2.0
Relationship with carers	4.6	2.4	3.4	2.4
Pro-social disposition	8.5	2.2	8.4	2.4
Total Score	24.8	10.1	19.2	1.0

The results in Table 5 compare the caseworker LAC ratings with the children's own ratings and the ratings of carers in the UK.

Table 5. Caseworker ratings On LAC subscales at Interview 2 and normative data from carer ratings for comparable group of 100 children in care (UK)

Subscale	Caseworker				Children's self-assessment		UK Carers	
	Mean	SD	range	n	Mean	SD	Mean	SD
Emotional problems	4.9	3.7	0–14	39	7.2	5.1	4.2	3.9
Conduct problems	4.4	3.0	0–11	41	4.1	2.9	3.4	2.7
Overactivity	5.7	3.0	0–12	40	5.5	2.4	4.7	3.0
Peer relationships	7.1	2.3	2–12	37	3.3	2.3	3.3	2.2
Pro-social disposition	4.3	3.0	0–9	40	8.5	2.2	8.0	2.7
Relationship with carers	2.7	2.0	0–8	40	4.6	2.4	3.0	2.2
Total score	23.3	11.3	5–50	36	24.8	10.1	19.8	1.2

While not compared statistically, the caseworker ratings provided some interesting contrasts with the children's own assessment. While the total LAC scores were similar, children reported more emotional problems than the caseworkers, and more problems with carers. The children, however, were more favourable in their ratings of their social skills and problems with peers.

In comparison with the base line ratings at entry to care, caseworker ratings recorded 18 months later on the LAC showed some significant improvements in three of the subscales, including emotional problems, conduct problems, and relationship with carers. On closer analysis, the majority of change in scores was attributable to girls, who did show significant change in total scores, whereas boys had significant changes in two domains only: emotional problems and relationship with carers.

Ability to build adaptive relationships

In relation to the second analysis, the data presented in Table 6 show how the children rated the extent to which they had 16 relationship-building skills. The skills have been ranked from most to least frequently endorsed. The data have been re-coded to be either "a lot or quite like me" versus "a bit or not at all like me." In Table 6, all the relationship-building skills are expressed in the positive version (i.e., if it was a negative characteristic like starts fights, "not like me" is written next to the item). The five relationship strengths most frequently reported by the children in Table 6 included their self-perceived ability to share or include others in their activities, their sense of appropriate relationship boundaries, and a sense of empathy, by being considerate of other's feelings. These relationship building skills were each reported by 75% or more of the children.

Table 6. Relationship-building skills reported by children at Interview 1

Rank		%
1.	Let others join in	88
2.	*Not* over friendly with others	85
3.	Considerate of other's feelings	81
4.	Like to share	77
5.	*Do not* Find it hard to mix with young people	75
6.	*Do not* Get into fights	70
7.	Comfort others who are upset	69
8.	Easy to make and keep friends	67
9.	Popular with young people	63
10.	*Not* Often angry and lose temper	59
11.	*Not* Extremely suspicious of motives	50
12.	*Not* Often in trouble	46
13.	Able to trust	41
Relationship with Carers		
1.	Like carers to show physical affection	70
2.	*Not* Impatient with carers	67
3.	Get reassurance from carers	48

The 16 relationship-building skills and abilities were also considered together as a further way of describing the children's relationship maturity. Each child reported a repertoire of between 4 and 15 positive relationship skills and abilities. Approximately a quarter (24%) of the children felt they had 8 or fewer of these skills and abilities and 61% had 9 to 12 of these skills. While a clear majority endorsed skills like sharing and letting others join in, 50% or more of the children, on their own reports, saw themselves as: often in trouble; extremely suspicious of others motives; unable to trust. Less than 50% felt able to look to their carers for reassurance. At the subsequent data gathering phase, the children were asked about the same range of skills and attributes that contribute to the development of adaptive relationships. At Interview 2, 7 skills were reported by more than 75% of the children. In particular, the children now reported feelings of empathy and support, such as comforting others, and being considerate of other's feelings (Figure 2). Further, "not getting in to fights" moved from the 6th ranked attribute at Interview 1 to the 2nd rank at Interview 2. "Being able to trust" remained the lowest ranked attribute, yet more than 50% of the children endorsed it. More than half of the children reported the positive skills toward their carers.

Figure 2. Illustrative examples of strengthening in relationship skills between Interview 1 and Interview 2

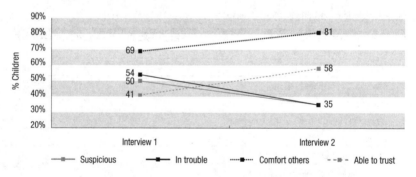

Concentration and behavioural problems

The children were asked about their experience of the six concentration and behavioural difficulties, outlined in the LAC Assessment Records, over the preceding three months

The most commonly acknowledged difficulty was "finding it difficult to stick at things for more than a few minutes," affecting just over a half (54%) of the children. The other more common difficulties included difficulties concentrating, impulsivity and restlessness, affecting between 44%

and 40%. At Interview 2, 60% of the children had one or no concentration difficulties compared with 44% at Interview 1.

Anxiety problems

The children were asked about their experience of eight different anxiety symptoms in the preceding three months. Change in appetite was the most frequently reported symptom. About half of the children reported worrying a lot or having anxiety-related somatic complaints. The number of symptoms of anxiety or distress is a further indicator of a child's emotional needs. Most children were experiencing two or three anxiety symptoms at the time of interview. Perhaps most telling was the fact that none of the children was free of anxiety symptoms. It is important to note that LAC is not intended as a diagnostic tool. It does, however, indicate that the majority of children experienced multiple anxiety symptoms at the time of entry to care. Statistically significant differences were observed in three areas: "feeling miserable or sad," "worry a lot," and somatic complaints were reported by significantly fewer children at Interview 2.

Factors associated with the children's adjustment at Interview 1

The data gathered about the child's background and history in care were analyzed to identify potential relationships with their adjustment at the initial interview. The analysis focused on the child's (1) self-assessed level of cohesion with their foster families; (2) LAC subscales; (3) relationship-building skills; and (4) current anxiety and concentration problems.

Cohesion with foster family

A series of analyses was used to examine factors associated with foster family cohesion. Because of the distribution of scores, with a major cluster in "very well" and then a spread of small frequencies in each other category, cohesion was recoded to two categories ("very well" and "other"), to try to identify contributing variables. Using chi-square (χ^2) analyses, no differences were detected between boys or girls, or older or younger children, in cohesion with their foster mother or foster father. There were no differences by age or sex in cohesion with children from the foster family. Children who reported more concentration and behavioural problems had less cohesive relationships with their foster fathers ($t = -2.85$, $df = 16$, $p = 0.012$) and foster mothers ($t = -2.62$, $df = 20$, $p = .016$). Children who reported more negative feelings about their initial separation at entry to care also had a less cohesive relationship with their foster fathers ($t = -2.09$, $df = 15, p = .054$).

Emotional and behavioural variables

Demographic factors (age, sex) and care history factors (number of pre-Barnardos placement, time in care, age at separation) were used to identify influences on emotional variables measured at Interview 1 (concentration/behavioural difficulties, anxiety problems). Girls were found to have significantly more anxiety problems ($M = 3.8$, $SD = 2.3$) than boys ($M = 2.0, SD = 1.9$) ($t = 2.09, df = 22, p = .049$).

Similarly, younger children (less than 10.5 years) were found to have more anxiety problems ($M = 3.7$, $SD = 1.9$) than older children ($M = 1.9$, $SD = 2.2$) ($t = 2.12, df = 22, p = .046$). Children's self-assessed relationship-building skills were inversely related to their self-rated behavioural problems ($r = -.67, p < .01$) and anxiety ($r = -.49, p < .05$). That is, children who reported they had many concentration and behavioural problems also reported fewer relationship-building skills. Similarly, children who were more anxious reported fewer relationship-building skills.

Factors influencing children's adjustment at Interview 2

Demographic variables

Age was significantly related to cohesion with the foster father ($r = .5$, $p = 0.01$), such that older children were less likely to report getting on "very well" with the foster father. This relationship did not extend to cohesion with other members of the foster family and there was no relationship between sex and cohesion. The child's cohesion with other children from the foster family, however, was significantly related to the child's number of placements since entering Barnardos' care. Children who got on very well with the children of the foster family had an average of 1.7 Barnardos placements ($SD = 0.8$), which was significantly fewer than children who did not get on very well (Mean places $= 2.9, SD = 1.2$; $t = -2.62, df = 17, p = .018$).

Interview 1 variables

Interestingly, the only significant relationship between cohesion at Interview 1 and cohesion at Interview 2 was between ratings for the foster fathers ($r = .50, p = .023$). There were significant relationships between the child's self-reported relationship-building skills and cohesion with the foster mother ($r = -.69, p < .01$) and the foster father ($r = -.63, p < .05$). That is, the more perceived skills at Interview 1, the more cohesive the relationships at Interview 2.

This is a clinically significant finding that points to an important area of supportive foster care and an accessible area for intervention. It suggests that where the children receive either well-modelled relationship skills in their earlier placements, or explicit teaching of these skills, the more likely they will develop cohesive relationships with later placements. Two other important findings were: (1) the number of each child's self-rated anxiety symptoms at Interview 1 predicted subsequent adjustment difficulties and, as such, gives guidance to targeted interventions; and (2) the importance for children's anxiety to be adequately acknowledged and supported within the foster family.

Key findings and implications for practice

The majority of the children had experienced significant instability in their young lives. First separated from their families of origin at a median of six years of age, more than half had had multiple care placements prior to entering the Barnardos "Find a Family" long-term foster care programme. Placement moves were accompanied by change of schools and consequent broken peer and adult attachments. Children in this study changed schools frequently, a pattern that jeopardizes their educational outcomes. This recurrent finding must give renewed impetus to foster care systems to strive for stability in schooling for children in care, and to train and support carers in helping their foster children achieve their educational potential.

As in the studies of Chapman et al. (2004) and Johnson et al. (1995), the children rated their cohesion with their current foster families highly. Approximately two thirds got on "very well" with their foster families. The decision on the part of the children to describe their relationships as anything but very well appears to be of clinical significance. The relationship with foster mothers remained very positive, especially among boys and younger children. Older children reported less cohesive relationships with their foster fathers. Care variables were also found to account for the difference in children's adjustment. Children who had more placements were less likely to get on well with other children in the foster family. Importantly, the nature of the relationship with the foster father at Interview 1 appears to have had an important developmental influence on the children, so if there was very good cohesion the child increased his or her relationship skills by Interview 2.

With regard to maintaining continuity of links with birth families, mothers and siblings were the key ongoing contact with the family of origin. One half of the children (52%) had no contact at all with their fathers and a further 19% saw their fathers on a yearly basis. Children in this study desired further contact. Findings indicate the need for a two-pronged approach to policy and practice—one that supports building children's cohesive relationships with foster parents while, at the same time, responding to children's needs for continued connection with significant members of their birth families. It is essential that attention be paid to both developing and existing attachments. In addition to working with vulnerable children, foster carers engage with the child's worker and birth family and, in many instances, other professionals working on behalf of the child. Clearly, carers need to be supported in building strong relationships with children while nurturing the latters' established relationships with birth parents.

Consistent with a resilience orientation that supports the search for positive indications of well-being, the study explored the children's experience of positive events and opportunities. It is encouraging to note that the findings highlighted positive attainments, with a third having more than 10 of these events. Knowledge about difficulties and strengths enables practitioners to maintain and improve children's assets and change the continuum of assets and risk factors.

As noted in the literature, children in care experience higher levels of psychological difficulties than the general population of children. The interviews here also suggested these children had high psychological needs. The children's LAC profiles were broadly comparable to, or greater than, the LAC scores reported for a sample of children in care in the UK. Between 30–40% of the children felt they had problems with anger, worry, sadness and trust. More than half also experienced multiple concentration and behavioural problems. However, approximately three quarters (76%) of the children felt they had a broad range of relationship-building skills, particularly inclusive skills like sharing.

Conclusion

In summary, the complex impact of growing up in care is well illustrated here. Children present to care placements with a high level of need. In some circumstances, this becomes more difficult developmentally, as children grow older and want more autonomy, or as they experience more placements, their sense of vulnerability increases, especially in relation to peer self-esteem. In other circumstances, the children benefit from cohesive early placements and develop relationship-building skills that consolidate their future relationships. At the second interview in this study there were, overall, encouraging signs of increased stability and positive change.

A strength of this study is that it generated data on the present experience of children currently in care. The voices of children added an important dimension to the study by bringing their lived experience into the research. Clearly, the children had individualistic views about the care experience, with different perceptions about a range of needs and hurts. This underlines the importance of listening to children and respecting their capacity for and right to self-expression (Gilligan, 2000; Morrow & Richards, 1996). Nevertheless, the conduct of research with children poses important ethical and methodological challenges (Grodin & Glantz, 1994), not least of which involves weighing the risks and benefits of the research for children, and recognizing the heterogeneity of children and young people and the range of knowledge needed to understand them from different perspectives.

Overall, the findings from this study indicate that, despite concerns related to emotional and behavioural development, academic performance and placement instability early in their care, the children in this sample displayed resilience in domains such as family and social relations and pro-social behaviours. There was evidence of emerging gains in academic and emotional and behavioural outcomes as they progressed in their care placements, supporting the optimistic trends noted in resilience studies (Newman, 2004; Masten & Reed, 2002; Garmezy, 1991).

A framework of resilience applied to out-of-home care enables child welfare practitioners to refocus assessments and develop strategic interventions that promote children's strengths and competence and enable them to recover from early adversity (Masten, chapter 1, this volume). Resilience-enhancing interventions may range from fostering children's relationship-building skills to supporting carers in acknowledging and reinforcing children's pro-social behaviours and self worth, or to finding turning points in their school experience through mentoring opportunities and positive peer and adult attachment relationships. Previous research has underlined the importance of fathers' ability to connect with their children's lives and worlds (Welsh et al., 2004). This research points to the need to explore factors that enhance foster father involvement and impact on child well-being.

Apart from bolstering children's resilience to beat the odds, policy and practice must strive to change the odds, whether this relates to placement breakdown, unscheduled school changes, or social exclusion. Daniel and

Wassell (2002) caution us about further pitfalls in the discourse on resilience, such as the possibility of minimizing or belittling children's experience of hurt and distress, or expecting all children to be resilient. There is also a danger that the concept of resilience may be used in public policy to withhold resources and supports (Walsh, 1998), based on the notion of individual efforts and responsibility.

References

Armsden, G. C., & Greenberg, M. T. (1987). The Inventory of Parent and Peer Attachment: Individual differences and their relationship to psychological well-being in adolescence. *Journal of Youth and Adolescence, 16*, 427–454.

Achenbach, T.M. (1991). *Manual for the Child Behaviour Checklist and 1991 Profile*. Burlington: University of Vermont.

AIHW. (2004). Retrieved March 4, 2004, from http://www.aihw.gov.au

Aldgate, J. (1990). Foster children at school: Success or failure. *Adoption and Fostering, 14*(4), 38–48.

Barber, J. G., & Delfabbro, P. H. (2004). *Children in foster care*, New York: Routledge.

Berridge, D., & Cleaver, H. (1987). *Foster home breakdown*. Oxford: Basil Blackwell.

Bullock, R., & Dartington Social Research Unit. (1998). *Children going home: The reunification of families*. Aldershot, England: Ashgate.

Cantos, A.L., Gries, L.T., & Slis, V. (1997). Behavioural correlates of parental visiting during family foster care. *Child Welfare, 76*, 309–329.

Chapman, M. V., Wall, A., & Barth, R.P. (2004). Children's voices: The perception of children in foster care. *American Journal of Orthopsychiatry, 74*, 293–304.

Cleaver, H. (2000). *Fostering family contact*. London: Her Majesty's Stationery Office.

Daniel, B., & Wassell, S. (2002). *Assessing and promoting resilence (in three parts: Early Years, Middle Years, Adolescence)*. London: Jessica Kingsley.

Delfabbro, P.H., Barber, J.G., & Cooper, L.L. (2002). Reassessing the role of parental contact in substitute care. *Journal of Social Service Research, 28*, 19–40.

Delfabbro, P.H., Barber, J.B., & Cooper, L.L. (2000). Placement disruption and dislocation in South Australian substitute care. *Children Australia, 25,* 16–20.

Fanshel, D., Finch, J., & Grundy, J. (1989). Foster children in a life-course perspective: The Casey Family Programs experience. *Child Welfare, 68,* 467–478.

Farmer, E., Moyers, S., & Lipscombe, J. (2004). *Fostering adolescents.* London: Jessica Kingsley.

Fernandez, E. (1996). *Significant harm: Unravelling child protection decisions and substitute care careers of children.* Avebury, England: Ashgate Publishing.

Fernandez, E. (1999). Representation and analysis of placement careers of children in care using event history models. *Children and Youth Services Review, 21,* 177–216.

Flynn, R. J., Ghazal, H., Legault, L., Vandermeulen, G., & Petrick, S. (2004). Use of population measures and norms to identify resilient outcomes in young people in care: An exploratory study. *Child and Family Social Work, 9,* 65–79.

Flynn, R., & Biro, C. (1998). Comparing developmental outcomes for children in care with those for other children in Canada. *Children & Society, 12,* 228–233.

Fratter, J., Rowe, J., Sapsford, D., & Thoburn, J. (1991). *Permanent family placement: A decade of experience.* London: British Association for Adoption and Fostering.

Garmezy, N. (1974). The study of competence in children at risk for severe psychopathology. In E. Anthony and C. Koupernik (Eds.), *The child in his family: Children at psychiatric risk (Vol. 3).* New York: John Wiley.

Garmezy, N. (1991). Resilience in children's adaptation to negative life events and stressed environments. *Pediatric Annals, 20,* 459–466.

Gilligan, R. (1997). Beyond permanency? The importance of resilience in child placement practice and planning. *Adoption and Fostering, 21,* 12–20.

Gilligan, R. (2000). The importance of listening to children in foster care. In G. Kelly & R. Gilligan (Eds.), *Issues in foster care: Policy, practice and research* (pp. 40–58). London: Jessica Kingsley.

Gilligan, R. (2001). *Promoting resilience*. London: BAAF.

Glaser, G., & Strauss, A. (1980). *The discovery of grounded theory*. Hawthorne, NY: Aldine de Gruyter.

Grodin, M.A., & Glantz, L.H. (1994). *Children as research subjects: Science, ethics and law*. Oxford: Oxford University Press.

Hare Self-Esteem Scale [HSS]. (1985). Hare B.R., In: Corcoran, K. & Fischer, J. (1987). *Measures for clinical practice: A sourcebook* (pp. 393–395). New York: Free Press

Heath, A., Colton, M., & Aldgate, J. (1994). Failure to escape: A longitudinal study of foster children's educational attainment. *British Journal of Social Work, 24,* 241–260.

Hughes, D. (1997). *Facilitating developmental attachment: The road to emotional recovery and behavioural change in foster and adoptive children*. N.J.: Jason Arouson.

Jackson, S. (2001). The education of children in care. In S. Jackson (Ed.), *Nobody ever told us school mattered: Raising the educational attainments of children in care* (pp. 11–53). London: British Association for Adoption and Fostering.

Johnson, P.R., Yoken, C., & Voss. R. (1995). Family foster care placement: The child's perspective. *Child Welfare, 74,* 959–974.

Luthar, S.S., & Zigler, E. (1991). Vulnerability and competence: A review of research on resilience in childhood. *American Journal of Orthopsychiatry, 61,* 6–22.

Masten, A.S., Best, K.M., & Garmezy, N. (1990). Resilience and development: Contributions from the study of children who overcame adversity. *Development and Psychopathology, 2,* 425–444.

Masten, A.S., & Coatsworth, J.D. (1998). The development of competence in favorable and unfavorable environments: Lessons from research from successful and unsuccessful children. *American Psychologist, 53,* 205–220.

Masten, A.S., & Reed, M.G. (2002). Resilience in development. In C. R. Snyder & S. J. Lopez (Eds.), *The handbook of positive psychology* (pp. 74–88). Oxford; Oxford University Press.

McAuley, C. (1996). *Children in long-term foster care*. Aldershot, England: Ashgate.

Menard, S. (1991). *Longitudinal research*. Newbury Park, CA: Sage.

Milham, S., Bullock, R., Hosie, K., & Haak, M. (1986). *Lost in care: The problems of maintaining links between children in care and their families.* Aldershot: Gower.

Morrow, V., & Richards, M. (1996). The ethics of social research with children: An overview. *Children and Society, 10,* 90–105.

Newman, T. (2004). *What works in building resilience?* Ilford, Essex, England: Barnardo's.

Parker, R.A., Ward, H., Jackson, S., Aldgate, J. & Wedge, P. (Eds.) (1992). *Looking After Children: Assessing outcomes in child care.* London: HMSO.

Pecora, P. J., Whittaker, J. K., Maluccio, A. N., Barth, R. P., & Plotnick, R. D. (2000). *The child welfare challenge* (2nd ed.). New York, NY: Aldine de Gruyter.

Quinton, D., & Murray, C. (2002). Assessing emotional and behavioural development of children looked after away from home. In H. Ward & W. Rose (Eds.), *Approaches to needs assessment in children's services.* London: Jessica Kinsley.

Rutter, M. (1985). Resilience in the face of adversity: Protective factors and resistance to psychiatric disorder. *British Journal of Psychiatry, 147,* 598–611.

Rutter, M. (1990). Psychosocial resilience and protective mechanisms. In J. Rolf, A. S. Masten, D. Cicchetti, K. H. Neuchterlein, & S. Weintraub (Eds.), *Risk and protective factors in the development of psychopathology* (pp. 181–214). Cambridge, MA: Cambridge University Press.

Rutter, M. (1999). Resilience concepts and findings: Implications for family therapy. *Journal of Family Therapy, 21,* 119–144.

Salahu-Din, S.H., & Bollman, S.R. (1994). Identity development and self-esteem of young adolescents. *Foster Care Child and Adolescent Social Work Journal, 11,* 123–135.

Stein, M. (1994). Leaving care, education and career trajectories. *Oxford Review of Education, 20,* 349–360.

Thorpe, R. (1980). The experience of parents and children living apart. In J.P. Triseliotis (Ed.), *New developments in foster care and adoption.* London: Routledge.

Walsh, F. (1998). *Strengthening family resilience.* New York: Guilford.

Ward, H. (1995). *Looking After Children: Research into practice.* London: HMSO.

Weinstein, E.A. (1960). *The self-image of the foster child.* New York: Russell Sage.

Welsh, E., Buchanan, A., Flouri, E., & Lewis, J. (2004). *Involved fathers and child well-being.* London: National Children's Bureau.

Werner, E. E., & Smith, R. S. (1992). *Overcoming the odds: High-risk children from birth to adulthood.* Ithaca: Cornell University Press.

Weyts, A. (2004). The educational achievements of looked after children: Do welfare systems make a difference to outcomes? *Adoption and Fostering, 28*(3), 7–19.

Wilson, L., & Conroy, J. (1999). Satisfaction of children in out-of-home care. *Child Welfare, 78,* 53–69.

Wyman, P.A., Cowen, E.L., Work, W. C., & Parker, G.R. (1991). Developmental and family milieu correlates of resilience in urban children who have experienced major life stress. *American Journal of Community Psychology, 19,* 405–426.

CHAPTER 9

Psychosocial well-being and placement stability in foster care: Implications for policy and practice

James G. Barber and Paul H. Delfabbro

Introduction

In Australia, child protection is the responsibility of State governments whose laws underwent extensive reform in the late 1980s following a shift in policy emphasis towards minimizing the role of the state. Criteria for government intervention were tightened across the country, so that children and adolescents who might previously have been supervised or confined by welfare authorities no longer received state protection. As a result, the number of children receiving out-of-home care in Australia declined by 28% between 1983 and 1993 (Australian Institute of Health & Welfare [AIHW], 2000). This decline in state care proceeded in spite of massive increases nationwide in the rate of child abuse (AIHW, 2000). It is important to note that the decline in the out-of-home care population that occurred during this time was almost entirely accounted for by residential (institutional) care, which had traditionally been the option of choice for disruptive or disabled children in Australia. In 1983, for example, there were 7,410 children in residential care nationwide, but that number had fallen to 2,455 by 1993. In contrast, the numbers in foster care remained relatively constant over the same period (AIHW, 2000).

In response to mounting public concern about children at risk following an alarming Royal Commission into youth homelessness (Burdekin, 1989), and following a series of highly-publicized child protection failures in the States of Victoria and New South Wales (see, for example, Review of Substitute-Care Services Committee, 1992), the numbers of children taken into foster care (but not residential care) began to rise after 1993 as Australian States were pressured to do more to protect their children. By 2000, the numbers in alternative care had returned to 1993 levels, but this was due entirely to increases in the number of children entering foster care (15,169 by the year 2000). Meanwhile, the numbers in residential care continued to fall throughout the period, reaching a mere 1,222 by the year 2000. In short, Australia's reliance on foster care had reached unprecedented levels by the early 1990s and foster care numbers have continued to rise since then. As the cheapest out-of-home care option available, foster care was (and still is) attractive to governments with an eye to controlling their outlays on child welfare.

Due to the closure of residential options, the influx of children into care has been accompanied by a change in the profile of Australian foster children. In South Australia, where our study was conducted, the proportion of children in receipt of a "special needs loading" doubled between 1994 and 1999. As its name implies, special needs loading is payable to children who require a level of care that goes beyond that which would normally be expected of foster parents. The most common reasons for applying the loading are conduct disorder and mental or physical disability—the very problems that would once have been hidden away in residential care.

Not only is the Australian foster care system taking on more difficult children, but the country's mounting reliance on foster care is at loggerheads with contemporary social and demographic realities. Perhaps the most important of these are the rises in women's workforce participation rates and in single-headed households (see Barber, 2003, ch. 1), both of which have shrunk the pool of volunteer foster parents. A less direct but almost as important influence has been an explosion in Australia's elderly population, because it has meant that women in particular are now increasingly torn between the care demands of their children and their ageing parents (Barber, 2003, ch. 11). Finally, changes in Australian workplace relations legislation has increased the demands at work, particularly in the service sector where women tend to be concentrated (see Barber, 2004). In view of these social forces, it is difficult to see how Australia's appetite for traditional family-based foster care can survive much longer—there are just too few carers to meet the needs of a population of children that is growing in number and complexity. Around a decade ago in 1994, the number of children in South Australian foster care was roughly equal to the number of carers; not five years later, there were around 25% more children than carers in the system. And the gap has widened further since then.

Against this social and political backdrop, the South Australian Foster Care Study set out to describe the well-being and psychosocial progress of children entering a very stretched foster care system. Although studies of this kind had been conducted before, a limitation of most of them has been their reliance on cross-sectional designs (see Altshuler & Gleeson, 1999, for a review). Most often, the functioning of children in care has been compared with that of children in the general population or comparable groups in the child welfare system at a single point in time (Kinard, 1994). Such designs provide no adequate baseline against which to compare change and often lead to sampling bias by over-representing children with longer and more unstable placement histories (Courtney, 1994; Goerge, 1990). This is problematic because children with long placement histories often have other characteristics that distinguish them from the rest of the children in care. For example, long-stay children tend to be older and to display poorer levels of psychosocial adjustment than short-stay children do. Thus, cross-sectional analyses involving snapshot profiles of children in care tend to produce an overly pessimistic view of long-term experiences and outcomes. This issue underscores the need for longitudinal designs that allow for comparison of outcomes over time. Most of the longitudinal studies that have been conducted to date, however, have been retrospective. Data have usually been obtained from large archival datasets, such as those routinely maintained by agencies, and used to generate social indicators of various kinds (Courtney, 1994, 1995; Courtney & Wong, 1996; Fernandez, 1999; Goerge, 1990). Although these studies have been highly effective in predicting changes in case status over time, they have been limited by the range of variables included, the sophistication of the measures available, and the absence of follow-up measures more proximal to the outcomes predicted.

Prospective longitudinal designs are therefore preferable, not only because they enable comparisons with a consistent baseline, but also because they are able to collect a greater volume of information, and choose the information collected. Although concerns can be raised about potential biases resulting from the selective loss of subjects over time, a prospective study has the capacity to identify, and potentially control for, any systematic differences between the retained sample and those who drop out. Testament to the effectiveness of the prospective longitudinal design is the landmark study undertaken by Fanshel and Shinn (1978), who tracked the progress of over 600 New York children placed into care during the late 1960s. In that study, outcome measures were administered annually for a total of five years, enabling the researchers to assess change in psychosocial adjustment and placement outcomes across time. Such was the richness of that study that much of what is now accepted practice in foster care emanates from that work.

The South Australian Foster Care Study

Overview

The overall project involved six mixed methods sub-studies that can be grouped into the following three categories: (1) worker and carer focus group studies involving approximately 24 carers and 50 workers; (2) a two-year tracking study of 235 children referred into foster care over a period of 12 months; and (3) three mixed-methods consumer feedback studies involving a total of 112 foster children.[1]

Worker and carer focus groups

The focus group component consisted of a series of group discussions conducted with government workers and foster care agencies in regional and metropolitan South Australia, as well as two carer focus groups. Sampling for carer and worker focus groups was purposive in both cases and designed to represent differences in region, child, carer and worker type. In total, 12 worker and 2 carer groups were held across a 12-month period and all of them followed a semi-structured format intended to elicit feedback on the administration and functioning of the foster care system.

The tracking study

The second and most extensive part of the project involved collecting detailed information about the placement movements and psychosocial outcomes of children in foster care. The fundamental object of the exercise was to identify who does well and who does poorly in family-based foster care in an era when more and more children are relying on out-of-home care. This kind of information is vital if the child welfare field is to develop care strategies that are matched to the developmental needs of its clients. The resultant tracking study involved 121 boys and 114 girls with a mean age of 10.8 years and an age range of 4 to 17 years. Children were selected if they were referred for a new placement between May 1998 and April 1999. Excluded from the sample were children on detention orders, children in supported accommodation, children referred for family preservation services, children with placements of less than two weeks' duration, and children under four years of age. The final sample represented the entire cohort of children meeting the selection criteria referred via the central referral agency from both metropolitan and regional areas of South Australia. The sample consisted of 40 (17.0%) Aboriginal children and 195 (83.0%) non-Aboriginal children. Sixty-three

(27%) were from the country areas of South Australia and 171 (73%) were from the metropolitan area of Adelaide. A breakdown of the sample by age showed that 65 (27.5%) were aged from 4 to 8 years, 79 (33.7%) were 9 to 12 years, and 90 (37.6%) were 13 to 17 years. Of the children, 37% ($n = 86$) were referred on short-term legal orders (< 12 months), and the rest 149 (63%) were on longer-term orders of at least 12 months' duration.

At intake, information was collected from foster care agency records and government databases and was verified with the child's social worker in a face-to-face interview. After the intake interview, follow-up interviews were conducted with the child's social worker at 4 months, 8 months, 12 months, and at 2 years post referral. Children remained in the study irrespective of their placement status, as long as there was an allocated worker from whom information could be obtained. Tracking only ceased when children had returned home or been discharged. Most of the information captured in intake assessments was collected either from case files or in the course of the one- to two-hour interviews routinely conducted with the foster child's social worker. Most of the variables were measured using standardized instruments and covered the following factors:

- demographic characteristics;
- client status variables (including legal status and placement type);
- placement history;
- presenting problem;
- family contact plan;
- degree of social dislocation (e.g., distance from old school and family);
- cognitive functioning (where a formal psychological assessment had been conducted);
- academic and social functioning at school;
- offending behaviour;
- global rating of physical health;
- substance use;
- sexualized behaviours;
- "Child Behaviour Checklist" subscales: conduct, hyperactivity and emotionality;
- social adjustment.

Consumer feedback studies

The final component of the project consisted of three small consumer feedback studies. In the first of these, 51 children in short- to medium-term care (23 girls, 28 boys) were interviewed using a semi-structured format to assess their satisfaction with their placements. These children were selected, based on availability, from our larger study sample. The children were interviewed approximately six months after they had entered the study and were asked a number of questions relating to their satisfaction with their social worker, such as: whether they knew the name of their worker; how often they saw that worker; whether their worker listened to them and cared for them; and how helpful their social worker had been. Children were also asked to rate their current placement on various dimensions, including, for example, the quality of caregiving received. In the second feedback study, a total of 48 children (23 girls, 25 boys) in long-term care were interviewed. These children were also selected from the larger tracking study based on availability and capacity to answer questions about their well-being. In this study, children were administered a standardized measure of child satisfaction derived from Stuntzner-Gibson, Koren, & DeChillo (1995). This latter measure consists of 11 items relating to the child's satisfaction with placement, including whether the child liked living with the foster family, was able to get help, have fun, and felt supported. Finally, separate in-depth interviews were conducted with 13 children and their foster carers who had experienced repeated placement disruption ostensibly because of the child's disruptive behaviour. The children were aged between 10 and 17 years and interviews with them covered: (1) the circumstances leading up to placement breakdown; (2) the point at which placement problems first became apparent to the child; (3) the child's emotional response to the breakdown; (4) whether and with whom the child had discussed placement problems, (5) positive and negative aspects of the placement, and (6) whether, in the child's view, any intervention might have enabled the placement to continue. Similar questions were put to the 19 carers who had terminated placements because of the child's behaviour and the responses were compared.

The following pages present data in relation to placement stability and psychosocial progress. Most of the data derive from the tracking study component of the project, although reference will also be made to findings from the consumer feedback.

Selected results

Placement moves

Analysis of placement moves revealed a very considerable level of placement instability during the first four months of care, with almost 40% of the sample moving at least once during that period. As expected, the degree of placement instability declined after that point as children either went home or settled into foster care. For the purposes of this study, a "stable" placement was defined as one where the child remained at a single address for the relevant period, and an "unstable" placement was one where at least one change of address occurred during the period. A striking feature of the placement data was the number of children who remained unstable in the foster care system a full two years after referral. Specifically, 50 children (around 20% of the remaining sample) still had not settled into a stable placement fully two years after referral into foster care. Table 1 presents the total number of placement moves as well as the reasons that were recorded in case files for these moves. It shows that in the early months, nearly half of all moves were planned. In other words, these moves were anticipated from the outset, for reasons such as: the initial placement was essentially emergency shelter while the social worker negotiated a more permanent arrangement; or because a parent required hospitalization for a short time. As time went by, however, the incidence of planned moves such as these declined, while the incidence of placement breakdown due to the child's putatively disruptive behaviour increased.

Table 1. Placement moves during each follow-up period

| | Follow-up period | | | |
	0–4 mths	4–8 mths	8–12 mths	1–2 years
Total number of placement moves	445	166	164	235
Reason for move	n (%)			
Planned move	216 (48.5)	54 (32.5)	44 (26.8)	53 (22.6)
Child's behaviour	79 (17.8)	31 (18.7)	53 (32.3)	60 (25.5)
Child wanted to leave	9 (4.2)	7 (4.2)	0 (0.0)	3 (1.3)
More suitable option found	16 (3.6)	31 (18.7)	27 (16.5)	68 (28.9)
Reunification with family	62 (13.9)	25 (15.1)	10 (6.1)	9 (3.8)
Child ran away	13 (2.9)	6 (3.6)	8 (4.8)	7 (3.0)
Foster carer couldn't cope	32 (7.2)	7 (4.2)	6 (3.7)	0 (0.0)
Child was arrested	2 (0.9)	0 (0.0)	10 (6.1)	29 (12.3)
Moved to independent living & other	16 (7.5)	5 (3.0)	6 (3.6)	6 (2.4)

Psychosocial progress

Table 2 summarizes some of the key findings of the psychosocial assessments that occurred at each follow-up point.

Table 2. Psychosocial outcomes of the sample as a whole

Follow-up period (in months)	Psychosocial well-being measures					Effect sizes
	Conduct	Hyperactivity	Emotionality	Social adjustment	School performance	
0–4 mths. (n = 164)	Improved	Improved	Improved	No change	Improved	Small
0–4–8 (n = 139)	Improved– Stable	Improved– Stable	Improved– Stable	No change– No change	Unavailable	Small– moderate
0–12 (n = 126)	Improved	No change	Improved	No change	Unavailable	Small– moderate
0–12–24 (n = 109)	Improved– Stable	No change	Improved– Stable	No change	Unavailable	Small– moderate

The statistical details behind this Table are available elsewhere (see Barber & Delfabbro, 2004) but it is important to point out that this is a summary table and, as indicated below, it masks some important individual differences. Nevertheless, the Table does show that the experience of foster care was accompanied by developmental gains across the sample as a whole. In the absence of a no-treatment control group, it is not possible to establish whether this improvement was attributable to foster care or some extraneous factor, such as maturation; nor is it possible to establish whether the improvement is greater or less than would be expected under alternate conditions. But the fact that there is improvement at all—rather than stagnation or decline—is encouraging nonetheless. Moreover, the generally sanguine picture suggested by Table 1 is consistent with our consumer feedback studies, which found that the overwhelming majority of respondents liked living with their foster families and felt well cared for and supported. Among the consumer feedback data, for example, was the surprising finding that foster children rated the quality of the caregiving received higher than did a normative sample of children from the general population living with their birth parents (Delfabbro, Barber, & Bentham, 2002). Furthermore, the overwhelming majority of foster children told a peer interviewer that they liked living with their foster family (90%), that they received the sort of care they had hoped for (98%), and that they felt wanted and supported by their foster family (94%) (Delfabbro et al., 2002).

Placement stability and psychological adjustment

Among the central issues under investigation in the tracking study was the association between placement instability and psychosocial well-being over time. Statistical analysis of this issue began with the construction of groups that varied in the level of placement stability experienced by foster children over different lengths of time in care. The first set of analyses was performed after eight months in care and the basic phenomenon identified is illustrated in Figure 1.

Figure 1. Placement stability and conduct disorder over the first 8 months in care

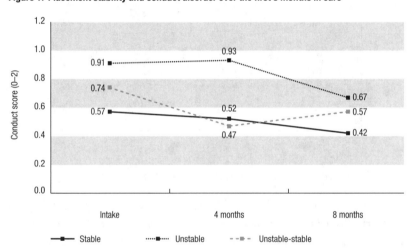

Figure 1 presents conduct disorder scores over the first eight months for three groups of children who differed according to level of placement stability. The first ("stable") group ($n = 49$) comprised children who were placed in foster care and remained in a single placement throughout the period. The second ("unstable") group ($n = 31$) consisted of children who had to change placement at least once during both follow-up periods (0–4 months and 4–8 months). The third ("unstable-stable") group ($n = 40$) was made up of foster children who had to change placement at least once during the initial four-month period but who settled into a stable placement thereafter. (One hundred and five children had either gone home by the eight-month point or were in some other kind of residential setting. A further 10 "stable-unstable" children were dropped from the analysis because of small sample size.) As would be expected, children in the "stable" group displayed lower levels of conduct disorder at intake. They also displayed steady improvement across the study period. Surprisingly, children in the "unstable" group displayed almost the identical developmental trajectory, while children in the "unstable-stable" condition displayed a quadratic pattern, with scores tending to improve in the first follow-up period and to deteriorate in the second.

Figure 2 illustrates our findings after two years.

Figure 2. Placement stability and hyperactivity after two years in foster care

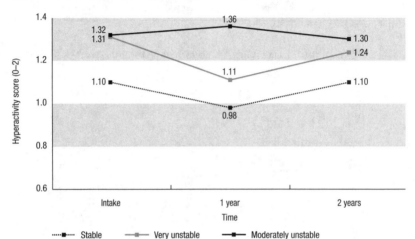

This Figure presents results of hyperactivity scores for three groups of foster children: (1) those who changed placement in at least two of the follow-up periods and/or were still unstable at two years (very unstable) ($n = 54$); (2) those who stayed in one placement throughout the period (stable) ($n = 35$); and (3) those who changed placements in one period only and were stable by the two-year point (moderately unstable) ($n = 26$).

Figure 2 therefore represents a crucial qualification to the picture that emerged in Figure 1. In a nutshell, when Figures 1 and 2 are considered together, it appears that whereas placement instability over the short-medium term is not generally associated with psychosocial decline (Figure 1), protracted instability clearly is (Figure 2). The key to understanding this phenomenon is contained in Table 1, which presented the reasons for placement change over time. As previously noted, most of the placement instability up to the eight-month point was actually planned, meaning that the majority of placement change occurred for positive reasons, such as moving closer to home or to a more stable living arrangement. Among those children remaining in care beyond the eight-month point, however, between one third and one quarter of all placement moves were the result of placement breakdown due to the child's behaviour. In other words, among those children who were initially unstable were individuals who were moving around for positive reasons; on the other hand, by the eight-month point most of these children had settled down, leaving a greater concentration of highly disruptive children among those who continued moving. It is to the psychosocial progress of these disruptive children that we now turn.

Serially evicted foster children

A profile of the placement histories of the 50 most disruptive children in the sample is presented in Table 3.

Table 3. Placement histories of the most disruptive children in foster care

Child #	0–4 months	4–8 months	8–12 months	1–2 years
1	F	FHFFR	RF	FFRFFFFRFFCC
2	FFFFH	H	H	H
3	FOM	OFMFMS	FCS	SCSCSC
4	FFFFH	H	H	H
5	F	FOF	FFFFH	FFFFFFF
6	FFFSYCYCSCO	OH	H	H
7	FIO	F	F	FI
8	FH	FFFFCC	C	C
9	FR	RFHR	RHFC	CF
10	F	F	FFF	FFFFCFFFC
11	F	F	FFFFF	FFFHFF
12	F	FFF	FFF	FFFO
13	FFFFC	CC	C	CC
14	F	F	FCFFHFFH	FYSISYSYSYSY
15	FFF	F	F	FCF
16	FHFFFFHFFF	FF	F	FFFFRFRFFC
17	FFFFFFFFF	FF	FFF	FFC
18	FFFSFCS	FFFFFFF	FFF	FCSCSCSCSCCSCSC
19	FFFFFF	FFFFFF	FF	FF
20	FF	FCCFF	FFFFFCSCSC	CM
21	FFFH	FHF	FHFFFFH	H
22	F	FF	F	FFFFFFF
23	FF	F	FFFFF	FFHFFFFFHFFF
24	FOM	MFF	MFY	YFF
25	FCFH	FH	YYYYOY	YH
26	FF	FFF	F	FH
27	FFFFFFFCF	FF	FF	FRYC
28	FFHCFHC	CFH	FF	FH

Table 3. Placement histories of the most disruptive children in foster care – *continued*

Child #	0–4 months	4–8 months	8–12 months	1–2 years
29	FFFF	F	F	F
30	FO	F	FF	FHFHRO
31	FFF	FCFF	F	FF
32	FH	H	FFH	FFHOHM
33	F	F	F	FFFFFCSCSCSYSYSYSYS
34	F	FFFFFFFFM	MRM	FFOSM
35	F	FFFFF	FMFMFOFFFF	MCY
36	FFFRFFFRCMCR	R	RMFFFFMSFM	MYHYS
37	FFFFF	FFFFFFFHFY	YC	CYCM
38	FFFHF	F	F	F
39	FYFFFFC	C	CF	FC
40	FFFFFFRFFFFF	F	FFFF	FF
41	FFMC	CC	C	C
42	F	F	FFF	FFF
43	F	FF	FF	FFF
44	F	F	FFF	FFFFFCF
45	FFFHF	FC	C	CFC
46	FF	FRF	FFOFFFFFF	FFFC
47	FFRFF	FYFFF	FFF	FFF
48	FOOF	FO	OI	I
49	FFFFFFFFFFFFFC	CY	Y	YSYSMSYSSSYSYM
50	FFFFFFFFRFFFFF FFFFF	F	FFFFFFFFFF	FFFFFFFFFF

C = Community residential; F = Foster care; H = Home; I = Independent living; M = Missing; O = Other; R = Relative care; S = Secure care; Y = Youth shelter

This Table is graphic evidence of the truly wretched conditions under which these foster children live. For example, one of the most disruptive children in the sample lived in 21 separate placements in his first four months in foster care. Not surprisingly, the psychosocial profile displayed by these children is very different from that of the overall sample presented in Table 2. Table 4 summarizes results of the statistical analysis of psychosocial data for the 50 most disruptive children and shows that improvement occurred in only one life domain (conduct disorder) together with deterioration in social adjustment. (This latter measure contained subscales on relationships with peers, carers and teachers). All the other domains remained unchanged and significantly inferior to the rest of the sample.

Table 4. Psychosocial outcomes of evicted children

Follow-up period (in months)	Psychosocial well-being measures					Effect sizes
	Conduct	Hyperactivity	Emotionality	Social adjustment	School performance	
0–4 mths.	No change	No change	No change	No change	Unavailable	
0–4–8	No change–Improved	No change	No change	No change	Unavailable	Moderate
0–12	Improved	No change	No change	Deterioration	Unavailable	Moderate (conduct) v. strong (social)
0–12–24	Improved–Stable	No change	No change	Deterioration–Further deterioration	Unavailable	Very strong

When we examined the predictors of "serial eviction" (Barber, Delfabbro, & Cooper, 2001), we found that evicted children tended to be older than the rest of the sample, marginally more likely to be male, and much more likely to record a high score at intake on our standardized measure of conduct disorder. No doubt because of their age, they were also less likely to be in care because of parental neglect. Perhaps most important, we found that *every* child who experienced at least two placement breakdowns due to his or her behaviour in the first four months of foster care went on to become a member of the serially evicted group (Barber & Delfabbro, 2004, ch. 11).

Summary and discussion

The purpose of this book, like that of the conference on which it was based, is to identify strategies for promoting resilience among children in care. In this respect, the data from the South Australian Foster Care Study contain some encouraging lessons and some ominous warnings. In the first place, the data suggest that the experience of family-based foster care promotes the psychosocial well-being of the majority of children who enter it. Not only did the majority of foster children display solid psychosocial progress across the two-year period, but the children themselves expressed very high levels of satisfaction with their quality of life in care. These findings question the very common assumption in child welfare policy that long-term foster care is antithetical to positive psychological adaptation. It follows that children in care can both develop in a positive direction and feel at home without necessarily terminating parental rights through adoption. This is hardly surprising since the attitudes and behaviour of the carer would be much more likely to influence the child's subjective quality of life than would the child's legal status.

Our findings in relation to placement stability were not entirely straightforward but they contain firm implications for practice nevertheless. To summarize, we found a very considerable level of placement disruption among foster children soon after their referral into care; however, much of this disruption was part of a broader case plan and (seemingly for that reason) was not generally associated with adverse psychosocial outcomes. All the same, as time went by, the incidence of what we might call "planned instability" declined, thereby resulting in a higher concentration of children who moved around because they were repeatedly evicted. Thus, placement instability need not necessarily be harmful to foster children but depends on the interrelated issues of how long the instability continues and why it occurs. As we have seen, there can be positive reasons to move placement and these reasons are likely to occur early in the placement. Thus, while social workers should be encouraged to achieve placement stability as soon as humanly possible, they should not be prevented from moving a foster child early in the placement, provided that the worker has a clear and positive rationale for doing so. Nevertheless, in a policy environment increasingly dominated by the concept of "permanency planning," there are legal and administrative disincentives to moving foster children except into adoption or back to their families of origin. Permanency planning has been defined as "a philosophy highlighting the value of rearing children in a family setting, preferably their biological families, [and] a theoretical framework *stressing that stability and continuity of relationships promote children's growth and functioning*" (Fein, Maluccio, Hamilton, & Ward, 1983, p. 197) (emphasis ours). While it is impossible to argue with the proposition that stable relationships are developmentally preferable to unstable ones, the current emphasis on permanency has been translated by some U.S. jurisdictions in particular into financial penalties against agencies that exceed often quite arbitrary rates of placement change (see Barber & Delfabbro, 2004).

If short-term instability is not necessarily harmful, protracted instability clearly is, and for more than one in five of our sample placement disruption continued for at least two years. It is no exaggeration to describe these children as effectively homeless in foster care. For those children (mainly boys) who enter placement with high levels of conduct disorder, eviction due to behaviour is likely to occur soon after arrival and to continue for as long as the child remains in care. In fact, the experience of "serial eviction" was found to be *inevitable* for children who experienced two such breakdowns within their first four months in care. We are therefore led to conclude that family-based foster care is unsuitable for disruptive children as operationally defined in this study and that the child welfare field urgently needs to find an alternative. The torrent of children currently entering the foster care system around the western world needs to be screened at intake and disruptive children redirected into something other than conventional, family-based foster care. And those foster children whom we have described as "homeless in care" need to be rescued from their plight as a matter of urgency and be provided with a civilized way of life. None of this implies that the oppressive, life-denying institutions of the past should be reopened, of course. Many alternatives to conventional family-based foster care now exist in the field, but few have been subjected to the kind of controlled experimentation necessary to identify their effectiveness or their application to the growing population of disruptive children entering care (see Barber & Delfabbro, 2004 for a review of this literature).

References

Altshuler, S. J. and Hawley, D. (1999). Completing the evaluation triangle for the next century: Measuring child "well-being" in family foster care. *Child Welfare, 78,* 125–147.

Australian Institute of Health and Welfare (2000). *Child protection in Australia 1998–99.* Canberra: Child Welfare Series no. 25; cat. No. CSW 11.

Barber, J. G. (2003). *Social work through the lifecycle.* Melbourne: Tertiary Press.

Barber, J. G. (2004). Australian industrial relations policy and workers with family responsibilities. *Community, Work & Family.*

Barber, J. G., Delfabbro, P. H., & Cooper, L. L. (2001). The predictors of unsuccessful transition to foster care. *The Journal of Child Psychology and Psychiatry, 42,* 785–790.

Barber, J. G., & Delfabbro, P. H. (2002). The plight of disruptive children in foster care. *Children's Services: Social Policy, Research and Practice, 5,* 201–212.

Barber, J. G., & Delfabbro, P. H. (2004). *Children in foster care.* London: Routledge.

Burdekin, B. (1989). *Our homeless children. Report of the national inquiry into homeless children.* Canberra: Australian Government Publishing Service.

Courtney, M. E. (1994). Factors associated with the reunification of foster children with their families. *Social Service Review, 68,* 81–108.

Courtney, M. E. (1995). Reentry to foster care of children returned to their families. *Social Service Review, 69,* 226–241.

Courtney, M. E. & Wong, Y. I. (1996). Comparing the timing of exits from substitute care. *Children and Youth Services Review, 18,* 307–334.

Delfabbro, P. H., Barber, J. G., & Bentham, Y. (2002). Children's satisfaction with out-of-home care in South Australia. *Journal of Adolescence, 25,* 523–533.

Fanshel, D., & Shinn, E. (1978). *Children in foster care: A longitudingal investigation.* New York: Columbia University Press.

Fein, E., Maluccio, A. N., Hamilton, V. J., & Ward, D. E. (1983). After foster care: Outcomes of permanency planning for children. *Child Welfare, 62,* 485–562.

Fernandez, E. (1999). Pathways in substitute care: Representation of placement careers of children using event history analysis. *Children and Youth Services Review, 21,* 177–216.

Goerge, R. M. (1990). The reunification program in substitute care. *Social Service Review, 64,* 422–457.

Kinard, E. M. (1994). Methodological issues and practical problems in conducting research on maltreated children. *Child Abuse and Neglect, 18,* 645–656.

Review of Substitute-Care Services Committee. (1992). *Report of the committee appointed by NSW Minister for Youth and Community Services.* Sydney, Australia: Ministerial Review Committee, NSW.

Stuntzner-Gibson, D., Koren, P. E., & DeChillo, N. (1995). The youth satisfaction questionnaire: What kids think of services. *Families in Society, 76,* 614–624.

---

1 More complete methodological details can be found in Barber, J.G., & Delfabbro, P.H. (2004) ch. 4.

CHAPTER 10

Positive life experiences that promote resilience in young people in care

Louise Legault and Shaye Moffat

Introduction

Much of the literature in psychology and social work focuses on negative life experiences in an attempt to clarify why some individuals have problems related to their upbringing. However, as Seligman and Csikszentmihalyi (2000) point out, "...psychology is not just the study of pathology, weakness, and damage; it is also the study of strength and virtue. Treatment is not just fixing what is broken; it is nurturing what is best" (p. 7). This is one of the main goals of the Looking After Children (LAC) approach. Introduced in Canada in the mid-1990s, the LAC approach endeavours to break away from the traditional negative assessment of children in care, instead recognizing that many fostered children and youths experience positive normal development and resilient characteristics in some areas of their lives. The LAC approach is resource-focused, highlighting positive achievements instead of focusing solely on negative outcomes of children in foster care (Ward, 1995). Newman (2004) notes that "[a] key protective factor for children who have experienced severe adversities is the ability to recognize any benefits that may have accrued, rather than focusing solely on negative effects, and using these insights as a platform for affirmation and growth" (p. 17). It is through the important LAC tool, the Assessment and Action Record (AAR), that it is now possible to obtain and explore the positive experiences that occur in fostered young people's lives.

Children and young people in foster care are a particularly at risk population for maladaptation (Bolger & Patterson, 2003). This population has faced numerous adversities including, but not limited to, developmental threats and/or maltreatment, being removed from their biological families, and being placed in an alternative care situation. Yet some demonstrate resilience by meeting age-salient development tasks in spite of serious threats to development (Flynn, Ghazal, Legault, Vandermeulen, & Petrick, 2004).

A Definition of Resilience

Masten and Coatsworth (1998) and Masten, chapter 1, this volume, define resilience as being comprised of two dimensions: one, that the person has been exposed to at least one adverse event, and two, that the individual's outcome was positive despite the adversity. Masten and Powell (2003) further note that resilience is a fluid concept that not all individuals are able to demonstrate at every moment of their life. The phenomenon of resilience is not a personal characteristic. Children are not born with resilient tendencies, they do not acquire resilience traits as they grow older, and they are not markedly different from others in the same position. Instead, the positive outcomes associated with resilience are generally attributed to protective factors at work in the environment as well as resources within the individual.

Research findings have shown that children who demonstrate resilience use various personal characteristics (e.g., cognitive capabilities and personality traits), as well as available resources (e.g., adult mentors and prosocial organizations), to foster their positive development (Masten & Reed, 2002). These children use what they are provided with to make some sense of their lives. Theoretically, these factors work to modify the effects of risk factors by favouring a child's development in a more positive direction toward successful adaptation. Moreover, resilience is the result of the operation of basic human adaptational systems (e.g., attachment relationships and parenting system; pleasure-in-mastery and motivational system; self-regulation of emotion, arousal, and behaviour; families; formal educational and community systems; cultural belief systems; and religious organizations [Masten & Reed, 2002, p. 82]). Subsumed within these systems are numerous protective factors identified in past research such as nurturing parents (Luthar & Zelazo, 2003; Masten, 2001), self-esteem (Cicchetti & Rogosch, 1997; Cicchetti et al., 1993), and access to good schools (Masten & Reed, 2002).

Basic human adaptational systems play a central role in the development and presence of assets characterizing children and young people who demonstrate resilience. These systems are also well established resources associated with well-being and development in general (i.e., under low-adversity conditions). For example, the attachment and parenting system comprises the asset of authoritative parenting style "...characterized by age-appropriate monitoring, closeness, and high expectations as opposed to neglect, rejection, and harshness" (Masten & Powell, 2003, pp. 14). Experiences of warmth and support favour perceptions of safety, encourage learning and exploration, and facilitate the development of adaptive coping strategies, self-control of emotions, and pro-social behaviours.

Findings from the above studies are difficult to directly apply to a fostered population because of distinctly different life experiences. The attachment and parenting system is the main system jeopardized for young people before, and sometimes after, they come into care. Given the particularly traumatic life experiences of fostered children and the evidence of resilience in this population (Flynn & Biro, 1998; Flynn et al., 2004), the exploration of naturally occurring factors that promote resilience seemed a worthwhile avenue to pursue.

Aims of This Research

The current study aimed to investigate assets and processes associated with resilience that are central in the lives of fostered young people. We argue that positive life events can be defined as naturally occurring environmental affordances that feed into basic human adaptational systems associated with positive development or resilience. Doyle, Wolchik and Dawson-McClure (2002) found positive life events were associated with the adjustment of adolescents living in reconstituted families. This association was found even after controlling for the effects of covariates and negative life events. In their study, adolescents and their mothers reported lower levels of internalizing behavioural problems co-occurring with positive life events. Further in-depth analyses revealed that specific categories of positive life events were differentially associated with psychological adjustment. For example, adolescents who experienced more positive events related to their relationship with their father or their mother were significantly less likely to be maladjusted (i.e., self-reported low levels of internalizing and externalizing behavioural problems; mother's report of few externalizing behavioural problems). Other researchers have also found healthier adjustment associated with positive life events experienced by children/adolescents living in various family configurations including intact, single-parent, and reconstituted families (Cohen, Burt, & Bjorck, 1987; Jackson & Warren, 2000; Kanner, Feldman, Weinberger, & Ford, 1987). Based on these promising findings, we sought to investigate the type of positive life events experienced by fostered children and young people.

As a first step in our research program, we searched for a validated measure of positive life events (uplifts) to include in the Assessment and Action Records. A literature review yielded few validated scales measuring positive life events. The existing scales were deemed inappropriate for our in-care population particularly because they included numerous items related to biological parents (e.g., Doyle et al., 2002). Heeding past researchers recommendations about developing typologies based on events identified as meaningful by the specific target group (Doyle et al., 2002; Seidman, Allen, Aber, & Mitchell, 1995), the decision was made to adopt a bottom-up research design.

Fostered young people were asked to identify positive life events they had experienced. Emerging themes from the data collected on positive experiences were the basis of our resilience research. Through the collective positive life experiences of children and young people currently in care, we hoped to deepen our understanding of resilience. How is it that some are able to face adversity and flourish, while others have less than ideal outcomes? What positive events are unique to an in-care population? Are there protective processes that can be provided for fostered children? And, is it possible to teach those who do not possess protective assets how to deal with the adversity that they face in their lives? The identification of experiences meaningful to an in-care population would allow researchers and practitioners to target areas in children's lives most likely to favour positive adjustment.

Method

Participants

Participants were part of the Looking After Children in Ontario (OnLAC; Flynn, Angus, Aubry, & Drolet, 1999) and in Canada (CanLAC; CWLC) projects during the year 2002-2003. The projects are longitudinal studies investigating developmental outcomes in fostered children and young people. In all, 924 Canadian children and young people were surveyed who had been placed in out-of-home care as a result of serious adversity in their families of origin.

The older group of respondents numbered 647 (334 males, 313 females). Their ages varied between 9 and 21 years ($M = 14$; $SD = 2.5$; 2 young people were 9 years old). The young people resided mainly in Ontario (95%), with a few living in PEI (2%), Alberta (2%), and Quebec (1%). The smaller sample of young people originating from provinces other than Ontario was due to the recent timing of the implementation or piloting of LAC in these provinces. The young people's admission to the current episode of out-of-home care was for reasons related to caregiver capacity (31%), physical/sexual abuse (23%), neglect (16%), abandonment

(13%), or emotional harm (5%). The current status of the great majority of these young people was court-ordered permanent care (85%), with a smaller number in court-ordered temporary care (4%) or voluntary temporary or permanent care (4%). The youths' current placements consisted mainly of foster homes (75%), with a smaller proportion living in group homes (10%) or independent living (10%). The young people had been living in their current foster placements from a few months to 17 years, with a mean of 3.7 years ($SD = 3.3$).

The younger group of children numbered 277 (154 males; 123 females). There were 203 children aged 5 to 9 ($M = 7.5$; $SD = 1.4$; 111 male, 92 female). Another 40 children were aged 3 to 4 ($M = 3.6$; $SD = .55$), with 21 males and 19 females. The remainder of the children were aged 1 to 2 ($n = 25$; 16 male, 9 female) or less than 12 months ($n = 9$; 6 male, 3 female). The children resided mainly in Ontario (85%), with a few living in PEI (8%), Alberta (5%), and Quebec (2%). Their admission to the current episode of out-of-home care was for reasons related to neglect (31%), caregiver capacity (29%), physical/sexual abuse (22%), abandonment (6%), or emotional harm (7%). The children's current status was mainly court-ordered permanent care (72%), with a smaller number in court-ordered temporary care (22%) or voluntary temporary or permanent care (3%). They resided mainly in foster homes (93%). A smaller proportion of children lived in homes under adoption probation (3%), group homes (1%), or other types of in-care placements (9%). The children had been living in their current foster placements from a few months to 9 years. On average, the mean length of time the children had lived in their current placements was 2.6 years ($SD = 1.8$) for children aged 5 to 9, and 1 year ($SD = 1.1$) for children aged less than 4 years.

It is important to note that the in-care sample (e.g., children and young people) was not random and therefore not truly representative of this population. All the participants had experienced at least two major negative life events, namely, separation from the biological family in addition to the condition(s) that had resulted in their removal from their family homes.

Procedure

A total of 27 agencies/jurisdictions had agreed to use the Assessment and Action Record (AAR-C2; Flynn, Ghazal, & Legault, 2004) to monitor children and young people in their care. As much as possible, child welfare workers were advised to select participants more likely to remain in care for the duration of the three-year longitudinal study. The final selection of fostered children and young people was left to each participating agency.

Administering the AAR-C2 took anywhere from one to four sessions, requiring on average a total of four hours to complete ($SD = 1.8$). Sessions took place in a variety of comfortable environments, including the foster or group home, restaurants, as well as other locales. Questions were to be answered within the context of a conversation between the caregiver(s), the child welfare worker and the young person (aged 10 and over) or, if appropriate, the younger child. Data were collected within a group format in deference to the LAC philosophy of promoting dialogue and partnership between the young person or child and those responsible for his/her well-being and care.

Informed consent was not required as analyses were done on secondary data. Anonymity was assured through the removal of all identifying information. This was done by the child welfare worker before sending a copy of the AAR-C2 to the researchers at the University of Ottawa. Once the copy was received, an individual identification number was given to the AAR-C2.

Instrument

The 2nd Canadian adaptation of the Assessment and Action Records (AAR-C2; Flynn et al., 2004) is used to annually monitor developmental outcomes among infants, children, and adolescents in out-of-home care. Multiple developmental outcomes assessed are subsumed under the dimensions of health, education, identity, family and social relationships, social presentation, emotional and behavioural development, and self-care. To allow for a more fine-grained assessment of children and avoid taxing respondents with irrelevant questions, six age-appropriate versions of the AAR-C2 were created: ages 0–12 months, 1–2 years, 3–4 years, 5–9 years, 10–14 years, and 15 or more years. Used yearly, the AAR-C2 enables child welfare workers and caregivers to pinpoint children and young people's individual needs, enhance the timeliness of the services they receive, and improve their developmental outcomes. The forms are designed to construct a thorough case record of the child/young person's development, as well as to provide the raw material to formulate a plan of care.

Measures

Positive life experiences were measured by means of two open-ended questions, namely: "What, to the best of the knowledge and in the joint opinion of [the child/youth], the foster parent, and the child welfare worker, is/are the most positive life event(s) that [the child/youth] has experienced in terms of promoting his/her positive development... (a) In the last 12 months? (b) Since birth, but more than 12 months ago?" (Flynn et al., 2002). For those aged under 10, the foster parent/group home worker and the child welfare worker answered the open-ended questions, although respondents were also instructed to include children in the conversation when appropriate. Young people aged 10 or older were encouraged to answer the open-ended questions in collaboration with their adult care-giver(s) and child welfare worker.

Demographic information was recorded for children and young people in the background information section of the AAR-C2. This information included gender, age, reason for coming into care, current legal status, type of placement, length of stay in current placement, and geographic location.

Data Analyses

All positive qualitative entries were listed in a database and separated by the time frame in which they were said to have occurred (in the past 12 months versus more than 12 months ago). Responses to these two questions were also analyzed separately for children aged 9 or less and young people aged 10 or more, in line with differences in the composition of respondents (adult respondents versus young people as well as adult respondents) All qualitative answers were analyzed and coded manually by two research assistants who were unaware of the resilience literature.

Categories were derived inductively from data in five steps. In step 1, a typology of positive life experiences was established. Two blinded coders independently analyzed line-by-line and categorized 25% of all responses into main themes. A subsequent comparison of themes generated by coders revealed identical emerging categories. The coders also arrived at identical themes of positive life events reported by respondents as occurring within 12 months and more than 12 months, although richer information was obtained from responses to events occurring within 12 months. To simplify qualitative data analyses, positive life events were collapsed across time.

In step 2, the coders categorized the remaining responses within the newly developed typology of positive life events. All responses were entered into as many themes as seemed fit.

In step 3, the coders sub-divided several categories to further delineate main themes and constructs that were evident within the broader category (e.g., the category of relationships was further divided into biological, foster, peer, etc.). This allowed for more refined categories to emerge while compressing the remaining categories. The analysis of the main themes was thereby clarified.

In step 4, the coders discussed all disagreements in categorizations until consensus was reached. Inter-rater agreement was 86%, indicating strong agreement among the two coders (Kvalseth, 1989; Landis & Koch, 1977, p. 165).

In step 5, once the data analyses were completed, the research team compared the generated typology of positive life events to Masten's resilience framework, which provided this study with a grounded theory approach.

Results

A total of 641 young people aged 10 and over provided responses in collaboration with their caregivers and child welfare workers. Of those who filled out an AAR-C2, 502 (78.3% of the total sample) identified a positive life event as having occurred during the past 12 months, and 402 (62.7%) said that a positive life event had occurred more than 12 months ago. In all, 1530 responses were analyzed and categorized. As for children aged 9 or less, 278 caregiver-child welfare worker teams listed positive life events. Of these, 232 responses (83.5%) named a positive life event occurring in the past 12 months, and 137 (49.3%) cited a positive life event occurring more than 12 months ago. A total of 599 responses were analyzed and categorized.

The responses provided by the children and young people were in a point-form format and generally comprised several themes. Typical responses were "Going to high school, making new friends, realizing foster parents cared," or "Long-term stable foster placement; being with biological brother," or "Moving into appropriate adult living space and get my own room with my own shelf." Fairly similar main themes emerged from the young children's adult respondents and the young people's answers, although differences in frequency were noted.

Qualitative data analyses yielded seven main themes for young people and six major themes for children (with a seventh minor theme). Approximately 24% of the young people nominated positive events focusing on activities/events, including playing a sport, participating in clubs, and going to camp or on trips. Similarly, 23% of the young people reported a relationship as being a key positive occurrence, nominating mainly biological family members (11.2%) and to a lesser extent foster family members

(5%). Closely related to the relationship category, living in a foster home was flagged as a positive event by a fair number of young people (18%). A smaller proportion specified living in the current placement as a positive life event (8%). Approximately 13% of young people identified education, particularly academic achievements (8%) such as graduating from school, receiving an award for good grades, or attending school (4%), as being a positive occurrence in their lives. An additional 8% of the nominated events reflected instances of personal growth, such as being in good health (3%), belonging to a religion or possessing a sense of spirituality (1%), or experiencing a life changing event such as, for example, going to prison (3%). One theme that was identified by young people (6%) as favouring their well-being comprised instances reflecting their coming of age (i.e., a transition to adulthood). Events grouped under this theme included being employed (3%) and acquiring personal possessions such as a bike or a stereo (2%). Finally, about 4% of the positive events cited involved activities with the biological family (2%) or the foster family (1%).

For children aged 9 or less, being in a foster home (37%) was the most frequent positive event cited by adult respondents (i.e., caregivers and child welfare workers). Events nominated as favouring children's positive development included achieving permanency (14%) or residing in the current placement (13%). The relationship category was also highlighted as an important positive event for a fair number of children (20%), in particular the relationship with the foster parent (9%) or with various biological family members (8%). Activities and events were nominated in 18% of responses, with participation in sport activities (6%) or some form of artistic activity (4%) being the most common examples (e.g., music, dance, arts). Approximately 12% of the adult responders identified education, particularly attending school (7%) or daycare (2%) or experiencing academic achievements (3%), as a being a positive occurrence in their fostered child's life. The personal development theme was found in approximately 8% of the responses, related mainly to health (1%) or personal growth, for example, gaining confidence and becoming more social (1%). Finally, the events cited involved activities with the foster family (4%).

Table 1 displays a complete breakdown of themes as a function of age group (9 years or less; 10 years and over). The reader is advised that a miscellaneous category was created for themes involving others due to the inability of coders to reliably determine the nature of the relationship between the child/young person and the person referred to in the text (e.g., the foster or biological brother).

Table 1. Frequency of emerging themes by age group

Major Themes	Total number of responses = 599 (100%)	Total number of responses = 1530 (100%)
Foster home	9 years and under	10 years and over
Permanency/stability	86 (14.2%)	47 (3.1%)
Admission to care	34 (5.7%)	54 (3.5%)
Placement	77 (12.9%)	126 (8.2%)
Change in placement/residence	30 (5.0%)	54 (3.5%)
Total	**227 (37.9%)**	**281 (18.4%)**
Relationships	9 years and under	10 years and over
Biological family		
Parent	17 (2.8%)	68 (4.4%)
Sibling	17 (2.8%)	46 (3.0%)
Extended family	13 (2.2%)	48 (3.1%)
Unspecified	—	11 (0.7%)
Foster family	55 (9.2%)	72 (4.7%)
Peers	7 (1.2%)	39 (2.6%)
Boy/girlfriend	n/a	16 (1.1%)
Teacher	—	6 (0.4%)
Unspecified relationship	10 (1.7%)	44 (2.9%)
Total	**119 (19.9%)**	**350 (22.9%)**
Personal development	9 years and under	10 years and over
Achievements	30 (5.0%)	81 (5.3%)
Health	2 (0.3%)	40 (2.6%)
Religion	6 (1.0%)	19 (1.2%)
Personal growth	6 (1.0%)	43 (2.8%)
Miscellaneous	3 (0.5%)	3 (0.2%)
Total	**47 (7.8%)**	**186 (12.2%)**
Education	9 years and under	10 years and over
Academic achievements	16 (2.7%)	116 (7.6%)
Daycare	7 (1.2%)	—
School	44 (7.4%)	59 (3.9%)
Special help	2 (0.3%)	24 (1.6%)
Total	**69 (11.5%)**	**249 (16.3%)**
Activities/events	9 years and under	10 years and over
Trips	16 (2.7%)	105 (6.9%)
Sports	35 (5.8%)	79 (5.2%)
Camp	13 (2.2%)	61 (4.0%)
Music/dance/arts	21 (3.5%)	41 (2.7%)
Special event	11 (1.8%)	52 (3.4%)
Clubs/activities	14 (2.3%)	23 (1.5%)
Total	**110 (18.4%)**	**361 (23.6%)**
Family activities	9 years and under	10 years and over
Biological family	—	30 (2.0%)
Foster family	22 (3.7%)	20 (1.3%)
Miscellaneous	—	5 (0.3%)
Total	**22 (3.7%)**	**55 (3.6%)**
Life transitions	9 years and under	10 years and over
Employment	n/a	43 (2.8%)
Future plans	n/a	6 (0.4%)
Independence	3 (0.5%)	24 (1.6%)
Material possessions	2 (0.3%)	22 (1.4%)
Volunteering	n/a	3 (0.2%)
Total	**5 (0.8%)**	**98 (6.4%)**

Discussion

For more than 30 years, numerous researchers have published work on the protective factors associated with the resilience demonstrated by some individuals. The events identified by young people and children's adult caregivers are very much in line with this resilience framework. As such, they provide preliminary empirical evidence that processes and basic human adaptational systems identified by Masten and colleagues (Masten, 2001; Masten & Reed, 2002; Masten & Powell, 2003; Masten, chapter 1, this volume) are an important part of the lives of children and young people in care.

The category of relationships was a very important one for the fostered children and young people. Despite their status as state wards, the children's and young people's relationships with biological family members were mentioned as key positive occurrences. To a lesser extent, foster family members were also cited. This emphasis on relationships mirrors Masten and colleagues' (2002; 2003) stress on the importance of the attachment relationship and parenting system in enhancing resilience. They state that "[r]elationship bonds to other competent and involved adults and also to prosocial peers are widely reported correlates and predictors of resilience" (Masten & Reed, 2002, p. 82). Masten (2001) also mentions that "…parent competence and parenting quality [are] strongly associated with resilience" (p. 232). More relevant to our in-care population, having a connection with a supportive adult (but not necessarily a parent) is a very important factor in promoting the well-being of children (Hetherington & Elmore, 2003; Luthar & Zelazo 2003). Additional relationships were also flagged by children's respondents and young people as being conducive to positive development. In particular, relationships with siblings, extended family and friends were mentioned. These findings replicate the results obtained by Caya and Liem (1998) on the importance of siblings when individuals are under stressful family situations. Likewise, Werner (1990) states that protective factors for children include friends, neighbours, and teachers, who provide emotional support, reward competence, and encourage self-esteem. Closely related to the relationships theme, being in-care was flagged as a positive event by the children's respondents and the young people themselves. This finding suggests that substitute parenting can fulfill the goals of providing a safe, caring, and sustained environment favouring the positive development of the children and young people in-care. The relationships and being in-care themes both feed into a healthy sense of belonging to a family unit or circle of friends.

Activities and events formed another important category that many children's respondents and young people nominated as being positive for their development. Gilligan emphasizes the importance of spare time activities as being helpful to young people because they increase self-esteem and self-efficacy by involving youth with external supports (1999, 2000, and chapter 2, this volume). These activities increase children's experiences of mastery and perceived control and as such, feed into Masten and colleagues' pleasure-in-mastery and motivational system (2002; 2003). More important, the value of pursuing activities "…also lies in the recognition that performance of the activity may earn, the relationships it may open up and the confidence it may generate" (Gilligan, 1999, pp. 188–189). As for events, Gilligan (2000) underlines the value of annual and seasonal celebrations because of their importance for social and symbolic enjoyment.

To a lesser extent, the young people and adult caregivers cited educational events as being conducive to positive development. By and large these events mostly referred to attending and doing well in school. Academic success has been found to be a key predictor of better outcomes of former young people in care (Jackson & Martin, 1998). School provides an additional forum wherein nurturing and supportive relationships may be developed (Gilligan, 1998). Rutter and colleagues established that positive school experiences could help alleviate the effects of stress at home (1979). Attending school with its routines and rituals may transmit a sense a safety and predictability to children experiencing turmoil and disruptions in their lives (Gilligan, 1998). Rutter (1990) furthered resilience research by recognizing the protective effects of achievements related to different life domains such as social success (taking of positions of responsibility) and success in non-academic pursuits (e.g., sports, music) in addition to traditional academic successes. In short, attending school may "have enduring and positive effects on students' friendships and social skills, lifetime interests and accomplishments, and opportunities and progress in the labour force" (Gilligan, 1998, p. 16). While academic successes feed into Masten's pleasure-in-mastery and motivational system, attending school nurtures multiple systems, including the attachment system, the self-regulation of emotion, arousal, and behaviour system and the educational system (Masten et al. 2002; 2003). Attending school may also serve to bolster a sense of belonging (i.e., to a circle of friends, a school, a community) and provides opportunities for the child/young person to develop a sense of identity beyond his or her life situation.

For the older age group, many references to events signalling a transition to adulthood were noted. The fostered young people cited getting a job, buying an expensive item (e.g., a stereo or a car), or moving into their own apartment as indicative of their positive development. These events are indeed hallmarks of the resilience process. Meeting age-salient development tasks is representative of Masten and colleagues' pleasure-in-mastery and motivational system (2002, 2003). Empirical research findings from a large study of high school students indicated that work experiences may enhance a sense of competence, promote adolescent well-being, and strengthen adolescent-parent relationships (Finch, Shanahan, Mortimer, & Ryu, 1991; Mortimer & Shanahan, 1994).

Future Directions

The current study presents several important limitations. The data were collected within a group-setting. The AAR-C2 is meant to be completed during a conversation occurring between the caregiver(s), the child welfare worker and young people, and when appropriate, older children. Within this group forum, it is quite possible that young people may not have disclosed sensitive life events that they considered positive (e.g., first sexual experience). A more complete list of positive life events could be obtained by conducting focus groups comprised of young people, or by providing them with a separate section that they could freely complete and send to the research team. While these alternate data collection strategies could increase response validity, they would nevertheless fail to meet LAC's philosophy of promoting dialogue and partnership between the young person or child and those responsible for his or her well-being.

A second limit is currently being addressed: approximately 8% of the young people did not take part in the completion of the AAR-C2. The qualitative data findings provided some indication that adult caregivers sometimes chose to respond in lieu of the young person. Recent revisions made to the AAR-C2 instructions now identify the young person as the main respondent to the positive life events questions. The decision was also made to measure lifetime positive events with one question to correct for the evident information saturation when this question was dichotomized as a function of time (e.g., less than 12 months; more than 12 months). These revisions are necessary in light of past research demonstrating differences in the opinions of adults and young people or children (Doyle et al., 2002).

The present research has contributed to ongoing refinement of the AAR-C2. The open-ended question on positive life events has been retained, and a list of positive life events has been added to the instrument. The development of this list will allow us to systematically study the relationships between various positive life event categories and resilient trajectories.

Conclusions

The importance of this type of research lies in its potential to inform us about the resources children/young people need for resilience. Masten and Reed (2002) outline four strategies for promoting resilience and bolstering positive adaptation. The first of these is to reduce the initial vulnerability and risk. This is best accomplished before the individual is exposed to the risk factor. Second, the authors advocate reducing stressors and the "pile-up" of negative life events that comes along with them. The third strategy includes increasing the individual's access to available resources for the facilitation of more positive adaptive outcomes. Finally, they suggest the mobilization of protective processes enabling the individual to buffer the effects of negative risk factors (Masten & Reed, 2002; Smokowski, 1998).

Our study of the positive life experiences of fostered children and young people concentrates on the possibilities offered in the third and fourth strategies. Our findings build upon previous research on resilience by exploring naturally occurring assets (e.g., positive life events) that can serve to inform child welfare practice and policies. Focusing on the positive will allow us to develop strategies that mobilize basic human adaptational systems so as to enact processes that favour competent and healthy development. More important, highlighting positive achievements forces us to recognize the resilient characteristics that fostered children and young people display. In child welfare, this means looking beyond the removal of a child or young person from an abusive situation—a strategy limited to removing or diminishing exposure to unsafe environments—to a more constructive perspective of building on fostered children's own strengths. As eloquently stated by Seligman "[r]aising children…is vastly more than fixing what is wrong with them. It is about identifying and nurturing their strongest qualities, what they own and are best at, and helping them find niches in which they can best live out these strengths" (Seligman & Csikszentmihalyi, 2000, p. 6).

Authors' note

We gratefully acknowledge the financial support for this research received from the Social Sciences and Humanities Research Council (strategic grant 828-1999-1008, awarded to Robert J. Flynn, principal investigator; co-investigators, Tim D. Aubry, Marie Drolet, and Douglas E. Angus), the Ministry of Community, Family, and Children's Services of the Province of Ontario, and Human Resources Development Canada. We thank our organizational partners: the Ontario Association of Children's Aid Societies (Toronto, Ontario), the Child Welfare League of Canada (Ottawa, Ontario), and Prescott-Russsell Services to Children and Adults (Plantagenet, Ontario). Special thanks are due to the young people, child welfare workers, foster parents, and group home staff and agencies who participated in the project. The authors also wish to express their appreciation to Robert Flynn for his helpful and thoughtful comments.

References

Bolger, K. E., & Patterson, C. J. (2003). Sequelae of child maltreatment: Vulnerability and resilience. In S. S. Luthar (Ed.), *Resilience and vulnerability: Adaptation in the context of childhood adversities* (pp. 156–181). New York: Cambridge University Press.

Caya, M., & Liem, J. (1998). The role of sibling support in high-conflict families. *American Journal of Orthopsychiatry, 68,* 327–333.

Cicchetti, D., & Rogosch, F. A. (1997). The role of self-organization in the promotion of resilience in maltreated children. *Development and Psychopathology, 9,* 797–815.

Cicchetti, D., Rogosch, F. A., Lynch, M., & Holt, K. (1993). Resilience in maltreated children: Processes leading to adaptive outcome. *Development and Psychopathology, 5,* 629–647.

Cohen, L., Burt, C., & Bjorck, J. (1987). Life stress and adjustment: Effects of life events experienced by young adolescents and their parents. *Developmental Psychology, 23,* 583–592.

Doyle, K.W., Wolchik, S.A., & Dawson-McClure, S. (2002). Development of the stepfamily events profile. *Journal of Family Psychology, 16,* 128–143.

Finch, M. D., Shanahan, M. J., Mortimer, J. T., & Ryu, S. (1991). Work experience and control orientation in adolescence. *American Sociological Review, 56,* 597–611.

Flynn, R. J., Angus, D., Aubry, T., & Drolet, M. (1999). *Improving child protection practice through the introduction of Looking After Children into the 54 local Children's Aid Societies in Ontario: An implementation and outcome evaluation.* SSHRC Strategic Grant No. 828-1999-1008. Centre for Research on Community Services, University of Ottawa.

Flynn, R.J., & Biro, C. (1998). Comparing developmental outcomes for children in care with those for other children in Canada. *Children & Society, 12,* 228–233.

Flynn, R. J., Ghazal, H., & Legault, L. (2004). *Looking After Children: Good Parenting, Good Outcomes, Assessment and Action Records (second Canadian adaptation)*. Ottawa, ON & London, UK: Centre for Research on Community Services, University of Ottawa & Her Majesty's Stationery Office.

Flynn, R.J., Ghazal, H., Legault, L., Vandermeulen, G., & Petrick, S. (2004). Use of population measures and norms to identify resilient outcomes in young people in care: An exploratory study. *Child and Family Social Work, 9,* 65–79.

Gilligan, R., (1998). The importance of schools and teachers in child welfare. *Child and Family Social Work, 3,* 13–25.

Gilligan, R. (1999). Enhancing the resilience of children and young people in public care by mentoring their talents and interests. *Child and Family Social Work, 4,* 187–196.

Gilligan, R. (2000). Adversity, resilience and young people: The protective value of positive school and spare time experiences. *Children & Society, 14,* 37–47.

Hetherington, E. M., & Elmore, A. M. (2003). Risk and resilience in children coping with their parents' divorce and remarriage. In S. S. Luthar (Ed.), *Resilience and vulnerability: Adaptation in the context of childhood adversities* (pp. 182–212). New York: Cambridge University Press.

Jackson, S., & Martin, P. Y. (1998). Surviving the care system: education and resilience. *Journal of Adolescence, 21,* 569–583.

Jackson, Y., & Warren, J. (2000). Appraisal, social support, and life events: Predicting outcomes behavior in school-age children. *Child Development, 71,* 1441–1457.

Kanner, A.D., Feldman, S.S., Weinberger, D.A., & Ford, M.E. (1987). Uplifts, hassles, and adaptational outcomes in early adolescents. *Journal of Early Adolescence, 7,* 371–394.

Kvalseth, T.O. (1989). Note on Cohen's Kappa. *Psychological Reports, 65,* 223–226.

Landis, J.R., & Kock, G.G. (1977). The measurement of observer agreement for categorical data. *Biometrics, 33,* 159–174.

Luthar, S. S., & Zelazo, L. B. (2003). Research on resilience. In S. S. Luthar (Ed.), *Resilience and vulnerability: Adaptation in the context of childhood adversities* (pp. 510–549). New York: Cambridge University Press.

Masten, A. S., & Coatsworth, J. D. (1998). The development of competence in favorable and unfavorable environments: Lessons from successful children. *American Psychologist, 53,* 205–220.

Masten, A. S., & Powell, J. L. (2003). A resilience framework for research, policy, and practice. In S. S. Luthar (Ed.), *Resilience and vulnerability: Adaptation in the context of childhood adversities* (pp. 1–25). New York: Cambridge University Press.

Masten, A. S., & Reed, M. J. (2002). Resilience in development. In S. Lopez & C. Snyder (Eds.), *Handbook of positive psychology* (pp. 74–88). Oxford University Press.

Masten, A. S. (2001). Ordinary magic: Resilience processes in development. *American Psychologist, 56,* 227–238.

Mortimer, J. T., & Shanahan, M. J. (1994). Adolescent work experience and family relationships. *Work & Occupations, 21,* 369–384.

Newman, Tony (2004). *What works in building resilience?* Ilford, Essex, England: Barnardo's.

Rutter, M. (1990). Psychosocial resilience and protective mechanisms. In Masten, A., Rolf, J., Cicchetti, D., Nuechterlein, K., & Weintraub, S (Eds.), *Risk and protective factors in the development of psychopathology* (pp. 181–214). New York: Cambridge University Press.

Rutter, M., Maughan, B., Mortimore, P., & Ouston, J. (1979). *Fifteen thousand hours: Secondary schools and their effects on children.* Cambridge, MA: Harvard University Press.

Seidman, E., Allen, L., Aber, L., & Mitchell, C. (1995). Development and validation of adolescent-perceived microsystem scales: Social support, daily hassles, and involvement. *American Journal of Community Psychology, 23,* 355–388.

Seligman, M. E. P., & Csikszentmihalyi, M. (2000). Positive psychology: An introduction. *American Psychologist, 55,* 5–14.

Smokoski, P.R. (1998). Prevention and intervention strategies for promoting resilience in disadvantaged children. *Social Service Review, 72,* 337–364.

Ward, H. (Ed.) (1995). *Looking After Children: Research into practice.* London, UK: HMSO.

Werner, E. E. (1990). Protective factors and individual resilience. In Shonkoff, J. P. & Meisels, S. J. (Eds.), *Handbook of early childhood intervention* (2nd ed.) (pp. 97–116). New York: Cambridge University Press.

Werner, E.E., & Smith, R.S. (2001). *Journeys from childhood to midlife: Risk, resilience, and recovery.* Ithaca, NY: Cornell University Press.

CHAPTER 11

Placement satisfaction of young people living in foster or group homes

Robert J. Flynn, Annie Robitaille, and Hayat Ghazal

Introduction

Out-of-home care is intended to improve the living situations of young people who, in many cases, have been neglected, abused, or abandoned in their families of origin. Although a good number of studies have examined the satisfaction of foster parents and child welfare personnel in their respective roles in child welfare (Brown & Calder, 1999; Denby, Rindfleisch, & Bean, 1999; Rindfleisch, Bean, & Denby, 1998; Sanchirico, Law, Jablonka, & Russell, 1998; Soliday, McCluskey-Faucett, & Meck, 1994), there appear to be only 10 published investigations (summarized in Table 1) that have assessed the level of satisfaction of young people with their foster or group-care placements (Kapp & Vela, 2000). These studies looked at aspects of out-of-home care such as how well the young people liked where they were living, the degree to which they saw their needs as being met, and the quality of their relationships with those with whom they were living. Only three of the 10 studies examined differences in the level of placement satisfaction between those in foster and group care. Overall, the relative lack of research on placement satisfaction is surprising, given that young people are willing and able to express their degree of satisfaction with where they are living and may perceive their placements differently from child welfare workers or caregivers (Stuntzner-Gibson, Koren, & DeChillo, 1995).

The 10 studies summarized in Table 1 were mainly contemporaneous in nature (i.e., focused on the young people's current level of placement satisfaction, without reference to the past or without being followed up from any prior time point). Three studies were, at least in part, retrospective (i.e., asked the participants to recollect and comment on their past experience), and only one was prospective (i.e., followed up the youths from an earlier starting point before asking them about their current placements). The placement satisfaction data were gathered mainly through interviews, as well as through group meetings or survey questionnaires. In the 1970s and

1980s, only three published investigations seem to have been conducted. In a small-sample exploratory study, Jacobson and Cockerum (1976) held a retrospective group meeting with seven young adults in their 20s and 30s who had previously spent many years in foster care. The young adults said that they had not received enough information and had not always been fairly treated. Moreover, they felt that some foster parents had taken in children for the wrong reasons (e.g., for extra money, help with chores, or enhanced feelings of status). In the next of these earlier studies, Gil and Bogart (1982) interviewed 50 young people living in foster care and 50 in

Table 1. Ten studies of young peoples' satisfaction with their out-of-home care, arranged in chronological order

Study	N	Age range	Country	Methodology	Type of placement	Level of placement satisfaction
Jacobson & Cockerum (1976)	7	20s & 30s	U.S.	Retrospective; data collected via group meeting	Foster care	Not mentioned
Gil & Bogart (1982)	100	8–18	U.S.	Contemporaneous; data collected via interviews	Foster care	High
Rice & McFadden (1988)	40	5–20	U.S.	Contemporaneous; data collected via group meetings	Foster care	High
Jonson, Yoken, & Voss (1995)	59	11–14	U.S.	Contemporaneous; data collected via interviews	Foster care	High
Chalmers (1996)	11	18–21	U.S.	Retrospective & contemporaneous; data collected via interviews	Foster care	High
Wedeven, Pecora, Hurwitz, Howell, & Newell (1997)	69	17–35	U.S.	Retrospective; data collected via questionnaires & interviews	Foster care	High
Baldry & Kemmis (1998)	71	6–14+	England	Contemporaneous; data collected via survey	Foster or group care	High; foster care > group care
Wilson & Conroy (1999)	1,100	5–18	U.S.	Contemporaneous; data collected via interviews	Foster or group care	High; foster care > group care
Barber & Delfabbro (2004), study 1	51	<10–15	Australia	Prospective; data collected via interviews	Foster or group care	High; foster care > group care
Barber & Delfabbro (2004), study 2	48	<10–11+	Australia	Contemporaneous; data collected via interviews	Foster care	High

group care about the quality of the care they were receiving. Eighty per cent of those in foster care reported feeling safe, and 81% said their current placement was the best place in which they had ever lived. Only 15% felt that living with their birth parents or relatives would have been the best option for them. Finally, in a series of group meetings, Rice and McFadden (1988) asked 40 young people about their foster care. The youths viewed their foster placements positively, despite missing their birth families and wishing that they could see their mothers more often. Some saw foster care as a better place for them, with fewer problems, than the homes they had known with their birth families.

In the first of five placement satisfaction studies published during the 1990s, Jonson, Yoken and Voss (1995) interviewed 59 young people in foster care. The latter viewed their placements positively, and many viewed foster care as an improvement over the living situations they had known previously with their birth parents. That is, foster care provided homes free of abuse or neglect, and also gave their birth parents an opportunity to resolve their problems and improve their parenting skills. In an exploratory study, based on interviews with 11 young adults in Minnesota, Chalmers (1996) found a high level of satisfaction with foster care. Similar results were reported by Wedeven, Pecora, Hurwitz, Howell and Newell (1997) who, in a retrospective study of 69 former foster care youths, found favourable views of foster placements. In London, England, Baldry and Kemmis (1998) surveyed 71 young people living in foster or group care. The youths were, in general, very satisfied with their living arrangements, with those in foster care expressing greater satisfaction than those in group care. Finally, Wilson and Conroy (1999) interviewed a large sample of 1100 children and adolescents in foster or group care in Illinois. Again, the participants tended to be very satisfied, with many stating that the quality of their lives and the level of satisfaction with their living situations had improved upon moving from the homes of their birth parents to out-of-home care. Once more, those in foster care were significantly more satisfied then those living in group care.

The most recent addition to the placement satisfaction literature appeared in Barber and Delfabbro's (2004) book, which describes a larger study of foster care in Australia. The authors report therein the results of two complementary placement satisfaction studies: one a prospective study of satisfaction with short- and medium-term foster or residential (group) placements, the other a contemporaneous study of satisfaction with long-term foster care. In their first investigation, 51 young people were interviewed. Twenty-nine per cent were 10 years of age or younger, and the other 71% were 11 to 15 years of age. They had been in care for approximately six months. All had started out in foster care but, by the time of the six-month interviews, 12 (24%) had moved to residential (group) care, while the other 39 (76%) remained in foster care. Virtually all the young people in foster care were satisfied with their placements, whereas those in residential care felt significantly less secure and less well-treated than those in foster care. Also, among those in foster care, the young people who rated the caregiving they received more highly were also significantly happier in their placements.

In their second study, of satisfaction with long-term foster care placements (in which the young people had spent an average [mean] of 5.1 years), Barber and Delfabbro (2004) found a high level of satisfaction with almost all aspects of the current placement. The young people described their foster homes as being highly nurturing, and their level of satisfaction was not related to the length of time they had been in care.

Overall, despite differences in the time period when the studies were conducted, the size of the samples used, or the rigour of the methodology employed, the studies reviewed converge on two conclusions. First, in all nine studies reporting on placement satisfaction among young people in foster care, the level of satisfaction was invariably high. Second, in all three investigations that compared placement satisfaction in foster care versus group care, foster care was rated more highly. We therefore adopted these conclusions as hypotheses in our own research, which appears to be the first quantitative Canadian investigation of placement satisfaction. We hypothesized that (1) satisfaction with foster home care would be high in our sample of young people in Ontario, and that (2) the level of satisfaction would be significantly higher in foster than in group homes.

In examining our hypotheses, we also controlled for a number of other factors that are of interest in their own right as well as possible confounds of the relationship between placement type and placement satisfaction. These controls included the standard demographic variables of the young person's gender and age. They also included the risk factor of the youth's level of physical aggressiveness because of its influence on the likelihood of placement in foster or group care (Barber & Delfabbro, 2004). Finally, we controlled for the young person's perception of the quality of his or her relationships with the female caregiver (because we had data from more female than male caregivers) and with friends.

Method

Participants

The sample was composed of 414 young people who were currently living in either a foster home (89%) or group home (11%) in the province of Ontario. Fifty-two per cent of the sample were male, 48% female. The participants ranged in age from 10 to 17 years ($M = 13.46$, $SD = 2.17$). (One nine-year-old participant was close to his 10th birthday and thus included in the sample.) The youths were receiving services from local Children's Aid Societies in Ontario, and most were in out-of-home care because of physical abuse, sexual abuse, or neglect in their families of origin. Their median age at the first out-of-home placement was eight years, and the median number of years that they had spent in their current placement was two years.

Procedures

Data collection procedure. The study sample was drawn from a larger group of young people who were in the care of 23 local Children's Aid Societies (CASs) in the province of Ontario, Canada, during 2001-2002. The CASs were taking part in a larger longitudinal study (Flynn, Angus, Aubry, & Drolet, 1999) of the implementation and outcomes of Looking after Children: Good Parenting, Good Outcomes. Looking After Children is a relatively new approach to out-of-home care originally developed in the UK that aims to improve the quality of substitute or "corporate" parenting (Parker, Ward, Jackson, Aldgate, & Wedge, 1991; Ward, 1995). Each participating CAS had agreed to use the second Canadian adaptation of the Assessment and Action Record (AAR-C2; Flynn, Ghazal, & Legault, 2004) from Looking After Children to assess the needs and monitor the progress of 25 children or adolescents in its care, or 10% of its in-care caseload, whichever was greater. In light of the longitudinal nature of the research, each CAS had also agreed to select, as much as possible, young people who were likely to remain in care for the duration of the study. The choice of which young people and child welfare workers would participate was left up to the CAS. After receiving training in the Looking After Children approach, the young person's child welfare worker used the AAR-C2 in a conversational interview that typically included the child and his or her caregiver (i.e., foster parent or group home worker) and covered 1 to 4 sessions.

Imputation of missing values procedure. When data were missing at the individual item level in the continuous measures described later (in the Measures section), the rate of missing data was low to very low (i.e., in the 0–5% range, and usually in the 1–3% range). To maximize sample size, when data values were missing, we followed the recommendation of Schafer and Graham (2002) and used the EM (Expectation-Maximization) algorithm. EM provides maximum-likelihood estimates for missing values and is an option in the missing-values routine in SPSS.

Instrument: Second Canadian adaptation of the Assessment and Action Record (AAR-C2)

The study variables and measures were assessed by means of the AAR-C2 (Flynn et al., 2004). Like the original version of the AAR developed in the UK (Ward, 1995), the AAR-C2 covers seven Looking After Children outcome domains: health, education, identity, family and social relationships, social presentation, emotional and behavioural development, and self-care skills. The participants in the present samples were assessed with the AAR-C2 form appropriate for young people aged 10–14 years or 15 years and over. To enable comparisons of the functioning of young people in out-of-home care with that of their age peers in the general Canadian population, the AAR-C2 incorporates a good number of standardized items and multi-item scales from the National Longitudinal Survey on Children and Youth (NLSCY; Statistics Canada & Human Resources Development Canada, 1995).

Variables and measures

As already mentioned, gender (1 = male; 0 = female), age (in years), and type of placement (1 = foster home; 0 = group home) were taken from the AAR-C2, as were the multi-item scales that follow.

Satisfaction with placement. A nine-item scale from the AAR-C2 was used to assess the young people's level of satisfaction with their current foster home or group home placement. The items are listed in Table 2. The response options were as follows: 0 = "Very little;" 1 = "Some;" 2 = "A great deal." The internal consistency (Cronbach's alpha) of the scale in the present sample was .90, and the total score could range from 0 (very low) to 18 (very high). The mean and standard deviation for this scale and the other measures are given later in Table 3.

Table 2. Responses (in percentages) to the nine items of the placement satisfaction scale, by type of placement

	Foster homes (*n* = 368)			Group homes (*n* = 46)		
	A great deal	Some	Very little	A great deal	Some	Very little
The next few questions have to do with your current living situation. Would you say that:						
1. You like living here?	78	17	5	39	41	20
2. You feel safe living in this home?	92	7	1	52	44	4
3. Your foster parents (or other adult caregivers) are interested in your activities and interests?	75	22	3	67	26	7
4. You would be pleased if you were to live here for a long time?	77	15	8	28	28	44
5. You are satisfied with the amount of privacy you have here?	78	17	5	50	28	22
6. You feel relaxed around the people with whom you are living?	76	22	2	39	39	22
7. You have a good relationship with the other people with whom you are living?	66	32	2	28	59	13
8. Your current living situation meets your needs?	83	14	3	54	33	13
9. Overall, you are satisfied with your current living situation here?	82	13	4	48	37	15

Note: With application of a Bonferroni correction, the chi-square for each item was tested at α = .006 (i.e., 05/9). The chi-square value for every item was significant, in fact, beyond the .001 level, except for item 3 (p = .42).

Physical aggression. A six-item measure drawn from the NLSCY was used to assess the young person's self-rated level of physical aggression. Sample items included "I get into many fights," and "I threaten people," with the following responses options: 0 – Never or not true; 1 – Sometimes or somewhat true; 2 = Often or very true. Cronbach's alpha was .80 in the present sample. The score could range from 0 (very low) to 12 (very high).

Relationship with the female caregiver. A four-item measure, also derived from the NLSCY, assessed the degree to which the youths saw their relationships with their female foster mothers or female group home workers as being close and of high quality. (The relationship with the female rather than the male caregiver was chosen because there were considerably more female than male caregivers.) Sample items included "How well do you feel that your foster mother (or other female caregiver) understands you?," and "How much affection do you receive from your foster mother (or other female caregiver)?" The response options were 0 = Very little; 1 = Some; 2 = A great deal. The internal consistency of the measure was .80 in this sample, and the total score could range from 0 (very poor) to 8 (excellent).

Relationship with friends. A four-item, NLSCY-derived scale assessed the young persons' perception of the quality of their friendship relationships.

Sample items included "I have many friends" and "I get along easily with others my age." The response options were 0 = False; 1 = Mostly false; 2 = Sometimes true/sometimes false; 3 = Mostly true; 4 = True. Cronbach's alpha was .87 in this sample. The total score could range from 0 (very poor) to 16 (excellent).

Results

Placement satisfaction in foster homes vs. group homes

Item-level comparisons. Table 2 displays the responses of the two groups of young people to the nine items of the placement satisfaction scale. Chi-square analyses revealed that the young people in foster homes evaluated their current placements more favourably than those in group homes on eight of the nine placement-satisfaction items ($p < .001$), even after application of a conservative Bonferroni correction that meant that each chi-square value was tested at the .006 level ($\alpha = .05/9 = .006$). The only exception was item no. 3, in which there was no significant difference ($p = .42$) between the two groups in the perceived level of interest shown by caregivers in the young person's activities and interests. The percentage of participants endorsing the various items ranged from a high of 92% to a low of 66% for the youths in foster care, compared with a high of 67% and a low of 28% for the young people in group care.

Total scale-level comparison. A *t*-test of the group means on the total score of the placement-satisfaction scale was significant ($t = 6.12$, conservative *df* for unequal variances = 51.22, $p < .001$). The mean level of satisfaction of the youths in foster homes ($M = 15.75, SD = 3.36$) exceeded that of the young people in group homes ($M = 11.48, SD = 4.58$) by an amount (4.27 points) that was more than one standard deviation unit (3.76, for the sample as a whole). In fact, the foster home mean was relatively close to the maximum possible satisfaction score of 18.

Predictors of placement satisfaction

Inter-correlations among variables. Before carrying out the correlational and hierarchical regression analyses, we screened the residuals for departures from normality by means of a preliminary regression. We eliminated three cases as outliers because they had standardized residuals greater than ±3.3 (Tabachnick & Fidell, 1996).

Table 3 shows the correlations among the variables. All but gender were significantly correlated with placement satisfaction. Older and more aggressive young people had lower levels of satisfaction, whereas those with higher-quality relationships with their female caregivers and friends were more satisfied. As expected, placement in a foster rather than a group home was associated with a lower level of physical aggression, reflecting, at least in part, a possible selection effect.

Table 3. Means (or percentages), standard deviations, and inter-correlations for all variables

Variable	1	2	3	4	5	6	7
1. Placement satisfaction	—						
2. Gender (1 = male, 0 = female)	−.03	—					
3. Age (years)	−.17***	−.05	—				
4. Physical aggression	−.15**	.24***	−.12**	—			
5. Type of placement setting (1 = foster home, 0 = group home)	.35***	−.15***	−.10*	−.19***	—		
6. Relationship with female caregiver	.73***	−.06	−.18***	−.12**	.13**	—	
7. Relationship with friends	.24***	−.10*	−.02	−.29***	.12**	.15***	—
Mean (or percentage)	15.35	52%	13.45	2.41	89%	6.53	11.91
SD	3.67	—	2.17	2.40	—	1.83	3.67

Note: N = 411 (after removal of three outliers).

*$p < .05$ **$p < .01$ ***$p < .001$

Hierarchical regression results. As Table 4 indicates, the young person's gender, age, and level of physical aggression were entered as the first step in the hierarchical regression. As a set, these variables accounted for a small but statistically significant amount (6%) of the variance in the total score of the placement satisfaction scale (F [3, 407] = 8.19, $p < .001$). When added at step 2, the type of placement (foster vs. group home) explained an additional 10% of the variance in placement satisfaction (ΔF [1, 406] = 45.79, $p < .001$). At step 3, the addition of the two relationship predictors—with the female caregiver and with friends, respectively—accounted for a further 46% of the variance in placement satisfaction (ΔF [2, 407] = 234.54, $p < .001$). The model as a whole explained 61% of the variance in place-ment satisfaction (adjusted R^2 = .60; F [6, 404] = 104.36, $p < .001$).

At step 3, the youth's perceived relationship with his or her female care-giver was the predictor with the largest beta coefficient (β = .68, $p < .001$), by a wide margin. Its beta was of nearly the same magnitude as its zero-order correlation with placement satisfaction (r = .73, $p < .001$; see Table 3). Foster versus group home placement remained predictive, even in the presence of the other variables (β = .25, $p < .001$), and the youth's perceived relationship with friends was also predictive, but only weakly so (β = .12, $p < .01$).

At step 3, age and physical aggression were no longer the significant pre-dictors of placement satisfaction that they had been at steps 1 and 2. This may be because the two relationship variables (and especially the relationship with the female caregivers) mediate the association that these two variables have with placement satisfaction (Baron & Kenny, 1986).

Table 4. Summary of hierarchical regression analysis for variables predicting young people's satisfaction with their current placements

Variable	β
Step 1	
Gender (1 = male, 0 = female)	−.00
Age (years)	−.19***
Physical aggression	−.17***
Step 2	
Gender (1 = male, 0 = female)	.03
Age (years)	−.15***
Physical aggression	−.11*
Type of placement setting (1 = foster home, 0 = group home)	.32***
Step 3	
Gender (1 = male, 0 = female)	.06
Age (years)	−.02
Physical aggression	.00
Type of placement setting (1 = foster home, 0 = group home)	.25***
Relationship with female caregiver	.68***
Relationship with friends	.12**

Note: $N = 411$ (after removal of three outliers). $R^2 = .06$ for Step 1; $\Delta R^2 = .10$ for Step 2; $\Delta R^2 = .46$ for Step 3 (all $ps < .001$).
*$p < .05$ **$p < .01$ ***$p < .001$

Discussion

Overall, our findings provide strong support for both research hypotheses. First, as predicted, the youths in foster homes reported a high level of satisfaction with their placements. Second, also as predicted, they were considerably more satisfied than those living in group homes. Our Canadian results are strikingly consistent with and thus confirmatory of the main findings of the small number of US, UK, and Australian studies that have examined placement satisfaction. We are apparently in the presence of a robust phenomenon that does not appear to be either sample-specific or country-specific. We thus concur with Barber and Delfabbro's (2004) judgment that "foster care is a positive experience for the majority of children" (p. 121), and we also agree with Wilson and Conroy (1999) and others who have found higher satisfaction in foster than in group settings.

Several methodological concerns in the present study should be mentioned. First, the data from the four self-report measures (i.e., placement satisfaction, physical aggression, relationship with the female caregiver, and relationship with friends) all came from the same source, namely, the young person. Source-specific effects, which can be seen as a variant of the broader problem of common-method variance, may thus have had some influence on the correlations among the four self-report scales, although we have no reason to think that any such impact was strong. However, we were able to rule out a conceptually related although different type of spuriousness—namely, item overlap—as an important confound. Upon removing the three relationship-related items from the placement satisfaction scale (items 3, 6, and 7, in Table 2), we reran the regression model in the sample of 441 youths (i.e., after removal of the three outliers) and found very similar results. The model explained almost as much of the variance in the six-item placement satisfaction scale (57%) as it had in the original nine-item scale (61%), and the beta weight for the key predictor, the relationship with the female caregiver, was virtually unchanged ($\beta = .66$, instead of .68). The relationship with friends was the only predictor whose status changed: its originally weak beta coefficient ($\beta = .12$, $p < .001$) was no longer significantly different from zero ($\beta = .06$, $p = .085$).

Second, a central component in Looking After Children—the notion of partnership between the young person in care and the adults charged with providing high-quality substitute parenting—meant that the youth's child welfare worker and caregiver usually participated with him/her in the AAR-C2 conversational interview. This, in turn, may have created demand characteristics that could have created some degree of socially desirable responding on the part of the young person. In our opinion, however, the striking convergence of our findings with those of the previous studies of placement satisfaction—which had been carried out at different times, in different countries, and with different methods or instruments—argues convincingly against the importance of any putative demand characteristic emanating from the Looking After Children approach or the AAR-C2 instrument.

Overall, we believe the present study has made at least two contributions to research on placement satisfaction. First, in what appears to be the first quantitative, large-sample Canadian study of placement satisfaction, we found that most young people in foster care are highly satisfied with their placements, considerably more so than those in group homes. This does not mean, however, that all young people should be placed in foster homes, although many should be. Barber and Delfabbro's (2004) important longitudinal study documented that while many young people do well in conventional family-based foster care, *disruptive youths* often do poorly in it and run a grave risk of serial eviction and progressive emotional deterioration. As a rule of thumb, Barber and Delfabbro (2004) suggest that after two placement breakdowns due to disruptive behaviour, a young person should be removed from conventional foster care and offered an alternative, such as therapeutic foster care (Meadowcroft, Thomlison, & Chamberlain, 1994; Hudson, Nutter, & Galaway, 1994), multisystemic therapy (Huey, Henggeler, Brondino, & Pickrel, 2000), or whole-family foster care (Barth, 2001). Unfortunately, rigorous evaluations of such alternatives are currently lacking and should be a top priority in future foster care research.

Second, we were successful in deriving a parsimonious model that, with only six predictors, was able to account for more than half the variance in placement satisfaction, an unusually large proportion in individual-level multiple regression models. The female caregiver emerged as having a particularly pivotal role, whether in foster or group care. General resilience theory suggests that it is highly plausible, even likely, that a young person's experience of the female caregiver as an understanding, fair, affectionate, and close parental figure will contribute greatly to the youth's positive adaptation. Masten (2000) has underlined the crucial role that caregivers play in a field such as child welfare:

> "The best-documented asset of resilient children is a strong bond to a competent and caring adult; however, this adult need not be a parent. For children who do not have such an adult involved in their lives, this is the first order of business."

Authors' note

We gratefully acknowledge the financial support for the Looking After Children in Ontario (OnLAC) project received from the Social Sciences and Humanities Research Council (Society, Culture and the Health of Canadians strategic grant 828-1999-1008, awarded to Robert J. Flynn, principal investigator; co-investigators, Tim D. Aubry, Marie Drolet, and Douglas E. Angus). We are also grateful for the additional financial support received from the Ministry of Children and Youth Services of Ontario (grant made to the Ontario Association of Children's Aid Societies [OACAS]), Social Development Canada (grant made to the Child Welfare League of Canada [CWLC]), and Prescott-Russell Services to Children and Adults (PRSCA). We also thank our organizational partners—OACAS,

CWLC, PRSCA—and the local Children's Aid Societies, as well as the many young people, child welfare workers, supervisors, foster parents, and group home workers who participated in the OnLAC project

References

Baldry, S., & Kemmis, J. (1998). Research note: What is it to be looked after by a local authority? *British Journal of Social Work, 28,* 129–136.

Barber, J. G., & Delfabbro, P. H. (2004). *Children in foster care.* London, UK: Routledge.

Baron, R. M., & Kenny, D. A. (1986). The moderator-mediator variable distinction in social psychological resarch: Conceptual, strategic and statistical considerations. *Journal of Personality and Social Psychology, 51,* 1173–1182.

Barth, R. P. (2001). Policy implications of foster family characteristics. *Family Relations: Interdisciplinary Journal of Applied Family Studies, 50,* 16–19.

Brown, J., & Calder, P. (1999). Concept-mapping the challenges faced by foster parents. *Children and Youth Services Review, 21,* 481–495.

Chalmers, M. L. (1996). Voices of wisdom: Minnesota youth talk about their experiences in out-of-home care. *Community Alternatives, 8,* 95–121.

Colton, M. (1989). Foster and residential children's perceptions of their social environments. *British Journal of Social Work, 19,* 217–233.

Denby, R., Rindfleisch, N., & Bean, G. (1999). Predictors of foster parents' satisfaction and intent to continue to foster. *Child Abuse & Neglect, 23,* 287–303.

Flynn, R. J., Angus, D., Aubry, T., & Drolet, M. (1999). *Improving child protection practice through the introduction of Looking After Children into the 54 local Children's Aid Societies in Ontario: An implementation and outcome evaluation.* SSHRC Strategic Grant No. 828-1999-1008 (awarded to Robert J. Flynn). Ottawa, ON: Centre for Research on Community Services, University of Ottawa.

Flynn, R. J., Ghazal, H., & Legault, L. (2004). *Looking After Children: Good Parenting, Good Outcomes, Assessment and Action Records.* (Second Canadian adaptation, AAR-C2.) Ottawa, ON, & London, UK: Centre for Research on Community Services, University of Ottawa & Her Majesty's Stationery Office (HMSO).

Gil, E., & Bogart, K. (1982). Foster children speak out: A study of children's perceptions of foster care. *Children Today, 11,* 7–9.

Hudson, J., Nutter, R., & Galaway, B. (1994). Treatment foster care programs: A review of evaluation research and suggested directions. *Social Work Research, 18,* 198–210.

Huey, S. J., Henggeler, S. W., Brondino, M. J., & Pickrel, S. G. (2000). Mechanisms of change in multisystemic therapy: Reducing delinquent behavior through therapist adherence and improved family and peer functioning. *Journal of Consulting and Clinical Psychology, 68,* 451–467.

Jacobson, E., & Cockerum, J. (1976). As foster children see it: Former foster children talk about foster family care. *Children Today, 42,* 32–36.

Jonson, P. R., Yoken, C., & Voss, R. (1995). Family foster care placement: The child's perspective. *Child Welfare, 74,* 959–974.

Kapp, S. A., & Vela, R. (2000). Measuring consumer satisfaction in family preservation services: Identifying instrument domains. *Family Preservation Journal, 4,* 19–37.

Masten, A. S. (2000). *Children who overcome adversity to succeed in life.* University of Minnesota Extension Service. Retrieved April 4, 2003, from www.extension.umn.edu/distribution/familydevelopment/components/7565_06.html.

Meadowcroft, P., Thomlison, B., & Chamberlain, P. (1994). Treatment foster care services: A research agenda for child welfare. *Child Welfare, 73,* 565–581.

Parker, R.A., Ward, H., Jackson, S., Aldgate, J. & Wedge, P. (Eds.) (1991). *Looking After Children: Assessing outcomes in child care.* London, UK: HMSO.

Rice, D. L., & McFadden, E. J. (1988). A forum for foster children. *Child Welfare, 67,* 231–243.

Rindfleisch, N., Bean, G., & Denby, R. (1998). Why foster parents continue and cease to foster. *Journal of Sociology and Social Welfare, 25*, 5–24.

Sanchirico, A., Lau, W. J., Jablonka, K., & Russell, S. J. (1998). Foster parent involvement in service planning: Does it increase job satisfaction? *Children and Youth Services Review, 20*, 325–346.

Schafer, J. L., & Graham, J. W. (2002). Missing data: Our view of the state of the art. *Psychological Methods, 7*, 147–177.

Soliday, E., McCluskey-Fawcett, K., & Meck, N. (1994). Foster mothers' stress, coping, and social support in parenting drug-exposed and other at-risk toddlers. *Children's Health Care, 23*, 15–32.

Statistics Canada & Human Resources Development Canada. (1995). *National Longitudinal Survey of Children and Youth: Overview of survey instruments for 1994-95, data collection cycle 1.* Ottawa, ON: Authors.

Stuntzner-Gibson, D., Koren, P. E., & DeChillo, N. (1995). The youth satisfaction questionnaire: What kids think of services. *Families in Society, 76*, 616–624.

Tabachnick, B. G., & Fidell, L. S. (1996). *Using multivariate statistics* (3rd ed.). New York: HarperCollins.

Ward, H. (Ed.). (1995). *Looking After Children: Research into practice.* London, UK: HMSO.

Wedeven, T., Pecora, P. J., Hurwitz, M., Howell, R., & Newell, D. (1997). Examining the perceptions of alumni of long-term foster care: A follow-up study. *Community Alternatives: International Journal of Family Care, 9*, 88–106.

Wilson, L., & Conroy, J. (1999). Satisfaction of children in out-of-home care. *Child Welfare, 78*, 53–63.

CHAPTER 12

Hope in young people in care: Role of active coping and other predictors

Angela Dumoulin and Robert J. Flynn

Introduction

Hope is the belief that one can find pathways to desired goals and become motivated to use those pathways (Snyder, Rand, & Sigmon, 2002). As such, hope can be seen as a platform for resilience because it is predictively—and probably causally—antecedent to a broad range of processes and outcomes linked to positive adaptation (Chang & DeSimone, 2001). Snyder et al. (2002) postulate that human actions are goal-directed, such that goals are the targets of mental action sequences and the cognitive anchors of hope theory. In order to attain desired goals, people must be able to see themselves as capable of thinking of one or more feasible routes to their goals. Snyder, Harris, Anderson, Holleran, Irving, and Sigmon (1991) term this process *pathways thinking*, which is exemplified by self-talk such as "I'll find a way to get this done!" Although important, especially when obstacles are encountered, pathways thinking is, by itself, insufficient. To reach their goals, people must also be able to see themselves as capable of using the pathways they have identified. Snyder et al. (1991) term this process *agency thinking*, the motivational anchor of hope theory. It is reflected in self-talk such as "I can do this!" or "I'm not going to be stopped!" (Snyder et al., 2002). In the face of difficulties, such agentic thoughts help the person apply the needed motivation to the best available pathway. During successful goal-pursuit sequences, pathways thinking is viewed as increasing agency thinking, which, in turn, promotes more pathways thinking, and so forth. Also, the person's perception that his or her goal pursuit is successful is a source of positive emotions, just as the perception of unsuccessful goal pursuit leads to negative emotions (Snyder et al., 2002). Developmentally, the acquisition of hopeful goal-directed thinking is seen as crucial in children, especially those who have known early adversity, if they are to survive and grow into thriving adolescents and adults.

Snyder, Hoza, Pelham, Rapoff, Ware, Danovsky et al. (1997) developed the Children's Hope Scale (CHS) in order to study the developmental roots of hope. They administered the CHS to two groups of children with serious physical illness (arthritis, sickle cell anaemia, or cancer), a third group with a psychological condition (ADHD), and two control groups. The mean scores ranged from a low of 25.5 in the ADHD group ($SD = 3.63$) to a high of 27.0 in one of the control groups ($SD = 4.51$), indicating little difference between the groups. Greater hope was associated with higher levels of academic achievement, social acceptance, athletic performance, physical appearance, and positive behaviour. Higher-hope children also exhibited greater internal control and fewer depressive symptoms.

Hope has been investigated much more extensively in adults than in children. Among adults, higher hope has been associated with more approach-oriented coping strategies (Chang, 1998; Chang & DeSimone, 2001), more positive school achievement (Snyder et al., 1997), better athletic performance (Curry, Snyder, Cook, Ruby, & Rehm, 1997), greater self-esteem and optimism (Snyder et al., 1991), more positive adjustment (Snyder, Sympson, Ybasco, Borders, Babyak, & Higgins, 1996), and greater life satisfaction (Chang, 1998). Higher hope has also been linked with lower levels of depressive symptoms (Snyder et al., 1991; Elliott, Witty, Herrick & Hoffman, 1991), less anxiety or negative affect (Stanton, Danoff-Burg, & Higgins, 2002), and decreased wishful thinking or social withdrawal (Chang, 1998).

The purpose of the present study, apparently the first of its kind in child welfare, was to investigate the level and predictors of hope in young people living in out-of-home care. More broadly, we saw the eventual results as contributing to a better understanding of the larger process of resilience itself, given that hopeful thinking presumably strengthens successful goal-pursuit, positive emotions, and, ultimately, resilient development among young people exposed to abuse or neglect early in life.

We drew on general hope theory and the mainly adult literature on which it is based (Snyder et al., 2002) to formulate an exploratory predictive model. We postulated that the following variables, from the most distal to the most proximal, would be significant predictors of hope among young people in care: gender, age, cumulative risk, physical aggression, type of placement (foster vs. group home), caregiver nurturance, relationship with the female caregiver, active coping, and avoidant coping.

Method

Sample

The sample consisted of 374 young people who were aged 10 to 17 ($M = 13.73, SD = 2.12$) and had complete data on all study variables. Fifty-one per cent were male, 49% female. They were living either in foster homes (90%) or group homes (10%) in Ontario, under the supervision of some 25 local Children's Aid Societies (CASs) in 2002–2003. The young people had been admitted to care because of a lack of caregiver capacity, physical or sexual abuse, neglect, or abandonment.

Instrument

Information was collected using the second Canadian adaptation of the Assessment and Action Record (AAR-C2; Flynn, Ghazal, & Legault, 2004) from Looking after Children (Ward, 1995). The AAR-C2 consists of measures designed to assess the needs and outcomes of young people in out-of-home care in seven developmental domains: health, education, identity, family and social relationships, social presentation, emotional and behavioural development, and self-care skills. These are the same dimensions used in the original version of the AAR from the UK (Ward, 1995). In the AAR-C2, however, the seven LAC dimensions have been operationalized in a "Canadianized" way through the incorporation of numerous standardized items and scales from the National Longitudinal Survey of Children and Youth (NLSCY; Statistics Canada & Human Resources Development Canada, 1995). This strategy allows comparisons to be made on many outcomes between young people in care and their age peers in the general Canadian population.

Measures

Children's Hope Scale. The Children's Hope Scale (CHS; Snyder et al., 1997) is a six-item self-report measure composed of three items that assess pathways thinking and three items that tap agency thinking. Intended for use with young people aged 8 to 17, the CHS is presented to respondents as "Questions About Your Goals." The six response options for each item range from 1 ("None of the time") to 6 ("All of the time"). The total score can thus run from 6 (low) to 36 (high), with the average (mean) for children being around 25, which is equivalent to hopeful thinking "a lot of the time." Internal consistency reliability coefficients in the .72 to .86 range, and test-retest reliability of .71 over a one-month interval, have been obtained in previous research (Snyder et al., 1997). Support for the validity of the CHS exists in the form of correlations with measures of related constructs such as self-perceived competence, locus of control, social acceptance, and athletic performance (Snyder et. al., 1997). In the present sample, the internal consistency of the CHS was .86 (Cronbach's alpha).

Adverse life events. The AAR-C2 measure of adverse life events consisted of a structured list of 17 items (e.g., death of a parent, divorce or separation of parents, physical or psychiatric illness in the birth family, violence, poverty, various types of abuse, or neglect). The young person (with assistance as needed from the caregiver or child welfare worker) could also identify an additional negative life event by responding to an open-ended question. Each negative event could have been experienced either "in the last 12 months" or "since birth but more than 12 months ago," to differentiate recent from past events. The items experienced by the young person in care were summed to form an overall measure of cumulative risk, with total possible scores ranging from 0 (low) to 36 (high). Internal consistency in the present sample was .70.

Physical aggression. This five-item scale was based on one from the NLSCY. The three response options were "Never or not true," "Sometimes or somewhat true," and "Often or very true." Sample items included, "I get into many fights," and "I kick, bite and hit other people my age." The total score could range from 0 (low) to 10 (high) and the internal consistency of the scale in the present sample was .79.

Parental nurturance. This seven-item scale, drawn from the NLSCY, was rated by the foster parent or group-home staff member to assess the level of caregiver warmth and acceptance towards the young person in care. Sample items were, "How often do you make sure that [the young person in care] knows that he/she is appreciated?" and "How often do you speak of the good things that he/she does?" The five response options were "Never," "Rarely," "Sometimes," "Often" and "Always." The internal consistency of the scale in the present sample was .78, with the total possible score ranging from 0 (low) to 28 (high).

Relationship with the female caregiver. On this four-item scale, taken from the NLSCY, the young person rated the quality of his or her relationship with the female caregiver. The latter was chosen in the present study because there were considerably more female than male caregivers. Sample items included, "How well do you feel your foster mother (or other female caregiver) understands you?," and "How much affection do you receive from your foster mother (or other female caregiver)?" The three response options were "A great deal," "Some," or "Very little." Internal consistency was .80 in the present sample, and the total score could range from 4 (low) to 12 (high).

Active and avoidance coping. The AAR-C2 active and avoidance coping scales were based on an established measure of general coping style (Ayers, Sandler, West, & Rosa, 1996), with the item content and wording tailored to an in-care population. Active coping (11 items) was assessed by items such as, "I think about different ways of solving my problem," and avoidance coping (8 items) by items such as, "I try not to think about my problem." The four response options ran from "Never" to "Most of the time" The internal consistency of the active coping scale was .83; for the avoidance coping scale, .75. On the active coping scale, the total score could range from 11 (low) to

44 (high); for avoidance coping, from 8 (low) to 32 (high).

Procedure

The child welfare workers responsible for administering the AAR-C2 had received prior training in Looking After Children and use of the AAR-C2. The instrument was administered in the form of a conversational interview, typically over several sessions, in which the young person, foster parent or other caregiver, and child welfare worker took part.

Results

Means and intercorrelations

Table 1 presents the means (or percentages), standard deviations, and zero-order correlations for the study variables. The mean hope score for the present sample was 25.82, corresponding to hopeful thinking "a lot of the time." All of the variables except gender, age, and cumulative risk were significantly related to hope, with active coping the single strongest predictor ($r = .56$).

Table 1. Means (or percentages), standard deviations and intercorrelations among all variables ($N = 374$)

Variable	1	2	3	4	5	6	7	8	9	10
1. CHS	—	.02	−.10	.00	−.33***	.27***	.20***	.28***	.56***	.38***
2. (1 = m; 0 = f)		—	−.08	−.02	.10	−.02	−.04	−.08	−.13*	.13*
3. Age (years)			—	.13*	−.10	−.08	−.05	−.07	.05	−.11*
4. Cumulative risk				—	.08	−.03	−.05	−.04	.09	.02
5. Physical aggression					—	−.22***	−.07	−.18***	−.28***	−.03
6. Type of home (1 = foster; 0 = group)						—	.09	.22***	.08	.06
7. Parental nurturance							—	.29***	.18***	.16**
8. Relationship with female caregiver								—	.19***	.22***
9. Active coping									—	.49***
10. Avoidant coping										—
Mean (or %)	25.82	51%	13.73	5.86	1.94	90%	23.02	10.67	28.31	20.14
SD	6.03	—	2.12	3.41	2.04	—	3.01	1.69	6.29	4.62

Note: CHS = Score on Children's Hope Scale

*$p < .05$ (two-tailed). **$p < .01$ (two-tailed). ***$p < .001$ (two-tailed)

Hierarchical regression

Hierarchical regression was used to test the predictive model. At step 1, the most distal variables were entered (i.e., gender and age), followed by cumulative risk at step 2, physical aggression at step 3, the type of home (foster or group) at step 4, parental nurturance and the young person's relationship with the female caregiver at step 5, and active and avoidant coping at step 6.

Table 2 shows the results of the hierarchical regression. Neither of the first two steps produced a significant increment in the amount of variance accounted for in hope. Beginning with step 3, however, each succeeding step added a significant increment: 12% at step 3, 4% at step 4, 5% at step 5, and 21% at step 6. The model as a whole accounted for 43% of the variance in the scores on the Children's Hope Scale. In the full model (i.e., at step 6), active coping was easily the most important predictor of hope, with a sizable beta coefficient of .44 ($p < .001$). At this final step, male gender, residence in a foster home, the young person's perception of the quality of his or her relationship with the female caregiver, and (especially) the frequency of the young person's active coping efforts in the face of difficulties were significant positive predictors of hopeful thinking, whereas older age and a higher level of physical aggression were significant negative predictors of hope.

Discussion

For several complementary reasons, the results of the present study can be interpreted as offering considerable support for our exploratory predictive model. First, the mean level of hope in our sample of young people in care was within the range reported by Snyder et al. (1997) for several normative groups of young people who either had physical or psychological health conditions or else were drawn from the general population. Second, four of the six steps in the hierarchical regression model produced statistically significant increments in the variance explained in young people's hopeful thinking. Third, the model as a whole accounted for an appreciable amount of the variance in hope (43%). Fourth, in the final regression model, six of the nine individual predictors had significant net relationships with hope.

Several results were consistent with previous findings in the literature. The fact that a higher-quality relationship with the female caregiver (as perceived by the young person) was predictive of higher hope agrees with abundant research linking social support to positive adaptation (Venters-Horton & Wallander, 2001; Cohen & Wills, 1985). Also, the fact that care-giver parental nurturance was a positive predictor of hope when it entered the regression model at step 5 is congruent with authoritative parenting theory. (The fact that parental nurturance became non-significant at step 6 suggested that its relationship with hope was mediated by active coping rather than that it was not important.) Last, the finding that more active coping was strongly predictive of a higher level of hopeful thinking is con-

Table 2. Summary of hierarchical regression analysis for variables predicting hope ($N = 374$)

Variable	β
Step 1	
Gender (1 = male, 0 = female)	.01
Age (years)	−.10
Step 2	
Gender (1 = male, 0 = female)	.01
Age (years)	−.10
Cumulative risk	.02
Step 3	
Gender (1 = male, 0 = female)	.05
Age (years)	−.14**
Cumulative risk	.05
Physical aggression	−.35***
Step 4	
Gender (1 = male, 0 = female)	.05
Age (years)	−.12*
Cumulative risk	.05
Physical aggression	−.31***
Type of home (1 = foster, 0 = group)	.20***
Step 5	
Gender (1 = male, 0 = female)	.06
Age (years)	−.10*
Cumulative risk	.06
Physical aggression	−.28***
Type of home (1 = foster, 0 = group)	.16***
Parental nurturance	.12*
Relationship with female caregiver	.16**
Step 6	
Gender (1 = male, 0 = female)	.09*
Age (years)	−.10*
Cumulative risk	.00
Physical aggression	−.17***
Type of home (1 = foster, 0 = group)	.16***
Parental nurturance	.05
Relationship with female caregiver	.09*
Active coping	.44***
Avoidance coping	.09

Note: $R^2 = .01$ at step 1 (n.s.); $\Delta R^2 = .00$ at step 2 (n.s.); $\Delta R^2 = .12$ ($p < .001$) at step 3;
$\Delta R^2 = .04$ ($p < .001$) at step 4; $\Delta R^2 = .05$ ($p < .001$) at step 5; $\Delta R^2 = .21$ ($p < .001$) at step 6.
For model as a whole, $R^2 = .43$ ($p < .001$); R^2 adjusted $= .42$.

*$p < .05$ (two-tailed)   **$p < .01$ (two-tailed)   ***$p < .001$ (two-tailed)

sistent with studies in which participants who coped more actively with health problems (Elliott, Witty, Herrick, & Hoffman, 1991; Drach-Zahavy & Somech, 2002) or with preparing for and writing examinations (Onwuegbuzie & Snyder, 2000) had greater hope.

Some of our findings, on the other hand, were unexpected. In our study, unlike others, gender was a significant (although weak) predictor of hope. This result emerged, however, only at step 6 of the regression model, when eight other variables had been statistically controlled. The failure of gender to predict hope in other studies may have been due to the fact that fewer factors had been controlled. Also contrary to expectation, the level of cumulative risk of the young person in care was not significantly related to hope. This is not consistent with prior research that has often found a greater number of risk factors to be associated with a larger number of problematic outcomes (see Masten & Powell, 2003).

Hopeful thinking among young people in care appears to be at a level comparable to that observed in other groups and seems especially predictable from the frequency with which youths in care cope with problems in an active rather than avoidant manner. Active coping skills can be learned and should be taught. Caregivers and child welfare personnel should also encourage young people in care to strive to reach their goals by engaging in pathways and agency thinking, particularly when confronted with obstacles. Having identified here a number of predictors of hopeful thinking, we plan in future to investigate a range of educational, interpersonal, and behavioural consequences that hope presumably has in its role as a broad platform for resilient outcomes.

Authors' note

We gratefully acknowledge the financial support for the Looking After Children in Ontario (OnLAC) project received from the Social Sciences and Humanities Research Council (strategic grant 828-1999-1008, awarded to Robert J. Flynn, principal investigator; co-investigators, Tim D. Aubry, Marie Drolet, and Douglas E. Angus). We are also grateful for the additional financial support received from the Ministry of Children and Youth Services of Ontario (grant made to the Ontario Association of Children's Aid Societies [OACAS]), Social Development Canada (grant made to the Child Welfare League of Canada [CWLC]), and Prescott-Russell Services to Children and Adults (PRSCA). We also thank our organizational partners—OACAS, CWLC, PRSCA, and the local Children's Aid Societies—as well as the many young people, child welfare workers, supervisors, foster parents, and group home workers who participated in the OnLAC project.

References

Ayers, T. S., Sandler, I. N., West, S. G., & Roosa, M. W. (1996). A dispositional and situational assessment of children's coping: Testing alternative models of coping. *Journal of Personality, 64,* 923–958.

Chang, E. C. (1998). Hope, problem-solving ability, and coping in a college student population: Some implications for theory and practice. *Journal of Clinical Psychology, 54,* 953–962.

Chang, E. C., & DeSimone, S. L. (2001). The influence of hope on appraisals, coping and dysphoria: A test of hope theory. *Journal of Social and Clinical Psychology, 20,* 117–129.

Cohen, S., & Wills, T. A. (1985). Stress, social support and the buffering hypothesis. *Psychological Bulletin, 98,* 310–357.

Curry, L.A., Snyder, C.R., Cook, D.L., Ruby, B.C. & Rehm, M. (1997). The role of hope in student-athlete academic and sport achievement. *Journal of Personality and Social Psychology, 73,* 1257–1267.

Drach-Zahavy, A., & Somech, A. (2002). Coping with health problems: The distinctive relationships of Hope sub-scales with constructive thinking and resource allocation. *Personality and Individual Differences, 33,* 103–117.

Elliott, T. R., Witty, T. E., Herrick, S., & Hoffman, J. T. (1991). Negotiating reality after physical loss: Hope, depression and disability. *Journal of Personality and Social Psychology, 61,* 608–613.

Flynn, R.J., Ghazal, H., & Legault, L. (2004). *Looking After Children: Good Parenting, Good Outcomes. Assessment and Action Records* (AAR-C2; second Canadian adaptation). Ottawa, ON & London, England: Centre for Research on Community Services, University of Ottawa & Her Majesty's Stationery Office (HMSO).

Masten, A. S., & Powell, J. L. (2003). A resilience framework for research, policy and practice. In S.S. Luthar (Ed.), *Resilience and vulnerability: Adaptation in the context of childhood adversities* (pp. 1–25). Cambridge, UK: Cambridge University Press.

Onwuegbuzie, A. J., & Snyder, C. R. (2000). Relations between hope and graduate students' coping strategies for studying and examination taking. *Psychological Reports, 86,* 803–806.

Snyder, C. R., Harris, C., Anderson, J. R., Holleran, S. A., Irving, L. M., Sigmon, S. T., et al. (1991). The will and the ways: Development and validation of an individual-differences measure of hope. *Journal of Personality and Social Psychology, 60,* 570–585.

Snyder, C. R., Hoza, B., Pelham, W. E., Rapoff, M., Ware, L., Danovsky, M., et al. (1997). The development and validation of the Children's Hope Scale. *Journal of Pediatric Psychology, 22,* 399–421.

Snyder, C. R., Rand, K. L., & Sigmon, D. R. (2002). Hope theory: A member of the positive psychology family. In C. R. Snyder & Lopez, S. J. (Eds.). *The handbook of positive psychology* (pp. 257–276). New York: Oxford University Press.

Snyder, C. R., Sympson, S. C., Ybasco, F. C., Borders, T. F., Babyak, M. A., & Higgins, R. L. (1996). Development and validation of the state hope scale. *Journal of Personality and Social Psychology, 70,* 321–335.

Stanton, A. L., Danoff-Burg, S., & Higgins, M. E. (2002). The first year after breast cancer diagnosis: Hope and coping strategies as predictors of adjustment. *Psych-Oncology, 11,* 93–102.

Statistics Canada & Human Resources Development Canada (1995). *National Longitudinal Survey of Children and Youth: Overview of survey instruments for 1994-95, data collection cycle 1.* Ottawa, ON: Authors.

Ventura Horton, T., & Wallander, J. L. (2001). Hope and social support as resilience factors against psychological distress of mothers who care for children with chronic physical conditions. *Rehabilitation Psychology, 46,* 382–399.

Ward, H. (Ed.) (1995). *Looking After Children: Research into practice.* London, UK: HMSO.

CHAPTER 13

Participation in structured voluntary activities, substance use, and psychological outcomes in out-of-home care

Robert J. Flynn, Julie Beaulac, and Jessica Vinograd

Introduction

Adolescence is a critical period for the development of identity, presenting opportunities for growth and self-affirmation as well as occasions for confusion and self-doubt (Compas, Hinden, & Gerhardt, 1995). For young people who have suffered abuse or neglect in their families of origin and been placed in out-of-home care, adolescence can be especially difficult. Knowledge of ways in which their positive psychological adaptation can be effectively promoted, especially through feasible and non-stigmatizing means, is obviously desirable.

About half of adolescents' waking hours is made up of free time (Larson & Seepersad, 2003), and the activities that occupy their free time have important implications for their well-being and development (Verma & Larson, 2003). Adolescents tend to spend most of their free time in unstructured voluntary activities, such as watching television, listening to music, or "hanging out" with friends. Unstructured activities such as these, however, may not have the same benefits as more structured voluntary activities and, in fact, may be associated with an increase in risky behaviours (Larson & Seepersad, 2003). Structured voluntary activities, on the other hand, appear to confer many developmental benefits. Larson (2000) defined the term *structured voluntary activities* (SVAs) as follows:

> "...activities that are organized by adults, such as extracurricular school activities and community youth activities, as well as structured activities that youth participate in on their own—such diverse things as hobbies, writing poetry, constructing a web site, or playing in a band with a group of friends. Our defining criterion for this category is activities that are voluntary (i.e., not required for school) and involve some structure, that is, where students' participation occurs within a system involving constraints, rules, and goals (p. 174)."

So defined, SVAs include sports (the most frequent SVA, occupying 4–6 hours per week of U.S. adolescents' time), arts, music, hobbies, and participation in organizations (accounting for 1–2 hours per week on average), and, during the summer, camps, classes, and sports leagues (Larson, 2000). SVAs are often known by other names, such as "after-school" activities (e.g., Kane, 2004) or "out-of-school time" programs (e.g., Chaput, Little & Weiss, 2004).

According to Larson (2000), involvement in SVAs is particularly important for young people because it involves three key elements—*intrinsic motivation, concerted attention*, and *a temporal arc of effort*—that, together, are conducive to the development of initiative and other positive outcomes. That is, the adolescent engaged in an SVA voluntarily chooses to participate, devotes thought and effort toward accomplishing a valued goal, and must re-evaluate and adjust his or her strategies over time to reach that goal. The simultaneous presence of these three elements differentiates SVAs both from academic activities at school (in which intrinsic motivation is often absent) and from unstructured leisure activities (e.g., watching television, spending time with friends), which typically do not require concerted attention.

In the general population, extensive research has indicated that more frequent participation in SVAs is associated with, and may be causally implicated in, many positive academic and non-academic outcomes (Chaput et al., 2004): higher academic achievement and grades; higher occupational expectations and university enrollment; greater attachment to school; lower levels of problem behaviour, cigarette smoking, and drug use; more volunteering; and better emotional adjustment, greater happiness, and more optimism about the future. Other benefits of SVAs include higher self-esteem, greater feelings of control over one's life, and lower rates of early school dropout (Larson, 2000; Holland & Andre, 1987; Gilman, 2001; Mahoney, 2000; Mahoney & Cairns, 1997; Anderson-Butcher, Newsome, & Ferrari, 2003).

In studies in Canada, the results have been similar to those just cited. In a large, nationally representative sample of 11,219 children aged 6 to 11 in the National Longitudinal Survey of Children and Youth (NLSCY; Statistics Canada & Human Resources Development Canada, 1995), Offord, Lipman and Duku (1998) found that more frequent participation in extracurricular activities was associated with better physical and psychological health. Other analyses from the NLSCY (Statistics Canada, 2001) have indicated that youth who participate in organized out-of-school-time activities have higher levels of self-esteem, better relationships with friends, and stronger performance in school. Conversely, those who rarely or never participate in organized leisure activities report lower self-esteem, greater difficulties with friends, and higher rates of cigarette smoking (Statistics Canada, 2001). Beauvais (2001) concluded, in a review of the Canadian literature on youth activities, that participation in such activities is associated with greater acceptance among peers, higher levels of self-empowerment, and a more positive self-concept.

In contrast to the abundance of research on youths in the general population, few studies have been carried out on the effects of participation in SVAs among young people living in out-of-home care. Gilligan (2000) and Newman (2004) are two child welfare researchers who have urged that involvement in SVAs be made available to youths in care as an important vehicle of resilient development. The purpose of the present study was to investigate the role of participation in SVAs in the psychological adaptation of young people in care. We did so in two ways: by testing a specific "main effect" hypothesis and by examining an exploratory "moderator effect" research question that complemented the hypothesis.

The *hypothesis* was the following: with controls for two basic demographic variables (gender and age), a prevalent risk factor (substance use), and a resilience-oriented protective factor (the youth's perception of the quality of his or her relationship with the foster mother or other female caregiver), we predicted that more frequent participation in SVAs would be associated with higher levels of self-esteem, pro-social behaviour, and happiness about the present and optimism about the future. The *research question* was as follows: with controls for the same demographic, risk, and protective factors, we asked whether the risk factor (substance use) or the protective factor (relationship with the female caregiver) would moderate (i.e., affect the strength of) the hypothesized relationship between the frequency of participation in SVAs and the three psychological outcomes. In a series of cross-sectional analyses, we tested the hypothesis by means of multiple regression and explored the research question through moderated hierarchical regression.

Method

Sample

The sample was composed of 442 young people living in out-of-home care in the province of Ontario in 2001-2002. Fifty per cent were males and 50% females, and they ranged in age from 10 to 17 years ($M = 13.55$, $SD = 2.20$).

The vast majority (82%) were living in foster homes, with another 9% in group homes, 3% in kinship care, 2% in independent living, 3% in other types of settings (e.g., psychiatric or young offenders' facilities), and 1% in unknown types of settings (on which data were missing). The young people had experienced serious adversity in their families of origin, including parental incapacity, physical, sexual, or psychological abuse, neglect, or abandonment. About 90% were "Crown wards," legal custody for whom had been transferred permanently to the government of Ontario. The government, in turn, had delegated the day-to-day exercise of its parental responsibilities to the local Children's Aid Societies taking part in the research.

Procedures

Data collection procedure. The sample was drawn from a larger group of young people who were in the care of 23 local Children's Aid Societies (CASs) in Ontario during 2001-2002. The CASs were partners in a larger longitudinal study (Flynn, Angus, Aubry, & Drolet, 1999) of the implementation and outcomes of Looking after Children: Good Parenting, Good Outcomes. Looking After Children is a new approach to out-of-home care, originally developed in the UK, that aims to improve outcomes through enhancing the quality of substitute or "corporate" parenting (Ward, 1995). Each participating CAS had agreed to use the second Canadian adaptation of the Assessment and Action Record (AAR-C2; Flynn, Ghazal, & Legault, 2004) from Looking After Children to assess the needs and monitor the progress of 25 children or adolescents in its care, or 10% of its in-care caseload, whichever was greater. Each CAS had agreed to select, as much as possible, young people who were likely to remain in care for the duration of the three-year study. The choice of which young people and child welfare workers would participate was left up to the CAS. After receiving training in the Looking After Children approach, the young person's child welfare worker used the AAR-C2 in a conversational interview that typically included the child and his or her caregiver (i.e., foster parent or group home worker) and covered 1 to 4 sessions.

Imputation of missing values procedure. The rate of missing data in the multi-item measures to be described later was low to very low (i.e., in the 0–5% range, and usually in the 1–3% range). We followed the recommendation of Schafer and Graham (2002) by imputing missing values with the EM (Expectation-Maximization) algorithm. EM provides maximum-likelihood estimates and is an option in the SPSS missing-values routine.

Instrument: Second Canadian adaptation of the Assessment and Action Record (AAR-C2)

The AAR-C2 (Flynn et al., 2004), like the original version of the AAR developed in the UK (Ward, 1995), covers seven Looking After Children outcome domains: health, education, identity, family and social relationships, social presentation, emotional and behavioural development, and self-care skills. The participants in the present sample were assessed with the AAR-C2 forms intended either for youths aged 10-14 or for those 15 years and over. To enable comparisons of the functioning of young people in out-of-home care with that of their age peers in the general Canadian population, the AAR-C2 incorporates numerous standardized items and multi-item scales from the National Longitudinal Survey on Children and Youth (NLSCY). This measurement strategy was adopted to allow the construction of population-based "growth charts" for young people in care on numerous outcomes, to facilitate the study of developmental progress and resilience among these youths. This strategy is also consistent with the basic principle of Looking After Children that outcome targets and expectations for young people in care should be set on the same level as those for young people in the general population, even though the needs of young people in care may often be greater.

Measures

Self-esteem. In the AAR-C2, self-esteem is part of the identity developmental dimension. Self-esteem was assessed by means of an eight-item scale, with the young people in care responding to each item by stating how closely they felt it described them. Sample items were "In general, I like the way I am," and "Other kids think that I am good looking." The scale had an internal consistency (Cronbach's alpha) of .87.

Pro-social behaviour. Part of the emotional and behavioural development section of the AAR-C2, the pro-social behaviour scale consisted of 10 items assessing the degree to which the young person saw himself or herself as helpful or considerate towards other young people who were in some type of need or difficulty. Sample items included "I try to help someone who has been hurt," and "I comfort another young person [friend, brother, or sister] who is crying or upset." Internal consistency (Cronbach's alpha) was .83.

Happiness/optimism. Two items from the identity section of the AAR-C2 made up this two-item scale, to which the young person responded. The items were "I am happy with how things are for me in my life now," and

"The next five years look good to me." Internal consistency was .72.

Substance use. Three items from the health section of the AAR-C2 formed the substance-use scale. The young person indicated the monthly or weekly frequency with which he or she currently smoked cigarettes, drank alcohol, or used marijuana or cannabis products. Internal consistency was .76.

Relationship with the female caregiver. A four-item scale from the family and social relationships section of the AAR-C2 was used to assess the young person's perception of the quality of his or her relationship with the female caregiver (i.e., foster mother or group home worker). The female rather than male caregiver was chosen to maximize sample size, as there were considerably more female than male caregivers. Sample items included "How well do you feel that your foster mother (or other female caregiver) understands you?" and "How much affection do you receive from your foster mother (or other female caregiver)?" Internal consistency was .80.

Index of frequency of participation in structured voluntary activities. This index was constructed from the six SVA items listed in Table 1 and taken from the education section of the AAR-C2. In terms of the classification of types of attendance measures developed by Chaput et al. (2004) in their research on out-of-school time activities, our six-item index was a measure of the *intensity* of participation in SVAs, because it assessed the cumulative number of times in an average week that the young person engaged in one or more of the six activities during the preceding 12-month period. The members of the sample reported participating in SVAs about seven times per week, on average ($M = 6.93, SD = 3.25$).

In addition, following a recommendation by Chaput et al. (2004), we also constructed a *breadth* measure of participation by counting the number of *different* SVAs in which each young person had been involved in an average week during the past year. The participants reported an average of between three and four different activities per week ($M = 3.52, SD = 1.54$).

The intensity and breadth indexes of participation proved to be extremely highly correlated (r [442] = .91, $p < .001$). After preliminary analyses had shown that the frequency (intensity) index was slightly more highly and more systematically correlated with the three psychological outcomes than was the breadth measure, we decided to use it alone in the present study. In other research contexts, however, with a different set of outcome measures, the breadth index, or a combination of the intensity and breadth measures, might be preferable (see Chaput et al., 2004).

Results

Frequency of participation in SVAs

Table 1 shows the frequency of participation in each of the six types of activities composing the index. Playing sports or carrying out physical activities without a coach or instructor was easily the most common activity, with 47% of the sample reporting a frequency of four or more times a week and 78% a frequency of at least once a week. On the other hand, half or more of the young people said that, outside of gym or others classes at school, they never took part in three of the six types of activities: art, drama or music groups, clubs or lessons (66% said "never"); dance, gymnastics, karate, or other groups or lessons (61%); and Guides or Scouts, 4-H club, community, church or other religious groups (50%).

Table 1. Frequency of weekly participation (in percentages) in six structured voluntary activities by young people in out-of-home care (*N* = 442)

Activity	Number of times per week (%)				
	4+	1–3	< 1	Never	Total
Outside of school, in the last 12 months, how often [per week] have you:					
1. Played sports or done physical activities *without* a coach or an instructor (e.g., biking, skate boarding, softball during recess, etc.)?	47	31	11	11	100
2. Played sports *with* a coach or instructor, other than for gym class (e.g., swimming lessons, baseball, hockey, school teams, etc.)?	8	40	11	41	100
3. Taken part in dance, gymnastics, karate or other groups or lessons, other than in gym class?	1	25	13	61	100
4. Taken part in art, drama, or music groups, clubs or lessons, outside of class?	4	20	10	66	100
5. Taken part in clubs or groups such as Guides or Scouts, 4-H club, community, church or other religious groups?	1	35	14	50	100
6. Done a hobby or craft (drawing, model building, etc.)?	17	33	30	20	100

Inter-correlations of study variables

Table 2 displays the inter-correlations among the study variables. The index of frequency of participation in SVAs was positively, significantly, but only modestly related to the three psychological outcomes. The latter were positively and significantly correlated with one another, although two of the three associations were weak. The frequency of participation in SVAs was negatively related to age and substance use, but positively to the young person's relationship with his or her female caregiver. Females had higher levels of pro-social behaviour. Older youths participated less frequently in SVAs and were also considerably more likely to engage in substance use. The role of substance use as a risk factor was underlined by its negative correlation with two of the psychological outcomes, self-esteem and happiness/optimism, and with the quality of the young person's relationship with the female caregiver. Conversely, the latter was significantly and positively correlated with all three positive psychological outcomes, consistent with its role as a protective factor.

Table 2. Means (or percentages), standard deviations, and inter-correlations for study variables ($N = 442$)

Variables	1	2	3	4	5	6	7	8
1. Self-esteem	—							
2. Pro-social behaviour	24***	—						
3. Happiness/optimism	47***	18***	—					
4. Gender (1 = male, 0 = female)	01	−27***	−02	—				
5. Age (years)	−17***	02	−08	−06	—			
6. Substance use	−18***	−04	−25***	−02	56***	—		
7. Relationship with female caregiver	34***	28***	46***	−04	−18***	−30***	—	
8. Index of frequency of participation in SVAs	20***	15***	20***	−01	−42***	−30***	21***	—
Mean (or percentage)	24.83	12.62	4.46	50%	13.55	3.52	6.52	6.93
SD	5.65	4.05	1.25	—	2.20	4.47	1.85	3.25

Note: Decimals omitted in correlations. SVAs = structured voluntary activities.

*$p < .05$ **$p < .01$ ***$p < .001$

Hypothesis test: Regression analyses

Table 3 shows the results of the regression analyses for the three outcomes. In each regression, following an initial run, we eliminated as multivariate outliers any cases with standardized residuals larger than ± 3.3 (Tabachnick & Fidell, 1996). In all three regression models, with controls for the demographic, risk, and protective factors, the frequency of participation in SVAs was a positive and significant predictor of better psychological outcomes, although the size of the beta coefficients was modest, ranging between .10 and .14. The protective factor—the young person's relationship with the female caregiver—was a positive and significant predictor of all three psychological outcomes, with sizable beta coefficients (.26 to .42). The risk factor—substance use—was a significant and negative predictor of happiness/optimism but was unrelated to the other two outcomes. Finally, female gender predicted greater pro-social behaviour.

Table 3. Multiple regression of positive psychological outcomes on demographic, risk, protective, and frequency-of-participation predictors

	Outcomes		
	Self-Esteem (N = 437)	Pro-Social Behaviour (N = 442)	Happiness/Optimism (N = 440)
Gender (1 = male, 0 = female)	.03	−.26***	−.01
Age (years)	−.06	.10	.12*
Substance use	−.03	.01	−.16**
Relationship with female caregiver	.30***	.26***	.42***
Index of frequency of participation in SVAs	.12*	.14**	.10*
R^2	.15***	.16***	.25***
Adjusted R^2	.14	.15	.24

Note: N is less than 442 in two of the three regressions because of the removal of outliers. SVAs = structured voluntary activities. Coefficients for the predictors, in the three columns, are beta (β) coefficients (i.e., standardized partial regression coefficients).

*$p < .05$ **$p < .01$ ***$p < .001$

Research question: Moderated regression analyses

We investigated the exploratory research question through the use of moderated regression analyses (Baron & Kenny, 1986; Cohen & Cohen, 1975) to discover whether the strength of the positive relationship found in testing the hypothesis between the frequency of participation in SVAs and the psychological outcomes was moderated by (i.e., varied with the level of) the risk factor (substance use) or the protective factor (the relationship with the female caregiver). At step 1 in a series of hierarchical regressions, we entered the predictors listed in Table 3, and then added, at step 2, a multiplicative term formed by multiplying the index of frequency of participation in SVAs by either the risk factor or the protective factor. We concluded that moderation was present when the addition of the multiplicative term produced a statistically significant increment in the amount of variance accounted for in any of the psychological outcomes.

We found no evidence of moderation in the regressions in which the protective factor was part of the multiplicative term. We did find evidence of moderation, however, in two of the three regressions in which the risk factor was a component of the multiplicative term, namely, in those for self-esteem and pro-social behaviour. First, in the regression for self-esteem, the addition at step 2 of the frequency-of-participation X substance-use multiplicative term produced a significant increment in the variance explained (ΔF [1, 430] = 4.15, $p < .05$). Follow-up analyses (see Cohen & Cohen, 1975, pp. 310–314, for a detailed discussion) revealed that the *lower* the level of substance use among the young people in out-of-home care, the *stronger* the positive association was between the frequency of participation in SVAs and self-esteem, and vice versa. Thus, when the level of substance use was *very low* (i.e., zero), the metric (i.e., unstandardized or *B*) coefficient for the regression of self-esteem on frequency of participation in SVAs was 0.33, indicating that for each unit increase in the frequency of participation, there was an increase in self-esteem of 0.33 units. When substance use was *average* (i.e., at the sample mean), the metric coefficient for frequency of participation was 0.21. And, when substance use was *high* (i.e., +1 *SD* above the sample mean), the metric coefficient for frequency of participation was nearly zero (0.05). These results meant that the average metric coefficient of 0.19 (which [not shown] is the unstandardized coefficient corresponding to the standardized beta coefficient of .12 in Table 3) had to be interpreted in light of the moderating effect of the level of substance use. Specifically, the average metric coefficient of 0.19 *underestimated* the strength of the relationship between the frequency of participation in SVAs and self-esteem when substance use was *low*, but *overestimated it* when substance use was *high*.

The second instance of moderation was found in the regression for pro-social behaviour. At step 2, the addition of the frequency-of-participation X substance-use multiplicative term produced a significant increment in the amount of variance explained in pro-social behaviour ($\Delta F[1, 435] = 3.89$, $p < .05$). Follow-up analyses showed that the *lower* the level of substance use, the *stronger* the positive association was between the frequency of participation and pro-social behaviour, and vice versa. Thus, when substance use by the young person was *very low* (zero), the metric coefficient for the regression of pro-social behaviour on the frequency of participation was 0.27, such that a one-unit increase in the frequency of participation was associated with an increase of .27 units in pro-social behaviour. When substance use was *average* (at the sample mean), the metric coefficient for frequency of participation was 0.19, and when substance use was *high* (+1 *SD* above the sample mean), the metric coefficient for frequency of participation was close to zero (0.07). These findings revealed that the average metric coefficient of 0.18 (i.e., the unstandardized metric coefficient [not shown] corresponding to the standardized beta coefficient of .14 in Table 3) *underestimated* the strength of the relationship between the frequency of participation and pro-social behaviour when the level of substance use was *low* but *overestimated* it when the level of substance use was *high*.

Discussion

Overall, the results supported our hypothesis that, net of the other predictors, the frequency (intensity) of participation in SVAs would be significantly and positively associated with the three psychological outcomes examined. However, these were average results for the sample as a whole that had to be qualified because the results of the exploratory research question showed that the risk factor of substance use moderated the strength of the relationship between participation and the outcomes of self-esteem and pro-social behaviour.

In line with the hypothesis, more frequent participation in SVAs positively and significantly (although only modestly) predicted better outcomes on self-esteem, pro-social behaviour, and happiness/optimism. These results contribute to the very limited amount of quantitative research on the role of healthy activities in promoting resilience among young people in care and are also consistent with the general resilience literature. Masten and Reed (2002), for example, have noted that the latter points to participation in pro-social organizations (i.e., school or community clubs, Guides or Scouts, etc.) as a recurring protective factor for children and adolescents at risk.

The findings from the moderated regressions added useful interpretive detail to the average picture emerging from the hypothesis test. Specifically, the frequency of participation in SVAs showed itself to be, in two out of three cases, a "protective but reactive" factor (Luthar, Cicchetti, & Becker, 2000), in that the psychological advantage of participation, clearly present when the level of risk (substance use) was low, virtually disappeared when the level of risk was high.

In the Looking After Children: Good Parenting, Good Outcomes framework, the immediate objective and key to improved short-term and long-term developmental outcomes is the enhancement of the quality of substitute or "corporate" parenting. A number of our findings are relevant to this issue. Most important, the young person's perception of the quality of his or her relationship with the female caregiver emerged as the best and most consistent predictor of positive psychological outcomes. This is congruent with Masten and Reed's (2002) comment that "The best-documented asset of resilient children is a strong bond to a competent and caring adult, who need not be a parent. For children who do not have such an adult involved in their lives, this is the first order of business" (p. 83). Second, this same protective factor was associated with lower levels of substance use and more frequent participation in SVAs.

For potential program design and intervention purposes, some of the results involving gender and age are worth noting. Female gender, as expected, was positively related to more pro-social behaviour, and older age was moderately strongly associated with more frequent substance use and less frequent participation in SVAs. Finally, two of the psychological outcomes, self-esteem and happiness/optimism, emerged in the correlation matrix as possibly protective against substance abuse.

The present study had three limitations. First, our correlational findings do not allow us to infer that the frequency of participation in SVAs had a causal effect on psychological outcomes, although they render such an effect more plausible. Second, the data gathered by means of our multi-item measures were derived from a single source, namely, the young person in care. Common method variance may thus have accounted for part of the associations observed. Third, the measures of intensity and breadth of SVA participation were so highly correlated ($r = .91$) that we could use only one (the former), thus foregoing an opportunity to explore the suggestion by Chaput et al. (2004) that more than a single facet of participation should be assessed whenever possible.

Despite these limitations, the present study is one of the first in the child welfare literature to have examined, in a quantitative way, the relationship between the frequency of participation in healthy activities and psychological resilience among young people in out-of-home care. Moreover, we used a relatively large sample and standardized population-based measures. Future research on SVAs in child welfare should include some well-designed and adequately funded experimental studies, in which issues of causal influence may be clarified through the random assignment of young people to different SVA frequencies or types. Additional psychometric research on participation would also be useful, with the aim of deriving more fine-grained measures that would be capable of capturing, beyond intensity and breadth, the motivational and quality-of-engagement aspects of participation. Such substantive and methodological efforts would advance our understanding of SVAs as vehicles of positive adaptation.

Authors' note

We gratefully acknowledge the financial support for the Looking After Children in Ontario (OnLAC) project received from the Social Sciences and Humanities Research Council (strategic grant 828-1999-1008, awarded to Robert J. Flynn, principal investigator; co-investigators, Tim D. Aubry, Marie Drolet, and Douglas E. Angus). We are also grateful for the additional financial support received from the Ministry of Children and Youth Services of Ontario (grant made to the Ontario Association of Children's Aid Societies [OACAS]), Social Development Canada (grant made to the Child Welfare League of Canada [CWLC]), and Prescott-Russell Services to Children and Adults (PRSCA). We also thank our organizational partners—

OACAS, CWLC, PRSCA—and the local Children's Aid Societies, as well as the many young people, child welfare workers, supervisors, foster parents, and group home workers who participated in the OnLAC project.

References

Anderson-Butcher, D., Newsome, W. S., & Ferrari, T. M. (2003). Participation in boys and girls clubs and relationships to youth outcomes. *Journal of Community Psychology, 31,* 39–55.

Baron, R. M., & Kenny, D. A. (1986). The moderator-mediator variable distinction in social psychological research: Conceptual, strategic and statistical considerations. *Journal of Personality and Social Psychology, 51,* 1173–1182.

Beauvais, C. (2001). *Literature review on learning through recreation.* Ottawa, ON: Canadian Policy Research Networks Inc.

Chaput, S. S., Little, P. M. D., & Weiss, H. (2004). *Understanding and measuring attendance in out-of-school time programs.* Cambridge, MA: Harvard Family Research Project.

Cohen, J., & Cohen, P. (1975). *Applied multiple regression/correlation analysis for the behavioral sciences.* New York: Wiley.

Compas, B.E., Hinden, B.R., & Gerhardt, C.A. (1995). Adolescent development: Pathways and processes of risk and resilience. *Annual Review of Psychology, 46,* 265–293.

Flynn, R.J., Angus, D., Aubry, T., & Drolet, M. (1999). *Improving child protection practice through the introduction of Looking After Children into the 54 local Children's Aid Societies in Ontario: An implementation and outcome evaluation.* SSHRC Strategic Grant No. 828-1999-1008, funded under the Society, Culture and the Health of Canadians program. Ottawa: Centre for Research on Community Services, University of Ottawa.

Flynn, R.J., Ghazal, H., & Legault, L. (2004). *Looking After Children: Good Parenting, Good Outcomes. Assessment and Action Record* (second Canadian adaptation). Ottawa, Ontario & London, England: Centre for Research on Community Services, University of Ottawa, & Her Majesty's Stationery Office (HSMO).

Gilligan, R. (2000). Adversity, resilience and young people: The protective value of positive school and spare time activities. *Children and Society, 14,* 37–47.

Gilman, R. (2001). The relationship between life satisfaction, social interest and frequency of extracurricular activities among adolescent students. *Journal of Youth and Adolescence, 30,* 749–767.

Holland, A., & Andre, T. (1987). Participation in extracurricular activities in secondary school: What is known, what needs to be known? *Review of Educational Research, 57,* 437–466.

Kane, T. J. (2004). *The impact of after-school programs: Interpreting the results of four recent evaluations.* New York: W. T. Grant Foundation.

Larson, R.W. (2000). Toward a psychology of positive youth development. *American Psychologist, 55,* 170–183.

Larson, R., & Seepersad, S. (2003). Adolescents' leisure time in the United States: Partying, sports, and the American experiment. *New Directions for Child and Adolescent Development, 99,* 53–64.

Luthar, S. S., Cicchetti, D., & Becker, B. (2000). The construct of resilience: A critical evaluation and guidelines for further work. *Child Development, 71,* 543–562.

Mahoney, J. L. (2000). School extracurricular activity participation as a moderator in the development of antisocial patterns. *Child Development, 71,* 502–516.

Mahoney, J. L., & Cairns, R.B. (1997). Do extracurricular activities protect against early school dropout? *Developmental Psychology, 33,* 241–253.

Masten, A. S. & Reed, M.G. J. (2002). Resilience in development. In C. R. Snyder & S. J. Lopez (Eds.), *Handbook of positive psychology* (pp. 74–88). New York, NY: Oxford University Press.

Newman, T. (2004). *What works in building resilience?* Ilford, Essex, England: Barnardo's.

Offord, D. R., Lipman, E. L., & Duku, E. K. (1998). *Sports, the arts and community programs: Rates and correlates of participation.* Ottawa, ON: Applied Research Branch, Human Resources Development Canada.

Schafer, J. L., & Graham, J. W. (2002). Missing data: Our view of the state of the art. *Psychological Methods, 7,* 147–177.

Statistics Canada. (2001). National Longitudinal Survey of Children and Youth: Participation in activities, 1998/1999. *The Daily,* May 30, 2001.

Statistics Canada and Human Resources Development Canada. (1995). *National Longitudinal Survey of Children and Youth: Overview of survey instruments for 1994-1995, data collection cycle 1.* Ottawa, ON: Authors.

Tabachnick, B. G., & Fidell, L. S. (1996). *Using multivariate statistics* (3rd ed.). New York: HarperCollins.

Verma, S., & Larson, R. (2003). Editors' notes. *New Directions for Child and Adolescent Development, 99,* 1–7.

Ward, H. (Ed.) (1995) *Looking After Children: Research into practice.* London, UK: HMSO.

CHAPTER 14

Foster parenting practices and foster youth outcomes

Julie Perkins-Mangulabnan and Robert J. Flynn

Introduction

A good deal of research has investigated the relationship between parenting practices and child development in the general population. Nurturance, conflict resolution, and parent-child cohesion have frequently been linked to positive outcomes in children. *Parental nurturance,* the consistent display by parents of loving, warm and accepting behaviour toward their children, is seen by many researchers as one of the most important components of effective parenting (Jackson, Fisher, & Ward, 1996; Miller, Jenkins, & Keating, 2002). It has been found related, in children, to greater academic achievement, psychosocial maturity, pro-social behaviour, and social-relationship quality, as well as less psychological distress and delinquent behaviour (Chao & Willms, 2002; Landy & Tam, 1996; Steinberg, Mounts, Lamborn, & Dornbusch, 1991). *Conflict resolution,* the settling of family problems through calm and open discussion, providing reasons for decisions, and considering everyone's point of view, has been linked, in children and adolescents, to more positive motor, cognitive, and social development, better psychological adjustment, higher-quality social relationships (Landy & Tam, 1996; Tesser, Forehand, Brody, & Long, 1989), and lower risk of psychopathology (Kashani, Burbach, & Rosenberg, 1988). *Parent-child cohesion,* consisting of closeness and understanding between parents and children (Gribble et al., 1993; Morrison & Cooney, 2002; Paulson, Hill, & Holmbeck, 1991; Shaw & Dawson, 2001), has been associated, in children, with higher levels of academic achievement and pro-social behaviour (Cook & Willms, 2002; Griswold, 1986) and lower levels of anxiety, conduct disorder, and indirect aggression (Cook & Willms, 2002; Hofferth & Sandberg, 2001; Racine & Boyle, 2002).

In foster care, the relationship between foster parenting practices and foster child outcomes has received virtually no attention (Haugaard & Hazan, 2002), despite the fact that young people in foster care are at higher risk of psychological and behavioural difficulties, such as anxiety, depression, or physical aggression (Flynn & Biro, 1998; Hulsey & White, 1989; McIntyre & Keesler, 1986; Stein, Rae-Grant, Ackland, & Avison, 1994) as well as academic problems, including school dropout and grade failure (Flynn & Biro, 1998). Smith (1994) found that positive foster parenting practices, including nurturance, were unrelated to young children's internalizing difficulties or receptive vocabulary but were associated with greater social competence and fewer externalizing difficulties. Flynn, Perkins, Biro, Lemay, and Lalonde (1999) found that negative foster parenting practices, such as yelling, were associated with higher levels of physical aggression, emotional distress and anxiety, and indirect aggression in foster youths, although positive parenting was unrelated to these foster youth outcomes.

The present study was intended to contribute to the very limited amount of research on the relationship between foster parenting practices and outcomes among young people in out-of-home care. We expected that effective substitute parenting would contribute to the attainment of resilient outcomes by youths in care, based on the assumption that the effects of foster parenting are similar (even if not identical) to those of parenting in the general population. We derived three hypotheses, by analogy, from the general-population parenting research. First, we hypothesized that foster parenting practices would account for a statistically significant increment in the variance accounted for in each of several foster youth outcomes, beyond that accounted for by the basic demographic variables of foster youth gender and age and two contextual variables, namely, the duration of the young person's current foster placement and the number of children (whether foster children or not) in the foster parent's household. Second, we hypothesized that more frequent engagement by foster parents in nurturant or cohesive parenting practices would be associated with more frequent foster youth pro-social behaviour and less frequent emotional disorder, conduct disorder, or indirect aggression. Third, we hypothesized that more frequent engagement by foster parents in conflictual parenting practices would be associated with less frequent foster youth pro-social behaviour and more frequent emotional disorder, conduct disorder, and indirect aggression.

Method

Sample

The participants were 367 young people (185 females and 182 males) who in 2001-2002 were living in foster homes that were either administered by not-for-profit Children's Aid Societies (CASs) in the province of Ontario

(91%) or operated by for-profit organizations (9%) in Ontario from which the CASs purchased foster care services. The young people in care ranged in age from 10 to 17 years ($M = 13.40$, $SD = 2.19$, $Mdn = 13$). Some of the youths had entered the foster care system at birth, while others had been adolescents at the time of entry ($M = 7.87$, $SD = 3.76$, $Mdn = 8$). The reasons most often cited for the current admissions to care were caregiver capacity (30%), physical/sexual harm by commission (26%), harm by omission (16%), and abandonment/separation (15%). The designations of their current foster care placements were as follows: *regular* (63%), *specialized* (17%, for youths with special needs), *special treatment* (12%, for youths with especially challenging behaviour), *provisional* (6%, for youths in special arrangements such as kinship care); and *other* (2%). Most of the young people were wards of the province of Ontario, either Crown wards (88%) or Society wards (7%). They had been in their current placements for several years, on average ($M = 3.38$, $SD = 1.49$, $Mdn = 2$). Parental responsibility had been legally and permanently transferred from the families of origin to the government of Ontario in the case of the Crown wards and temporarily in the instance of the Society wards (most of whom were in the process of becoming permanent Crown wards). The government of Ontario, in turn, had delegated the day-to-day exercise of its parenting responsibility to the local Children's Aid Societies that were partners in the research. Most of the foster parents taking care of the young people had considerable experience as foster parents ($M = 7.88$, $SD = 6.87$, $Mdn = 6$). The total number of children in their households, including their own children as well as their foster youths, ranged from 1 to 8 ($M = 3.38$, $SD = 1.49$, $Mdn = 3$).

Procedures

Data collection procedure. The study sample was drawn from a larger group of young people in the substitute care of 23 local Children's Aid Societies (CASs) in Ontario during 2001-2002. The CASs were partners in a larger longitudinal study of the implementation and outcomes of Looking after Children: Good Parenting, Good Outcomes (Flynn, Angus, Aubry, & Drolet, 1999). Looking After Children is a developmentally oriented approach to out-of-home care that originated in the UK and has the goal of improving outcomes through enhancing the quality of substitute or "corporate" parenting (Ward, 1995). Each participating CAS had agreed to use the second Canadian adaptation of the Assessment and Action Record (AAR-C2; Flynn, Ghazal, & Legault, 2004) from Looking After Children to assess the needs and monitor the progress of 25 children or adolescents in its care, or 10% of its in-care caseload, whichever was greater. In light of the longitudinal nature of the research, each CAS had also agreed to select, as much as possible, young people who were likely to remain in care for the duration of the three-year study (2001-2004). The choice of which young people and child welfare workers would take part was left up to each local CAS. After receiving training in the Looking After Children approach, the young person's child welfare worker completed the AAR-C2 in the context of a conversational interview that typically included the youth in care, the foster parent who was most knowledgeable about the young person's daily routine and functioning, and the youth's child welfare worker. The conversational interview lasted from 1 to 4 sessions.

Imputation of missing values procedure. In the measures to be described later (in the *Measures* section), the rate of missing data at the item level was typically low to very low, in the 0-6% range, and most often in the 1-3% range. In imputing missing values, we followed Schafer and Graham's (2002) recommendation and used the EM (Expectation-Maximization) algorithm, an option in SPSS that provides maximum-likelihood estimates for missing values.

Instrument: Second Canadian adaptation of the Assessment and Action Record (AAR-C2)

Like the original version of the AAR developed in the UK (Ward, 1995), our version of the tool, AAR-C2 (Flynn et al., 2004), covers seven Looking After Children outcome domains: health, education, identity, family and social relationships, social presentation, emotional and behavioural development, and self-care skills. The participants in the present sample were assessed with the AAR-C2 forms intended for youths between 10 and 4 years of age or for those 15 years of age and over.

To enable ready comparisons between the functioning of young people in out-of-home care and that of their age peers in the general Canadian population, the AAR-C2 has incorporated numerous standardized items and multi-item scales from the National Longitudinal Survey on Children and Youth (NLSCY; Statistics Canada & Human Resources Development Canada, 1995). This measurement strategy allows comparisons, on many developmental outcomes, of the progress made by young people in care with that of their age peers in the general Canadian population. The availability of the general population of children and youths as a normative comparison group greatly facilitates the study of resilience among youths in care (Flynn, Ghazal, Legault, Vandermeulen, & Petrick, 2004). It is also consistent with the basic principle of Looking After Children that outcome targets and expectations for young people in care should be on the same level as those for young people in the general population, even though the needs of young people in care may often be greater.

Measures of foster parenting practices

It is important to note that in the AAR-C2, the foster parent rather than the foster youth was the respondent for the three parenting measures, whereas in the NLSCY, the youth rather than the parent responded to these measures. This was an exception to our general rule, according to which the source of information (i.e., the parent or the youth) for AAR-C2 measures was the same as in the NLSCY (for the same measures). We made an exception to this principle in constructing the parenting practice measures for two reasons. First, we wished to avoid a potentially negative reaction on the part of foster parents who, we feared, might have objected to what they may have seen as an evaluation of their parenting practices by their foster youths. Second, by obtaining data from two different sources, we wanted to avoid the "method effect" (i.e., inflated correlations) that would probably have been produced had the source of information been the same for the parenting practice and outcome measures.

Parental nurturance. We used factor analysis and reliability analysis to derive this six-item scale and the other two foster parenting scales to which the foster parents responded during the AAR-C2 conversational interview. It was a slightly shorter version of the original NLSCY nurturance scale, from which we omitted one item because it overlapped conceptually with an item in the parent-child conflict scale. The six-item scale had good internal consistency reliability in the present sample (Cronbach's alpha = .80). Sample items included "How often do you praise [your foster child]?" and, "How often do you make sure that [your foster child] knows that he/she is appreciated?" The response options, on a five-point scale, ranged between "Never" and "Always," with a total possible scale score between zero and 24. A higher score indicated more frequent use of a warmer, more nurturant foster parenting style.

Parent-child conflict. We derived this eight-item measure through psychometric analyses, omitting two items from the original 10-item NLSCY scale because they appeared to us to be ambiguous and lacking in construct validity in the context of foster care. The eight-item scale had acceptable internal consistency in the present sample (Cronbach's alpha = .75). Foster parents rated the frequency of their behaviour and that of their foster youths on items such as "We make up easily when we have a fight" (reversed) and, "When we argue, we stay angry for a very long time." The response options, on a five-point scale, ranged from "Not at all" to "Almost all or all of the time," with the total possible score running from zero to 32. A higher score indicated more frequent engagement in conflictual parenting.

Parent-child shared activities. We constructed this six-item scale as a shorter version of the original eight-item NLSCY parent-child cohesion scale. The first item that we dropped had ambiguous content and the second was not applicable to foster families. We changed the name of the scale to reflect the fact that the AAR-C2, like the NLSCY, had operationalized the concept of "cohesion" in terms of "shared activities." The six-item scale had a somewhat low but still acceptable level of internal consistency in the present sample (Cronbach's alpha = .64). Foster parents rated the frequency with which they engaged in shared activities with their foster youths. Sample items were "How many days a week do you watch television together?" and, "How many days a week do you do a family project or family chores together?" The six response options ranged from "Every day" to "Rarely or never," with a total possible scale score between zero and 30. A higher score signified more frequent shared activities.

Measures of foster youth outcomes

Preliminary factor and reliability analyses showed that the AAR-C2 youth outcome measures, taken from the NLSCY, could be used without change. As in the NLSCY, it was the youth who responded to these AAR-C2 outcome measures.

Pro-social behaviour. This scale, consisting of 10 items, had good internal consistency in the present sample (Cronbach's alpha = .84). Sample items included "I try to help someone who has been hurt" and, "I encourage other people my age who cannot do things as well as I can." The three response options for this scale and the other outcome scales were "Never or not true," "Sometimes or somewhat true," and "Often or very true." The total scale score could range from zero to 20, with a higher score signifying that the foster youth assisted or comforted other young people more frequently.

Emotional disorder. This eight-item scale had good internal consistency in the present sample (Cronbach's alpha = .81). Sample items included "I am unhappy, sad or depressed" and, "I worry a lot." The total score could range from zero to 16, with a higher score indicating more frequent anxious or depressive behaviour on the part of the foster youth.

Conduct disorder. This six-item scale had good internal consistency (Cronbach's alpha = .80). Sample items included "I get into many fights" and, "I am cruel, I bully, or I am mean to others." The total score could range from zero to 12, with a higher score indicating more frequent physically aggressive behaviour on the part of the foster youth.

Indirect aggression. This five-item scale had good internal consistency (Cronbach's alpha = .78). Sample items included "When I am mad at someone, I try to get others to dislike him/her" and, "When I am mad at someone, I say bad things behind his/her back." The total score could range from zero to 10, with a higher score indicative of more frequent indirect or "relational" aggression.

Data analysis

To test the study hypotheses, we used a two-step hierarchical regression procedure. At step 1, we regressed each of the outcome variables on two demographic variables (the foster youth's gender and age) and two contextual variables (the number of years the foster youth had been in his or her current placement, and the total number of children in the household in which the foster youth resided). (In preliminary analyses, we also explored two other contextual variables: the foster parent's educational level, and his or her years of experience as a foster parent. These were never statistically significant, however, and were dropped.) At step 2, we added the three parenting practice variables to the regression model, to discover whether the three foster parenting practices would account for a statistically significant increment in each of the outcome variables, beyond the variance already explained by the four demographic or contextual variables. We also conducted exploratory moderated-regression analyses, to discover whether the demographic or contextual variables moderated (i.e., affected the strength of) the relationships between the three foster parenting practices and the four foster youth outcomes.

Results

Intercorrelations. Table 1 shows the correlations among the study variables, in the full sample of 367 youths (i.e., before the removal of outliers in two of the four hierarchical regression analyses). Gender was not related to any of the three parenting practices but was significantly correlated with three outcome variables: girls reported higher levels of pro-social behaviour and emotional disorder, whereas boys reported higher levels of conduct disorder. Age was significantly related to one foster parenting practice and two foster youth outcomes: older youths were less likely to be involved in parent-youth shared activities and also reported lower levels of conduct disorder and indirect aggression. The total number of children in the household was negatively related to one parenting practice, parental nurturance, and one youth outcome, emotional disorder. A greater number of years spent by the youth in his or her current placement was positively related to one parenting practice, parent-child conflict, and negatively to two youth outcomes, emotional disorder and indirect aggression.

Table 1. Intercorrelations among four demographic or contextual variables, three foster parenting practices, and four foster youth outcomes ($N = 367$)

Variable	1	2	3	4	5	6	7	8	9	10	11
1. Gender (m = 1, f = 0)	—										
2. Age (in years)	−08	—									
3. Total number of children in household	−15**	−06	—								
4. Youth's years in current placement	00	03	−03	—							
5. Parental nurturance	01	−04	−11*	01	—						
6. Parent-youth conflict	08	−05	−06	15**	−28***	—					
7. Parent-youth shared activities	08	−27***	−01	07	23***	−08	—				
8. Youth pro-social behaviour	−26***	01	−02	10	22***	−10	07	—			
9. Youth emotional disorder	−11*	03	−13*	−21***	−14**	14**	−08	−11*	—		
10. Youth conduct disorder	20***	−12*	00	−10	−15**	31***	04	−33***	34***	—	
11. Youth indirect aggression	−06	−17***	07	−17***	−17***	13*	04	−18***	35***	48***	—
Mean (or %)	49.59%	13.40	3.38	3.26	19.35	5.40	14.86	12.68	4.78	2.24	2.19
SD	—	2.19	1.49	2.90	2.77	3.98	4.65	4.08	3.31	2.35	2.19

Note: Decimals omitted in correlations.
*$p < .05$ (two-tailed) **$p < .01$ (two-tailed) ***$p < .001$ (two-tailed)

Of the parenting practices, nurturance was significantly correlated with all four youth outcomes, with greater nurturance predictive of more frequent pro-social behaviour, as expected, and less frequent emotional disorder, conduct disorder, and indirect aggression, also as expected. Greater parent-child conflict was not related to the youth's level of pro-social behaviour but, as anticipated, was associated with higher levels of the three negative outcomes. Finally, contrary to expectations, more frequent engagement in parent-child shared activities was not related to any of the youth outcomes.

Hierarchical regression analyses. In preliminary analyses, we carried out log and square-root transformations in the case of skewed variables, namely, years in current placement, parent-child conflict, conduct disorder, and indirect aggression. These transformations reduced skewness but produced unacceptably high kurtosis and, moreover, failed to eliminate all outliers. Thus, instead of employing data transformations, we adopted the alternative procedure of carrying out screening regression runs on the untransformed (i.e., raw) variables, examining the standardized residuals, and eliminating as outliers all cases that had standardized residuals larger than ± 3.3 (Tabachnick & Fidell, 1996). There were no outliers in the regressions for pro-social behaviour and emotional disorder, four in that for conduct disorder, and two in that for indirect aggression. The results of the regressions with the untransformed variables, in which any outliers had been removed, proved to be virtually identical to the regressions with the transformed variables. We thus report here only the findings obtained with the untransformed (raw) variables, because they are considerably easier to interpret.

As the note at the bottom of Table 2 indicates, the foster parenting practices, introduced as a set at step 2, accounted for a significant increment in the variance in each of the youth outcomes beyond that accounted for by the demographic variables of gender and age and the contextual variables of total number of children in the household and the number of years the child had been in the current placement. The increments due to the set of three foster parenting practices were 5% in the case of youth pro-social behaviour, 4% for emotional disorder, 11% for conduct disorder, and 5% for indirect aggression.

Regarding the predictive power of the demographic and contextual variables, at step 2 male gender predicted less frequent pro-social behaviour and lower emotional disorder ($p < .06$), as well as greater conduct disorder. Older age was associated with lower indirect aggression, whereas a larger number of children in the household predicted more frequent emotional disorder. A longer time spent by the youth in the current placement was related to greater pro-social behaviour ($p < .06$) and lower emotional disorder, conduct disorder, and indirect aggression.

Concerning the three foster parenting practices as predictors, a higher level of nurturance was associated with greater pro-social behaviour and lower conduct disorder and indirect aggression. Greater parent-child conflict predicted higher levels of all three negative foster youth outcomes, emotional disorder, conduct disorder, and indirect aggression. Finally, the level of parent-child shared activities was unrelated to any of the outcomes.

Moderated regression analyses. We explored the possibility that the demographic and contextual variables may have moderated (i.e., affected the strength of) the relationship between the foster parenting practices and the foster youth outcomes. We formed multiplicative terms by multiplying each of the three parenting practices by each of the demographic and contextual variables (i.e., by the potential moderators [Baron & Kenny, 1986]). For each potential moderator (e.g., gender), we entered the set of three multiplicative terms involving that variable as an additional (i.e., third) step in the previously described regression equations, for each of the four youth outcomes. In no instance did the set of multiplicative terms account for a statistically significant increment in the amount of variance explained in any of the four youth outcomes. Thus, there was no evidence that the demographic or contextual variables moderated the relationship between the foster parenting practices and the foster youth outcomes.

Discussion

Overall, the results provided some, albeit mixed, support for our hypotheses. On the one hand, there were three supportive findings. First, the three foster parenting variables, as a set, did indeed account for a statistically significant increment in the variance explained in each of the youth out-

Table 2. Summary of hierarchical regression of four foster youth outcomes on four demographic or contextual variables and three foster parenting practices

Step and Predictors	Youth pro-social behaviour ($N = 367$)	Youth emotional disorder ($N = 367$)	Youth conduct disorder ($N = 363$)	Youth indirect aggression ($N = 365$)
Step 1				
Gender (m = 1, f = 0)	−.27***	−.09	.22***	−.07
Age	−.02	.04	−.11*	−.17***
Total number of children in household	−.06	.11*	.04	.04
Youth's years in current placement	.10[a]	−.21**	−.10[a]	−.16**
Step 2				
Gender (m = 1, f = 0)	−.27***	−.10[a]	.19***	−.09
Age	.00	.04	−.09	−.15**
Total number of children in household	−.04	.11*	.04	.03
Youth's years in current placement	.10[a]	−.23***	−.14**	−.18***
Parental nurturance	.19***	−.08	−.11*	−.18***
Parent-youth conflict	−.04	.16**	.30***	.11*
Parent-youth shared activities	.04	−.02	.03	.06

Note: In the regressions for conduct disorder and indirect aggression, the sample size (N) was less than 367 because outliers had been removed. Coefficients are beta (β) coefficients (i.e., standardized partial regression coefficients). In the hierarchical regression for pro-social behaviour, $R^2 = .08$ ($p < .001$) for step 1; $\Delta R^2 = .05$ ($p < .001$) for step 2. For emotional disorder, $R^2 = .07$ ($p < .001$) for step 1; $\Delta R^2 = .04$ ($p < 001$) for step 2. For conduct disorder, $R^2 = .07$ ($p < .001$) for step 1; $\Delta R^2 = .11$ ($p < .001$) for step 2. For indirect aggression, $R^2 = .06$ ($p < .001$) for step 1; $\Delta R^2 = .05$ ($p < .001$) for step 2.

*$p < .05$ (two-tailed) **$p < .01$ (two-tailed) ***$p < .001$ (two-tailed) [a]$p < .06$ (two-tailed)

comes, beyond that accounted for by the demographic and contextual variables. Moreover, these significant increments were not attributable to the use of a single source of information (i.e., to method variance), given that the foster parents provided the information on the parenting practices whereas the foster youths furnished the data on the outcomes. Second, parental nurturance was a significant predictor of more frequent pro-social behaviour and less frequent conduct disorder and indirect aggression. Third, parent-child conflict was a predictor of more frequent emotional disorder, conduct disorder, and physical aggression.

On the other hand, three results were contrary to our hypotheses. First, more frequent parental nurturance was unrelated to emotional disorder. Second, less frequent foster-parent engagement in conflict with their foster youths was unrelated to the frequency of the youths' pro-social behaviour. Third, more frequent participation by fosters parents in activities with their foster youths was unrelated to any of the youth outcomes.

The increments of between 4 and 11% in the variance in the outcomes attributable to the parenting practices were consistent, in that they were found for each of the outcomes. Except in the case of conduct disorder, however, these increments were relatively modest. This latter finding is congruent with the results reported in many general-population studies (Maccoby & Martin, 1983). Lamborn, Mounts, Steinberg, and Dornbusch (1991) and Steinberg et al. (1991), for example, found consistent but only modest effects of parenting in large samples of US adolescents. In addition, several specific factors in the present research context may also help explain the modest increments in the variance accounted for that we observed. First, the young people had been in their current placements for an average (median) of two years, such that the behaviour of many, like the parenting practices of many of their foster parents, may have stabilized, with the resultant low behavioural variability explaining the modest correlations observed. Stronger covariation between foster parenting practices and foster youth outcomes might be found during times of transition, such as during the first few weeks or months of a new placement. Second, it is possible that moderators other than those examined here (e.g., foster youth age at first admission to care, or reason for admission; foster parent gender, socio-economic status, ethnic match with the youth in care, or amount of training for the foster parent role; or nature of the foster care placement, such as regular vs. specialized) may moderate (i.e., affect) the strength of the relationship between foster parenting practices and foster youth outcomes. We intend to investigate these possibilities, both cross-sectionally and longitudinally, in future analyses of our growing data base. Third, the fact that our parenting data came from the foster parents, whereas the outcome data came from the foster youths, probably reduced or eliminated the inflated correlations that are likely to be present in studies in which either parents or youths serve as the single source of data.

The fact that neither age nor gender moderated the relationship between foster parenting practices and foster child outcomes was congruent with the results of other studies (e.g., Lamborn, Mounts, Steinberg, & Dornbusch, 1991). This finding was contrary to the meta-analysis of Rothbaum and Weisz (1994), however, who found that the association between the quality of parenting and the absence of externalizing difficulties was stronger among older children and preadolescent boys (although only in analyses involving mothers rather than fathers).

Regarding the contextual variables, a lack of prior research on these variables as moderators made interpretation of our exploratory results difficult. Moreover, in the wider parenting literature, the number of children in the household has been used mainly as a predictor rather than as a moderator. Cook and Willms (2002) found that this variable was associated with higher parental nurturance and cohesion, whereas Racine and Boyle (2002) found that it was unrelated to family functioning. The length of time the youth has been in his or her current placement, on the other hand, has been studied mainly as an outcome rather than as a predictor or moderator, in placement-disruption research aimed at identifying factors related to greater placement stability (e.g., Lipscombe, Farmer, & Moyers, 2003).

Another issue to be addressed in future analyses, when we have accumulated sufficient longitudinal data, is that of the causal direction of effects. For example, the fact that in the present study youths who had been in their current placements for a longer period of time had greater pro-social behaviour as well as lower levels of emotional disorder, conduct disorder, and indirect aggression may reflect either a beneficial effect of foster care (i.e., foster care may have led to improvements across the four youth behaviours), or a selection effect (i.e., more difficult youths may have been removed from foster care), or both. The cross-sectional nature of our data does not allow us to decide which of these possibilities is the most tenable. We plan to examine this issue in the future longitudinally.

How best to assess foster parenting practices in a scientifically valid and clinically feasible fashion should become a research priority, especially for the resilience-oriented Looking After Children approach, the subtitle of which ("Good Parenting, Good Outcomes") emphasizes the central role that foster parenting is assumed to play in improving foster youths' adaptation. In the present study, the measure of parent-child shared activities (our

NLSCY-derived operationalization of the construct of parenting cohesion) was unrelated to any of the outcomes. This finding was contrary to previous research which, although limited (Larson & Verma, 1999), has suggested that the frequency of certain parent-child activities is related to outcomes such as pro-social behaviour (Cook & Willms, 2002), emotional difficulties (Cook & Willms, 2002; Hofferth & Sandberg, 2001), and resilience to stress (Gribble et al., 1993). The fact that we did not find such links may be because shared parent-youth activities are simply not relevant to foster youth outcomes or, more probably, because of a lack of construct validity in our measure of this parenting practice. That is, the construct of parent-child shared activities (which has also been referred to as cohesion, engagement, or involvement) has been considered by some (Shaw & Dawson, 2001) to be poorly defined. As a result, we have only limited understanding of its most salient features, such as the key family aspects to be assessed, their duration, or the intensity of parental involvement in them (Cook & Willms, 2002; Larson & Verma, 1999). Thus, the results of our study may mean that the sheer *frequency* of shared activities is less important in foster care as a facet of parent-youth cohesion than the *quality and meaning* of such activities for the participants, especially the young person in care. Other studies point in this direction. Steinberg et al. (1991) stated that children's experience of their parents' behaviours is just as important, developmentally, as the way in which the parents characterize their own behaviours. Flynn, Robitaille, and Ghazal (2006) found that the perceptions of young people in care of their female foster parents as understanding, fair, affectionate, and close to them were very strongly related to the young people's satisfaction with their current placements ($r[409] = .73, p < .001$).

To improve the measurement of foster parenting in the AAR-C2, we have incorporated into the most recent (2005) revision of the instrument a new measure (answered by the foster parent) of the degree to which foster parents monitor the behaviour and peer relationships of their foster youths. We have also added a similar measure to which foster youths will respond. These new measures replace one (responded to by the foster parent) that had unacceptably low internal consistency in the present study, precluding its use. We hope that these and other ongoing improvements in the AAR-C2 will lead to enhanced understanding of the influence of foster parenting practices on resilient outcomes among young people in care. Important in its own right, this issue is crucial for Looking After Children, with its emphasis on the benefits of high-quality substitute parenting.

Authors' note

We gratefully acknowledge the financial support for the Looking After Children in Ontario (OnLAC) project received from the Social Sciences and Humanities Research Council (strategic grant 828-1999-1008, awarded to Robert Flynn, principal investigator; co-investigators, Tim Aubry, Marie Drolet, and Douglas Angus). We are also grateful for the additional financial support received from the Ministry of Children and Youth Services of Ontario (grant made to the Ontario Association of Children's Aid Societies [OACAS]), Social Development Canada (grant made to the Child Welfare League of Canada [CWLC]), and Prescott-Russell Services to Children and Adults (PRSCA). We also thank our organizational partners—OACAS, CWLC, and PRSCA—and the participating local Children's Aid Societies, as well as the many young people, child welfare workers, supervisors, foster parents, and group home workers who have been or remain participants in the OnLAC project.

References

Baron, R. M., & Kenny, D. A. (1986). The moderator-mediator variable distinction in social psychological research: Conceptual, strategic and statistical considerations. *Journal of Personality and Social Psychology, 51*, 1173–1182.

Chao, R. K., & Willms, J. D. (2002). The effects of parenting practices on children's outcomes. In J. D. Willms (Ed.), *Vulnerable children: Findings from Canada's National Longitudinal Survey of Children and Youth* (pp. 149–165). Edmonton, AB: University of Alberta Press.

Cook, C., & Willms, J. D. (2002). Balancing work and family life. In J. D. Willms (Ed.), *Vulnerable children: Findings from Canada's National Longitudinal Survey of Children and Youth* (pp. 183–197). Edmonton, AB: University of Alberta Press.

Flynn, R. J., Angus, D., Aubry, T., & Drolet, M. (1999). *Improving child protection practice through the introduction of Looking After Children into the 51 local Children's Aid Societies in Ontario: An implementation and outcome evaluation.* SSHRC Strategic Grant No. 828-1999-1008. Ottawa, ON: Centre for Research on Community Services, University of Ottawa.

Flynn, R. J., & Biro, C. (1998). Comparing developmental outcomes for children in care with those for other children in Canada. *Children & Society, 12*, 228–233.

Flynn, R. J., Ghazal, H., & Legault, L. (2004). *Looking After Children: Good Parenting, Good Outcomes, Assessment and Action Records* (second Canadian adaptation, AAR-C2.) Ottawa, ON, & London, UK: Centre for Research on Community Services, University of Ottawa, & Her Majesty's Stationery Office (HSMO).

Flynn, R. J., Ghazal, H., Legault, L., Vandermeulen, G., & Petrick, S. (2004). Use of population measures and norms to identify resilient outcomes in young people in care: An exploratory study. *Child & Family Social Work, 9,* 65–79.

Flynn, R. J., Perkins, J. N., Biro, C., Lemay, R. A., & Lalonde, D. (1999). *Foster parenting practices and foster child outcomes: Cross-sectional and longitudinal analyses.* Unpublished manuscript. Ottawa, ON: University of Ottawa, School of Psychology.

Flynn, R. J., Robitaille, A., & Ghazal, H. (2006). Placement satisfaction of young people living in foster or group homes. In R. J. Flynn, P. M. Dudding, & J. Barber (Eds.), *Promoting resilience in child welfare.* Ottawa, ON: University of Ottawa Press.

Gribble, P. A., Cowen, E. L., Wyman, P. A., Work, W. C., Wannon, M., & Raoof, A. (1993). Parent and child views of parent-child relationship qualities and resilient outcomes among urban children. *Journal of Child Psychology and Psychiatry, 34,* 507–519.

Griswold, P. A. (1986). Family outing activities and achievement among fourth graders in compensatory education funded schools. *Journal of Educational Research, 79,* 261–266.

Haugaard, J., & Hazan, C. (2002). Foster parenting. In M. H. Bornstein (Ed.), *Handbook of parenting. Volume 1: Children and parenting* (pp. 313–327). Mahwah, NJ: Lawrence Erlbaum Associates.

Hofferth, S. L., & Sandberg, J. F. (2001). How American children spend their time. *Journal of Marriage and Family, 63,* 295–308.

Hulsey, T. C., & White, R. (1989). Family characteristics and measures of behavior in foster and non-foster children. *American Journal of Orthopsychiatry, 59,* 502–509.

Jackson, S., Fisher, M., & Ward, H. (1996). Key concepts in Looking After Children: Parenting, partnership, outcomes. In S. Jackson & S. Kilroe (Eds.), *Looking After Children: Good Parenting, Good Outcomes reader* (pp. 5–17). London, UK: HMSO.

Kashani, J. H., Burbach, D. J., & Rosenberg, T. K. (1988). Perception of family conflict resolution and depressive symptomatology in adolescents. *Journal of the American Academy of Child and Adolescent Psychiatry, 27*, 42–48.

Lamborn, S. D., Mounts, N. S., Steinberg, L., & Dornbusch, S. M. (1991). Patterns of competence and adjustment among adolescents from authoritative, authoritarian, indulgent, and neglectful families. *Child Development, 62*, 1049–1065.

Landy, S., & Tam, K. K. (1996). Yes, parenting does make a difference to the development of children in Canada. In Statistics Canada & Human Resources Development Canada, *Growing up in Canada* (pp. 103–118). Ottawa, ON: Human Resources Development Canada & Statistics Canada.

Larson, R. W., & Verma, S. (1999). How children and adolescents spend time across the world: Work, play, and developmental opportunities. *Psychological Bulletin, 125*, 701–736.

Lipscombe, J., Farmer, E., & Moyers, S. (2003). Parenting fostered adolescents: Skills and strategies. *Child and Family Social Work, 8*, 243–255.

Maccoby, E. E., & Martin, J. A. (1983). Socialization in the context of the family: Parent-child interaction. In P. H. Mussen (Ed.), *Handbook of child psychology: Socialization, personality, and social development* (Vol. 4, pp. 1–101). New York: Wiley.

McIntyre, A., & Keesler, T. Y. (1986). Psychological disorders among foster children. *Journal of Clinical Child Psychology, 15*, 297–303.

Miller, F., Jenkins, J., & Keating, D. (2002). Parenting and children's behaviour problems. In J. D. Willms (Ed.), *Vulnerable children: Findings from Canada's National Longitudinal Survey of Children and Youth* (pp. 167–181). Edmonton, AB: University of Alberta Press.

Racine, Y., & Boyle, M. H. (2002). Family functioning and children's behaviour problems. In J. D. Willms (Ed.), *Vulnerable children: Findings from Canada's National Longitudinal Survey of Children and Youth* (pp. 199–209). Edmonton, AB: University of Alberta Press.

Rothbaum, F., & Weisz, J. R. (1994). Parental caregiving and child externalizing behaviour in non-clinical samples: A meta-analysis. *Psychological Bulletin, 116,* 55–74.

Schafer, J. L., & Graham, J. W. (2002). Missing data: Our view of the state of the art. *Psychological Methods, 7,* 147–177.

Smith, M. C. (1994). Child-rearing practices associated with better developmental outcomes in preschool-age foster children. *Child Study Journal, 24,* 299–326.

Statistics Canada & Human Resources Development Canada. (1995). *National Longitudinal Survey of Children and Youth: Overview of survey instruments for 1994-1995, data collection cycle 1.* Ottawa, ON: Authors.

Stein, E., Rae-Grant, N., Ackland, S., & Avison, W. (1994). Psychiatric disorders of children "in care": Methodology and demographic correlates. *Canadian Journal of Psychiatry, 39,* 341–347.

Steinberg, L., Mounts, N. S., Lamborn, S. D., & Dornbusch, S. M. (1991). Authoritative parenting and adolescent adjustment across varied ecological niches. *Journal of Research on Adolescence, 1,* 19–38.

Tabachnick, B. G., & Fidell, L. S. (1996). *Using multivariate statistics* (3rd ed.). New York: HarperCollins.

Tesser, A., Forehand, R., Brody, G., & Long, N. (1989). Conflict: The role of calm and angry parent-child discussion in adolescent adjustment. *Journal of Social and Clinical Psychology, 8,* 317–330.

Ward, H. (Ed.). (1995). *Looking After Children: Research into practice.* London, UK: HMSO.

CHAPTER 15

Costs and outcomes for looked-after children

Lisa Holmes and Harriet Ward

Introduction

Social services departments in the United Kingdom are accountable to central government and are required to provide annual statistical returns concerning the children for whom they provide a service. We therefore have extensive data sets on the placements and outcomes for children looked after. With virtually no private expenditure on social services in England, almost all child welfare placements are provided by the public sector. For many years the data on costs in children's social care have been regarded as insufficient; since 1999, local authorities have been required to provide information to the Government for "Best Value," a quality assurance initiative aimed at making better use of resources and increasing transparency of expenditure.

Not only national data sets, but also a wide body of research, have demonstrated that outcomes for looked-after children can be less than satisfactory. Although some do well, many children who spend long periods in care or accommodation achieve a poor standard of education (Jackson, 2001; Social Exclusion Unit, 2003). They may also become socially isolated (Millham et al., 1986; Bullock, Little, & Millham, 1993). Their health may be indifferent or poor, and emotional or behavioural difficulties may deteriorate during the period in which they are looked after (Butler & Payne, 1997; McCann et al., 1996; Ward et al., 2002).

Findings that seem to demonstrate disappointing outcomes for children who are placed in care or accommodation are compounded by information concerning the high costs of providing such a service. The numbers of children looked after away from home peaked in England and Wales at 96,000 in 1977 (Bebbington & Miles, 1989) and then started to decline; between 1988 and 1994 they fell by almost a quarter (Department of Health, 1999). However, this decline in numbers has been accompanied by an increase in costs per child, as those who are looked after remain in care or accommodation for longer periods (Department for Education and Skills, 2003). Particular concerns have been expressed about the widespread use of agency placements, which are often more costly than those provided by local authorities, although as yet providing little evidence of better outcomes (see Ayres, 1997). However, research by Sellick and Connolly (2002) suggests that when the exceptional needs of the children concerned and the services provided to meet those needs are taken into account, the disparities in costs are less extensive.

In an attempt to address many of the issues outlined above, the Government in England introduced the *Children in Need Census* in 2000, a census of all children who were either looked after or supported in families or independently by local authorities during a selected week. The aim was to collect information that assists local authorities to manage the services they provide and compare their performance. The data are also aggregated at a national level for monitoring and policy purposes. The Government has also funded a research initiative that complements the *Children in Need Census*. This initiative, "Costs and Effectiveness of Services for Children in Need," began in 1999 and aims to explore and explain variation in the use of resources and develop a better understanding of the cost and effectiveness of different interventions provided to children in need. The 13 studies funded under the initiative fall into three broad groups: children in the community, children who are or have been looked after, and general studies of resource use.

The remainder of this chapter will focus on the methodology and findings from one of the studies in the initiative, Costs and Consequences of Different Types of Child Care (Ward et al., 2004). The aims of the study were to assess how far variations in the cost of different types of placement are reflected in the quality of care experienced by looked-after children with different needs, and to use the findings to develop a methodology to enable local authorities to calculate the cost consequences of different types of placements and services.

Methodology

A prospective longitudinal study was undertaken, designed to explore both quantitative and qualitative data concerning the background, needs and experiences of a population of 478 children looked after by three matched pairs of local authorities between the first two *Children in Need Census* dates of February 2000 and October 2001. The sample was restricted to children aged 10 years and over and was weighted to include disproportionate numbers of children in residential units in order to provide sufficient data for meaningful analysis. Data on children's needs, experiences and the services they received were collected from local authority computer records (management information systems), case files and from structured interviews with the children and young people and their carers.

Costs methodology

The cost of providing a placement constitutes only a proportion of the total cost incurred by social services to look after a child. The remainder is associated with all the activities undertaken by social workers, managers and administrative staff to support the children during the time they are looked after.

The eight processes for which the unit costs were derived for this study are based on the nine case management operations that underpin the task of looking after children outlined in the Core Information Requirements, Process Model (Department of Health, 2001). These processes are set out in Table 1 below.

Table 1. Social work processes to support looked-after children

Process	
Process One	Decide child needs to be looked after and find first placement
Process Two	Care planning (including care plan, personal education plan and health assessment)
Process Three	Maintaining the placement
Process Four	Exit from care/accommodation
Process Five	Find a subsequent placement
Process Six	Review
Process Seven	Legal processes
Process Eight	Transition to leaving care services

Activity to support these processes was based on the policy and procedure documents supplied by the six local authorities participating in the study. Specific data were then gathered from structured group discussions with social services personnel to ascertain who carries out the identified activities to support the children and the time taken to complete them.

Information was obtained from 17 focus groups, attended by 104 social workers, 23 family placement workers, 13 team managers and 2 independent reviewing officers. This information was then verified at a workshop attended by representatives from four of the participating authorities; a follow-up questionnaire was also completed by representatives from five authorities. The average amount of time spent by each of the workers on each of the processes was then costed as a proportion of their salary and overheads using the schema outlined by Netten and Curtis (2003). The total activity was added together for each of the eight processes to calculate standard unit costs. In addition, the costs of providing the placement, including placement fees and allowances paid to carers, were added to the cost of maintaining the placement (Process Three).

Variations in activity

The focus group approach to gather information from social services personnel proved to be robust in that there was little variation between staff concerning the amount of time they spent completing standard tasks. However, substantial variations in activity were identified to support children with different needs and to arrange and support different placement types. Variations in local authority procedures and circumstances also had a bearing on the level of activity and therefore the costs of completing certain tasks.

Local authority factors

Local authority factors that led to variations in activity were attributed to local geography, policy and procedures, staffing, and the availability of resources. The geography of the authority was found to have an impact on the travelling times for statutory visits and other direct contact with the children and their families. For example, local authorities in England and Wales vary considerably in size. Staff identified that a visit to a child placed in a different area of a shire (i.e., county) authority can take a full working day, while travelling time in a small unitary authority was rarely more than 20 minutes.

Differences in authority procedures also had a bearing on the level of activity and therefore the costs of completing certain tasks. For example, there were substantial variations in the level of management at which decisions for funding agency placements were made.

Both the salaries paid to staff and the allowances paid to carers were found to vary between the authorities that participated in the study. Furthermore, all authorities reported difficulties in both recruiting and retaining front-line workers and managers. Consequently, some of the authorities were employing high numbers of temporary agency staff, resulting in increased expenditure on staffing.

Placement provision

The cost of providing a placement, including fees or charges, salary and capital costs along with all the activity to support the child were included in the unit cost of Process Three (maintaining the placement). This process was found to account for between 92% and 96% of the total cost of a care episode, although there were substantial variations in the cost of different placement types. The standard unit cost to maintain a child for a week in a residential placement was eight times that of the cost of foster care, nine and a half times that of a placement with friends or relatives, and twelve and a half times that of a placement with the child's own parents.

Placing children out of the area of the authority was also found to have an impact on costs. Supporting children in these placements was particularly expensive because of the travelling time involved for statutory visits, review meetings, and other direct contact with the child.

Child-related factors

Children's specific needs are likely to affect both the types of placement they are offered, and the additional support services provided by other agencies such as health, education, and mental health. Information from workers and managers indicated that the prevalence of children within the care population who display different identified needs (disabilities; emotional or behavioural difficulties; offending behaviour)—or combinations of them—is likely to have a direct impact on the cost of placements. Unaccompanied children seeking asylum were also identified as a group whose circumstances, rather than their attributes, engender a different pattern of costs. Of course, in any population of looked-after children, some children will display none of these additional support needs.

Prevalence of factors that potentially affect costs

Eleven groups of different costing profiles emerged according to the children's identified needs: five simple groups of children who displayed none or one of the additional needs expected to affect costs; and six complex groups of children who displayed two or more additional support needs. The findings indicated that the higher the proportion of looked-after children with complex needs in an authority, the greater the costs of providing care or accommodation.

Of the children in the sample, 129 (27%) showed no evidence of additional support needs—an important point to note both because the prevalence of such children in the care system is often ignored and because this is the group who are most likely to have relatively simple pathways through care, incurring few additional costs either to social services or to other agencies. Two hundred and fifteen (45%) of the children displayed one high support need; 124 (26%) children displayed combinations of two; and a very small group (10:2%) displayed combinations of three or more.

Care episodes

After standard unit costs for each of the eight processes were calculated and the variations outlined above were identified, it was then possible to calculate costs of care episodes, based on the frequency with which the processes occur, the placement provided, and the provision of other support services. Not all looked-after children will go through all the processes during a care episode, although all will go through Processes One to Four. In every case, a decision has to be made as to whether a child needs to be looked after, and a first placement has to be agreed and found. Decisions are based primarily on the core assessment, which has been costed separately, as a process outside this study (see Cleaver & Walker, 2004). When children are looked after, more specialist assessments should be made of their health, educational and developmental status. These assessments need to be linked to the overall care plan for a looked-after child, and to the placement plan, specific to each individual placement. In this study, they were included in Process Two (Care Planning). Once a child is in placement, work has to be done to ensure that both the carers and child are adequately supported (Process Three). There is also a process undertaken at the end of the care episode when the child ceases to be looked after (Process Four).

Additional processes are undertaken for some children: many will move to new placements during the time they are looked after (Process Five); under British legislation, those who remain looked after for a month or more will be subject to the review process (Process Six); and some will require legal interventions such as care orders (Process Seven). Young people in England and Wales who come under the provision of the *Children (Leaving Care) Act* 2000, will also be entitled to leaving care services (Process Eight). Some of these processes will be repeated as children remain in the care system and their progress is monitored or circumstances change.

Child A

Child A was aged 14 at the start of the study. He first became looked after at the age of six, as the result of neglect. Since then he has been placed with the same local authority foster carers, a placement that had lasted eight years by the start of the study. A care order was obtained in 1992. He completed his statutory schooling in summer 2001 and obtained seven GCSEs, six of them at Grade C or above. Child A attended mainstream school until summer 2000. He then progressed to further education to start an "A" level course. He has fortnightly contact with his birth mother and occasional contact with his elder brother.

Timelines

Costs for this study could therefore be calculated over specific periods of time. These can be translated into timelines that provide an illustration of the differences between costs, experiences and outcomes for individual children with different needs. The timelines depict the level of activity and the services provided by both social services and other agencies over 20 months. Furthermore, they also illustrate how costs can accrue over time when children show increasingly complex combinations of need.

Children with no evidence of additional support needs

Child A (see case study below) was one of the 129 (27%) children in the sample who showed no evidence of additional support needs. The children and young people in this group tended to incur lower costs and have the most positive outcomes. They experienced fewer changes of placement and were also more likely to be placed within the area of the authority, either in a kinship placement (with relatives or friends) or with local authority foster carers. The costs of placements and the eight social work processes to support these children in their placements are therefore likely to be lower than for children with more complex needs.

The timeline on this page provides an illustration of the placements, processes and services provided to support this young man during the time-

Timeline for Child A

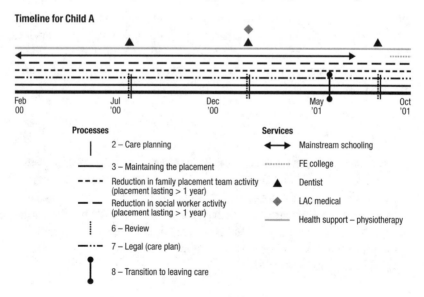

frame of the study and demonstrates how these might be costed. It is noteworthy that Child A had a relatively inexpensive placement with local authority foster carers. He incurred some educational costs, in that he attended school, and some health care costs, but there was no exceptional expenditure. Having been placed with the same carers since the age of six, he is likely to have developed a secure attachment while also retaining a relationship with one of his birth parents and a sibling. He is also likely to have gained maximum life chances from educational opportunities, and health and social care.

Table 2. Costs for Child A (1 pound sterling = $2.25 CAN. [June 2005])

Process	Cost to social services	Total £	Cost to other agencies	Total £
Care Planning	£104 × 3	312	£128 × 3	384
Maintaining the placement	£421 × 87 weeks minus £5,188 [1]	31,439		
Review	£353 × 3 + £10 [2]	1,069	£41 × 3	123
Legal	£ 4.10[3] × 87 weeks	357	£ 7.60[4] × 87 weeks	661
Transition to leaving care	£1,006	1,006		

Support service	Cost to social services		Cost to other agencies	
Mainstream schooling			£19.30[5] per day	5,501
FE College			£19.60[6] per day	608
Dentist			£ 6.50[5] × 3	19.50
Looked-after child			£ 21	21
Medical				
Physiotherapy			£ 44 × 87 weeks	3,828
Total	**£34,183**		**£11,146**	

1 This cost includes the payment made for the placement and all activity to support the placement. There is a reduction in cost as a result of reduced activity once the placement has lasted for more than one year.

2 An additional cost is incurred for the first 16+ review.

3 The cost of obtaining a care order has been divided over the total number of weeks between admission and the child's 18th birthday.

4 Costs taken from Selwyn, J., Sturgess, W., Quinton, D. & Baxter, K. (forthcoming) *Costs and Outcomes of Non-Infant Adoptions*, Bristol: Bristol University.

5 Costs taken from Berridge, D. *et al* (2002) *Costs and Consequences of Services for Troubled Adolescents: An Exploratory, Analytic Study*, Luton: University of Luton.

6 Provisional cost based on the cost of mainstream schooling taken from Berridge, D. et al. (2002) *Costs and Consequences of Services for Troubled Adolescents: An Exploratory, Analytic Study*, Luton: University of Luton.

Children with complex needs

The cost of looking after children may be substantially increased if they display a combination of additional support needs, both because they may require specialized, more costly placements and also because additional support services may be necessary.

Of the children who displayed a combination of additional support needs, the highest proportion were found to have both a disability and emotional or behavioural difficulties ($n = 46$, or 10%), or emotional or behavioural difficulties plus offending behaviour ($n = 72$, 15%). Information from social services personnel indicated that children with both a disability and who were displaying emotional or behavioural difficulties were the most difficult to place. They often required specialist placements provided by independent agencies.

Child G

Child G was aged 15 at the start of the study. He first became looked after at the age of 11 when his parents needed relief. This young man had a history of absconding from placements and had also been remanded to the care of the authority on one occasion prior to the start of the study. During the time he was looked after he had five separate placements in secure accommodation. He had also been placed in various residential homes, residential schools and foster placements, many of which had broken down. As a consequence he had been classified as "difficult to place" and there was evidence on his file that several residential units had refused to take him because of his behaviour. During the study period this young man refused all statutory medicals and dental appointments. He also refused any mental health support. He had a history of alcohol and drug use, including solvents, and smoked regularly. He had a statement of special educational needs but did not complete his statutory schooling because of numerous exclusions, school changes and non-attendance. Child G experienced four unscheduled school changes during the timeframe of the study. Prior to the start of the study, he had a history of offending; this continued throughout the study, during which time he committed 10 separate criminal offences. Because of his offending behaviour he was subject to a criminal supervision order. He ceased being looked after in summer 2001 when he refused to return to his placement, or any other placement provided by the authority, and he went to live with a family friend.

Child G (see case study above) is one of the 72 children and young people who were committing criminal offences and also had emotional or behavioural difficulties during the timeframe of the study. The timeline on the next page demonstrates the costs and experiences of this young man, although he ceased to be looked after three months before the end of the study. Costs to social services were extremely high, both because he moved through a number of very expensive placements, and because finding new placements involved a substantial amount of activity. Although he retained contact with family members, this young man had high additional needs and appeared to be alienated from all efforts to provide effective support.

Timeline for Child G

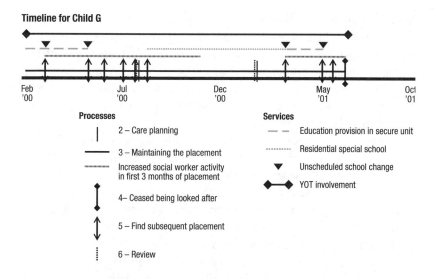

Processes

| | 2 – Care planning
—— 3 – Maintaining the placement
·········· Increased social worker activity in first 3 months of placement
↕ 4 – Ceased being looked after
↕ 5 – Find subsequent placement
⋮ 6 – Review

Services

— — Education provision in secure unit
·········· Residential special school
▼ Unscheduled school change
◆—◆ YOT involvement

Table 3. Costs for Child G

Process	Cost to social services	Total £	Cost to other agencies	Total £
Care Planning	£104 × 2	208	£124 × 2	248
Maintaining the placement	£202,221 plus £909[1]	203,130	£41 × 74 weeks[2]	3,034
Ceased being looked after	£228	228		
Find subsequent placements	£6724[3]	6,724		
Review	£353 + £705	1,058	£149 × 2	298
Support service[4]	**Cost to LA**		**Cost to other agencies**	
YOT involvement/ criminal costs			£841[5] × 74 weeks[2]	62,234
Total	**£211,348**			**£65,814**

1 This cost includes the payment made for the placement and all activity to support the placements. There is an increase in cost in the first three months of a placement due to increased social worker activity.

2 Child G ceased being looked after in July 2001, therefore the time period being costed is 74 weeks.

3 Child G experienced nine changes of placement during the timeframe of the study.

4 There are no additional education costs because these are included in the costs of the placements in Process Three.

5 Costs taken from Liddle, M. (1998) *Wasted Lives: Counting the Cost of Juvenile Offending*, London: NACRO.

Apart from the very small group of children who tended to skew the costs for the whole authority (see below), the costs for this group (children with emotional or behavioural difficulties and who were offending) were among the highest and outcomes the least favourable. The children in the sample with these identified needs experienced frequent changes of placement and were the least likely to complete statutory schooling; many of them had either been excluded from schooling or had chosen not to attend. Furthermore, these children were the least likely to access either routine or specialist health or mental health support, often because they refused input. For this group, a vicious circle could be identified whereby outcomes deteriorated as costs increased.

On average, the children with emotional or behavioural difficulties who were also offending were nearly two years older (when they started to be looked after) than those without any additional support needs. This finding corroborates those of other studies that suggest that concerns over both the potentially adverse outcomes and the spiralling costs had led some local authorities to overlook the increasingly damaging consequences of leaving children in circumstances detrimental to their well-being or of allowing them to return to them (see Packman & Hall, 1998; Sinclair, Baker, Wilson, & Gibbs, 2003; Ward et al., 2003). While there is increasing evidence that postponing the decision to place children and young people with this profile is a false economy in the long term, there is as yet no clear indication as to which interventions are most likely to meet their needs. Treatment foster care following the Oregon model is currently being piloted in England, and it is possible that this may prove to be a more successful type of placement than those currently on offer.

Child J

Child J was aged 15 at the start of the study. He has both physical and learning disabilities, a rare genetic disorder and conduct disorder, and also displays challenging behaviour. He first became looked after before his first birthday. From then onwards he was continuously looked after under a care order and experienced 10 different placements. Four of these placements were with foster carers, and five in residential units. He also spent a night in a secure unit when an alternative placement could not be found. Nine placements were out of the area of the authority. He had previously absconded from placements and on one occasion committed a criminal offence. In order to meet his needs, he now has a placement in a specialist one-bed residential unit where he has two-to-one supervision at all times. He has a statement of special educational needs and has been excluded from numerous education provisions. During the timeframe of the study, he was receiving one hour a day of home tuition. He was also receiving mental health support (clinical psychologist). This young person has had no contact with his birth family for a number of years.

Skewed costs

Within each of the authorities there were a few children (around 2%) with very complex needs. Providing placements and associated support services for them could skew the budget for all looked-after children. This is particularly likely to happen where children displayed a combination of three additional support needs. Child J, whose case study is shown below, had both a disability and emotional or behavioural difficulties. He also committed a criminal offence within the timeframe of the study.

The costs of looking after Child J are shown below. They are markedly higher than for the majority of other children in the sample. The greatest amount of expenditure came from the series of residential placements and foster homes provided by independent agencies, the monthly charges for which ranged between £3,302 and £10,504 ($7,415 and $23,585 CAN. as at June 2005). These were out of the area of the authority, and therefore required high levels of social work time to support them. Due to the number of placements and the complexity of his needs, Child J was classified as "difficult to place" and increasing amounts of social work time had to be spent on finding the rare placements that were able to meet his needs or were prepared to accept him. The costs of changing placements for this young man were calculated at over £1,000 ($2,250 CAN.) per move.

Timeline for Child J

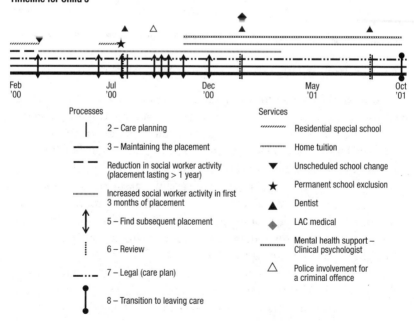

Table 4. Costs for Child J

Process	Cost to social services	Total £	Cost to other agencies	Total £
Care Planning	£52 × 3	156	£128 × 3	384
Maintaining the placement	£386,611 plus £992[1]	387,603		
Finding subsequent placements	£ 8,674	8,674	£70 × 8[3]	556
Review	£ 705 × 3	2,115	£302 × 3	906
Legal	£ 2.60[2] × 87 weeks	226	£4.70[4] × 87 weeks	412
Transition to leaving care	£1006	1,006		

Cost of services	Cost to social services		Cost to other agencies	
Home tuition			£ 33[5] per hour	6,270
Permanent exclusion			£ 112[6]	112
Dentist			£ 6.50[5] × 3	19.50
Looked-after child Medical			£ 21	21
Clinical psychologist			£ 69 per hour for 52 weeks	3,588
Police costs for criminal offence			£173[7]	173
Total		**£399,780**		**£12,443**

1 This cost includes the payment made for the placements and all activity to support the placements. There is an increase in cost in the first three months of a placement due to increased social worker activity.

2 The cost of obtaining a care order has been divided over the total number of weeks between admission and the child's 18th birthday.

3 Child J experienced eight changes of placement during the timeframe of the study.

4 Costs taken from Selwyn, J., Sturgess, W., Quinton, D. and Baxter, K. (forthcoming) *Costs and Outcomes of Non-Infant Adoptions*, Bristol: Bristol University.

5 Costs taken from Berridge, D. *et al* (2002) *Costs and Consequences of Services for Troubled Adolescents: an exploratory, analytic study*, Luton: University of Luton.

6 Parsons, C. and Castle, F. (1998) The Cost of School Exclusion in England. *International Journal of Inclusive Education*, 2 (4), 277-294.

7 Costs taken from Liddle, M. (1998) *Wasted Lives: Counting the Cost of Juvenile Offending*, London: NACRO.

Although the charges for some residential units included on-premises education for the six months before he was moved to his specialist placement at the end of the study timeframe, Child J was excluded from this provision. During this time, he received only one hour a day home tuition and one session a week with a clinical psychologist; these were not included in the placement charge. His very high additional support needs make it difficult to assess the impact of interventions on his education or his emotional or behavioural development; however, it should be noted that after 15 years of care, this young man had no contact with his birth family and no substitute relationships with carers.

Both the last two case studies (Child G and Child J) illustrate instances where young people have very high support needs, and it is difficult to assess how successful extremely costly services are in influencing long-term outcomes. There are several possible explanations why outcomes for these young people may appear to be unsatisfactory (see also Selwyn et al., forthcoming; Sinclair & Gibbs, 1998). It may be that service responses are too reactive—offering too little, too late, instead of responding proactively to need. It may also be that some placements are extremely expensive—not because they provide a high-quality service, but because they are the only provision that will take some children with very extensive needs. On the other hand, it might be that some children's needs are so great that almost any interventions will be ineffective.

Much of the difference in costs between these illustrative cases is attributable to the different types of placement that the children received. It is noteworthy that the children placed in residential units (Child G and Child J) incurred substantially higher costs than those in other groups. The two children also had numerous changes of placement during the study period, thereby incurring high (and therefore costly) levels of social work activity. There was no guarantee that the very expensive placements adequately met children's needs any more than did the less expensive placements with birth parents or relatives.

Messages for policy and practice

The findings from this research have implications for the development of policy and practice at both national and local levels and for the strategic planning of services. They demonstrate the importance of adopting a systems approach to analyzing the costs of looking after children. Authorities that place only a small number of children away from home may be restricting placements to those with high support needs and thereby incurring high average costs per child looked after. They may also need to increase expenditure on family support to meet the needs of children who otherwise have been placed in care or accommodation.

A systems approach should also demonstrate how costs are spread across agencies so that reducing the costs to one may increase the costs to another. Policies that promote better integration of both services and budgets should introduce greater transparency concerning how costs are divided and make it possible to consider how different configurations could improve the effective deployment of resources.

Authorities need to monitor how far reductions in costs represent true savings and how far they simply represent a failure to offer an appropriate and timely response to need. By being able to cost children's placements accurately, it is possible to compare the relative value, both in terms of costs and quality, of different packages of care. Accurate cost data can make it easier to compare the value of alternative options, such as replacing the very expensive residential placements with a package of specialist foster care, accompanied by extensive support from psychotherapeutic and special education services.

References

Ayres, M. (1997). *Report on the review of children's agency placements conducted during July and August 1997.* Suffolk: Suffolk Social Services Department.

Bebbington, A., & Miles, J. (1989). The background of children who enter local authority care. *British Journal of Social Work, 19,* 349–368.

Berridge, D. et al. (2002). *Costs and consequences of services for troubled adolescents: An exploratory, analytic study.* Luton: University of Luton.

Bullock, R., Little, M., & Millham, S. (1993). *Going home: The return of children separated from their families.* Aldershot: Dartmouth Publishing Company.

Butler, I., & Payne, H. (1997). The health of children looked after by the local authority. *Adoption and Fostering, 21,* 28–35.

Cleaver, H., Walker, S., & Meadows, P. (2004). *Assessing children's needs and circumstances: The impact of the Assessment Framework.* London: Jessica Kingsley Publishers Ltd.

Department for Education and Skills. (2003). *The Children Act report 2002.* Nottingham: DfES Publications.

Department of Health. (1999). *Children looked after by local authorities: Year ending 31 March 1998 England.* London: Department of Health.

Department of Health. (2001). *Children's social services core information requirements process model.* London: Department of Health.

Jackson, S. (Ed.) (2001). *Nobody ever told us school mattered: Raising the educational attainments of children in care.* London: BAAF.

Liddle, M. (1998). *Wasted lives: Counting the cost of juvenile offending.* London: NACRO.

McCann, J., James, A., Wilson, S. & Dunn, G. (1996). Prevalence of psychiatric disorders in young people in the care system. *British Medical Journal, 313*, 1529–1530.

Millham, S., Bullock, R., Hosie, K., & Haak, M. (1986). *Lost in care: The problems of maintaining links between children in care and their families.* Aldershot: Gower.

Netten, A., & Curtis, L. (2003). *Unit costs of health and social care 2003.* University of Kent: Personal Social Services Research Unit.

Packman, J., & Hall, C. (1998). *From care to accommodation: Support, protection and control in child care services.* London: The Stationery Office.

Parsons, C., & Castle, F. (1998). The cost of school exclusion in England. *International Journal of Inclusive Education, 2*, 277–294.

Sellick, C., & Connolly, J. (2002). Independent fostering agencies uncovered: The findings of a national study. *Child and Family Social Work, 7*, 107.

Selwyn, J., Sturgess, W., Quinton, D., & Baxter, K. (forthcoming). *Costs and outcomes of non-infant adoptions.* Bristol: Bristol University.

Sinclair, I., Baker, C., Wilson, K. & Gibbs, I. (2003). *What happens to foster children? Draft report.* University of York: Social Work Research and Development Unit.

Sinclair, I., & Gibbs, I. (1998). *Children's homes: A study in diversity.* Chichester: Wiley.

Social Exclusion Unit. (2003). *A better education for children in care.* London: SEU.

Ward, H., Holmes, L., Soper. J., & Olsen, R. (2004). *Costs and consequences of different types of child care provision.* Loughborough University: Centre for Child and Family Research.

Ward, H., Munro, E.R., Dearden, C., & Nicholson, D. (2003). *Outcomes for looked-after children: Life pathways and decision-making for very young children in care of accommodation.* Loughborough University: Centre for Child and Family Research.

Ward, H., Jones, H., Lynch, M., & Skuse, T. (2002). Issues concerning the health of looked-after children. *Adoption and Fostering, 26*(4), 8–18.

CHAPTER 16

Resilience and young people leaving care: Implications for child welfare policy and practice in the UK

Mike Stein

Introduction

This paper will explore the bridges and barriers to promoting the resilience of young people leaving care. It will begin by defining resilience and summarizing the factors associated with the resilience of young people from disadvantaged family backgrounds identified in the international literature. This will provide a framework for reflecting upon research studies of care leavers completed during the last 20 years, including those studies that have captured their experiences and views. The paper will adopt a life course perspective to consider the different stages of young peoples' journeys to adulthood: their lives in care; their transitions from care; and their lives after care. Finally, drawing upon this material, the implications for child welfare law, policy and practice in the UK will be discussed.

What is resilience?

Resilience can be defined as the quality that enables some young people to find fulfilment in their lives despite their disadvantaged backgrounds, the problems or adversity they may have undergone or the pressures they may experience. Resilience is about overcoming the odds, coping and recovery, that is, "positive patterns of functioning or development during or following exposure to adversity, or, more simply, good adaptation in a context of risk" (Masten, 2006, this volume). But resilience is only relative to different risk experiences—relative resistance as distinct from invulnerability—and is likely to develop over time (Rutter, 1999; Schofield, 2001). Also, as has been recognized by a review of the literature on self-esteem, single causal factors, although popular, usually oversimplify complex associations—for example, as discussed below, the close relationship between resilience and attachment theory (Elmer, 2001; Luther et al., 2000).

Why some young people cope better than others is complex, and there may well be innate and linked personal attributes we do not understand. In the UK, the resilience of young people from very disadvantaged family backgrounds has been found to be associated with a redeeming and warm relationship with at least one person in the family—or secure attachment to at least one unconditionally supportive parent or parent substitute; positive school experiences; feeling able to plan and be in control; being given the chance of a "turning point," such as a new opportunity or break from a high-risk area; higher childhood IQ scores; lower rates of temperamental risk; and having positive peer influences (Rutter et al., 1998).

A research review of the international literature on resilience factors in relation to the key transitions made by children and young people during their life cycle has added to this picture. As well as the first three factors identified above, the authors conclude that children and young people who are best equipped to overcome adversities, will have strong social support networks; a committed mentor or person from outside the family; a range of extra-curricular activities that promote the learning of competencies and emotional maturity; the capacity to re-frame adversities so that the beneficial as well as the damaging effects are recognized; the ability—or opportunity—to make a difference, for example, by helping others through volunteering, or undertaking part-time work; and exposure to challenging situations that provide opportunities to develop both problem-solving abilities and emotional coping skills (Newman and Blackburn, 2002a; 2002b).

But what of young people from care backgrounds? Although there have been some descriptive accounts and very useful practice guides (Gilligan, 2001) and an important study applying the concept of resilience to 40 adults who grew up in foster care (Schofield, 2001), there has been little exploration of research focusing solely upon the resilience of young people who have been in care and the implications of these findings for promoting the resilience of care leavers. To begin with, how has living in care helped or hindered young people?

Living in care

First, young people who experience stable placements providing good-quality care are more likely to have positive outcomes than those who have experienced further movement and disruption during their time in care (Biehal et al., 1995; Sinclair et al., 2003). Stability has the potential to promote resilience in two respects. First of all, by providing the young person with a warm and redeeming relationship with a carer—a compensatory secure attachment that may in itself reduce the likelihood of placement breakdown (Rutter et al., 1998). Second, and not necessarily dependent on the first, stability may provide continuity of care in young people's lives, which may give them security and contribute to positive educational and career outcomes (Jackson, 2002; Jackson et al., 2003). In promoting resilience, providing stability and continuity may be as important as secure attachment, depending on the age of the young person on entry to care and his or her history, including the quality of family relationships and links. Indeed, research on adoptions has shown that not all adopted children and young people are able to form secure attachments—but they can benefit from stability and continuity in their lives (Department of Health, 1999).

Conversely, instability is a barrier to promoting resilience, associated with poor outcomes. For too many young people, their experiences of care, far from helping them overcome the damaging emotional legacy of family problems, have rendered them unable to form the very relationships they need so much. A consistent finding of studies of care leavers since the 1980s has been the 30 to 40% of young people who experience four plus moves and within this group the 6 to 10% who have a very large number of moves—as many as 10 or more (Stein & Carey, 1986; Stein 1990; Biehal et al., 1995; Dixon & Stein, 2002).

The consequence of movement and disruption for many of these young people is to leave them emotionally polarized between dependence and independence and denied through their experiences of family and care the emotional flexibility to find satisfaction in a range of different relationships. As Downes has suggested in her study of attachment relationships in foster care, many of these young people have great difficulties in using other people's help: either they are only able to fend for themselves, or they repeatedly subvert their own efforts to cope and to make satisfying relationships. Her study showed that the difficulties young people had in making alliances with helpful adults and peers were likely to put them at a disadvantage when they were trying to make their way in the world as young adults (Downes, 1992).

Second, helping young people develop a positive sense of identity, including their self-knowledge, self-esteem and self-efficacy, may also promote their resilience. And although not explicitly recognized as a variable in the research literature on resilience, identity could be seen as connected to, as well as a component of, key associations: feeling able to plan and be in control; the capacity to re-frame adversities so that beneficial as well as damaging effects are recognized; personality—or lower rates of temperamental risk (Rutter et al., 1998; Newman & Blackburn, 2002a; 2002b).

Indeed, identity formation is an ongoing challenge for all young people, as society has become more complex in terms of industrial change, more consumerist in its ideals and less certain in class, gender, geographical and ethnic identities. In what has been described as today's "risk society," identity formation is a dynamic and reflexive process, less given and pre-determined—but it is a society in which the family plays a central and increasingly extended role (Beck, 1992; Giddens, 1991).

Helping care leavers develop a positive identity will be linked, first of all, to the quality of care and attachments experienced by looked-after young people—a significant resilience promoting factor discussed above; second, to their knowledge and understanding of their background and personal history; third, to their experience of how other people perceive and respond to them; and finally, how they see themselves and the opportunities they have to influence and shape their own biography. Research into young people leaving care has shown that the main barrier to helping them achieve a secure sense of identity, in addition to instability, is the failure of those entrusted with their care to help them understand *why* their parents had abused or neglected them or were unable to care for them, and how this had influenced subsequent events—to understand, if possible, their feelings of rejection and resentment (Biehal et al., 1995).

Family relationships are a major dilemma for many of these young people. They need and want to have a sense of family—not surprising given the centrality of "the family" in ideology, policy and practice—yet many have been damaged by their experiences (Biehal & Wade, 1999). They also need to be able to commit themselves to their carers and then move on to new relationships (Sinclair et al., 2003). In promoting their resilience, a deeper and more profound story is required, often through professional help, to assist many of these young people make sense of their past, including their fractured family relationships, and look to the future.

Third, having a positive experience of school (including achieving educational success) is associated with resilience among young people from disadvantaged family backgrounds and young people living in care (Rutter et al., 1998; Newman & Blackburn, 2002; Sinclair et al., 2003; Masten, 2006). Research studies completed on young people leaving care since the beginning of the 1970s show low levels of attainment and participation beyond the minimum school leaving age. Good outcomes are associated with placement stability, gender (young women do better than young men, as reflected in the UK national data), a carer committed to helping the young person, and a supportive and encouraging environment for study. This may also include the foster families own children providing help and acting as role models (Biehal et al., 1995; Department of Health, 2001; Jackson et al., 2003).

There is also evidence that young people who have had several placements can achieve educational success if they remain in the same school, and this also meant they were able to maintain friendships and contacts with helpful teachers. As well, late-placed young people who may have experienced a lot of earlier placement disruption can succeed in foster care, although this was seen by young people and their foster carers as more of a service relationship than a substitute family (Jackson et al., 2003). The main barriers to educational success identified by research studies included placement movement leading to a disruption in education, negative or unsupportive attitudes of teachers and carers, labelling young people as trouble makers, or patronizing them as deserving cases (Jackson, 2001; Stein, 1994).

Fourth, care or school itself may also provide turning points (Rutter et al., 1998), open the door for participation in a range of leisure or extra curricula activities that may lead to new friends and opportunities (including the learning of competencies and the development of emotional maturity), and thus promote their resilience (Newman & Blackburn, 2002). Indeed, resilient young people have often been able to turn their negative experiences at home, or in care, into opportunities, with the help of others.

Fifth, preparation for leaving care may also provide young people with opportunities for planning, problem solving and the learning of new competencies, all resilience-promoting factors (Rutter et al., 1998; Newman and Blackburn, 2002a; 2002b). This may include the development of self-care skills—personal hygiene, diet and health, including sexual health; practical skills—budgeting, shopping, cooking and cleaning; and inter-personal skills—managing a range of formal and informal relationships. Preparation should be holistic in approach, attaching equal importance to practical, emotional and interpersonal skills—not just, as in the past, practical independence training for young people to manage on their own at 16 (Stein & Carey, 1986; Stein & Wade, 2000). Other barriers to positive preparation include over-protective care, including a lack of opportunity for supported risk taking and participation by young people.

Transitions from care

Emerging adulthood provides opportunities for what Masten, at the Ottawa conference, called "late blooming resilience". However, in comparison to their peers in the general population, most young people leaving care have to cope with the challenges and responsibilities of major changes in their lives, in leaving foster care or residential care and setting-up home, in leaving school and entering the world of work, or (more likely) being unemployed and surviving on benefits, and being parents, at a far younger age. In short, many have compressed and accelerated transitions to adulthood. This represents a barrier to promoting their resilience in that they are denied the psychological opportunity and space to focus—to deal with issues over time—which, according to empirically tested focal theory, is how most young people cope with the challenges of transition (Coleman and Hendry 1999). However, there are two related dimensions of transition that have an impact upon young people leaving care and also need to be considered.

First, as the Joseph Rowntree Foundation Young People in Transition research program shows, patterns of transition into adulthood have been changing fast during the past 20 years: the major decline in the youth labour market based on manufacturing and apprenticeship training; the extension of youth training through further and higher education; and the reduction in entitlements to universal welfare benefits for young people. These changes have resulted in young people being more dependent on their families for emotional, financial and practical support, often into their early twenties (Joseph Rowntree Foundation, 2002). In today's "risk" society, parents, grandparents and other relatives are increasingly occupying a central role at different life stages, yet, young people leaving care, who are the most likely to lack the range and depth of help given by families, are expected to cope at a far younger age than young people living with their families.

Second, the process of social transition has traditionally included three distinct, but related stages: leaving or disengagement; transition itself; and integration into a new or different social state. However, due to the changes outlined above—especially in relation to education, employment and housing—the overall process for many young people is becoming more extended, connected and permeable. For example, further and higher education is taking place over a longer period of time, young people are returning home after higher education, and there is growth in temporary and short-term employment markets.

The second stage, transition itself, is critical to this process, preparing young people for the "risk" society. What anthropologists call a "liminal state" or opportunity to "space out" provides a time for freedom, exploration, reflection, risk taking and identity search. For a majority of young people today, this is gained through the experience of further and higher education. Yet, as discussed above, many care leavers, as a consequence of their pre-care and care experiences, are unable to take advantage of educational opportunities. Instead, there is too often the expectation of instant adulthood on leaving care, a conflating of the three distinct stages of social transition into the final stage, to be achieved by the preparatory rigours of domestic combat courses when young people reach just 15, 16 or 17 years of age.

The implications of focal theory and greater awareness of transitions point to the need for more recognition of the nature and timing of young people's transitions from care. This will include giving young people the emotional and practical support they will need into their early twenties, providing them with the psychological space to cope with changes over time, as well as recognizing the different stages of transitions, including the significance of the middle stage, transition itself, and the implications of the increased uncertainties, risks and more fluid nature of social transitions.

Life after care

The resilience of young people after leaving care is closely associated with their care experience and the support they may receive. Drawing upon studies completed during the last 20 years suggests three outcome groups can be identified (Stein & Carey, 1986; Stein, 1990; Biehal et al., 1995; Dixon & Stein, 2002; Sinclair et al., 2003; Pecora et al., 2004).

First, the "moving on" group are likely to have had stability and conti-nuity in their lives. They have welcomed the challenge of independent liv-ing and gaining more control over their lives—often contrasting this with the restrictions imposed while living in care, including the lack of opportu-nities to make or participate in decisions that affected their lives. They have seen this as improving their confidence and self-esteem. In general, their resilience has been enhanced by their experiences after care and they have been able to make good use of the help they have been offered, often main-taining contact and support from former carers (Schofield, 2001; Sinclair et al., 2003). The experiences of these young people resonate with Masten's three predictors of late-blooming resilience, based on her research into transitions to adulthood in the United States: planfulness; motivation and aspiration to achieve; and connections to support.

The second group, the "survivors," have experienced more instability, movement and disruption while living in care than the "moving on" group. What made the difference to their lives was the personal and professional support they received after leaving care. Specialist leaving care workers, key workers, as well as mentors—the latter identified in the international literature as a resilience promoting factor (Masten, 2006; Newman & Blackburn, 2002)—and different family members, or some combination of support networks, could help them overcome their very poor starting points at the time of leaving care and thus promote their resilience (Biehal et al., 1995; Clayden & Stein, 2002; Marsh & Peel, 1999).

The third group, the "victims," were the most disadvantaged group. They had the most damaging pre-care family experiences and, in the main, care was unable to compensate them, to help them overcome their past difficulties. After leaving care they were likely to be unemployed, become homeless, and have great difficulties in maintaining their accommodation. They were also highly likely to be lonely, isolated and have mental health problems. Aftercare support was unlikely to be able to help them overcome their very poor starting points and they also lacked or alienated personal support. But it was important to these young people that somebody was there for them.

The *Children (Leaving Care) Act 2000*

The findings from research studies in the different UK jurisdictions contributed to an increased awareness of the problems faced by care leavers, including the limitations of discretionary child welfare and social policy legislation and the wide variations between areas in the quality of leaving care services (Broad, 1998; Biehal et al., 1995; Pinkerton & McCrea, 1999; Stein, 1999; Stein et al., 2000; Dixon & Stein, 2002).

Following the revelations of widespread abuse in children's homes, the Labour government (elected in 1997) committed itself to legislate for new and stronger duties for care leavers through its response to the Children's Safeguards Review. Sir William Utting, who chaired the Review, had drawn attention to the plight of 16-year-old care leavers "unsupported financially and emotionally, without hope of succour in distress" (Utting, 1997).

The proposed changes, detailed in the consultation document, *Me, Survive, Out There?*, were to build upon Labour's modernization program for children's services in England (Department of Health, 1999). This included the Quality Protects initiative introduced in 1998, providing substantial central government funding linked to specific service objectives. In relation to young people leaving care, objective 5 was to "ensure that young people leaving care, as they enter adulthood, are not isolated and participate socially and economically as citizens" (Department of Health, 1998).

Three performance indicators linked to this objective were "for young people looked after at the age of 16, to maximize the number engaged in education, training or employment at 19; to maximise the number of young people leaving care after their sixteenth birthday who are still in touch... on their nineteenth birthday; to maximize the number of young people leaving care on or after their sixteenth birthday who have suitable accommodation at the age of 19" (Department of Health, 1998).

As well, wider government initiatives in England to combat social exclusion (including the introduction of the Connexions Service) and initiatives to tackle youth homelessness, under-achievement in education, employment and training, and adolescent parenthood are intended to have an impact upon care leavers (Social Exclusion Unit 1998, 1999). Indeed, the changing economic climate, combined with the restructuring of post-16-year-old education and training, has resulted in reductions in youth unemployment—although there continue to be regional variations, as well as stratification by class, gender, disability and ethnicity, and the continued expansion of low-paid jobs in the service industries: more opportunities and more risks?

Against this background, the *Children (Leaving Care) Act 2000* was introduced in England and Wales in October, 2001. Its main aims are to delay young people's transitions from care until they are prepared and ready to leave; strengthen the assessment, preparation and planning for leaving care; provide better personal support for young people after care; and improve the financial arrangements for care leavers.

To meet these aims, the main provisions of the Act apply to different groups of "eligible," "relevant," "former relevant," and "qualifying" young people—(see Chapter 2 of the Guidance for a clear explanation of who gets what [Department of Health, 2001]). The key responsibilities are to assess and meet the needs of young people in and leaving care; pathway planning; the appointment of personal advisers to provide advice and support to young people, to participate in needs assessment and pathway planning, to coordinate services, to be informed about progress and well-being and to keep records of contact; assistance with education and training up to the age of 24; financial support for "eligible" (young people looked after at 16 and 17) and "relevant"(16- and 17-year-old young people who have left care); maintenance in suitable accommodation; and a duty to keep in touch by the "responsible authority," that is by the local authority that "looked after" the young person.

All the provisions of the Act apply to England and Wales whereas, under devolution, only the financial provisions are mandatory in Northern Ireland and Scotland. However, both these jurisdictions are also considering strengthening their existing legislation.

Research trends, the *Children (Leaving Care) Act 2000*, and specialist leaving care approaches in the UK

What are the implications of the main trends from the research findings, from the early studies to the most recent, for the Children (Leaving Care) Act and the development of specialist leaving care approaches in the jurisdictions of the UK?

First, the Act by itself cannot improve outcomes for young people leaving care. It will have to build upon the foundations of good-quality substitute care—the resilience-promoting factors identified above—of which providing stability is critical. But, as detailed above, the research evidence from studies completed since the 1970s consistently shows the great difficulty in responding to this very basic need for many looked-after young people, with over a third experiencing four or more placement moves and only 10% having just one move before leaving care.

Second, and linked to the point above, the contribution of specialist leaving care approaches will be closely linked to the quality of substitute care and young people's opportunities for gradual transitions from care. The relationship between care and specialist leaving care provision has been potentially problematic for three reasons since the development of specialist projects during the 1980s.

To begin with, many young people currently move on to accommodation provided by specialist schemes and projects when they are just 15 or 16 years of age. Not only does this build in additional movement and disruption and accelerate young people's transitions from care, but it also may contribute to the re-definition of foster or residential care (as being for young people only up to 15 years of age). Second, there is evidence that preparation for leaving care may be viewed as the responsibility of specialist workers rather than carers, again, separating leaving care from ordinary care. Third, the development of specialist leaving care schemes may be seen by authorities as the answer to meeting the needs of care leavers, shifting the focus from the quality of substitute care.

Leaving care should be reclaimed by carers. As the research evidence clearly shows, it is they who can provide the stability and continuity young people need during their journey to adulthood. The role of specialist advisers and their teams should not be to take over from them but to assist them in preparing and supporting young people during their transition. Their main role would shift from being a provider of direct care to servicing those who provide care.

Third, the new legal framework provides an opportunity for improving services and thus the level of resources for young people leaving care. Surveys of the work of leaving care teams carried out before and after the Act point to improvements in financial support, increases in the proportion of young people entering post-16 education, and related reductions in those not in education, employment or training. There has also been a strengthening and clarification of roles towards care leavers through needs assessments and pathway planning and a greater involvement in inter-agency work (Allard, 2002; Broad, 1994, 1998, 2003; Hai & Williams, 2004). However, the research evidence also reveals a wide degree of variation in the funding, range and quality of services between local authorities. Such territorial injustices are likely to remain a major challenge, although one way of assessing the impact of the Act could be by the reductions in such inequalities.

Fourth, what is also important, along with quantity, is the quality of resource relationships. As the discussion of the "moving on" group of young people shows, those who had successful transitions out of care not only had more access to resources; they also had a lot more interactive relationships. They were, for example, able to negotiate decent housing, derive meaningful employment or work, participate in community and leisure activities, and engage in education. Also, they were able to participate in "general" or open-access community activities and opportunities as distinct from "specialist" leaving care provision—although the latter can often pave the way for the former. There is a lot of practice evidence from the 1980s onwards showing that leaving care services have played a major role in involving young people at different levels: policy consultation, training, as well as in individual practice (Stein & Wade, 2000). The Act should continue this momentum. But on a more cautionary note, there is a balance to be achieved between young people's rights to participation through greater involvement and meeting their emotional and developmental needs. Neither a shallow and token legalism that rejects all needs in favour of rights, nor a crude and narrow pathologizing that reduces young people to receptacles of professionally defined need, will serve these young people well.

Fifth, not all groups of young people are benefiting equally under the Act. There is research evidence that young disabled people are being denied access to mainstream leaving-care services partly as a consequence of poor communication between care teams responsible for youths with disabilities, leaving-care services, and adult services (Hai & Williams, 2004). The Act has also been criticized for not including young disabled people who are "high-level" respite users (Priestley et al., 2003). Also, some young and unaccompanied young people who seek asylum may be excluded from the Act if they are being supported under Section 17 of the *Children Act 1989* instead of being accommodated.

The needs of specific groups of care leavers could also be given more prominence: the racism experienced by minority ethnic young people; the lack of support for young parents, in their own right, not just as an extension of child protection concerns; and the mental health of young care leavers. There has been, albeit more recently, research evidence of the mental health problems of looked-after young people (McCann et al., 1996; Cheung & Buchanan, 1997; Dumaret et al., 1997; Koprowska & Stein, 2000; Meltzer et al., 2003). For most of these young people, such problems will be associated with their damaging pre-care experiences within their families. These mental health problems are likely to have contributed to the reasons for them coming into care in the first place as well as being associated with poor outcomes after care. These connections, as with education, demonstrate the need for interventions across the life course of young people and their families, to address problems within families when they arise, to improve the quality of care and provide skilled help for young people after they leave care.

Finally, a connecting theme arising from the body of research findings discussed in this paper is that leaving care should be at one with a common developmental journey, from being a young person to becoming an adult. Those looked-after young people who experienced such a common journey are the most likely to find fulfilment in their careers and personal lives and overcome the damaging consequences of familial problems, abuse or neglect. They are able to become more independent, not in an emotionally isolated way but "move on" from care into education, employment or parenthood and thus achieve an "ordinary" or "common" identity—not just coping as "survivors," or, as too many young people are, trapped within welfare identities as "victims."

References

Allard, A. S. (2002). *A case study investigation into the implementation of the Children (Leaving Care) Act 2000*. NCH, London.

Beck, U. (1992). *Risk society: Towards a new modernity.* London: SAGE.

Biehal, N., Clayden, J., Stein, M., & Wade, J. (1995). *Moving on: Young people and leaving care schemes.* London: Her Majesty's Stationery Office.

Biehal, N., & Wade, J. (1996). Looking back, looking forward: Care leavers, families and change. *Children and Youth Services Review, 18,* 425–445.

Broad, B. (1994). *Leaving care in the 1990's: The results of a national survey.* Royal Philanthropic Society, Westerham.

Broad, B. (1998). *Young people leaving care: Life after the Children Act 1989.* London: Jessica Kingsley.

Broad, B. (2003). *After the Act: Implementing the Children (Leaving Care) Act 2000*. Action on Aftercare Consortium and De Montfort University, Leicester.

Cheung, S. Y., & Buchanan, A. (1997). Malaise scores in adulthood of children and young people who have been in care. *Journal of Child Psychology and Psychiatry, 38*, 575–580.

Clayden, J., & Stein, M. (2002). *Mentoring for care leavers, evaluation report*. Prince's Trust, London.

Coleman, J., & Hendry, L. (1993). *The nature of adolescence*. London: Routledge.

Department of Health. (1998). *Quality Protects: Framework for action*. London: DoH.

Department of Health. (1999). *Adoption now: Messages from research*. London: DoH.

Department of Health. (1999). *Me, survive, out there? New arrangements for young people living in and leaving care*. London: DoH.

Department of Health. (2001). *Children Act Report 2000*. London: DoH.

Department of Health (2001). *Children (Leaving Care) Act 2000: Regulations and guidance*. London: DoH.

Dixon, J., & Stein, M. (2002). *A study of throughcare and aftercare services in Scotland: Scotland's children, Children (Scotland) Act 1995*. Research Findings No. 3, Edinburgh: Scottish Executive.

Downes, C. (1992). *Separation revisited*. Aldershot: Ashgate.

Dumaret, A.-C., Coppel-Batsch, M., & Courand, S. (1997). Adult outcomes of children reared for long long-term periods in foster families. *Child Abuse and Neglect, 20*, 911–927.

Elmer, N. (2001). *Self-esteem: The costs and causes of low self-worth*. York: Joseph Rowntree Foundation.

Giddens, A. (1991). *Modernity and self-identity: Self and society in the late modern age*. Cambridge: Polity Press.

Gilligan, R. (2001). *Promoting resilience: A resource guide on working with children in the care system*. London: BAAF.

Hai, N., & Williams, A. (2004). Implementing the Children (Leaving Care) Act 2000: The experience of eight London boroughs. London: National Children's Bureau.

Jackson, S. (Ed.). (2001). Nobody ever told us school mattered: Raising the educational attainments of children in care. London: BAAF.

Jackson, S. (2002). Promoting stability and continuity of care away from home. In D. McNeish, T. Newman, & H. Roberts (Eds.), *What works for children?* Buckingham: Open University Press.

Jackson, S., Ajayi, S., & Quigley, M. (2003). *By degrees: The first year, from care to university.* London: The Frank Buttle Trust.

Joseph Rowntree Foundation. (2002). The youth divide: Diverging paths to adulthood. *Foundations.* York: Joseph Rowntree Foundation.

Koprowska, J., & Stein, M. (2000). The mental health of "looked after" young people. In Aggleton, P., et al. (Eds.), *Young people and mental health.* Chichester: Wiley.

Luthar, S. S., Cicchetti, D., & Becker, B. (2000). The construct of resilience: A critical evaluation and guidelines for future work. *Child Development, 71,* 543–562.

Marsh, P., & Peel, M. (1999). *Leaving care in partnership: Family involvement with care leavers.* London: Her Majesty's Stationery Office.

Masten, A. S.(2006). Promoting resilience in development: A general framework for systems of care. In R. J. Flynn, P. M. Dudding, and J. G. Barber (Eds.), *Promoting resilience in child welfare.* Ottawa, ON: University of Ottawa Press.

McCann, J. B., James, A., Wilson, S., & Dunn, G. (1996). Prevalence of psychiatric disorders in young people in the care system. *British Medical Journal, 313,* 1529–1530.

Melzer, H., Corbin, T., Gatward, R., Goodman, R., & Ford, T. (2002). *The mental health of young people looked after by local authorities in England.* National Statistics, London.

Newman, T., & Blackburn, S. (2002a). *Interchange 78—Transitions in the lives of children and young people: Resilience factors.* Edinburgh: Scottish Executive.

Newman, T., & Blackburn, S. (2002b). *Transitions in the lives of children and young people: Resilience factors.* Report for the Scottish Executive Education and Young People Research Unit: Edinburgh: www.scotland.gov.uk/library5/education/ic78-00.asp

Pecora, P. J., Williams, J., Kessler, R. J., Downs, A., O'Brien, K., Hiripi, E., et al. (2004). *Assessing the effects of foster care: Early results from the Casey National Alumni Study.* Casey Family Programs, Seattle, WA (http://www.casey.org).

Pinkerton, J., & McCrea, J. (1999). *Meeting the challenge? Young people leaving care in Northern Ireland.* Aldershot: Ashgate.

Priestley, M., Rabiee, P., & Harris, J. (2003). Young disabled people and the "new arrangements" for leaving care in England and Wales. *Children and Youth Services Review, 25,* 863–890.

Rutter, M., Giller, H., & Hagell, A. (1998). *Antisocial behaviour by young people.* Cambridge: Cambridge University Press.

Rutter, M. (1999). Resilience concepts and findings: Implications for family therapy. *Journal of Family Therapy, 21,* 119–144.

Schofield, G. (2001). Resilience and family placement: A lifespan perspective. *Adoption and Fostering, 25*(3), 6–19.

Sinclair, I., Baker, C., Wilson, K., & Gibbs, I. (2003). *What happens to foster children? Report to the Department of Health.* York: University of York.

Social Exclusion Unit. (1998). *Rough sleeping.* London: The Stationery Office.

Social Exclusion Unit. (1999). *Teenage pregnancy.* London: TSO.

Stein, M. (1990). *Living out of care.* Ilford: Barnardo's.

Stein, M. (1994). Leaving care, education and career trajectories. *Oxford Review of Education,* 20:3.

Stein, M. (1999). Leaving care: Reflections and challenges. In O. Stevenson (Ed.), *Child welfare in the UK.* Oxford: Blackwell.

Stein, M., & Carey, K. (1986). *Leaving care.* Oxford: Blackwell.

Stein, M., Pinkerton, J., & Kelleher, J. (2000) Young people leaving care in England, Northern Ireland, and Ireland. *European Journal of Social Work, 3,* 235–46.

Stein, M., & Wade, J. (2000). *Helping care leavers: Problems and strategic responses.* London: Department of Health.

Utting, W. (1997). *People like us: The report of the review of the safeguards for children living away from home.* London: HMSO.

Part 3:

Resilience and the Implementation of Innovative Approaches to Child Welfare Policy and Practice

Training, experience, and supervision: Keys to enhancing the utility of the Assessment and Action Record in implementing Looking After Children

Sarah Pantin, Robert Flynn and Vivien Runnels

Introduction

Looking After Children (LAC) has been an important initiative internationally in child welfare over the last decade because of its central focus on improving substitute parenting and developmental outcomes for young people in care (Parker, Ward, Jackson, Aldgate, & Wedge, 1991; Ward, 1995). LAC has also been a key vehicle for promoting resilience, with its emphasis on maximizing young people's competence and setting outcome targets on the same level as those for young people in the general population.

Within the LAC theoretical framework, the Assessment and Action Record (AAR) is the main instrument used for assessing the needs of young people in care and monitoring their developmental outcomes (Parker et al., 1991; Ward, 1995). The AAR operationalizes the LAC approach on three interrelated levels, each corresponding to a major AAR function. First, on the level of the *individual child or youth*, the AAR has the *clinical function* of assisting child welfare staff and caregivers to assess the young person's strengths and needs comprehensively, prepare a high-quality, updated plan of care for the coming year, and monitor the young person's ongoing progress (Flynn, Ghazal, Moshenko, & Westlake, 2001). Second, on the level of the local *child welfare organization*, the AAR has the *managerial function* of enabling managers and board members to monitor the progress of a group of children or youth, compare actual developmental outcomes with those targeted, and make evidence-based decisions to improve service relevance and young people's lives (Flynn, Lemay, Ghazal, & Hébert, 2003). Third, at the level of a provincial or national *child welfare system*, the AAR has the *policy function* of encouraging decision makers to monitor young people's outcomes on a system-wide basis, evaluate these outcomes in light of expected progress, and formulate improved policies and practices.

The successful implementation of any social innovation is likely to depend on many factors, such as the size of the organization, the voluntary versus mandatory nature of the new approach, the support of senior management, and a culture that encourages participation in decision making by supervisory and direct-service personnel. To date there have been a number of studies that have looked at levels of implementation of LAC (see Jones, Clark, Kufeldt, & Norman, 1998; Kufeldt, Vachon, & Simard, 2000; Moyers, 1998; Ward, 1996; Wheelaghan, Hill, Borland, Lambert, & Triseliotis 1999; Wise, 1999), investigating implementation at the level of the individual by assessing the perceived usefulness of the approach for foster carers, workers and foster youth (Wheelaghan, Hill, Borland, Lambert, & Triseliotis, 1999; Wise, 1999) and carrying out audits of levels of use of LAC documentation (Moyers, 1998).

Taken together, these studies have identified several process variables that appear to influence the success of implementation (Donovan & Ayres, 1998; Wheelaghan, Hill, Borland, Lambert, & Triseliotis, 1999). In an especially informative study, Wheelaghan and colleagues (1999) evaluated the implementation of LAC in six local authorities in Scotland. They found that the initial uptake of LAC was influenced by staffing levels, support from managers and supervisors, the ability to integrate LAC into pre-existing recording procedures, and the quality of training. According to Wheelaghan et al. (1999), trainees felt the LAC philosophy was well covered in their training but that certain more practical aspects, such as the completion of the LAC forms, were less adequately handled. Moreover, when practitioners had to use the new approach with some cases but maintain the old procedures with others, they complained of redundancy and duplication. Finally, the use of LAC in supervision was seen as crucial, so that direct-service workers would perceive it as useful for practice.

In Canada, Kufeldt, Vachon, & Simard (2000) reported the results of a three-year project in which LAC was implemented on a pilot basis in six Canadian provinces (Ontario, Quebec, New Brunswick, Nova Scotia, Prince Edward Island, and Newfoundland and Labrador). Based on their experience in the Canadian project, Kufeldt et al. (2000) made a number of suggestions for improving implementation that they thought would be helpful for virtually any jurisdiction wishing to implement LAC. These suggestions included: managers showing workers that AAR data could be aggregated and used to plan positive changes; allowing project coordinators sufficient time to provide training and consultation; changing from a crisis-driven to a strengths-oriented approach to practice; and ensuring that supervisors discuss the information in the AAR on a regular basis with direct-service workers to improve decision making and guide interventions. Wise (1999), reporting on a pilot project in Australia, also highlighted the need for all care providers and workers to have a commitment and understanding of the LAC approach so they could appreciate the necessity for adopting the new system.

The present research was part of a larger "OnLAC" project, the goal of which was to evaluate the implementation of LAC in Ontario as a policy reform initiative aimed at improving service practices and young people's developmental outcomes in the 51 local Children's Aid Societies (CASs) in the province (Flynn, Angus, Aubry, & Drolet, 1999). The purpose of the present study was to investigate the relationship between several modifiable process variables and an important LAC *impact* (i.e., an intermediate objective essential to achieving individual-level outcomes; Steckler & Linnan, 2002). The impact, itself an important component of LAC implementation, was the degree to which child welfare workers and supervisors view the AAR as useful in their supervisory work. The process variables that we saw as possible influences on the impact were, in order: the amount of LAC training that child welfare personnel receive; the quality of their LAC training; the amount of experience they gain in using the AAR in practice; and the frequency with which they discuss information from the AAR in supervision.

Like many service reform initiatives, the OnLAC project took training as its basic point of entry into the system change process (Kirkpatrick, 1998). LAC training was seen as a feasible means of affecting many other aspects of implementation, such as motivating CAS staff to participate fully in the OnLAC project, adhering faithfully to its key principles and values, and, ultimately, helping to improve young people's outcomes. We thus viewed the quantity and quality of training, post-training experience, and supervisory encouragement as probably important influences on the degree to which practitioners would accept LAC and the AAR as innovations and succeed in integrating them into their daily practice. Finally, our thinking was shaped by a central assumption in Azjen's (1991) theory of planned behaviour, namely, that more favourable attitudes towards innovations such as LAC and the AAR, combined with a climate that is supportive of the innovation, are likely to result in higher levels of use of the LAC approach by workers and foster carers.

To summarize, based on the general theoretical perspectives of Kirkpatrick (1998) and Azjen (1991) and the specific LAC research of Wheelaghan et al. (1999) and Kufeldt et al. (2000), we assumed that the overall process of LAC implementation would be strengthened to the extent that, all other things being equal, child welfare workers and supervisors saw the main LAC needs-assessment and outcome-monitoring tool (the AAR) as useful in their work with young people in care, foster parents, or other caregivers. Our specific hypothesis was that a more favourable evaluation by child welfare personnel of the utility of the AAR would be positively related to higher levels of four modifiable process variables, namely, the amount of LAC training obtained, the quality of such training, the amount of experience accumulated in using the AAR, and the frequency with which information from the AAR was discussed in supervision.

Method

Participants

As is described in greater detail in the section on data collection, we invited the following CAS personnel to participate in a survey in 2004: all child welfare workers and supervisors who had been involved in the OnLAC project during its second year (July 2002 to June 2003) and who had completed or used in supervision, during that year, the second Canadian adaptation of the Assessment and Action Record (AAR-C2; Flynn, Ghazal, & Legault, 2004). Of the 229 child welfare workers and supervisors invited to participate, 146 provided useable survey responses, for an effective response rate of 64%. We excluded from the present study, however, 10 respondents who said they had never used the AAR and another 10 who reported they had never received any LAC training. Thus, the research sample was composed of the 126 respondents who had used the AAR and had also received some LAC training, such that they were in a position to evaluate the quality of LAC training and the utility of the AAR.

Of the study sample of 126 respondents, 93 (74%) were child welfare workers, 30 (24%) were supervisors, and 3 (2%) had assumed other positions (e.g., coordinator of training) within their local agencies. Overall, the participants were relatively experienced, 52% having worked in child welfare for more than 10 years, 18% for 6-10 years, 29% for 1-5 years, and only 1% for less than 2 years. Most had been employed for a substantial amount of time at the local CAS where they were working at the time of the survey in 2004: 48% had been at their local CAS for more than 10 years, 18% for 6–10 years, 32% for 2–5 years, and only 2% for less than 2 years. The size of the active caseload ranged from zero (in the case of 20% of the participants who occupied exclusively supervisory or other non-direct-service roles), through 1–10 young people in care (9% of the participants), 11–15 (10%), 16–20 (22%), 21–25 (26%), and more than 25 (13%).

Instrument

The four-page survey form requested that the child welfare workers and supervisors indicate for how many young people in care they had ever completed the AAR or used it in supervision. For most respondents, the AAR in question was the AAR-C2 (Flynn et al., 2004), which has been the only version of the AAR used in the OnLAC project since early 2001 Besides the background questions already mentioned (i.e., the amount of work experience in child welfare and at the local CAS, and the size of the active caseload), the survey form also asked for the following information: the length of time respondents had been using the AAR; the amount of LAC training they had ever received; the length of time since their last LAC training; the frequency with which they discussed the information in the AAR in supervision; whether they had ever presented LAC training to others; and their evaluation of two implementation-related matters (i.e., how well their training had covered key LAC issues, and how useful the AAR was in their work as child welfare workers or supervisors). On the last page of the survey form, respondents were invited to add open-ended comments about LAC and the AAR.

Measures used in the present study

Amount of LAC training. This was measured by a single item that asked respondents how many days of training they had ever received in the LAC approach. The response options ranged from "never received training" to "three days or more". (As noted earlier, the 10 respondents reporting they had never received any LAC training were excluded from the study sample.)

Quality of LAC training. On this three-item measure, the respondents indicated how well, in their opinion, their LAC training had covered three core issues, all reflecting fidelity to the overall LAC approach: the key values and principles of LAC; the adequacy with which the training had prepared them to complete the AAR or use it in supervision; and the adequacy with which the training had prepared them to construct or approve plans of care. The three response options for each item were "Very well," "Well," and "Poorly." The total score could range from 3 to 9, with a higher score indicating higher-quality LAC training. The internal consistency of the three-item scale was good (Cronbach's alpha = .74).

Amount of experience in using the AAR. A single item asked respondents to report the total number of young people in care for whom they had completed the AAR or used it in supervision. The response options ran from "1" to "more than 20." (Also as noted previously, the 10 respondents who said they had never completed the AAR or used it in supervision were excluded from the study sample.)

Frequency of discussion in supervision of the information in the AAR. On a single item, the child welfare workers and supervisors indicated how frequently they discussed the information in the AAR in supervision. The three response options were "Rarely or never," "From time to time," and "Often or always."

Utility of the Assessment and Action Record. This seven-item scale asked the respondents to indicate how useful they found the AAR in their work as child welfare workers or supervisors (e.g., in helping them to understand their foster youths' needs better or to become more aware of their youths' progress). The response options were "Very useful," "Useful," and "Not very useful." The total score could range from 7 to 21, with a higher score signifying greater AAR utility. The internal consistency of the scale was very high (Cronbach's alpha = .95).

Data collection procedure

We used a modified version of Dillman's (1978) Total Design Method. A package of individually addressed envelopes was mailed in 2004 to the LAC coordinator ("lead hand") in each of the CASs that had taken part in the OnLAC project during its second year, 2002-2003. The lead hand was asked to distribute an envelope containing a survey questionnaire, accompanying letter, two copies of an informed consent form, and a stamped, self-addressed return envelope, to the CAS worker or supervisor whose name appeared on the envelope. A total of 229 CAS staff members received an envelope. The letter explained that the respondent's responses would be seen only by members of the research team. The respondent was invited to complete the questionnaire, sign both copies of the consent form and keep one, and return the questionnaire and the other copy of the consent form in the return envelope, which was to be placed in the out-mail box at the local CAS. A second letter was sent approximately a week later, thanking those who had already mailed back their questionnaires and inviting the others to do so. About two months later, a new package of individually addressed envelopes was sent to the LAC lead hands, for distribution to all non-respondents. Because we did not wish to overburden CAS staff who had not responded, we decided not to send out the fourth "wave" called for by Dillman (1978). After three waves, we received a total of 146 useable responses from the pool of 229 potential participants, for an effective response rate of 64%.

Data analysis

The rate of missing data in the returned questionnaires was very low (less than 3%) for virtually all the items. To impute missing values in the items composing the scales assessing the quality of LAC training and the utility of the AAR, we used the EM (Expectation-Maximization) procedure (Schafer & Graham, 2002) that is an option in the Missing Values Analysis routine in SPSS. In analyzing the data, we proceeded as follows.

First, we carried out descriptive analyses on the predictor variables (i.e., the amount of LAC training, quality of LAC training, amount of experience in using the AAR, and frequency of discussion of the information in the AAR in supervision) and on the criterion variable (utility of the AAR). Second, to test the study hypothesis, we carried out a four-step hierarchical regression, to evaluate, for each of the four predictors, the sign and magnitude of its beta coefficient and the size of the increment that it added to the variance accounted for in the criterion variable. In order, the predictors were the amount of LAC training, the quality of LAC training, the amount of experience in using the AAR, and the frequency of discussion of AAR information in supervision. Third, we carried out exploratory analyses to examine the possible mediating role (Baron & Kenny, 1986) of the variables introduced in steps 2 to 4 of the hierarchical regression and to investigate in greater detail the relationship between the strongest predictor (the frequency of discussion in supervision of AAR information) and the utility of the AAR.

Results

Descriptive results

Amount of LAC training received. Ten per cent of the 126 core respondents said they had received less than one day of LAC training, 29% had had one day, 34% two days, and 27% had received 3 or more days of training.

Quality of LAC training received. On this three-item measure, which could run from a low of 3 to a high of 9, the mean score was 6.54 ($SD = 1.46$, $Mdn = 6$). The proportion of the study sample rating the training as having handled each of the three key LAC fidelity-related issues either "Very well" or "Well" was as follows: 98%, for coverage of the key values and principles of LAC; 88%, for preparing trainees to complete the AAR; and 79%, for preparing trainees to construct (or contribute through supervision to) more useful plans of care.

Amount of experience in using the AAR. Seven per cent of the study sample had completed the AAR or used it in supervision with only one young person in care, while 11% had used it with 2 young people, 14% with 3, 16% with 4 or 5, 16% with 6–9, 20% with 10–15, 2% with 16–20, and 14% with more than 20 young people in care.

Frequency of discussion in supervision of information in the AAR. Of the 93 child welfare workers, only 8% reported that they discussed the information in the AAR in supervision "often or always," whereas 46% did so "From time to time" and 46% "Rarely or never." The 30 supervisors, on the other hand, were considerably more likely to discuss AAR information in supervision: 23% said they did so "Often or always," 70% "From time to time," and only 7% "Rarely or never" ($\chi^2[2] = 17.15$, phi coefficient = .35, $p < .001$).

Utility of the AAR. On this seven-item measure, which could range from a low of 7 to a high of 21, the mean score was 13.34 ($SD = 4.21$, $Mdn = 14$). Overall, between three quarters and two thirds of the study sample said that completing the AAR, or (for supervisors) using it in supervision, was either "Very useful" or "Useful" in helping them carry out a range of important tasks. The percentage of respondents rating the AAR as "Very useful" or "Useful" in the accomplishment of these tasks was as follows: 77%, in helping them better understand the needs of the young person in care; 73%, in helping them collaborate more effectively (directly or through supervision) with the foster parent or other caregiver in implementing the young person's plan of care; 70%, in helping them prepare (or contribute through supervision to) more useful plans of care; 70%, in helping them assist the young person in planning his or her future; 66%, in helping them to do their direct-service or supervisory work more effectively; 64%, in helping them have more targeted discussions with the young person in care; and 64%, in helping them become more aware of the young person's progress.

Hypothesis test

Intercorrelations. Table 1 shows the correlations among the study variables. The sample size was 125 rather than 126 because an initial regression screening run had revealed that one of the 126 cases had a standardized residual outside the recommended limits of ± 3.3 (Tabachnick & Fidell, 1996). We removed this outlier from the correlational and hierarchical regression analyses. From Table 1, it can be seen that all four predictors were positively and significantly related to the utility of the AAR. The frequency of discussion of AAR information in supervision had the strongest association with the utility of the AAR ($r = .57$).

Table 1. Correlations among study variables (N = 125)

Variable	1	2	3	4	5
1. Amount of LAC training received	—				
2. Quality of LAC training received	.36***	—			
3. Amount of experience in using AAR	.27**	.21*	—		
4. Frequency of discussion in supervision of information in AAR	.31***	.38***	.43***	—	
5. Utility of the AAR	.33***	.45***	.33***	.57***	—
Mean	3.77	6.52	5.62	1.74	13.39
SD	0.96	1.45	2.09	0.63	4.19

Note: LAC = Looking After Children; AAR = Assessment and Action Record.

$*p < .05$ (two-tailed) $** p < .01$ (two-tailed) $***p < .001$ (two-tailed)

Hierarchical regression. As Table 2 shows, the beta coefficient for each of the predictors was positively and significantly related to the criterion variable, the utility of the AAR, at the step at which the predictor entered the model. Moreover, as the note to Table 2 indicates, each predictor, when added to the regression model, produced a statistically significant increment in the amount of variance accounted for in the criterion. The largest increments, in order, were due to the quality of LAC training (13% of the variance), the frequency of discussion of AAR information in supervision (also 13%), the amount of LAC training received (11%), and the amount of experience gained in using the AAR (4%). The model as a whole accounted for 40% of the variance in the criterion.

Table 2. Summary of hierarchical regression analyses for variables predicting scores on the Utility of the Assessment and Action Record scale (N = 125)

Step and Variables	β
Step 1 Amount of LAC training received	.33***
Step 2 Amount of LAC training received	.19*
Quality of LAC training received	.39***
Step 3 Amount of LAC training received	.14
Quality of LAC training received	.36***
Amount of experience in using AAR	.21**
Step 4 Amount of LAC training received	.09
Quality of LAC training received	.25**
Amount of experience is using AAR	.07
Frequency of discussion of information in AAR in supervision	.42***
R^2	.40***
R^2 (adj.)	.38

Note: LAC = Looking After Children; AAR = Assessment and Action Record.

$R^2 = .11$ for Step 1 $(p < .001)$; $\Delta R^2 = .13$ for Step 2 $(p < .001)$; $\Delta R^2 = .04$ for Step 3 $(p < .01)$; $\Delta R^2 = .13$ for Step 4 $(p < .001)$.

$*p < .05$ (two-tailed) $**p < .01$ (two-tailed) $***p < .001$ (two-tailed)

Exploratory analyses

Mediation analyses. Preacher and Leonardelli (2005, p. 1) define mediation as follows: "A variable may be considered a *mediator* to the extent to which it carries the influence of a given independent variable (IV) to a given dependent variable (DV)." Generally speaking, mediation can be said to occur when: (1) the IV significantly affects the mediator; (2) the IV significantly affects the DV in the absence of the mediator; (3) the mediator has a significant unique effect on the DV; and (4) the effect of the IV on the DV shrinks upon the addition of the mediator to the model. As previously noted, the beta coefficient for each of the predictors was significantly different from zero at the step in which the predictor entered the regression model. Thus, the fact that at later steps these betas were either no longer significantly different from zero, or else were reduced in size, indicated that mediation was occurring among the predictors. To explore this issue, we used Preacher and Leonardelli's (2005) Internet-based interactive tool to calculate Sobel's (1982) test for mediation. Using the causal order of the predictors implied by the hierarchical regression model, we carried out the 6 possible mediation tests (i.e., 1 at step 2, 2 at step 3, and 3 at step 4). Five of the six mediation tests were significant ($ps < .05$ to $.001$). In the case of the sole exception, the amount of the participant's experience in using the AAR was found not to mediate ($p > .05$) the effect of the quality of LAC training on participants' evaluation of the utility of the AAR.

These analyses suggested that the frequency with which participants discussed information from the AAR in supervision mediated the three other predictors, carrying their effects to the dependent variable, the utility of the AAR. In addition, both the quality of LAC training and the amount of experience gained in using the AAR mediated the effect of the amount of LAC training on participants' assessment of the usefulness of the AAR in their work.

Role of frequency of discussion in supervision of information in the AAR. Given that this variable had emerged as the best predictor of the utility of the AAR and also mediated the influence of the other predictors, we explored its role in greater detail. In a univariate ANOVA, the three levels of the frequency with which respondents discussed AAR information in supervision served as the independent variable, the utility of the AAR as the dependent variable, and the three other variables as covariates. As shown in Figure 1, the frequency with which participants discussed AAR information in supervision was strongly related to participants' evaluation of the usefulness of the AAR (F [2, 119] = 13.05, partial eta squared = .18, $p < .001$), even after the means had been adjusted for the three covariates. Pair-wise comparisons among the adjusted means were carried out, with a Bonferroni correction applied (Tabachnick & Fidell, 1996) to keep the overall alpha level at the .05 level in the pair-wise comparisons. The respondents who frequently ("Often or always") discussed AAR information in supervision ($M = 17.47$) evaluated the utility of the AAR significantly more favourably than those who did so only occasionally ("From time to time"; $M = 13.86, p < .01$) or virtually never ("Rarely or never"; $M = 11.52, p < .001$). Also, those who discussed AAR information in supervision occasionally rated the utility of the AAR more highly than those who rarely or never did so ($p < .01$).

Figure 1. Mean scores (adjusted for covariates) on the Utility of the AAR scale, as a function of the frequency of discussion of information in the AAR in supervision ($N = 125$)

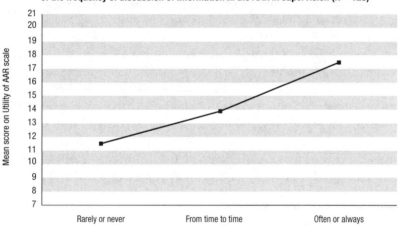

Frequency of discussion of information in AAR in supervision

Discussion

The results of the hierarchical regression provided strong support for our hypothesis that each of the four implementation-process variables—the amount and quality of LAC training, amount of experience in using the AAR, and frequency of discussion of AAR-derived information in supervision—would be positively and significantly related to a more favourable evaluation of the AAR. Each of the process variables had a positive beta coefficient upon entering the regression model and together they accounted for fully 40% of the variance in the criterion. In particular, more frequent discussion of AAR information emerged as an especially important predictor, both in its own right and as a mediator of the other process variables.

Our findings are consistent with but also extend those of Wheelaghan et al. (1999) and Kufeldt et al. (2000). Most of our respondents rated the AAR as useful in their work. However, the data they provided also point to several concrete ways in which the utility of the AAR, and thereby the implementation of LAC, can be enhanced. First, child welfare workers and supervisors must receive a sufficient amount of LAC training, in order to make optimal use of the AAR. In our sample, however, only 61% had received what is currently considered the minimally adequate amount of LAC training, namely, two full days. Our results suggest that had all the participants received at least this minimum, their overall assessment of the utility of the AAR would have been even more favourable. Second, the fidelity and overall quality of LAC training should be increased. Although virtually all the participants rated the coverage of the basic LAC philosophy very highly, their responses indicated that LAC training should place more emphasis on using the AAR in practice and on constructing plans of care. Moreover, our findings suggest that a new module on how to optimize the usefulness of the AAR through discussion in supervision should be added to the basic LAC training curriculum. Third, the fact that greater experience in using the AAR contributed to a more favourable evaluation of its utility is important, both for LAC training and AAR users. In our sample, however, almost half (48%) of the participants had used the AAR with five or fewer young people. A more experienced sample of AAR users would presumably assess it even more positively. Fourth, the moderately large beta coefficient, sizable incremental effect, and important mediational role of the frequency of discussion of AAR information in supervision all suggest that maximizing the impact of this variable is most crucial of all for enhancing the utility of the AAR and LAC implementation. Because LAC training to date has not realized the importance of this factor and given it due coverage, it is not surprising that participants in our sample made far less use of the AAR in supervision than would be optimal. Of the child welfare workers, almost half (46%) said they almost never discussed the AAR in supervision, another 46% said they did so only occasionally, and a mere 8% reported doing so on a frequent basis. The situation was somewhat better among the supervisors, perhaps because the AAR provided them with information that, in the absence of first-hand contact with the young person in care, they would otherwise have lacked. Nevertheless, even here there was considerable room for improvement. Only 23% of the supervisors discussed information from the AAR on a frequent basis in supervision, while 70% did so occasionally, and 7% virtually never. Once again, and as is strongly suggested by Figure 1, regular use of the AAR in supervision would be likely to lead to an even more positive view of its usefulness and improved LAC implementation.

The present study had two important limitations. First, our cross-sectional data do not allow us to make causal inferences, although the temporal and causal ordering that we assumed among our predictors in structuring the hierarchical regression renders such inferences more plausible. We suspect, in fact, that many of the associations noted (e.g., between the utility of the AAR and the frequency with which it was discussed in supervision) were actually reciprocal in nature, with higher levels of one variable leading to higher levels of the other, and vice versa. Second, despite a response rate of 64%, which is similar to those reported elsewhere in the literature (Dillman, 1991), a third of our potential respondents did not participate in the survey. Their views and use of the AAR may have been somewhat different than those of the individuals who chose to take part in the study.

Despite these limitations, the present research has made several contributions to the literature on LAC implementation. It proposed and predictively validated a model consisting of a chain of process variables that was able to explain an appreciable amount (40%) of the variance in an important facet of LAC implementation, namely, the opinion held by child welfare workers and supervisors of the utility of the AAR for their work. Our study also employed a hypothesis-testing and quantitative methodology that complements the descriptive studies of LAC implementation conducted previously. Both types of approaches are necessary to build the knowledge base required for the effective and efficient implementation of a social innovation as complex as LAC.

Two final points are worth noting. Since year 2 of the OnLAC project (2002-2003), we have continued to revise the AAR-C2, in response to ongoing feedback from the field. Although similar to the version evaluated in the present study, the most recent version of the AAR-C2 is somewhat shorter, takes less time to administer, and assesses an even wider range of strengths and assets in young people in care. The initial reactions from users have been encouraging, such that evaluations of the utility of the AAR based on this newest version would probably be even more positive than the favourable assessments found in the present study.

Using the promising results of the OnLAC project to date as a springboard, the Ontario Association of Children's Aid Societies, in collaboration with its member agencies and the Ontario Ministry of Children and Youth Services, is now engaged in implementing LAC and the AAR in all 53 local AARs, with a target of full implementation across the province by April 1, 2007. This initiative has generated many new actual or planned activities, including the creation of an Ontario LAC Council to oversee the process of implementation; formal plans to implement LAC in a growing number of CASs; more frequent LAC training sessions for child welfare personnel, foster parents, and other caregivers; new LAC training modules for supervisors and senior managers; increased attention to informing young people in care about LAC; project-management training for LAC coordinators in local CASs; computerization of the AAR, plan of care, and other recording procedures; data-analysis training for local CASs to encourage the use of AAR data for evidence-based decision-making and service planning; and local and province-wide outcome monitoring, with systematic feedback of results to local CASs and provincial policy makers. In this exciting new context, the demand for solid knowledge of how best to implement LAC and the AAR is growing rapidly. Rigorous and informative applied research on the process of implementation, and rapid dissemination of the new knowledge gained, must become a sustained priority in the knowledge-intensive field that is child welfare.

Authors' note

We gratefully acknowledge the financial support for the Looking After Children in Ontario (OnLAC) project received from the Social Sciences and Humanities Research Council (strategic grant 828-1999-1008, awarded to Robert J. Flynn, principal investigator; co-investigators, Tim Aubry, Marie Drolet, and Douglas Angus). We are also grateful for the additional financial support received from the Ministry of Children and Youth Services of Ontario (grant made to the Ontario Association of Children's Aid Societies [OACAS]), Social Development Canada (grant made to the Child Welfare League of Canada [CWLC]), and Prescott-Russell Services to Children and Adults (PRSCA). We also wish to thank the child welfare workers and supervisors who responded to the survey and Pamela Murray for her help with data management.

References

Azjen, I. (1991). The theory of planned behavior. *Organizational Behavior and Human Decision Processes, 50,* 179–211.

Baron, R. M., & Kenny, D. A. (1986). The moderator-mediator variable distinction in social psychological research: Conceptual, strategic and statistical considerations. *Journal of Personality and Social Psychology, 51,* 1173–1182.

Dillman, D. A. (1978). *Mail and telephone surveys: The Total Design Method.* New York: Wiley.

Dillman, D. A. (1991). The design and administration of mail surveys. *Annual Review of Sociology, 17,* 225–249.

Donavan, D., & and Ayres, M. (1998). Implementing Looking After Children in an English local authority. *Children and Society, 12,* 247–248.

Flynn, R. J., Angus, D., Aubry, T., & Drolet, M. (1999). *Improving child protection practice through the introduction of Looking After Children into the 54 Local Children's Aid Societies in Ontario: An implementation and outcome evaluation.* SSHRC Strategic Grant No. 828-1999-1008. Ottawa: Centre for Research on Community Services, University of Ottawa.

Flynn, R.J., Ghazal, H., & Legault, L. (2004). *Looking After Children: Good Parenting, Good Outcomes. Assessment and Action Record* (second Canadian adaptation). Ottawa, ON & London, UK: Centre for Research on Community Services, University of Ottawa & Her Majesty's Stationery Office (HMSO).

Flynn, R. J., Ghazal, H., Moshenko, S., & Westlake, L. (2001). Main features and advantages of a new, "Canadianized" version of the Assessment and Action Record from Looking After Children. *Journal of the Ontario Association of Children's Aid Societies, 45*(2), 3–6.

Flynn, R. J., Lemay, R., Ghazal, H., & Hébert, S. (2003). A performance measurement, monitoring, and management system for local Children's Aid Societies. In K. Kufeldt & B. McKenzie (Eds.), *Child welfare: Connecting research, policy, and practice* (pp. 319–330). Waterloo, ON: Wilfrid Laurier University Press.

Jones, H., Clark, R., Kufeldt, K., & Norman, M. (1998). Looking After Children: Assessing outcomes in child care—The experience of implementation. *Children and Society, 12,* 212–222.

Kirkpatrick, D. L. (1998). *Evaluating training programs: The four levels* (2nd ed.). San Francisco: Berrett-Koehler.

Kufeldt, K., Simard, M., & Vachon, J. (2000). *Looking After Children in Canada: Final report.* Submitted to Social Development Partnerships, Human Resources Development Canada. St. John, NB & Québec, QC: University of New Brunswick & Université Laval.

Moyers, S. (1998). Auditing the implementation of Looking After Children. *Children and Society, 12,* 238–239.

Parker, R.A., Ward, H., Jackson, S., Aldgate, J., & Wedge, P. (Eds.). (1991). *Looking After Children: Assessing outcomes in child care.* London, UK: HMSO.

Preacher, K. J., & Leonardelli, G. J. (2005). *Calculation for the Sobel test: An interactive calculation tool for mediation tests.* Retrieved March 10, 2005, from: http://www.unc.edu/~preacher/sobel/sobel.htm

Schafer, J. L., & Graham, J. W. (2002). Missing data: Our view of the state of the art. *Psychological Methods, 7,* 147–177.

Sobel, M. E. (1982). Asymptotic intervals for indirect effects in structural equations models. In S. Leinhart (Ed.), *Sociological Methodology 1982* (pp. 290–312). San Francisco: Jossey-Bass.

Steckler, A., & Linnan, L. (Eds.) (2002). *Process evaluation for public health interventions and research.* San Francisco; CA: Jossey-Bass.

Tabachnick, B. G., & Fidell, L. S. (1996). *Using multivariate statistics* (3rd ed.). New York: Harper Collins.

Ward, H. (Ed.) (1995) *Looking After Children: Research into practice.* London, UK: HMSO.

Ward, H. (1996). Constructing and implementing measures to assess the outcomes of looking after children away from home. In J. Aldgate and M. Hill (Eds.) *Child welfare services: Developments in law, policy, practice and research.* Bristol: Jessica Kingsley.

Wheelaghan, S., Hill, M., Lambert, L., Borland, M., & Triseliotis, J. (1999). *Looking After Children in Scotland.* Edinburgh, Scotland: The Scottish Office Central Research Unit.

Wise, S. (1999). *The UK Looking After Children approach in Australia.* Australian Institute of Family Studies [on line] http://www.aifs.gov.au/institute/pubs/resreport2/main.html

The needs of children in care and the Looking After Children approach: Steps towards promoting children's best interests

Marie Drolet and Mélissa Sauvé-Kobylecki

Ontario's child-centred legal framework

The child welfare system in Ontario has changed significantly since 1998. In keeping with the primacy accorded to children's rights in the 1989 *UN Convention on the Rights of the Child*, ratified by Canada in 1991 (Farris-Manning & Zandstra, 2003), promoting the best interests of the child[1] became the primary objective of the Ontario *Child and Family Services Act* (CFSA) in 2000. This amendment triggered an increase in the number of placements of children at risk of abuse or neglect, or both.

The CFSA (2000) also prescribed stricter limits with respect to the maximum amount of time that children can stay in temporary care. This provision aims to ensure that arrangements for permanency planning[2] are made for each child as quickly as possible. The Children's Aid Society (CAS) investigates to determine whether children would best be returned to their biological parents or be designated Crown wards eligible for adoption. If these children are be made Crown wards sooner than in the past, they should benefit from a greater level of stability in their lives by being adopted. When they are designated by a court as Crown wards, they live in foster care until they are adopted or reach the age of majority. The CAS becomes then their legal "parent" responsible for their well-being and development. With the intent to promote the best interests of children, the Ministry of Community and Social Services (MCSS) recommended that CAS agencies adopt the Looking After Children (LAC) approach for assessing the needs of the children and planning for their care.[3]

This new legal framework, as well as the various child-welfare issues currently facing social workers, led us to question the concept of the best interests of the child as it applies to the situation of children in foster care. Because the LAC approach and its corresponding tool—the Assessment and Action Record (AAR)—are still relatively new, it is important to highlight the views of the social workers who have been using this tool. Besides reviewing the literature on out-of-home placement and on the concept of the best interests of the child, we propose to identify (a) what practitioners consider to be the needs of children in care and (b) how they view the AAR as a support tool for assessing children's needs and planning their care. Finally, we will examine recommendations that may help social workers using the AAR to continue taking steps towards promoting children's best interests.

Placement of children in out-of-home care

In 2003, 18,126 children were placed in the care of CAS agencies in Ontario. One of the various placement arrangements, and the particular focus of this study, is the foster family.[4] Since 1998, the number of available foster families has not increased in proportion to the growing number of children requiring placement in out-of-home care (Farris-Manning & Zandstra, 2003). In fact, the number of children placed in care has grown by 40% since 1998, while the number of foster families has risen by only 29% (Ontario Association of Children's Aid Societies [OACAS], 2003). This disproportion is due mainly to problems with recruiting and retaining foster families (OACAS, 2002).

A generation ago, cared-for children manifested more problems with behaviour and aggression, attention-deficit and hyperactivity disorders, emotional problems and anxiety disorders than their peers (Flynn & Biro, 1998, in Perkins-Mangulabnan, 2003; Tremblay, 1999). Nevertheless, Farris-Manning and Zandstra (2003) report that children in need of protection today have more complex problems and stay in care much longer than did the preceding generation.

Moreover, 44% of the children removed from their biological families because of abuse or neglect were made wards of the Crown (OACAS, 2003). The average age of these children was 9.1 years (Lodermeier et al., 2002). When these children have access orders to their biological parents, they cannot get adopted. On the other hand, the lack of available adoption resources for older children and for those demonstrating significant behavioural problems also results in these children staying in care until they reach the age of majority, i.e., for an average of 10 years (Lodermeier et al., 2002). Foster children are displaced once every 23.4 months on average (Plunkett & Osmond, 2004), which can lead to four or five displacements during their care (National Youth In Care Network, 2001[5]; Tremblay, 1999). Children also change social workers once every 22.3 months, which has a negative impact on their sense of security and stability (Plunkett & Osmond, 2004). This instability clearly explains why permanency planning and the best interests of those children are key objectives in the CFSA (2000).

Child's best interests

It is well known that placement in substitute care causes major changes in children's lives (limited contact with the biological family, neighbourhood, friends, or school). In turn, these disruptions have a significant impact on their well-being (Byrne, 1997). The negative effects of long-term foster care have also been addressed by many authors (Lodermeier et al., 2002; Tremblay 1999; Trocmé et al., 2002). In view of all these issues, achieving the best interests of children in foster care continues to be a major challenge facing CAS workers.

The concept

The concept of the child's best interests is rooted in child custody disputes rather than child welfare legislation (Swift, 1995). In Ontario, this concept first appeared in the 1978 amendment to the *Child Welfare Act*. It became a guiding principle for the measures to be taken when children are considered to be in need of protection (Walter et al., 1995). It was not until 2000, however, that this concept became the primary goal of the child welfare system. The aim of the *Child and Family Services Act* is now to "promote the best interests, protection and well-being of the child" (CFSA 2000, para. 1[1]:5).

Under the CFSA (2000), children's best interests are defined by 13 circumstances to be taken into account in any decisions made concerning these children. Chiefly included here are the needs that are intrinsic to children's well-being, that is, "their physical, mental and emotional needs, and the appropriate care or treatment to meet those needs" (CFSA 2000, para. 3[1]:5). Other factors to be taken into consideration are "the child's physical, mental and emotional level of development and cultural background" (CFSA 2000, para. 3[2–3:5]). The Act also sets down five guiding principles for arranging long-term care for children receiving child-welfare services. The Act refers, among other principles, to "the importance of continuity in the child's care and the possible effect on the child of disruption of that continuity" (CFSA 2000, para. 3[5–8 and 10:5]). Stability (especially in terms of the children's living arrangements) and a permanent plan for the future (adoption or return to a parent) are viewed as two of the needs associated with their well-being.

Despite this legislative framework, there is still no firm consensus as to what constitutes children's best interests, owing to the great complexity of this concept (Parker, 1994). In the *Convention on the Rights of the Child*, this concept is defined in terms of protecting children and providing the care they need to ensure their well-being, safety and health (art. 3[2–3]:1 in Cloke & Davis, 1995). The Convention also lists three categories of rights: the right to healthy development (art. 6); the right to freedom of expression (art. 13); and the right to freedom of thought (art. 14). For Miller (1993), the psychology permeating various child-welfare laws focuses on both the importance that forming significant relationships has for children and on their development, by meeting the needs intrinsic to their well-being. Children's best interests are thereby linked to their resilience. In line with these perspectives, we will define children's best interests chiefly in terms of their needs, well-being and stability. Ensuring children's well-being is therefore equated with meeting their needs with the aim of fostering their development and helping them to achieve their full potential.

Looking After Children (LAC) and the Assessment and Action Record (AAR)

The Looking After Children (LAC) approach adopted in the United Kingdom in 1991 (Ward, 1995) was introduced to Canada in the mid-1990s (Child Welfare League of Canada [CWLC], 2002). In the wake of the amendments to the child welfare system instituted since 1998, and reflecting the importance of children's best interests, the Ontario Ministry of Community and Social Services (MCSS) recommended that CAS agencies use the Assessment and Action Record (AAR) when dealing with the children placed in their care (OACAS, 1999). This approach was developed for the purposes of assessing children's needs, planning their care, and following their progress (Flynn et al., 2001, p. 1). In 2003, half the agencies were already using it.

Advocates of the LAC approach (Flynn et al., 2001; Norgaard & Balla, 2002; Parker et al., 1991) maintain that it helps children in care to reach their full potential (CWLC, 2002). In fact, this child-centred and needs-centred approach focuses on long-term planning and on providing opportunities for developing life skills (Perkins-Mangulabnan, 2003). Based on children's resilience, it is designed to follow their progress in relation to developmental goals deemed important to their well-being (Ward, 1995).

The AAR is based on seven developmental dimensions: health, education, identity, family and social relationships, social presentation, emotional and behavioural development, and self-care skills (CWLC, 2002; Ward, 1995). Each dimension of the report is filled out annually (CWLC, 2002);

all dimensions are associated with specific pre-defined objectives designed to help child welfare workers prepare annual care plans for the children (Perkins-Mangulabnan, 2003). The AAR also specifies the different steps and persons involved in achieving these objectives (Kufeldt et al., 2003).

Nevertheless, even if the best interests of the child are at the core of the child welfare system (CFSA, 2000), placement issues reveal that applying this principle in a way that fosters the well-being and resilience of children in care is a major challenge. It was this concern that led to the implementation of LAC and the AAR. Because this approach is still relatively new in Canada, it is important to highlight the views of the child welfare workers who have been using it. More specifically, the question must be asked whether or not they believe this tool provides them the support they need to ensure the best interests of the children in their care. To answer this question, our first objective was to determine the needs of foster children as perceived by clinical practitioners in daily contact with those children. Such perceptions of needs would give us a clearer picture of the best interests of the child in care. Our second objective was to examine the implementation of the AAR carried out in two CAS agencies (and specifically the part that dealt with the children's needs and best interests).

Methodology

To answer these questions, we conducted in-depth qualitative interviews with 14 social workers caring for children who had been made Crown wards because of the abuse or neglect they had experienced in their families of origin. These practitioners were recruited from two Ontario CAS agencies and selected because they were all using the AAR. The initial sample group had consisted of 20 volunteers (Mayer & Deslauriers, 2000), comprising 6 managers and 14 child welfare social workers. The latter represented one third of those from the two agencies whose duties made them eligible as interview candidates (Pires, 1997). Only the data collected from these 14 social workers will be examined in this paper since they are the ones who have daily contact with children in care.

The group included 11 women and 3 men. The participants were between the ages of 24 and 50: one belonged to the 20–24 age group; six to the 25–29 age group; three to the 30–34 age group; two to the 35–39 age group; none to the 40–44 age group; one to the 45–49 age group; and one to the 50+ age group. Three of the respondents held a master's degree in social work; seven had a bachelor's degree in social work; and four had a bachelor's degree in social sciences. With respect to their work experience with children in permanent care, six of the respondents had between 0 and 4 years of experience; seven had between 5 and 9 years; none had between 10 and 14 years; and one had 15 or more years. Finally, three of the interviewees had been using the AAR for 4 or more years, three for 3 years, five for 2 years, and three for 1 year.

The interviews focused on determining social workers' impressions of both the AAR and the needs of the children in their care. This study took place within the framework of a comprehensive Canadian research project, "Improving Child Protection Practice Through the Introduction of 'Looking After Children': An Implementation and Outcome Evaluation" (Flynn, Angus, Aubry, & Drolet, 1999). A structured interview grid was designed by the principle investigators from the different provinces to evaluate the implementation of LAC and the use of the AAR. The grid contained 40 open-ended questions covering four predetermined dimensions. It was adapted in order that in-depth interviews could be conducted with our sample group.

Held in the winter of 2004, the interviews lasted a minimum of 60 minutes and were conducted in either French or in English. The verbatim transcripts were sorted by NVivo 1.3 and coded using content analysis (Huberman & Miles, 1991; Mayer & Deslauriers, 2000). Results were analyzed deductively and inductively. Only the analysis dealing with the AAR and the children's best interests and needs will be examined.

As with other qualitative research studies, the results of this study can theoretically be generalized (Pires, 1997) to all social workers using the AAR in the two participating agencies. Although the theoretical saturation level of the data was reached, empirical generalization must be approached with caution (Pires, 1997), in view of the small number of participants in this study. The dynamic forces prevailing in other contexts are also difficult to predict.

Social workers' perceptions of foster children's needs

The concept of children's best interests is primarily linked to their needs. Because need is a relative concept (Colton, Drury, & Williams, 1995), we asked the social workers to describe their perceptions of the needs that must be met in order to ensure the well-being and best interests of the children in the care of CAS agencies. The 14 practitioners interviewed identified the following needs: (1) physiological needs; (2) emotional needs such as affection, love, acceptance, a sense of belonging, support and attention; (3) the need for stability in terms of both foster home and social worker; and (4) the need for social integration, in light of their experience as children in care.

Food, clothing and shelter correspond to basic physiological needs

(Maslow, in Hill & Tisdall, 1997; Seaberg, 1990). Only five practitioners (5/14) mentioned these basic needs as being important for the children in their care. The fact that over half the participants failed to mention these needs presumably means that they follow the same logic as does Pringle's child-needs model (1980, in Hill & Tisdall, 1997), which excludes them because they are considered self-evident.

Eight (8/14) practitioners mentioned the emotional needs (Seaberg, 1990) of the children in their care. Some of them specified that children in care need love, acceptance and a sense of belonging to a group: "They must be capable of receiving love to be able to give love." Similarly, some of them stated that children in care need to be heard and supported: "They need support, they need to feel that someone is there to support them and to listen to them." These children feel a particular need to share their many concerns with someone they trust (Hill, 1999). Removed from their biological families by force of law (CFSA, 2000), the children often have to adjust to this particular situation (Hill, 1999). Some social workers explained that children who have experienced abuse and neglect feel a great need to talk, to be heard and to be guided so they can overcome this ordeal and maximize their potential:

> Listening to these children—I think that's a vital need because some of our kids have really been put through the mill. I think we have to spend time with them, one on one, to give them the chance to air out their feelings, the chance to talk, the chance to get it all off their chest. That's what they need.

Meeting these children's affective and emotional needs gives them a sense of security, enhances their self-esteem (Pringle, 1980, in Hill & Tisdall, 1997) and helps build their resilience (Cyrulnik, 1998). Meeting their affective needs goes hand in hand with providing them with stability, either in the form of a permanent home or in the form of one or more significant relationships (Trocmé et al., 1999). The vast majority of the social workers (12/14) recognized that stability is a fundamental need for children in care and that the principle of permanency guides their practice:

> Even as adults, we need stability, we need to know where we're heading in life and to have stable relationships with the people around us. And that's even truer for children who are 3, 4, 5 or 10 years old. That's what they need.

Still on the topic of stability, the respondents talked about the children's need for someone to be there for them, to be available to them. These children need someone who can support and guide them until they reach the age of majority so they can achieve a functional level of autonomy: "They need to be surrounded by people capable of supporting them. They need a life teacher, someone who can help them, support them, teach them." In view of these needs, the high turnover of child welfare staff has an effect on children in care:

> If you're responsible for a Crown ward, you don't want to keep chang-
> ing their social worker because many of these children have several. The
> nature of our job means that these kids might have three or four social
> workers while they're in care.

As for the foster-care experience, this is in itself an unusual situation and underscores a final need. Children in care admittedly face a situation that other young people do not experience. The stigmatization and marginaliza-tion they experience in their community and in the school system have an impact on their self-esteem and trigger a process of social exclusion (Plunkett & Osmond, 2004). Some practitioners (4/14) brought out the special need to support children in normalizing their situation and helping them fit into society. They mentioned that they work actively with the children, especially in their care settings, to minimize the negative labels attached to being in care and to provide opportunities for them to achieve their full potential. Interestingly enough, none of the practitioners identified the need for the children to maintain ties with their biological families when possible. Yet, maintaining contact with the biological family is apparently a crucial factor in facilitating children's social integration (Farris-Manning & Zandstra, 2003; Plunkett & Osmond, 2004) as well as stability in foster families.

Assessment and Action Record (AAR): Benefits

Now that we have described what the practitioners perceive as the needs of children in care within the child-welfare system, we will now examine whether they believe that the Assessment and Action Record (AAR) is an effective tool for ensuring children's best interests. (Note that the AAR used in both CASs was the AAR-C2, the second Canadian adaptation [Flynn, Ghazal, & Legault, 2004]). More precisely, the data presented in this section relate to whether the AAR is able to support the social workers' interven-tions aimed at meeting the needs of the children in their care. Since the LAC approach and the AAR were developed for the purposes of assessing chil-dren's needs, planning their care, and following their progress (Flynn et al., 2001) across seven developmental dimensions (Ward, 1995), the AAR is in essence a step in the direction leading to the promotion of children's best interests. Yet how do the social workers perceive the AAR in the context of their regular contact with children in care?

First, all the practitioners we interviewed stated that this tool allows them to touch upon elements in the children's lives that would generally have received less attention in the past. Four out of five child-welfare workers (11/14) admitted that the AAR enhances their awareness of these elements. They describe this as a positive experience for all the parties concerned (social workers, children, foster parents).

> There are a lot of questions that I would never have thought to ask my kids and I think that once you manage to get people to open up, a lot of information comes out, and you can see how people react to certain questions.

As was also revealed by the data on foster children's needs, one of the aspects that practitioners used to pay less attention to was the family of origin. This is a difficult issue to broach: "Often, if our kids don't have access to their biological families, we tend to keep that door closed and not talk about it. On the other hand, it's clear that they do think about their biological families." Doucet (1999) suggested that child welfare workers are afraid of how the children will react and therefore avoid this issue. Two of the practitioners mentioned that the AAR does give them support in dealing with this sensitive topic.

Furthermore, the majority (9/14) stated that this tool allows everyone to share the same "language" when discussing how to best meet the children's needs in order to foster their development and maximize their potential. Most of them pointed out that they already bear in mind the seven dimensions covered by the AAR when they work with the children: "Maybe everyone thinks that we don't refer to these dimensions, but we actually do." "We could put away that tool right now and I'd still think about these dimensions."

According to LAC advocates (Flynn et al., 2001; Norgaard & Balla, 2002), this instrument allows practitioners to remain objective when evaluating the needs of the children in their care. Until the AAR was implemented, social workers had to make decisions on the basis of their own criteria, impressions and interpretations of children's needs to ensure their well-being. One practitioner admitted appreciating the objectivity afforded by this tool for the following reasons:

> It's very subjective when social workers arrive with their own set of values and ideas, and they end up doing what they believe is best for that particular child. Well, I think the AAR is a good tool ... which is nevertheless objective. I think it's intended above all for the child's well-being.

Besides providing support in evaluating the needs of children in care, the AAR also has the clinical objective of helping social workers develop care plans that match the children's potential and give them opportunities to develop life skills (Flynn et al., 2001). As such, it helps in the planning of their care and in tracking their progress.

There is almost a consensus (13/14) among those interviewed that the AAR helps them develop more detailed plans of care. They noted a positive difference compared with their former plans: "When we use the AAR, our care plans are much more complete. They used to fill up a single page. Now there's a minimum of seven pages."

A majority of the participants (9/14) stated that the AAR helps them formulate objectives tailored to children's specific needs and resilience. They emphasized that it supports them in developing their care plans by giving them new goals to reach during the year that are specific to each child and to the child's level of development: "I definitely put more emphasis on goals that relate specifically to the child's needs, instead of general goals. You find out much more information about the child and you work on those specific things."

Similarly, two of the practitioners explained that they were now much better able to establish long-term objectives. "The advantage is being able to look further ahead, not just day by day … but what do we want to see in one year or five years from now." Their care plans can now be formulated with greater emphasis on the children's potential and thus their best interests.

Furthermore, half of the respondents (7/14) stated that the AAR allows them to see progress in the children in their care. Some claim not to see real change from one year to the next. Still others said that they appreciate the fact that this more detailed care plan allows them to see the progress made by the children, limited as it may be: "It helps us see the progress the children have made. And there is progress, I must admit." By highlighting the steps the children have taken, they are able to emphasize the positive aspects in the children's lives, which serves to encourage them: "In that way, you can identify positive things, and I think that that's very good for the kids to see."

Other practitioners (5/14) are more sceptical about the overall usefulness of the tool for developing their care plans. They maintain that their expertise already allows them to identify what children need for their well-being. Moreover, owing to the nature of social work with foster children and the amount of the work to be done, administrative tasks must sometimes be carried out in a rush.

The Assessment and Action Record (AAR): Critical viewpoints

The third part of this paper presents respondents' viewpoints that are more critical of the implementation of the AAR as promoting children's best interests. They question the tool's ability to assess the needs of maltreated children placed in the foster-care system.

Most of those interviewed (9/14) feel that the AAR is not particularly well adapted to some of the special needs of children in care. It would seem to be less effective with children with cognitive deficits, major behavioural problems and concentration problems. This tool is also apparently more challenging to use with young people who live on their own, in detention facilities or in group homes. In agreement with Garrett (1999) and Knight and Caveney (1998), they share the same feeling as one participant who stated: "I have the impression that the AAR is designed for children who function well, who we think will cooperate."

With respect to its use on a yearly basis (CWLC, 2002), a little over half (8/14) of the respondents criticize such timing, saying they do not need this tool to evaluate the needs of children annually. In fact, they see little change from one year to the next among children in stable placements. They nevertheless support the annual use of the AAR in cases where children have experienced several upheavals during the year. Moreover, these practitioners state that using this tool every year could even become an annoyance for the children and others involved in the process, and thereby is not in the child's best interest. The following are comments that touch upon the very validity of the annual exercise: "The fourth time around, I'd say it's pretty repetitive. The kids don't want to do it any more, they say whatever pops into their head, so the tool loses its validity." "It'll be done quickly and poorly. It'll be done in a way that wasn't intended. The whole purpose of the tool is to foster discussion, and that won't happen any more."

In line with Garrett (1999), 9 out of 14 commented that the AAR does not help meet the need to normalize the foster-care experience:

> Children in care already talk about the fact that they feel different because they have a social worker and at different times they have to make a care plan and all these things that "normal" children don't need to do; unfortunately, the [AAR] reinforces that because now the three of us [including the foster parent] have to sit down and fill out a huge document that's more than 50 pages long and that's going to make them feel even more different.

The AAR also touches upon aspects of children's lives that can be very personal (Wise 2003). Children may feel intimidated and uncomfortable: "The children will feel stripped bare ... emptied out, like an open book. Because young people, if they're aware, are going to ask, where's my integrity in all of this?" As a result, those interviewed agree with Wise (2003) that it is sometimes very difficult to involve the children in the process or yet again to obtain honest answers about their situations, as they may choose to remain silent or to lie. These questions about the implementation of this tool challenge its usefulness for evaluating children's needs and best interests.

In another respect, some of the practitioners (6/14) explained that although the AAR helps them explore the needs of the children, the ensuing intervention is even more important. They raised the ethical issue that the services needed to respond to the needs identified in the AAR are not always available. This becomes a major obstacle to achieving some of the objectives in the care plans. And indeed, owing partly to the growing number of children taken into care, most agencies are not in a position to provide the quantity, quality or frequency of the services required (Wise 2003). This is also a dilemma for the community.

As previously mentioned, the child welfare system is experiencing problems ensuring stable living arrangements for maltreated children. In this respect, Jackson (1998) confirms that a tool such as the AAR is necessary because it allows social workers to gather information about these children in order to guarantee continuity in terms of their placement and best interests. Some practitioners (4/14) do not share this optimism and instead stress children's need for stability and the need to avoid displacements.

Summary and recommendations

On the whole, the need for stability is considered the core issue with respect to children in the care of CAS agencies. This point is evident throughout the literature on placement, the principle of permanency planning enshrined in the CFSA (2000), and the perceptions of the 14 practitioners consulted on the needs of the children in their care. Some social workers added that their priority consideration in achieving placement stability is finding a good match between the foster home and the child:

> Foster care stability is the top priority. That stability relies on the match between the child and the foster parents. It's all very well to find a foster family but if the match isn't right, that gets us nowhere. Without stability and a good match the children will have a hard time making progress and meeting the objectives specified in their care plans.

In fact, a relatively good match between the foster family and the child's personality and between their cultures, values and needs is necessary to increase the chances that the placement will succeed (Barratt, 2002). In their study, Lodermeier et al. (2002) suggested that an evaluation of children's needs, a successful match and the availability of placements contribute to achieving the objective of permanency planning. For that reason, the current lack of foster homes and the difficulty of recruiting and retaining foster families have a definite impact on the quality and stability of placements (Farris-Manning & Zandstra, 2003). On the other hand, several of the social workers interviewed insisted that a good match will have a beneficial impact on foster children's sense of security and that responding to the children's affective and emotional needs, and to their need to integrate into society, is a key target in promoting their best interests and well-being and actively intervening in favour of their resilience (Cyrulnik, 1998).

With respect to the Assessment and Action Record (AAR), this tool allows social workers to identify aspects of the children's needs that had been accorded less attention in the past. They are able to base their interventions on a common frame of reference built upon the seven developmental dimensions specified in the AAR. They now develop much more detailed care plans and include objectives that target more specific needs. Progress is noticed on the part of the children as a result of this more precise plan. With its clearly identified steps, the plan encourages the children to make an effort; most important, it offers them different developmental opportunities aimed at helping them maximize their potential. Consequently, the AAR achieves the objectives of its implementation and contributes to the best interests of children. A tool, such as the AAR, is needed in order to satisfy the legal responsibilities of foster care in a pro-active way.

On the other hand, a large number of practitioners maintain that the AAR is less adapted to certain children's special needs. Several raised two different issues tied directly to administering the tool. First, using the AAR every year can become annoying, so they recommended it to be used less often and in a shorter way:

> We should use it every two years at the very most and then put only the relevant questions in a condensed version so that there's more time for discussion. Of course if a child has gone through a lot or experienced several changes in the past year, we could then use the full AAR.

Some of the features of the AAR make young people uncomfortable. The practitioners suggested limiting the use of measurement scales such as those for self-esteem and problem solving. They also mentioned that greater discretion is needed when dealing with sensitive topics like sexuality and drug use. They recommended the use of open-ended questions when discussing the children's living arrangements and future. They stressed that support should be provided sooner and organized more readily for young people turning 18 and facing the transition between the foster system and total independence. The respondents pointed out an issue that is somewhat overlooked by the AAR, and should be reviewed: the ethnic and cultural diversity of young Canadians and the work that needs to be done to help them strengthen their cultural ties and heritage.

The respondents also indicated that even though the AAR is instrumental in evaluating children's needs, the ensuing intervention is much more important. Since meeting the needs identified by the AAR is clearly in the children's best interest, responding to these needs calls for appropriate resources in relation to each of the seven developmental dimensions of children in care. Furthermore, these resources must be pooled together, planned, implemented, coordinated, followed up and maintained (Turcotte & DeLuca, 1993).

Once again, social workers juggle the limited time they have with reaching out to and supporting the children, the foster families and the resource persons identified in the care plans. However, social workers affirm that providing support to those involved in the care plan comprises the form of intervention that most effectively favours children's best interests and resilience. Barber and Delfabbro (2004) propose that even the informal support network of foster families is associated with more positive results.

Nevertheless, heavy caseloads and frequent changes in social worker staff (given the nature of the job) hinder the important work of stimulating support: establishing beneficial relationships between foster families, children in care and networks demands a lot of time and effort. Given that all this is occurring in the midst of an increase in the number of children being placed in care, and in the wake of the Hurwitz and Cresswell report (2001), they recommend a reduction in their administrative tasks as a means of alleviating their workload.

Conclusion

In conclusion, given that the paramount purpose of the CFSA (2000) is to promote the best interests of the child, and that the principle of permanency planning is clearly spelled out in the Act, we must continue to reflect on the best interests of children in terms of stability and support for that stability. The first encouraging steps have been taken in that direction— the main one being the implementation of the Looking After Children approach and the opportunities it presents for supporting the development and resiliency of children in care. All the same, the recommendations proposed by the social workers should be carefully considered so that the best interests of the child will become truly enshrined in our daily reality.

Authors' note

The authors gratefully acknowledge the financial support received from the Social Sciences and Humanities Research Council (strategic grant no. 828-1999-1008, awarded to Robert J. Flynn, principal investigator; co-investigators Tim D. Aubry, Marie Drolet and Douglas E. Angus). We thank especially the child welfare practitioners from the two Ontario Children's Aid Societies who graciously consented to participate in the interviews upon which this study was based. The authors also thank Louise Legault, Caroline Lemieux and the School of Social Work of the University of Ottawa for their contributions.

References

Barber, J. G., & Delfabbro, P. H. (2004). *Children in foster care*. London: Routledge.

Barratt, S. (2002). Fostering care: The child, the family and the professional system. *Journal of Social Work Practice, 16*, 163–173.

Byrne, B. A. (1997). *Le bien-être des jeunes placés sous les soins de la Société de l'aide à l'enfance d'Ottawa-Carleton: Parole aux jeunes!* Unpublished master's thesis, University of Ottawa, Ottawa, ON, Canada.

Cloke, C., & Davies, M. (1995). *Participation and empowerment in child protection*. London: Pitman Publishing.

Child and Family Services Act (CFSA), ch. C.11. (1990 [2000]).

Child Welfare League of Canada. (2002). S'occuper des enfants. *Mise à jour canadienne, 1*(1), 1–5. Retrieved July 2004 from: http://cwlc.no-profit.ca.net/html/french/LAC-French.pdf

Colton, M., Drury, C., & Williams, M. (1995). Children in need: Definition, identification and support. *British Journal of Social Work, 25*, 711–728.

Cyrulnik, B. (1998). *Ces enfants qui tiennent le coup*. Revigny-sur-Ornain, France : Hommes et perspectives.

Doucet, M. (1999). Des adolescents témoignent de l'abandon parental. *Prisme, 29*, 110–121.

Farris-Manning, C., & Zandstra, M. (2003). *Children in care in Canada.* Ottawa, ON: Child Welfare League of Canada,

Flynn, R. J., Angus, D., Aubry, T., & Drolet, M. (1999). *Improving child protection practice through the introduction of Looking After Children into the 54 Local Children's Aid Societies in Ontario: An implementation and outcome evaluation.* SSHRC Strategic Grant No. 828-1999-1008. Ottawa, ON: Centre for Research on Community Services, University of Ottawa.

Flynn, R.J., Ghazal, H., & Legault, L. (2004). *Looking After Children: Good Parenting, Good Outcomes. Assessment and Action Record* (second Canadian adaptation). Ottawa, ON & London, UK: Centre for Research on Community Services, University of Ottawa & Her Majesty's Stationery Office (HMSO).

Flynn, R., Ghazal, H., Moshenko, S., & Westlake, L. (2001). Main features and advantages of a new "Canadianized" version of the Assessment and Action Record from Looking After Children. *Ontario Association of Children's Aid Societies Journal, 45*(2), 1–5.

Garrett, P. M. (1999). Mapping child-care social work in the final years of the twentieth century: A critical response to the 'Looking After Children' system. *British Journal of Social Work, 29,* 22–47.

Hill, M. (1999). What's the problem? Who can help? The perspectives of children and young people on their well-being and on helping professionals. *Journal of Social Work Practice, 13,* 135–145.

Hill, M., & Tisdall, K. (1997). *Children and society.* London: Longman.

Huberman, M. A., & Miles, M. B. (1991). *Analyse des données qualitatives: Recueil de nouvelles méthodes.* Brussels: De Boeck Université.

Hurwitz, H., & Cresswell, D. (2001). Workload measurement project report. *Ontario Association of Children's Aid Societies Journal, 45*(1), 8–38.

Jackson, S. (1998). Looking After Children: A new approach or just an exercise in form filling? A response to Knight and Caveney. *British Journal of Social Work, 28,* 45–56.

Knight, T., & Caveney, S. (1998). Assessment and Action Records: Will they promote good parenting? *British Journal of Social Work, 28,* 29–43.

Kufeldt, K., Simard, M., Tite, R., & Vachon, J. (2003). The "Looking After Children in Canada" project: Educational outcomes. In K. Kufeldt & B. Mckenzie (Eds.), *Child welfare: Connecting research, policy and practice* (pp. 177–189). Waterloo, ON: Wilfred Laurier University Press.

Lodermeier, J.-A., Hammond, D., Henderson, H., & Carvalho, N. (2002). Factors affecting timely permanency planning for children in care. *Canadian Social Work, 4,* 136–153.

Mayer, R., & Deslauriers, J.-P. (2000). Quelques éléments d'analyse qualitative. L'analyse de contenu, l'analyse ancrée, l'induction analytique et le récit de vie. In R. Mayer, F. Ouellet, M.-C. St-Jacques, D. Turcotte, et al. (Eds.). *Méthodes de recherche en intervention sociale* (pp. 159–190). Montréal, Québec : Gaétan Morin Éditeur.

Miller, G. (1993). The psychological best interests of the child. *Journal of Divorce and Remarriage, 19*(1–2), 21–36.

National Youth in Care Network. (2001). *Who will teach me to learn: Creating positive school experiences for youth in care.* Retrieved July 2004 from www.youthincare.ca

Norgaard, V., & Balla, S. (2002). Looking After Children Canadian-style. *Ontario Association of Children's Aid Societies Journal, 46*(1), 3–4.

Ontario Association of Children's Aid Societies. (OACAS). (1999). Child welfare reform agenda: A progress report. *Ontario Association of Children's Aid Societies Journal, 43*(1), 4–13.

Ontario Association of Children's Aid Societies. (OACAS). (2002). *Workload management project report, Phase III final report.* Retrieved July 2004 from http://www.oacas.org

Ontario Association of Children's Aid Societies (OACAS). (2003). *CAS Facts. April 1, 2002—March 31, 2003.* Retrieved July 2004 from http://www.oacas.org/resources/CAS%20Facts%20Ap02Mar03.pdf

Ontario Association of Children's Aid Societies (OACAS). (2003-2004). Looking After Children. Background information on youth aged 10–15. *Ontario Association of Children's Aid Societies Journal, 47*(3), 34.

Ontario "Looking After Children" Project (OnLAC). (2003). *Agency recruitment, 4*(2), p. 2.

Parker, S. (1994). The best interest of the child—Principles and problems. *International Journal of Law and Family, 8,* 26–41.

Parker, R., Ward, H., Jackson, S., Aldgate, J., & Wedge, P. (1991). *Looking After Children: Assessing outcomes in child care.* London: HMSO.

Perkins-Mangulabnan, J. (2003). *Foster parenting practices as predictors of foster child outcome.* Unpublished doctoral thesis proposal, University of Ottawa, Ottawa, ON, Canada.

Pires, A. (1997). Échantillonnage et recherché qualitative : essai théorique et méthodologique. In Poupart et al. (Eds.), *La recherche qualitative : enjeux épistémologiques et méthodologiques* (pp. 113–169). Gaétan Morin Éditeur.

Plunkett, R., & Osmond, M. (2004). Permanency planning: Choosing between long-term foster care and adoption. *Ontario Association of Children's Aid Societies Journal, 48*(1), 7–14.

Seaberg, J. R. (1990). Child well-being: A feasible concept? *Social Work, 35,* 267–272.

Swift, K. (1995). *Manufacturing "bad mothers": A critical perspective on child neglect.* Toronto, ON: University of Toronto Press.

Tremblay, G. (1999). L'impact du placement d'enfants. Une recension des écrits. *Travail social canadien, 1*(1), 90–99.

Trocmé, N., Fallon, B., MacLaurin, B., & Copp, B. (2002). *The changing face of child welfare investigations in Ontario: Ontario incidence of reported child abuse and neglect 1993/1998.* Toronto, ON: Centre of Excellence for Child Welfare, Faculty of Social Work, University of Toronto.

Trocmé, N., Nutter, B., MacLaurin, B., & Fallon, B. (1999). *Child Welfare Outcome Indicator Matrix.* Bell Canada Child Welfare Research Unit.

Turcotte, D., & DeLuca, T. (1993). *L'implantation du plan de services individualisé en protection de la jeunesse. Le cas du C.S.S de l'Outaouais.* Québec, QC: École de service social de l'Université Laval.

Walter, B., Isenegger, J. A., & Bala, N. (1995). "Best interests" in child protection proceedings: Implications and alternatives. *Canadian Journal of Family Law, 12,* 367–439.

Ward, H. (1995). *Looking After Children: Research into practice.* London: HMSO.

Wise, S. (2003). An evaluation of the trial of Looking After Children in the state of Victoria, Australia. *Children and Society, 17,* 3–17.

1   The general term "children" will be used to designate both children and youths (adolescents) for the purpose of simplifying the text. In 2003, 76% of the children involved with the AAR were between the ages of 10 and 17 (OACAS, 2003).

2   Permanency planning is defined as "the systematic process of carrying out, within a limited period, a set of goal-directed activities designed to help the children and youths live in families that offer a continuity of relationships with nurturing parents or caretakers, and the opportunity to offer life-time relationships" (Mallucio et al., 1986, in Farris-Manning & Zandstra, 2003:10).

3   In 2003, close to half (25/52) of Ontario CAS agencies had already taken part in the LAC implementation project (OnLAC, 2003).

4   73% of 410 children interviewed with the AAR in 2003 lived with foster families; 80% of them were Crown wards. The children averaged 7 years of age when they were first placed in care (OACAS, 2003).

5   This figure is based on a sample of 100 young people between the ages of 12 and 23, with the average age being 17 (National Youth In Care Network, 2001).

CHAPTER 19

Managing change: Implementing Looking After Children at Prescott-Russell Services to Children and Adults

Raymond Lemay, Beverly Ann Byrne and Hayat Ghazal

Introduction

Looking After Children (LAC) is a strength-based, resilience-focused approach that systematically operationalizes good parenting for children and youth who are in the care of the state (Lemay & Ghazal, 2004). The Assessment and Action Record (AAR) (Flynn, Ghazal, & Legault, 2004), which is the comprehensive assessment tool that is part and parcel of the LAC approach, is sometimes used as a stand-alone individual clinical assessment and service planning tool. It also provides the possibility of data aggregation and program and outcome monitoring. LAC is a different way of providing residential services: it is an important change in approach requiring a different mind-set from staff and foster parents. Moreover, using the AAR takes on average about 3.5 hours, which is a considerable time investment at the front end of the service process. As Jane Scott (1999) reported in her implementation audit in the United Kingdom, "the cultural and organizational shift required to implement Looking After Children cannot and should not be underestimated" (p. 29).

The Looking After Children approach was first developed for child welfare authorities in the United Kingdom (Parker, Ward, Jackson, Aldgate, & Wedge, 1991), but has since been adopted in a number of other jurisdictions including Hungary, Australia and Canada. Flynn, Ghazal, Moshenko and Westlake (2001) have written a useful description of the features of the second Canadian version of the AAR (i.e., the AAR-C2).

This article reviews the implementation of Looking After Children in a medium-sized Canadian child welfare organization, identifies implementation strategies that seem to have been effective, and relates these to themes that recur in the management literature. One book in particular, by R. Luecke (2003), *Managing Change and Transition*, provides an interesting conceptual framework for managing change that is quite relevant to the experiences in Prescott-Russell described above. Other important management sources that will be referred to in this part include Buckingham and Coffman (1999), Collins (2001a), Gladwell (2000/2002) and Hage (1999).

The local context

Prescott-Russell Services to Children and Adults is the result of a recent amalgamation of child and adult developmental services and child and family mental health services with an Ontario Children's Aid Society (CAS). When Looking After Children was first introduced into the organization, the latter was known by its original corporate name of the *Prescott-Russell Children's Aid Society* or la *Société de l'aide à l'enfance de Prescott-Russell*. Founded in 1935, the Prescott-Russell Children's Aid Society (PRCAS) was responsible for delivering child protection services in the United Counties of Prescott and Russell in accordance with the *Child and Family Services Act* of Ontario. The United Counties of Prescott and Russell have a population of approximately 80,000 people (c. 2001), of whom a majority are francophone (approximately 75%). The United Counties are in the easternmost part of the province of Ontario, an hour west of Montreal, Quebec, and 45 minutes east of Ottawa, Ontario. It is a mostly rural region, with the majority of the population spread out in some 30 villages and with 3 small urban clusters (each 10,000 people and fewer) at the extremities of the geographic region. Several social indicators suggest that the United Counties of Prescott and Russell are an economically depressed area in Ontario, including a high placement rate for children in care, high suicide rate, below-average family income, and high unemployment (Lalande and Bertrand, 2003).

The organization has a history of using mostly foster care as a residential option. Foster care has accounted for more than 90% of the total days of care since the mid-1980s in a province where the use of foster care by local CASs ranges from 30% to 91% of total days care, with an average of less than 50% for the province as a whole (Lemay, 1999).

Evaluation of Child Welfare Outcomes Project (ECWO)

LAC was initially a component of a larger agency-wide initiative that proposed to first ascertain and then improve client outcomes. In late 1994, the Prescott-Russell Children's Aid Society, along with Professor Robert J. Flynn of the University of Ottawa, submitted a proposal, *Evaluating Child Welfare Outcomes/Évaluation des Résultats de l'Aide à l'Enfance* (Flynn & Biro, 1996), to the Ontario Ministry of Community and Social Services for a "foster care demonstration grant." At the outset, it was decided that the methods of outcome monitoring and measurement of program effectiveness could not be so costly as to reduce direct service time to clients. Moreover, it was felt that whatever monitoring and measurement system was set up had to involve employees, foster parents, and volunteers from the organization. The Evaluating Child Welfare Outcomes (ECWO) project also provided for the administration of a program evaluation tool called PASSING (Wolfensberger & Thomas, 1983), with a first assessment conducted in 1997 (Osburn, Caruso, & Reidy, 1997) as well as the piloting of a cost-benefit measure (Beecham & Flynn, 2000). Since then, the amalgamated organization has gone on to systematically using a briefer version of PASSING (Flynn, Guirguis, Wolfensberger, & Cocks, 1999) for all of its programs. Eventually, the organization developed a comprehensive program measurement, monitoring and management system described by Flynn, Lemay, Ghazal and Hébert (2003).

In 1994, the Prescott-Russell Children's Aid Society obtained an early version of the U. K. Assessment and Action Record of LAC and piloted its use with two children in care and their foster families, as well as with one child who was not in residential services but still living with his own parents. This early experience suggested to the management team that the tools were very powerful in refocusing intervention toward a positive and strengths-based approach that could be very useful clinically for front-line staff. The AAR systematically gathered information on service outputs, activities and outcomes. Moreover, the AAR answer format allowed data aggregation. In April of 1995, PRCAS was awarded a three-year "foster care demonstration grant" that allocated to the agency approximately $235,000 to help support the ECWO project. It is important to note that none of this money was used by the organization to add any extra human resources to administer AAR assessments or even to implement the approach. Rather, the money was devoted to the first Canadian adaptation and translation of the Assessment and Action Record (Biro & Lemay, 1996a, 1996b), to establish a data aggregation capacity, and helped pay for a validity and reliability study carried out by Flynn and Biro (1998). PRCAS implemented LAC without any additional staffing or funding. Robert Flynn and Chantal Biro (1996) then reported on the early history of the ECWO project.

Dissatisfaction and the need for change

Looking After Children was introduced to PRCAS in a period of great tension and because there was considerable dissatisfaction with the *status quo*. The board of directors was dissatisfied with the lack of information about program effectiveness. In 1989, Mr. Claude Mainville, then Chairman of the Board, proposed that the organization should change its focus from the monitoring of inputs and service volumes to the measurement of outputs and the monitoring of outcomes. His stated rationale was simple: Board members had for years been approving important increases in expenditure and budgets with no sense that the money being spent was in fact leading to improvements in the lives of the children and families served by the organization. Mr. Mainville and the members of the Board instructed the Executive Director and his management team to develop a new way of monitoring and measuring the organization's effectiveness.

For their part, agency employees were dissatisfied for a whole variety of reasons. Staff had unionized in 1987 following the specialization of certain service functions (intake and residential services). At PRCAS, case loads were high and, as in all Ontario Children's Aid Societies, the organization was then struggling with important budget and salary constraints. By 1995, the relations between staff and management were in great difficulty; as they were unable to come to a new collective agreement, staff went on a bitter 15-week strike. Moreover, there was an ongoing general malaise about service results, particularly for children and youth in care. Since the agency had no outcome data to speak of, a few situations of poor service outcomes generated a considerable amount of acrimonious debate.

Nevertheless, such situations are not exceptional. Most private for-profit organizations are mediocre performers and do not achieve excellent results (Buckingham & Coffman, 1999; Collins, 2001a, Foster & Kaplan, 2001). Though there are few similar studies of the not-for-profit sector, some of these suggest that most human service organizations do not perform better (Flynn, Guirguis, Wolfensberger, & Cocks, 1999; Lemay, 2001; Wolfensberger, 1978). Not surprisingly, many managers work with staff who are somewhat cynical and critical of the service processes in which they are involved and the impact that services might have on clients.

Dissatisfaction is at times the order of the day in many organizations, and the good news is that this dissatisfaction can be marshalled in the cause of innovation and change. There might be better times to introduce change, but if things are going well, people would tend to be satisfied. Moreover, as Luecke (2003) points out, satisfaction breeds continuity because if people are satisfied with what is going on, there are few good reasons for change. In fact, one of the most important change strategies in an organization is to first make the case for change. When it comes to Looking After Children, that case can be made on the basis that the outcomes on which we do have some data are not very good (Lemay & Ghazal,

2004) or, at the very least, could be much better. It should not be surprising that the LAC initiative was first developed in the UK following highly publicized problems in the child welfare system. The dissatisfaction in the UK was broad and touched upon issues of outcomes and accountability.

There are not many systematic data about how well or how poorly looked-after children and youth are doing while in the care of the state, and there is not much information about their outcomes when they leave care (Lemay & Ghazal, 2004). The little research that does exist suggests important experiential and outcome gaps between looked-after children and youth and typical Canadian kids (Flynn & Biro, 1998). This is certainly borne out by some of the recent data coming from Looking After Children that show, for instance, that about 50% of children and youth in care in Ontario have significant school problems compared to only about 7% of children in the general population (Ghazal & Petrick, 2003 & 2004).

Collins (2001a) suggests that, at least in his large sample of for-profit corporations, organizations that perform well are those that systematically attend to the bad results and problems, that it is more important to scrutinize failure than celebrate success. Similarly, hospital medicine requires a practice of systematically reporting and discussing medical errors through regularly held "Morbidity and Mortality" conferences (Gawande, 2002). Hage (1999) and Luecke (2003) point out that employees in private for-profit industry can be motivated to improve performance and to take on innovation for altruistic reasons. Luecke (2003) proposes that appealing to employee's better motives helps in bringing about change. He points out that many organizations in the for-profit sector have lofty goals that propose benefits to the community rather than just to shareholders. He provides the example of 3M, which has as its purpose to "solve unsolved problems innovatively." Cargill's mission is "to improve the standard of living around the world;" Hewlett-Packard wants "to make technical contributions for the advancement and welfare of humanity;" and McKinsey & Company seeks "to help leading corporations and governments to be more successful." These lofty ideals can play a role in creating the impetus for improvement in the business world, and human services should certainly attempt to motivate their staff and stakeholders by appealing to important values and broad goals. After all, many people become involved in human services precisely to do some good and to make a difference. So, dissatisfaction with current results on the one hand, and the positive motivation that brings most people to the field on the other, can be used to set the scene for the introduction of innovation and change.

This was certainly the case at PRCAS where, despite a strike that could have seriously jeopardized the introduction of LAC (at least in the medium term), employees were by and large willing, and some were even enthusiastic, at the idea of implementing Looking After Children. Indeed, the LAC initiative was one thing that an otherwise divided workforce could come together on. Very simply, Board members, managers, and staff (in the children services team, particularly) could not help but observe some of the difficulties that our organization was having in garnering positive outcomes for looked-after children and youth; they concluded that change was needed and LAC worth considering. A number of front-line staff quickly identified themselves as champions for change and were the first to try out the Assessment and Action Record in the piloting stage; they eventually became quite vocal supporters of the change process.

That is not to say there were no naysayers among the employees; quite the contrary: a number of them voiced concerns and talked about the difficulties of introducing the Assessment and Action Record. These difficulties centred on high caseloads and on the notion that the AAR seemed to be a lot of additional bureaucracy that would keep them away from clients. Luecke (2003) argues that naysayers have important information to convey: though they have an agenda for stopping change, the information they provide is critical and can help identify some of the difficulties that might be encountered during the change process. Critical individuals can often identify real stumbling blocks to change that are best identified early on, rather than encountered later by surprise. Thus, the critics and naysayers play an important role and should be listened to. Indeed, after the training, and in response to some of the concerns voiced by some staff, the management team conducted a review of the forms and reports that were part of the required documentation process. The conclusion of this review was a very public, almost celebratory, removal of many of the forms, an action that was well received by staff and foster parents.

Why change is difficult

The best time for introducing change could very well be when things are difficult; however, that does not mean that change will be easy. Luecke (2003) acknowledges that most organizations view change and innovation as being difficult. For instance, change and innovation require that employees and other stakeholders take up new work practices and abandon habitual processes with which they have developed competence and comfort, that is, leaving the known to take up the unknown. As Luecke argues, most people equate new and different work processes with more work and this is, in fact, most probably the case because of learning curves. Habitual practices require less effort and deliberation, whereas new practices require a great deal of concentration, persistence, and effort to master.

Hage (1999) adds that innovation and change are easier in some organizations than others and that this is in part due to issues of structure. He suggests that centralization and formality in organizations inhibit change, and he documents that decentralized and informal organizations are more comfortable with change and innovation and seem to experience a great deal more of it. Indeed, Collins (2001a) found that high-performing organizations, or so-called "good-to-great" companies, were not large, complex, highly bureaucratized organizations with multiple levels of hierarchy; rather, they were fairly flat and collegial. By and large, child welfare organizations are relatively hierarchical and centralized, and relationships, particularly those between front-line staff and front-line supervisors, are fairly formal (for instance, because of standardized work processes), suggesting initial barriers to change. With its amalgamation in 2001, Prescott-Russell Services to Children and Adults opted for a flattened management structure. It comprised four self-directed teams of front-line managers directing services and an ambitious program of change and innovation that would relatively quickly lead to an integrated model of service inspired, at least in part, by LAC's positive strengths-based approach.

But earlier, in 1995-1996, when it was decided to implement LAC, the situation was quite different. The agency had a traditional management structure and had not, until then, experienced much change. In fact, the last important service process to be changed at the agency dated back to 1987 with the specialization of the intake function and the creation of specialized residential services teams; these changes were quite dramatic and led to unionization. Implementing LAC affected mostly residential services, but at the time, this touched upon the work of most professional staff in the organization. Moreover, in 1997, the Ontario government implemented an important and labour-intensive service and funding reform strategy (which included the use of a risk assessment tool and a standardized child protection investigation process) affecting mostly non-residential services. All of a sudden, much was going on; some of it was unexpected, and this might have lead to delays or even to abandoning the LAC approach.

Planning... But a preference for action

Luecke (2003) quotes *Patten's law* which reads "a good plan today is better than a perfect plan tomorrow." A number of management authors (Collins, 2001a; Coutu, 2003) have argued against overplanning and preparing for every eventuality. Organizations are complex and embedded in communities and in jurisdictions that provide for a lot of unpredictability. Though some planning is needed, it is important for a plan to be flexible, to evolve over time, and especially to engage key people in action. In Prescott-Russell, the implementation plan evolved in stages. The members of the management team and staff were well aware of where they wanted to end up—full implementation—but did not plan more than one stage at a time. Thus, PRCAS field tested the draft AAR, which then led to the development of a project proposal that was eventually funded by the government. Managers then planned for training and a later pilot stage. As the pilot was going forward, planning proceeded and prepared the organization for various degrees of implementation. Full implementation ended up taking about 24 months, which is a fairly tight time frame under the circumstances.

Communications

Feedback and communication are, at all times, critical management issues in most organizations (Buckingham & Coffman, 1999). Talking up and communicating the need for change, both the plan for change and the progress of change are important factors in keeping an implementation plan on track (Luecke, 2003). The issue of dissatisfaction discussed above requires a good communication plan that highlights the need for change by talking up some of the difficulties encountered in service provision and in service outcomes. Poor outcomes and the lack of data that confront most agencies are good places to sensitize staff, foster parents, and management about the need for organizational change. Communications are also important to ensure that organizations are not surprised by changes taking place. As implementation progresses, feedback is critical, particularly for the staff and foster parents directly involved in the change strategy. Finally, it is important to ensure that all stakeholders know about implementation successes as they occur: talking up success is vital, particularly early on as momentum is building.

Since the Prescott-Russell agency was of moderate size and since the initial implementation of Looking After Children would mostly concern two teams of social workers and a group of foster parents, communications were rather simple and fairly contained. Nonetheless, it was important to keep the Board of Directors apprised of the developments in implementing Looking After Children, and it was particularly important to allow all involved in the implementation to review and savor the data when they were finally available in 1997. The research coordinator produced yearly reports and a newsletter (Biro, Flynn, Lemay, & Lalonde, 1997, 1998) that kept stakeholders apprised of developments and data as they became available. Through the years numerous meetings were held to show and discuss the data with employees, foster parents, youth in care, Board members and funders. It was of great importance to share the data and put them to immediate clinical and managerial use (see Flynn, Lemay, Ghazal, & Hébert [2003] for a description of this process), if only to ensure that staff were directly getting the benefit of their work; otherwise, it was feared that they might conclude they were investing a lot of time on a mere research project (Martin [1993] provides an in-depth discussion of how systematically gathered data may improve decision-making). Many employees and foster parents commented on the fact that just seeing the data for the first time made the work and the effort seem worthwhile. At the same time, communications emphasized that the data-gathering activities were very secondary to the individual assessment and service plan process, which most participants found helpful and engaging. In supervision and team meetings, the AAR, the assessment process, and the resulting individual service plan were often the subject of probing discussion.

The initial data were quite compelling and readily suggested two initial conclusions about reading and out-of-school activities: looked-after children and youth did not seem to be reading much, and they were not involved in many after-school or weekend activities. Front-line staff recommended that the agency promote the purchase of books and magazines as presents for children and youth in care, and the idea was promoted at subsequent meetings with foster parents and through memos. Child protection workers were encouraged to purchase reading materials that they would give to the children and youth. The board of directors also liberalized the agency's expense reimbursement policies in order to further promote the purchase of reading materials, subscriptions to periodicals, and the enrollment of children and youth in extra-curricular activities. Staff and foster parents were encouraged to address both of these issues when writing up plans of care, and these were then reviewed in supervision. This early attention to the data, and the resultant decisions and expenditures, were very important in getting staff, foster parents, managers and board members involved in Looking After Children.

Piloting: A developmental model of implementation

Change is best understood according to what we could call a *developmental model* where the organic organization is called upon to move through stages of development. Change requires momentum. Momentum is built up one step at a time with small successes leading to big successes (Collins, 2001a). Such a developmental model also allows individuals and groups to progress along their learning curves: to practice new skills, develop competence and, finally, mastery. It also allows a good planner to initially involve the enthusiastic or at least the committed, then, at a later stage, the willing, and, finally, everybody else.

Piloting

Piloting is a particularly powerful strategy for cutting one's teeth on a new, innovative service practice that one has yet to master. Piloting comes with the notion that one starts small before growing the change project into larger components. Piloting provides an opportunity for the enthusiastic and the committed to try out and play with an innovation, to garner success and, of course, to communicate that success to others. Piloting and the accumulation of small successes help make change eventually inevitable in an organization. Successful piloting creates momentum. At PRCAS, the piloting went through a number of stages. In 1994, Danielle Lalonde, a front-line supervisor, tested the draft version of the British AAR with two youth in care, and with a family receiving child welfare services. These early trials demonstrated the feasibility of using the AAR with looked-after children and youth, but also made clear that the tools would require major modifications for use in non-residential services (an idea which the organization eventually abandoned). Indeed, the 1994 testing of the AAR created enthusiasm in the management team and gave the agency its first LAC champion: Mrs. Lalonde.

During 1995 and part of 1996, the AAR was adapted and translated by Chantal Biro and Raymond Lemay (1996a & 1996b). After the initial training in 1996, staff members who had seemed to respond best to the training were approached individually and asked to pilot the Assessment and Action Record with two children of the 5-to-9 age group in their case loads. We wanted to keep the pilot stage as simple as possible and only use one of the AAR age-group categories. From June to October 1996, eight children and youth in care were assessed, and then individual service plans were developed from the Assessment and Action Record information.

In November 1996, the organization went to full implementation, at least for all looked-after children and youth who were permanently in care (termed "Crown wards" in the *Child and Family Services Act*). Thus, in this first 12-month period, 65 looked-after children and youth were assessed.

In 1997, Chantal Biro administered an abridged version of the *National Longitudinal Survey of Children and Youth* (NLSCY; Brink & McKellar, 2000; Willms, 2002) to 43 looked-after children and youth and their foster parents. This exercise was done first and foremost as a validity exercise for the AAR, but was also used to confirm the developmental gap that was thought to exist between children and youth in residential care with typical Canadian children and youth (Flynn and Biro, 1998, reported on this assessment).

In 1998, full implementation continued, with all 94 permanent (Crown) wards being assessed. In 1999, full implementation was broadened, and all looked-after children and youth who had been in care for one year or more were assessed. This brought the number up to 155 out of a total of 182 children.

During this time, the Centre for Research on Community Services at the University of Ottawa developed the infrastructure for data aggregation, which was later expanded and used for the Ontario Looking After Children Project, and Phase II of the Canadian Looking After Children Project. Indeed, as early as the end of 1997, Chantal Biro was presenting first-year data to front-line staff and foster parents, managers, and the Board of Directors (Biro, Flynn, Lemay, & Lalonde, 1997, 1998).

Working groups, leadership and champions

Implementing change and innovation requires getting many people involved in moving the change forward. Martin (1993) suggests that achieving organizational objectives may be facilitated by a team approach that has a clear mandate and direction from senior management. Choosing the right persons to represent the various stakeholders is of great importance and should as much as possible bring together people who have demonstrated enthusiasm and engagement in the organization and in the change and innovation process (Luecke, 2003). This can be done by creating a working group with a composition that should include front-line staff, foster parents, youth in care, and senior managers. Thus, broad stakeholder representation ensures that every group that might have a stake in the change is involved in planning, implementing, and evaluating it. Such a working group becomes a leadership group which, in turn, requires terms of reference and empowerment from the organization's leadership. At PRCAS, the Board of Directors was overwhelmingly supportive, and the executive director was directly involved in a number of the implementation initiatives.

During implementation, the agency's project champions had a lot of support, which lead to a sure-footed path of implementation. Working group leaders, or champions, must have special qualities. Luecke (2003) calls these individuals "change agents" and he suggests that they "articulate the need for change; are accepted by others as trustworthy and competent; see and diagnose problems from the perspective of their audience; motivate people to change; work through others in translating intent into action; stabilize the adoption of innovation; and, foster self-renewing behavior and others so that they can 'go out of business' as change agents" (p. 77). Collins (2001b) suggests that leadership requires humility and a "fierce resolve."

Moreover, a champion—an individual who in a sense personifies the change that is being proposed—should lead the group. In Prescott-Russell, a number of individuals played this role at different times. We were particularly fortunate in hiring Chantal Biro and then Hayat Ghazal as our project coordinators, but members of management—Danielle Lalonde, and (since 2000) Beverly-Ann Byrne—as well as other front-line staff have also been champions.

PRCAS did not really set up a formal working group, though a fair amount of time was devoted to meeting with stakeholders to keep them apprised of developments and listen to advice and concerns. In retrospect, a formal working group would probably have ensured even quicker implementation.

Training

Hage (1999) points out that innovative organizations tend to spend a lot of money on research and development but also spend a fair amount of money, time and effort in transferring new knowledge and new innovations to employees through in-house training. It is a question of eliminating the research-practice gap, and ongoing training becomes the vehicle for ensuring up-to-date practice. This concept, when transferred to the child welfare realm or at least to Looking After Children, is probably best understood as providing staff, foster parents, and even youth in care with the knowledge and the skills required to use the AAR effectively and to integrate the LAC approach. Indeed, recent research on the implementation of the AAR in Ontario (Pantin & Flynn, 2004; Pantin, Flynn, and Runnels, 2006, this volume) shows that staff and foster parents who receive the complete two-day training program on LAC perceive this training as being of higher quality. Because of the training, they see the revised Canadian Assessment and Action Record as being helpful in their roles as child protection workers or foster parents. Finally, the training leads them to view the work they and their service partners do with the young person as being more successful in achieving the broad goals and priorities of LAC (Pantin & Flynn, 2004).

With Looking After Children, what professionals, foster parents, and other stakeholders are called upon to do is to provide improved day-to-day parenting (the humble tasks of parenting), which becomes the primary mode of intervention rather than other competing modalities such as treatment, therapy, etc. The AAR is not only a comprehensive interview guide, but also very pedagogic: its many questions lay out, in operational terms, the expected behavior of a partnership of adults engaged in the parenting of a looked-after child or youth. Thus, every administration "teaches" an effective form of parenting.

Looking After Children requires a very proactive approach to assessment: the AAR is not administered after the fact (after a crisis or after a problem), but rather it is a yearly assessment activity that attempts to ascertain the current life conditions and experiences of children and youth (the quality of the parenting that they are receiving) and the outcomes they are achieving. It is done at the beginning of the service cycle rather than as a reaction to a crisis.

The AAR is a direct service tool; in other words, the assessment is conducted with the full participation of the caregiver, and with the child or youth (starting at age 10), as an extended conversation about the child or youth's current situation as well as about his or her future. The individual service plan that comes from this exercise is constructed with the full participation of the individuals who will carry it out, including the child or youth. There is probably a greater likelihood of implementation if the persons who will do the work feel some ownership for the plan. Youth in residential care are also quite vocal in wanting to have a say about the plans we make for them (Byrne & Lemay, 2005).

LAC requires that a foster parent and child protection worker hold and communicate high and positive expectations to a child or youth in care. The tool and the approach stress strengths and assets rather than deficits and pathology. The AAR systematically describes normative parenting as the expected service output, and the age categories direct the participants to measure age-appropriate outcomes. Resilience—"a dynamic process encompassing positive adaptation within the context of significant adversity" (Luthar, Cicchetti, & Becker, 2000, p. 543)—is the expected outcome. The AAR comprehensively articulates normative parenting and suggests that typical life experiences and conditions, such as those that are taken for granted by most Canadian children and youth, will counter the effects of past adversity and lead to better outcomes. Some researchers suggest that putting an end to adversity, and providing typical life conditions and experiences, will be sufficient to promote positive development and resilience (Clarke & Clarke, 2000; Lemay & Ghazal, 2001). LAC is quite consistent with Masten's (2001) observations on resilience: "Resilience does not come from rare and special qualities, but from the everyday magic of ordinary, normative human resources in the minds, brains, and bodies of children, in their families and relationships, and in their communities" (p. 235). All of the above constitutes an important innovation that requires a shift in thinking and practice, which cannot be achieved without an important investment of time for training.

Initially, in February 1996, Harriet Ward and Helen Jones conducted (mostly in French) two days of training to 25 front-line workers, foster parents, supervisors, and managers of the Prescott-Russell Children's Aid Society. Professor Ward and Ms. Jones were both involved in the development of Looking After Children and had first-hand knowledge of the reasons for its development. They were very powerful trainers and made a compelling case for the changes required by the Looking After Children approach. The training was very well received. Subsequently, employees from the PRCAS were instrumental in developing a Canadianized LAC training Curriculum (Lemay, Ghazal, & Westlake, 1999) and more recently a *Practitioners Guide* (Lemay & Ghazal, 2004) that link the AAR and its seven developmental dimensions to four important theoretical components: the developmental model, the power of positive expectancies, parenting, and resilience. Many front-line staff were recently involved in revising the training curriculum (Lemay, Ghazal, & Byrne, 2005) and are currently involved in delivering training modules to new foster parents and staff.

All in all, the training experience in Prescott-Russell was of great importance and was certainly one of the key factors for mobilizing staff, foster parents, and managers in the initial pilot and eventual implementation of Looking After Children. The training demystified Looking After Children, explained the core concepts, allowed participants to role play the AAR interview, was reassuring and, in the end, energized a number of individuals to take up this important change. It led to an important change of discourse where child protection workers would come to openly celebrate the numerous successes of looked-after children and youth and de-emphasize shortcomings and difficulties. Indeed, in 2004, our residential services sector held a two-day retreat with front-line staff where participants shared stories of looked-after child and youth resilience, and how we might learn from these and apply such insights to other challenging case situations. This resilience discourse has been infectious and heartening.

Partnering and corporate parenting

The originators of Looking After Children make clear that the parenting done by organizations, or what they term *corporate parenting* (Jackson, & Kilroe, 1995), is a particular challenge. That which is done informally, intuitively, and well enough by most adults playing the parent role needs to be conducted more deliberately and more formally by organizations that are complex and that bring together many stakeholders. Looked-after children and youth depend on professional staff, their supervisors, foster parents, and other caregivers and potentially many other people to take up the various responsibilities for parenting. Thus, the Looking After Children approach requires bringing together, as partners, a number of stakeholders to ensure the job gets done. This partnership best begins during the early phases of implementation.

The Prescott-Russell experience was one of partnering, where stakeholders, as much as possible, were involved in the change process. Early meetings were held with Board members, staff, managers, foster parents and the youth in care group to talk up the need for change and how LAC provided an interesting solution to the organization. Mostly, the stakeholders were involved in the training and all of these stakeholders received feedback. It is interesting to note that Hage (1999) points out that organizations that are open to partnering with other organizations are particularly successful at innovation and change. PRCAS's ongoing research relationship with Prof. Robert Flynn and the Centre for Research on Community Services at the University of Ottawa, and then the later collaboration with the Ontario Association of Children's Aid Societies, proved to be important factors in the successful implementation. Such openness to the community allows for the sharing of ideas and the sharing of knowledge which, according to Hage, accelerates change and innovation.

The resilient organization

Many organizations are interested in improving performance and outcomes and achieving excellence. A quick perusal of the management section in most bookstores will lead one to a number of titles in the management literature on developing effectiveness and excellence in organizations. However, despite these numerous guides, recent studies by Collins (2001a) and Buckingham and Coffman (1999) point out that excellence is relatively rare (Lemay, 2001). Though organizations are complex and change requires effort and deliberation, the fact of the matter is that sometimes just one important change (or just a few) can lead an organization to radically change its culture and its performance. Gladwell (2000/2002) calls it *Tipping Point* decision-making (see also Kim & Mauborgne, 2003), and he highlights instances where just a few key decisions in large organizations lead to profound change for the better. Hage (1999) argues that research and development leads to constant change, and Foster and Kaplan (2001) have linked high performance—doing better than average—with organizational acceptance of continuous change, or as they term it "creative destruction." The experience of Prescott-Russell suggests that taking up and implementing Looking After Children can have a very beneficial impact not only on services to children and youth in care, but as well on the organization as a whole. It is a comprehensive and positive approach that aims to improve the outcomes of otherwise very vulnerable clients. Moreover, if organizations take up the possibility of aggregating the Assessment and Action Record data, they provide themselves with a whole new source of systematic information upon which to base organizational decision-making on important strategic issues such as resource allocation and program development. It is not enough, however, to have access to data. There must be a decision to pay it some attention through the setting up of a formal and regular (and even ritualistic) data review process (such a process is described in Flynn, Lemay, Ghazal, & Hébert, 2003). When the data are seen and discussed, they will invariably beg for some form of decision or action: one can hardly remain passive before well-documented poor results (recall the above example about the data on reading and out-of-school activities), just as one will be compelled to celebrate good outcomes.

This regular access to performance data might very well lead to further and indeed continuous, innovation and change (Luecke, 2003). Organizations are made up of individuals and are thus organic. Accordingly, access to data or information about service activities and client benefits (outcomes), and relating these to decision-making, can be empowering. It means that an organization exerts some proactive control over what can otherwise be a turbulent and unpredictable environment. Much of the developmental process described above resembles the "collective self-efficacy" concept described by Albert Bandura (1995), where organizations come to exercise agency and a modicum of self-determination along a developmental path. Thus, implementing LAC may be the decision that leads an organization to move beyond adversity and experience resilience.

References

Bandura, A. (Ed.), 1995. *Self-efficacy in changing societies.* Cambridge: Cambridge University Press.

Beecham, J., & Flynn, R.J. (2000). *The costing of child welfare services.* Invited paper presented at an invitational meeting on revisions to the instruments used in the Looking After Children initiative. Windsor Park, England, April.

Biro, C., Flynn, R., Lemay, R., et Lalonde, D. (1997). *Evaluating child welfare outcomes (ECWO)/Évaluation des résultats de l'aide à l'enfance (ERAE): Newsletter/Bulletin no. 2,* Plantagenet, ON: Société de l'aide à l'enfance de Prescott-Russell/University of Ottawa.

Biro, C., Flynn, R., Lemay, R., et Lalonde, D. (1998). *Projet d'évaluation des résultats de l'aide à l'enfance (ERAE : Résultats de la première année de collecte de données.* Plantagenet: Société de l'aide à l'enfance de Prescott-Russell.

Biro, C., & Lemay, R. (1996a). *Looking After Children: Assessment and Action Record – Canadian adaptation and French translation.* Ottawa: University of Ottawa (with permission from Her Majesty's Stationery Office, London).

Biro, C., & Lemay, R. (1996b). *S'occuper des enfants: Cahier d'évaluation et suivis – Adaptation et traduction canadienne.* Ottawa: University of Ottawa (avec la permission du HMSO, London).

Brink, S., & McKellar, S. (2000). NLSCY: A unique Canadian survey. *Isuma Canadian Journal of Policy Research, 1*(2), 111–113.

Buckingham, M., & Coffman, C. (1999). *First, break all the rules: What the world's greatest managers do differently.* New York: Simon & Schuster.

Byrne, B.-A., & Lemay, R. (2005). *Parole aux jeunes: Les jeunes nous disent ce qu'il faut pour assurer le succès du placement résidentiel.* Paper submitted for publication.

Clarke, A.M., and Clarke, A.D.B. (2000). *Early experience and the life path.* London: Jessica Kingsley Publishers.

Collins, J. (2001a). *Good to great: Why some companies make the leap…and others don't.* New York: Harper Business.

Collins, J. (2001b). Level 5 leadership: The triumph of humility and fierce resolve. *Harvard Business Review, 80* (1), 66–76, 175.

Coutu, D. (2003). Sense and reliability: A conversation with celebrated psychologist, Karl E. Weick. *Harvard Business Review, 81*(4), 84–90, 123.

Flynn, R. J., & Biro, C. (1996). *Évaluation des résultats de l'aide à l'enfance (EREA): Résultats de la phase pilote.* Actes du colloque de recherche : Maintien des liens familiaux et placement d'enfants. Québec: Université Laval.

Flynn, R. J., & Biro, C. J. (1998). Comparing developmental outcomes for children in care with those for other children in Canada. *Children and Society, 12,* 228–233.

Flynn, R. J., & Ghazal, H. (2001). *Looking After Children in Ontario: Good Parenting, Good Outcomes—Assessment and Action Record.* (Second Canadian adaptation.) Ottawa, ON: Centre for Research on Community Services, University of Ottawa (developed under licence from Department of Health, London, England; HSMO copyright, 1995).

Flynn, R. J., Ghazal, H., & Legault, L. (2004). *Assessment and Action Record from Looking After Children: Second Canadian adaptation (AAR-C2).* Ottawa, Canada & London, UK: Centre for Research on Community Services, University of Ottawa & HSMO.

Flynn, R.J., Ghazal, H., Moshenko, S., & Westlake, L. (2001). Main features and advantages of a new, "Canadianized" version of the Assessment and Action Record from Looking After Children. *Ontario Association of Children's Aid Societies Journal, 45*(2), 3–6.

Flynn, R. J., Guirguis, M., Wolfensberger, W., & Cocks, E. (1999). Cross-validated factor structures and factor-based subscales for PASS and PASSING. *Mental Retardation, 37,* 281–296.

Flynn, R. J., Lemay, R., Ghazal, H., & Hébert, S. (2003). A performance measurement, monitoring, and management system for local children's Aid Societies. In K. Kufeldt & B. McKenzie (Eds.), *Child welfare: Connecting research, policy, and practice* (pp. 319–330). Waterloo: Wilfrid Laurier University Press.

Flynn, R. J., Perkins-Manguladnan, J., & Biro, C. (2001). Foster parenting styles and foster child behaviours: cross-sectional and longitudinal relationships. Paper presented at the 12th biennial conference of the International Foster Care Organisation, Veldhoven, The Netherlands, July.

Foster, R., & Kaplan, S. (2001). *Creative destruction: Why companies that are built to last underperform the market—And how to successfully transform them.* New York: Doubleday

Gawande, A. (2002). *Complications: A surgeon's notes on an imperfect science.* New York: Metropolitan Books (Henry Holt and Company).

Ghazal, H., & Petrick, S. (2003 & 2004). *Looking After Children: Good Parenting, Good Outcomes.* Ontario provincial report series, young people aged 10–21, 5–9, and 0–4 years. Ottawa, ON: Centre for Research on Community Services, University of Ottawa.

Gladwell, M. (2000/2002). *The tipping point: How little things can make a big difference.* Boston: Little, Brown and Company.

Hage, J. T. (1999). Organizational innovation and organizational change. *Annual Review of Sociology, 25,* 597–622.

Kim, W.C., & Mauborgne, R. (2003). Tipping point leadership. *Harvard Business Review,* April, pp. 60–69.

Jackson, S., & Kilroe, S. (Eds.) (1995). *Looking After Children: Good Parenting, Good Outcomes reader.* London, UK: HSMO.

Lalande, L., et Bertrand, R. (2003). *L'intégration des services de santé communautaires au sein des Services aux enfants et adultes de Prescott-Russell.* Plantagenet, ON : Services aux enfants et adultes de Prescott-Russell.

Lemay, R. (1999). *Placement types and children's needs: Is there any matching going on?* Unpublished manuscript, Prescott-Russell Services for Children and Adults, Plantagenet, ON.

Lemay, R. (2001). Good intentions and hard work are not enough: Review of Levy, P. F., (2001). The Nut Island effect: When good teams go wrong. *SRV-VRS: The International Social Role Valorization Journal, 4*(1&2), 94–97.

Lemay, R. (2004). Managing change and transition. Book review of Luecke, R. (2003), Managing change and transition, Harvard Business School Publishing, Boston. *OACAS (Ontario Association of Children's Aid Societies) Journal, 48*(1), 2–6.

Lemay, R., & Biro-Schad, C. (1999). Looking After Children: Good parenting, good outcomes. *OACAS (Ontario Association of Children's Aid Societies) Journal, 43*(2), 31–34.

Lemay, R., & Ghazal, H. (2001). Resilience and positive psychology: Finding hope. *Child & Family, 5*(1), 10–21.

Lemay, R., & Ghazal, H. (2004). *Looking After Children in Canada: A practitioner's guide* (experimental edition). Plantagenet, ON: Prescott-Russell Services to Children and Adults.

Lemay, R., Ghazal, H., & Byrne, B.-A. (2005). *Introduction to Looking After Children (LAC): A Canadian training curriculum.* Plantagenet, ON: Valor Institute.

Lemay, R., Ghazal, H., & Westlake, L., (1999). *Introduction to Looking After Children (LAC): A training curriculum.* Toronto, ON: Ontario Association of Children's Aid Societies.

Luecke, R. (2003). *Managing change and transition* (Harvard Business Essentials). Boston: Harvard Business School Publishing.

Luthar, S.S., Cicchetti, D., & Becker, B. (2000). The construct of resilience: A critical evaluation and guidelines for future work. *Child Development, 71,* 543–562.

Martin, L. (1993). *Total quality management in human service organizations.* Newbury Park: SAGE Publications.

Masten, Ann S. (2001). Ordinary magic: Resilience processes in development. *American Psychologist, 56,* 227–238.

Osburn, J., Caruso, G., & Reidy, D. (1997). *PASSING: Assessment of the Prescott-Russell Children's Aid Society.* Plantagenet, ON: Prescott-Russell Children's Aid Society.

Pantin, S., & Flynn, R. J. (2004). *Importance of training in the Implementation of Looking After Children: Two surveys of foster parents and child welfare workers in Ontario.* Paper presented at the conference, Promoting Resilient Development In Children Receiving Care, Ottawa, August 16–19.

Pantin, S., Flynn, R. J., & Runnels, V. (2006). Training, experience, and supervision: Keys to enhancing the utility of the Assessment and Action Record in implementing Looking After Children. In R. J. Flynn, P. M. Dudding, & J. G. Barber (Eds.), *Promoting resilience in child welfare.* Ottawa, ON: University of Ottawa Press.

Parker, R.A., Ward, H., Jackson, S., Aldgate, J. & Wedge, P. (Eds.) (1991). *Looking After Children: Assessing outcomes in child care.* London, UK: HMSO.

Scott, J. (1999). *Report of the audit of implementation of Looking After Children in Year 3: 1997/98.* University of Leicester, September.

Statistics Canada (1995). *National Longitudinal Survey of Children and Youth (NLSCY)*. Ottawa: Statistics Canada & Human Resources Development Canada.

Ward, H. (Ed.) (1995). *Looking After Children: Research into practice: The second report to the Department of Health on assessing outcomes in child care*. London: HMSO.

Ward, H. (1996). Constructing and implementing measures to assess the outcomes of looking after children away from home. In J. Aldgate & M. Hill (Eds.), *Child welfare services: Developments in law, policy, practice and research*. London, UK: Jessica Kingsley.

Willms, J. D. (2002). *Vulnerable children: Findings from Canada's National Longitudinal Survey of Children and Youth*. Edmonton: University of Alberta Press.

Wolfensberger, W. (1978). The ideal human service for a societally devalued group. *Rehabilitation Literature, 39*(1), 15–17.

Wolfensberger, W., & Thomas, S. (1983). *PASSING* (program analysis of service systems' implementation of normalization goals*): Normalization criteria and ratings manual (2nd ed.)*. Toronto: National Institute on Mental Retardation.

CHAPTER 20

On becoming strength based in service delivery and program culture

Simon Nuttgens

> "…darkness has a hunger that's insatiable,
> and lightness has a call that's hard to hear."
> —Indigo Girls, song *Closer to Fine*

Introduction

In recent years, there has been increased interest within the helping professions in what is commonly referred to as the strengths perspective, or strength-based paradigm. Although the basic tenets of this perspective can be traced back to at least the 1940s when Carl Rogers began writing about a client-centred approach to psychotherapy, it has only been within the last 10 years or so that these ideas have been developed to resemble a coherent theoretical model. As such, the strengths perspective is still very much in an early, evolving stage of development (Chazin, Kaplan, & Terio, 2000; Saleebey, 1998). Because of its youthful status, there is still considerable work to be done to clarify, articulate, and expand upon what it means to be strength based in one's service delivery and program culture.

In what follows, I put forward one agency's experience of adopting the strength perspective. I begin by discussing the history behind our decision to adopt this philosophy of practice, followed by an examination of the reservations associated with its alternative, the deficit paradigm. I then propose that the strengths perspective can usefully be characterized by five areas of focus that arise through a cross-disciplinary survey of associated theories and models. Finally, I discuss ways to encourage a strengths perspective through addressing common misunderstandings that, if not addressed, may impede its implementation.

The Salvation Army Children's Village is a multi-disciplinary mental health agency that offers a broad range of services to emotionally and behaviorally troubled children and their families. Over the past five years, the Children's Village has dedicated itself to the goal of adopting and developing a strengths perspective in its therapeutic and supportive services.

The formal beginnings of this project date back five years ago to the arrival of our current Director of Children's Services, who recalls reading our program manual and thinking, "I cannot imagine myself sitting down with one of our clients and reading through what is written on these pages." Littered through the document was a cold, detached, technical language, rife with the jargon of 1970s and 80s behaviourism. It held little resemblance to the work that was actually being done, or the beliefs and values that informed this work. The search began for a theoretical model that would be compatible with our existing philosophy of working with children and families.

In the early stages of this exploration, our attention was drawn to the developmental assets literature associated with the Search Institute in Minneapolis (Scales & Leffert, 1999). About the same time, we also seized upon the growing interest in resiliency theory (e.g., Masten, Best, & Garmezy, 1990; Werner, 1993; Werner & Smith, 1992). Yet, despite the impressive research tradition and compelling therapeutic utility of these two approaches, their inclination towards cataloguing and tallying up empirically derived qualities of person and environment as a means to counter risk with opportunity left more to be desired. We needed recourse not only to ideas of "what" can be done, but of "how" we might do it. In other words, we needed a larger, more encompassing model that would inform, at a more personal and practical level, how we carry out our work with clients on a daily basis. Although aspects of resiliency theory and the developmental assets approach remain relevant to our work—and indeed are subsumed within the strength-based perspective as outlined in this chapter—neither could provide a stand-alone theoretical model upon which to base and identify our practice. Something more was needed and the something that seemed the most natural and comfortable fit was the strength-based paradigm.

Through the ensuing years, it has been an ongoing task to articulate at a practical and theoretical level what it means to embrace a strength-based perspective in our work with children and families. We are committed to the idea of a strengths perspective, though we recognize that ample room remains to pull under its umbrella a host of additional ideas and practices that share an affinity with its primary aspirations. Indeed, one aspect of the strength-based paradigm is its inclusive approach to other theories; that is, it makes room for and use of other theories so long as they uphold its therapeutic and ethical praxis. In part, the need to develop a clear account of the strengths perspective is a necessary step toward its implementation. However, it is also useful to reflect on our rationale for distancing ourselves from its alternative, the deficit paradigm.

The deficit paradigm

The deficit paradigm—variously labelled the "medical model," "pathology model," or "damage model"—is predicated on the notion that children and families come to our service because of underlying disorder or dysfunction that must be treated before health can be restored or attained. Both its research and clinical tradition are set within a medical scientific methodology that asserts a causal relationship between all natural phenomena and which, given time and procedural rigour, will expose these relationships in a neutral and objective manner. This methodology enjoys widespread application in the arena of therapeutic practice: for every spoken or observed problem, there is an identifiable cause that must be discovered, named, and declared before efforts to help may profitably commence. As Madsen (1999) notes, the notion of true causes of an individual or family's problems rests on normative assumptions that inevitably, though perhaps inadvertently, lead to a deficit outlook.

> A deficit model assumes certain knowable norms for family organization and interaction. Whatever deviates from these norms is assumed to be defective. Therapy then focuses on fixing that which is in need of repair, inadvertently reinforcing a focus on dysfunction. (pp. 22–23)

In conventional terms, it is said that assessment necessarily precedes intervention, where assessment refers to the technical application of empirically validated assessment measures. In the aftermath of assessment, we are typically left with an extensive inventory of shortcomings that are then expected to illuminate the road to recovery. When our attention is directed toward and held captive to all that appears to be wrong, we begin to feel stuck: every corner is a dead end, every hole without a ladder. It is difficult to sustain such a gaze without becoming discouraged, deflated and jaded, at which time we either turn away and detach, or succumb to professional burnout. Fixating on what is wrong or broken simultaneously diminishes the hope and inspiration of both client and practitioner (Wolin, 2002). A sense of therapeutic inertia takes over, leaving both wondering what, if anything, might break such a crushing spell.

It is also apparent that many of the families arrive through our doors with prior experiences of feeling blamed and shamed by the very professionals to whom they have turned for help. Through their experiences, they have received implicit and explicit messages that they are the cause of their child's ailment and that if it were not for a deficiency in parenting skill or character dysfunction, this would never have occurred. I have no misgivings that the family's previous professional helper was not scrupulously committed to theoretically and ethically sound practice and proceeded with full intention of serving his or her client well, though at the same time I acknowledge that at least for some of the people we serve, oppression becomes an unintended side-effect of intervention (Austin, Bergum, & Nuttgens, 2003). It is my belief and that of others (e.g., Saleebey, 1998; Madsen, 1999) that an undue emphasis on deficit and pathology inadvertently directs parents to the conclusion, if not already present, that they are the sole and malevolent cause of their children's problems. Whether or not one believes this to be the true and best explanation, beginning a relationship under such pretence rarely sets the stage for an enduring and effective therapeutic relationship.

Not only does subscribing to a deficit paradigm undermine the therapeutic relationship, it may well have a detrimental influence on the personal identities of those with whom we work. Authors such as Gergen (1991), Sarbin (1986), and Polkinghorne (1991) have increasingly turned toward narrative as an organizing metaphor for personal identity, that is, to explain the development and consistency of identity over time. Accordingly, a narrative conceptualization of identity asserts that personal identity is a function of the stories we hold of our lives. These stories are socially constructed through language, culture, and our relationships with others. It is thought that the story of self becomes a filter of sorts that censors, accepts, and rejects new information according to its ability to cohere with existing storylines and the dominant story of self. When we as helping professionals enter into a relationship with our clients, we can never do so benignly with respect to a client's story of self. Through mutual engagement, we become part of their story and are thus conferred considerable responsibility to handle it with care; that is, to engage in ways that advance virtuous rather than deleterious descriptions of self. Moreover, given the real and perceived power we as supposed authorities have over their lives, it is all the more important not to pander to the vulnerabilities of an unhelpful storyline. Ultimately, we endeavour not to leave the impression that we have authorship rights to our clients' lives. Rather, we strive to transfer this power back such that they become first-person narrators of their story with enhanced volition to improve their lives.

Shifting paradigms

Contemplation of the deficit paradigm's limitations and drawbacks leads us to a greater appreciation of the strengths perspective and towards greater zeal in its implementation and development. At the Children's Village, direct feedback from our clients and stakeholders convinces and reassures us that we are headed in the right direction. And one does not need to spend much time within the walls of the Children's Village to sense that something is different, that there is a distinct philosophy of therapeutic practice and relationship at work here. When you have been with other agencies, you appreciate this "something different," even if you cannot readily define it. When I first came to the Salvation Army Children's Village to work in the Bridges Program,[1] it seemed impossible to go a day without hearing the language of strength based: "Are we being strength based here?" "What would be a strength-based approach to this situation?" How could we think about this person's struggles as a possible strength?" Yet at the same time, many questions remained regarding what was meant by the term "strength based" and how this approach might be practised in our daily work. As the cliché goes, *We weren't all on the same page,* and not surprisingly there was a sense that discrepant understandings were hindering our ability to embrace and usefully implement these ideas. As our current Director of Children's Services commented, "The question became, how do we reconcile the various notions of what it means to be strength based? People mean different things, so how to bring divergence to convergence?"

To help answer this question, an all-day managers and directors retreat was held specifically to move closer to a common understanding of being strength based. I recall this retreat as a very dynamic and impassioned affair, in which each comment and observation sparked the flame of another. The themes that arose through this discussion were collated and presented at our next staff forum (an all-staff meeting intended to share program and agency developments of mutual interest). In close conjunction with this meeting was a presentation solely to the Bridges program from two senior staff who shared their ideas on strength-based practice. Through such efforts, it was anticipated that a sense of shared understanding would ensue with a concomitant decrease in any lingering practices associated with the deficits paradigm; this, however, did not occur to the extent that was hoped. Thus, we stepped back to survey the landscape. It now seemed that a crucial step had been missed. No one, it seemed, had a clear and solid grounding as to the theoretical basis of the strengths perspective. Through proceeding in a very organic, grassroots fashion, we had neglected to delve into the literature base. To establish a shared understanding of the strengths perspective, theory and research needed to come first.

Thus, I was summoned to undertake the task of finding out "what was out there." What I found—or should say, did *not* find—surprised me. I thought I would come across (with little effort to my search) a one-stop, tell-it-all resource, the definitive book or article that would explain the strength-based model in detail. I did not. I thought I would find legions of articles describing the theory and practice of the strengths perspective applied to a variety of mental health settings. I did not. The closest approximation was the writing of Saleebey (1996, 1998) in social work and, to a lesser extent, Laursen (2000, 2003) in child and youth care. Indeed, I found Saleebey's writing to offer a very powerful and instructive case for adhering to a strengths perspective in social service and mental health programming, though his accounts were perhaps more theoretical than practical in their focus. What struck me as I read Saleebey's articles was the degree of communion, overlap, and compatibility between what he termed the "strengths perspective in social work" and other ideas described in related disciplines—even if such ideas were not identified as strength based, per se. Indeed, what I discovered was a kinship of ideas within the various helping professions (family therapy, psychology, social work, counselling, and child and youth care), all of which spoke to a paradigm shift away from pathology-driven models towards an emphasis on strengths.

Presented next are five areas of focus that I have pulled together "so far" which, through my readings of the literature and practice as a therapist, seem to coalesce across and within various disciplines to inform a strengths-based perspective in mental health service.

A focus on language

The hallmark of what has been described as social constructionist therapies within counselling, psychotherapy and family therapy is a focused and relentless interrogation of language use, noting, as Anderson (1996) does, that "language is not innocent," that it can intentionally and unintentionally "be used by people to justify, separate, control, and castigate" (Gergen, 1994, p. 414). Kenneth Gergen, a key proponent of social constructionism, argues convincingly against a representationalism perspective of language in which there is a one-to-one correspondence between words and real world objects and events. Instead, he reminds us of the metaphorical quality of words where meaning is acquired through social convention and consensus. Words, as Gergen (1994) points out, are not regarded as intractable truths. Rather, they are looked upon as arbitrary applications of meaning that are open to differing options for use and definition. Thus, it is with specific intent that we pay close attention to the words we use to describe people and our modes of practice. For example, we might choose not to use a term such as "Parenting Skills Class" to denote a group intended to share child-rearing ideas with parents. Implicit in this title is the message that our parents are unskilled and in need of a healthy dose of professional knowledge. Such a notion may play upon the worries of many of our parents who fear that they have irreparably damaged their children due to various failures in parenting.

Given their emphasis on language, social constructionist therapies maintain a cautious stance when it comes to diagnosis, ever wary that the labels used are ripe with potential to become "totalizing" accounts of one's identity (Gergen, Hoffman, & Anderson, 1996). Moreover, the pathology models associated with diagnosis often treat people's problems and struggles as static, enduring, and constitutional, versus a more fluid, temporal manifestation of human experience. This is a trap inadvertently set through the linguistic shortcomings inherent in the notion of psychopathology. Indeed, the entire premise of successful diagnosis rests on the notion that we must discover and highlight relatively fixed conceptualizations of personhood, leaving little room for other stories (discussed next) that might better service our therapeutic ambitions.

A focus on story

Not only does a strengths perspective pay close attention to how language is used to describe and identify our clients' life experiences, it also concerns itself with language in the broader sense of narrative and the stories our clients come to live by.

The application of narrative as a metaphor for therapy is generally associated with Australian family therapist, Michael White, and his New Zealand counterpart, David Epston. Their book, *Narrative Means to Therapeutic Ends* (1990), has generated much ardour and enthusiasm among adherents to their therapeutic model. Central to their use of "narrative" is the notion that stories of self guide how people act, think, feel and make sense of their past and present lives. In White and Epston's view, clients typically come to therapy under the influence of a "problem-saturated" story that, due to its hold on the individual or family, leaves little room for the resolution of problems or facilitation of healing. The indeterminate nature of story—that is, the idea that there are many, rather than just one story that informs one's experiences—provides the means of escape from the problem-saturated story and its "rules" for how one should live his or her life. The notion of multiple versus singular stories of experience has direct implications for strength-based practice. Believing that there is more than one story to be heard and told by our clients attunes us to the idea that stories of deficit and pathology are but one of many possible stories, and that through careful consideration and determined exploration there are always alternative—more affirming—stories to be had. Thus the question, "What is it that we see when we engage with clients?" becomes less a question of what is physically or imaginatively present and more one of how we orient our eyes and ears when undertaking our work. From a practice stand point, Michael White (1995) often talks about the therapeutic skill of "double-listening" to describe the ability to hear, appreciate, and keep in mind serious concerns on one hand, while listening for alternative stories of strength, knowledge and ability on the other.

The inherent qualities of narrative also support a strengths perspective through its ability to expand, broaden, and contextualize what often begins as a very brief, circumscribed, and problem-focused account of a person's life or current situation. As stories unfold in breadth and detail, a greater understanding and appreciation of our clients' lives emerge such that their perceived failings of will or character come to make "perfect sense" given their particular life stories (Nuttgens, 2004). Coming to know a person's actions and attitudes to be the expected consequences of their given constellation of life experiences imparts feelings of compassion and understanding, rather than the reproach and condemnation that may ensue when only part of the story is known.

A focus on strengths, abilities and resources

It is understood that a strengths perspective focuses on strengths, abilities, and human resourcefulness. This focus manifests as a firm and committed belief that all people of all ages, and all families of all types, possess ability, competence, and other special qualities regardless of their life experience or current situation (Cohen, 1999; Laursen, 2003; Saleebey, 1998). An emphasis on strengths does not imply that adherents of other theoretical models are unaware that people have strengths, abilities, and the alike, for in many instances such qualities are obvious. What differentiates the strengths perspective from other models of helping is its tenacity to discover strengths in people and situations where it is anything but obvious and yet where doing so often kindles desperately needed hope and healing. A strengths perspective also *attends* to strengths in a different way, viewing them as laden with therapeutic promise, rather than as encouraging though perhaps incidental information.

Intuitively we know it to be the case that all people have strengths of some sort, whether present and accounted for, or hidden and dormant. Research in the area of resiliency backs this intuition with scientific credence. There is now considerable evidence to support the notion that given the right constellation of protective factors, positive adaptation can occur for children despite the presence of significant risk or adversity (Masten, Best, & Garmezy, 1990; Masten, chapter 1, this volume). Authors such as Norman (2000), Fraser and Galinsky (1997), and Saleebey (1996) have noted the close affinity between resiliency research and a strengths perspective. Chazin, Kaplan and Terio (2000) go so far as to string both terms together to name a single entity ("strengths perspective/resiliency enhancement paradigm"). The resiliency literature highlights and reminds us that strengths are not only present but are exceedingly important in bringing understanding to how people come to thrive despite terrible life experiences.

A focus on strengths also finds its place within the theory and practice of solution-focused therapy (Berg, 1991; de Shazer, 1991). Indeed, De Jong and Miller (1995) note that, "It is hard to imagine a tighter fit between philosophy and practice than that between the strengths perspective and solution focused interviewing." The basic premise of solution-focused therapy asserts that all individuals and families have strengths, abilities, and knowledge, and that it is more efficacious to focus on what clients can and are doing to manage their lives than to emphasize and address what is going wrong. Similar to narrative therapy, adherents of solution-focused therapy hold that there is always "another side of the story" where exceptions reside and can be used to build solutions to one's problems.

A focus on collaboration

A central feature of the strengths perspective, and one that also finds its place within the other theoretical models discussed thus far (solution-focused therapy, narrative therapy, and the strengths perspective in social work) is the belief in the merits of collaboration. In family therapy, the collaborative language-systems approach (Anderson & Goolishian, 1988) has promoted collaboration in reaction to perceived power differentials between therapist and client and has adopted the colonial metaphor to highlight ways in which therapy proper may unwittingly mimic the colonial mentality of conquest and suppression. Multicultural and feminist therapies have also strongly advocated for collaborative practice as a means to counter discrimination and prejudice directed towards people perceived to be different from a white, monocultural norm (Sue, 1998; Arrendondo et al., 1996; Arthur & Stewart, 2001). In all three therapeutic approaches (multicultural, feminist, and collaborative language systems), there is an acute sensitivity towards intended and unintended acts of oppression and a commensurate striving to level manifestations of hierarchy and their resultant marginalization.

Many writers who discuss collaborative practices within the helping professions draw on the writings of cultural anthropologist Clifford Geertz. In his seminal work, *The Interpretation of Cultures,* Geertz (1973) draws attention to two types of knowledge: expert knowledge, in which the locus of knowing rests within professional academic discourse; and local knowledge, in which the locus of knowing rests within people's daily experience and learning. Though acknowledging a role for expert knowledge, the strengths perspective spends more time in the company of local knowledge, taking care to listen and learn of the ways that ordinary people accomplish extraordinary things through their own resourcefulness and ingenuity. It should be noted, however, that collaborative therapists "are not against expertise *per se* [original italics], but against nonreflective, taken-for-granted impositions of expertise." (Lowe, 2004, p. 30)

A collaborative approach to mental health services acknowledges that our clients have a view of the presenting complaint, its potential solutions, and ideas about the how the change process should unfold. In other words, they have a personal theory of change (Miller, Duncan, & Hubble, 1997). Hearing, accepting, and working with the client's theory of change increases active participation, which is considered the most important determinant of outcome in any therapeutic endeavour (Duncan, Hubble, & Rusk, 1994).

A focus on relationship

The areas of focus mentioned thus far lead toward and perhaps culminate in the definitive aspect of a strengths perspective, that is, the centrality of relationship. A focus on relationship in mental health services is, indeed, nothing new. Ever since Carl Roger's early writings in the 1940s and 50s, most every therapeutic model proposed has similarly espoused the need for a healthy rapport (or working alliance) between therapist and client before therapy can begin. Relationship, as I often say, is the "first therapy" that leads the way for all subsequent therapeutic aspirations.

Increasingly, however, a healthy therapeutic alliance is being regarded as more than just a precursor to good therapy; rather, it is being looked upon as therapeutic by itself. The writings of Hubble, Duncan, and Miller (1999) are instructive in this matter. Through their research efforts and review of other's research, they propose four common factors that contribute to effective therapy. In order of their relative contribution to change, these include:

(a) Extra-therapeutic factors: the clients' strengths and resources, beliefs about the change process, and the occurrence of change-producing events in their lives (40%);

(b) Client-therapist relationship: an empathic, warm relationship, in which goals, method and pace of therapy are collaboratively established (30%);

(c) Hope and expectancy: the client's belief in the possibility of change (15%); and

(d) Structure/model and/or technique: The unique ways that a therapeutic approach organizes the therapeutic process in a manner acceptable to the client (15%).

Taken together, extratherapeutic factors and the therapist-client relationship account for 70% of therapeutic change, whereas, contrary to what is often believed, the theoretical model accounts for only 15%. The relevance of this finding is twofold. First, research findings regarding extratherapeutic factors serve not only as a reminder that all clients have strengths, abilities and resources, but that these alone represent the greatest contribution to therapeutic change. Second, the literature on common factors underscores the key role that relationship plays—in and of itself—in sponsoring change. In effect, this line of research tells us that people do have strengths and that heeding them is central to the task of creating a solid therapeutic relationship, which in turn helps to facilitate change.

Moving forward with a strengths perspective

At the Salvation Army Children's Village, we are committed to the strengths perspective and have already come a long way in developing it as the theoretical basis of our work. Acknowledging that we are "not quite there yet" is to acknowledge a continued need to articulate what it means to be strength based, such that the ideas can be implemented and practiced effectively and with intent. When it appears that, as a team or as individuals, we are not operating from a strengths perspective, it is likely not because we do not subscribe to the model, but because we are uncertain of its nature. While acknowledging that these lines are not always obvious or easily drawn, it remains necessary that we possess to the greatest degree possible a shared set of ideas and assumptions regarding theory and practice.

Some of the questions and concerns that have arisen in our efforts to endorse a strength perspective are similar to those noted by Saleebey

(1996). These include the view that a strengths perspective is merely positive thinking in disguise, simply attempts to reframe deficit and misery, is "Pollyannaish," and ignores the harsh reality of people's lives. In the Bridges program, there is sometimes a feeling that we must edit conversations regarding the challenges, difficulties, and calamities that come to view, or even that serious issues such as domestic violence and child abuse must be downplayed in the name of "remaining positive." When it comes to this, the strengths perspective acquires a tenor of social control, a self-righteous "do-gooder" mentality that leaves little room for our felt reactions to certain people and their situations; it becomes a form of censorship where all that is said and done falls under the surveillance of the "strengths police." The strengths perspective does not subscribe to such ambitions, for it is not about denying, distorting, or deflecting from the tremendous amount of hardship, cruelty, injustice and mistreatment that exists in this world. Rather, the strengths perspective is more fruitfully thought of as a manner of positioning ourselves relative to those whom we serve. It is a way of being with the other that honours all facets of their personhood, respecting though not dignifying their struggles, while encouraging and celebrating their strengths.

The questions from staff that come forth through the process of becoming strength based are natural, expected, and welcomed—welcomed in the sense that the very nature of a strengths perspective requires us to make room for all voices as we continue to question and reflect on the assumptions that guide our practice. Being strength based is not about finding a perch to rest on, as if we have arrived at some final answer or solution to this work, comforting as this thought may be.

Future considerations

In this paper, I examined one mental health agency's experience of becoming strength based in their delivery of service. To this end, one of our greatest lessons has been the need to have a coherent and shared understanding of the theories and research that informs this way of working. Through examining the relevant multi-disciplinary literature, I have come to believe that strength-based practice is best thought of as a collection of complementary ideas and practice identified through five areas of focus.

When people first read about or experience the strengths perspective, there is often a sense of communion with these ideas; they seem to fit, make sense, and be useful in a practical sort of way. For those schooled in the more prevalent deficit-based models of mental health service, coming to know the strengths perspective and experience it firsthand may impart feeling of liberation indeed feelings of vindication: "I knew there had to be another side to the story. I knew there must have been something more to people than their perceived failings and misery." The risk, as is always the case with the terminology that accompanies new directions in thinking and practice, is that the word or words associated with such trends become hackneyed, and hence rejected, even before their full potential is realized. Caution must be exercised to ensure that the strengths perspective does not succumb to this fate, becoming little more than a slogan—a sterile directive to be followed, bereft of its rich clinical and theoretical utility. The challenge is to keep the words alive and breathe meaning and purpose into them, such that they can withstand and outlast the winds of faddism while remaining open to the regenerative spirit that should accompany any theory of practice.

References

Andersen, T. (1996). Language is not innocent. In F.L. Kaslow (Ed.), *Handbook of relational diagnosis and dysfunctional family patterns* (pp. 119–195). New York: John Wiley & Sons.

Anderson, H., & Goolishian, H. (1988). Human systems as linguistic systems. *Family Process, 27,* 371–395.

Arrendondo, P., Toropek, R., Brown, S.P., Jones, J., Locke, D.C., Sanchez, J., & Stadler, H. (1996). Operationalization of the multicultural counselling competencies. *Journal of Multicultural Counselling and Development, 24,* 42–78.

Arthur, N., & Stewart, J. (2001). Multicultural counselling in the new millenium: Introduction to the special theme issue. *Canadian Journal of Counselling, 35* (1), 3–14.

Austin, W., Bergum, V., & Nuttgens, S.A. (2004). Addressing oppression in psychiatric care: A relational ethics perspective. *Ethical Human Sciences and Services* (in press).

Berg, I.K. (1994). *Family-based services: A solution-focused approach.* New York: Norton.

Chazin, R., Kaplan, S., & Terio, S. (2000). Introducing a strengths/resiliency model in mental health organizations. In E. Norman (Ed.), *Resiliency enhancement: Putting the strengths perspective into social work practice.* New York: Columbia University Press.

Cohen, B. (1999). Intervention and supervision in strengths-based social work practice. *Families in Society, 80,* 460–466.

De Jong, P., & Miller, S.D. (1995). How to interview for client strengths. *Social Work, 40,* 720–736.

de Shazer, S. (1991). *Putting differences to work.* New York: Norton.

Duncan, B.L., Hubble, M.A., & Rusk, G. (1994). To intervene or not to intervene: That is not the question. *Journal of Systemic Therapies, 13,* (4), 22–30.

Fraser, M.W., & Galinsky, M.J. (1997). Toward a resiliency-based model of practice. In Mark W. Fraser (Ed.), *Risk and resilience in childhood.* Washington, DC: NASW Press.

Geertz, C. (1973). *The interpretation of cultures.* New York: Basic Books.

Gergen, K.J. (1991). *The saturated self: Dilemmas of identity in contemporary life.* New York: Basic Books.

Gergen, K.J. (1994). Exploring the postmodern: Perils or potentials? *American Psychologist, 49,* 412–416.

Gergen, K.J., Hoffman, L., & Anderson, H. (1996). Is diagnosis a disaster? A constructivist trialogue. In F.L. Kaslow (Ed.), *Handbook of relational diagnosis and dysfunctional family patterns* (pp. 102–118). New York: John Wiley & Sons.

Hubble, M., Duncan, B., & Miller, S. (1999). *The heart and soul of change: What works in therapy.* Washington, DC. American Psychological Association.

Laursen, E.K. (2000). Strength-based practice with children in trouble. *Reclaiming Children and Youth, 9*(2), 70–75.

Laursen, E.K. (2003). Frontiers in strength-based treatment. *Reclaiming Children and Youth, 12*(1), 12–17.

Lowe, R. (2004). *Family therapy: A constructive framework.* London: SAGE Publications.

Madsen, W.C. (1999). *Collaborative therapy with multi-stressed families.* New York: The Guilford Press.

Masten, A.S., Best, K.M., & Garmezy, N. (1990). Resilience and development: Contributions from the study of children who overcome adversity. *Development and Psychopathology, 2,* 425–444.

Miller, S.D., Duncan B.L., & Hubble, M.A. (1997). *Escape from Babel.* New York: Norton.

Norman, E. (2000). *Resiliency enhancement: Putting the strengths perspective into social work practice.* New York: Columbia University Press.

Nuttgens, S.A. (2004). *Life stories of Aboriginal adults raised in non-Aboriginal families.* Unpublished dissertation: University of Alberta, Edmonton, Alberta, Canada.

Polkinghorn, D.E. (1991). Narrative and self-concept. *Journal of Narrative and Life-History, 1,* 135–153.

Saleebey, D. (1996). The strengths perspective in social work practice: Extensions and cautions. *Social Work, 41*(3), 296–305.

Saleebey, D. (Ed.) (1998). *The strengths perspective in social work practice.* New York: Longman.

Sarbin, T.R. (Ed.) (1986). *Narrative psychology: The storied nature of human conduct.* New York: Praeger.

Scales, P.C., & Leffert, N. (1999). *Developmental assets: A synthesis of scientific research on adolescent development.* Minneapolis: Search Institute.

Sue, D.W. (1998). *Multicultural counselling competencies.* Thousand Oaks, CA: SAGE Publications.

Walsh, F. (1998). *Strengthening family resilience.* New York: Guilford.

Werner, E.E. (1993). Risk, resiliency, and recovery: Perspectives from the Kauai longitudinal study. *Development and Psychopathology, 5,* 503–515.

Werner, E.E., & Smith, R.S. (1992). *Overcoming the odds: High-risk children from birth to adulthood.* Ithaca, NY: Cornell University Press.

White, M. (1995). *Re-authoring lives: Interviews as essays.* Adelaide: Dulwich Centre Publications.

White, M., & Epston, D. (1990). *Narrative means to therapeutic ends.* New York: W.W. Norton.

Wolin, S. (2002). Shifting paradigms: Easier said than done. *Paradigm,* Summer, 10–11.

---

1 The Bridges Program is a day-treatment program for pre-school children identified with serious emotional and behavioural concerns.

CHAPTER 21

Developing a common assessment approach to the early identification of children in need: The Swansea, Wales, case study

Andrew Pithouse

Background and rationale

A core element of Welsh Assembly Government and UK government policy in child and family services is the notion of multi-agency collaboration in order to meet the needs of children and adults (Welsh Assembly Government, 2004). The Welsh and UK governments are both required by the *Children Act 2004*, s.25(2) to provide and/or promote effective services to improve the well-being of children with regard to their: (1) physical, mental and emotional well-being; (2) protection from harm and neglect; (3) education, training and recreation; (4) contribution to society; and (5) social and economic well-being. To achieve these five policy priorities will require new or improved information-sharing techniques, stronger joint efforts, and more openness and shared goals between relevant agencies. This emphasis on collaboration is thus at the heart of UK and Welsh government policy and is endorsed in the UK government Green Paper *Every Child Matters* (Department for Education and Skills, 2003) and the subsequent *Children Act 2004*. Indeed, *Every Child Matters* proposed the introduction of a national common assessment framework as a critical element of a strategy to achieve the above five priorities. Our study is thus closely linked to current policy ambitions, and the results have informed UK government consultation (Department for Education and Skills, 2004) on the design and implementation of a national common assessment model.

Essentially, the pre-referral common assessment is a tool to help child and family professionals from different organizations undertake a basic assessment with a child or young person who may have additional needs that require the involvement of partner agencies. Of particular interest to our study were referrals of children in need made by health, education, police and the voluntary sector to the local authority social services department. Children in need and their families are the subject of planned inter-vention through what is known in the UK as the Assessment Framework (National Assembly for Wales, 2000; DoH, DfEE, and Home Office, 2000). This Framework contains domains, dimensions and measures to identify needs that are conceived as inter-related in regard to the individual child, the child's family, and the child's environment. The Framework comprises initial and core assessment procedures for which local authority social serv-ices have lead responsibility and whose staff will investigate in depth a range of issues related to a child's welfare. However, children have in the first place to be referred to a local authority with social services responsibil-ities in order for such assessments to occur, and thus the role of referrers (e.g., teachers, health staff, police, voluntary sector, courts) is crucial in children's coming to local authority notice and obtaining a service.

Children in need

Until recently, referrers in Wales and England have tended to operate with their own criteria about the sorts of needs or circumstances that should trigger their contact with social services about a child. Such criteria may (or may not) have been agreed with the local authority or indeed stem from local authority guidance on referral making. The point, however, is that there are few examples of a pre-referral assessment procedure shared by local agencies that will help identify appropriate cases to refer to social services. The aim of this study, therefore, was, through collaboration with Swansea local authority social services and local referring agencies, to design, implement and evaluate a *pre-referral common assessment protocol* compatible with the Assessment Framework. We believed this would help generate standardized procedures and promote appropriate referrals to the local authority social services, thereby resulting in better targeting of resources to children in need. The latter, as defined by the *Children Act 1989*, s.17, include (a) children unlikely to achieve or maintain, or to have the opportunity of achieving or maintaining, a reasonable standard of health or development without the provision for the child of services by a local authority; (b) children whose health or development is likely to be significantly impaired, or further impaired, without the provision for the child of such services; or (c) children who are disabled. Furthermore, under s.47, social service departments are required to make enquires if they have reason to believe a child in their area is suffering or likely to suffer signifi-cant harm. It can be argued that the social services are often not necessari-ly in the best position to identify who these children are. Very often it is health providers and education departments who provide a more universal children's service and who have more contact with the families concerned.

A major debate within the field of UK child care (Peel & Ward, 2000) concerns the way an emphasis on child protection investigations has tended to overshadow a more preventive and needs-led intervention thought likely to promote family stability and reduce crises, so the well-being of all children in need is thought to have been affected adversely. Thus, a major issue for social services is how to refocus practice toward a more preventive approach via the notion of "children in need," whereby child protection is but one part of a continuum of provision to meet need rather than the dominant element. Indeed, as a means of helping to re-balance provision, the Assessment Framework was launched by the Department of Health in England in 2000, and by the National Assembly in Wales in 2001(DoH, DfEE, & Home Office, 2000; National Assembly for Wales, 2000). The Framework tools and guidance (see DoH & Cleaver, 2000; DoH, DfEE and Home Office, 2000, p. 63) stress that children's needs and their families' circumstances will require inter-agency collaboration to generate full appreciation of what is happening and to ensure an effective response (see Hudson et al., 1999).

The pre-referral common assessment tool: Building on Loughborough

Our purpose was to complement the Assessment Framework initiative by enhancing the way the early identification of need is understood and shared between a wide variety of practitioners, working in numerous agencies. Thus, our project aimed to generate commonly agreed standards against which needs can first be identified and prioritized in order to determine whether a situation warrants referral to social services or some other agency. We sought to do this by developing, piloting and evaluating a pre-referral common assessment protocol that would help standardise the way in which children in need who are aged 0–4 and 5–9 years come to notice. We did not think it feasible in the time available to address the broad spectrum of needs of children and young people aged 0–18. Nor did we include child protection referrals in our initial piloting of this project in Swansea, although it was our belief that such a scheme could properly encompass child protection referrals once we were confident it operated effectively.

Our study built on work undertaken by the Centre for Child and Family Research, Loughborough University, between 1996 and 2002 with two northern local authorities in England (Peel, 1999; Peel & Ward, 2000; Ward

& Peel, 2002). Results from these pilots suggested that initial fears that the new approach would require extensive additional investment of time and resources from child welfare practitioners, or that social services would be overwhelmed by new referrals, proved unjustified. In fact, in both authorities there was a drop in child concern referrals during the pilot period. The reasons for this cannot be attributed solely to the pilot scheme, but it does seem evident that many professionals concluded from their use of common assessment standards that a referral to the local authority social services was not necessary (see Peel & Ward, 2000).

Significantly, there was no corresponding rise in child protection referrals (see also Hardiker et al., 1996). There was also in one authority a clear decrease in the number of referrals where "no further action" was recorded. The Loughborough pilots, together with more general guidance on assessment techniques (Meyer, 1993; Millner & O'Byrne, 1999; Waterhouse & McGhee, 2002), were pivotal in our development of tools and methods of assessment accessible to practitioners from different agencies. To be effective, such tools must be organized around well understood ideas about child development and those factors that promote or inhibit successful progress, based on research evidence and integrated with policies and procedures. Thus, our aim was to pilot a pre-referral common assessment tool that would help ensure that referrals to social services had some consistency over concepts and thresholds, thereby reducing inappropriate referrals and helping target scarce resources. The scheme would also help determine if the matter could be dealt with by the agency first involved or should be referred to some other organization.

As a first stage search procedure, its primary aim was to identify those needs of children aged 0–4 and 5–9 years that might require additional services and refer these needs to Swansea social services, who would decide if the matters presented warranted further attention via the Assessment Framework initial and core assessment tools into which they would incorporate the information from the pre-referral common assessment.

Common assessment domains and thresholds

Thus, the focus of the common assessment was the child and the key categories were drawn from the Assessment Framework dimensions. These categories structured the common assessment document and included the child's:

- health;
- education;
- identity and social presentation;

- family and social relationships;
- emotional and behavioural development and self care; and
- physical and social environment.

These six core categories were each connected to (a) indicators of parenting capacity; (b) key areas of child development; and (c) thresholds of concern—mild, moderate and serious (see below). These materials were crafted as an age-band specific document for children who were either 0–4 or 5–9 years old. Professionals would be asked to enter their comments across the categories in relation to thresholds of concern about parenting capacity and child development insofar as they had relevant and appropriate knowledge. It is important to note that the formats require professionals to stress child and family strengths as well as needs, and to outline any advice to social services they may have about the sorts of intervention that might best assist the child. These elements of the common assessment were first introduced and tested in the Loughborough studies (Peel &Ward, 2000; Rose & Ward, 2003). These formats then became the subject of consultation with key stakeholders in Swansea, and an adjusted version was agreed (Pithouse et al., 2004) and introduced through a sequence of training.

The training of local child care professionals in the undertaking of common assessments was predicated upon principles of partnership and openness; such essentials speak both to service users and providers (Lloyd & Taylor, 1995; Peel & Ward, 2000). Service users often evince distrust of local authority social services (Cleaver & Freeman, 1995; Smith, 2001) and experience some discomfort in having to explain their circumstances to different professionals. Our scheme addressed these issues directly as the tool required clear involvement of parents and children in the assessment process and their agreement in a referral being made, unless there were overriding concerns about significant harm.

In order to agree on indicators of parenting capacity and key areas of child development linked to thresholds of concern (mild, moderate or serious) in relation to the above categories of assessment, we needed to take into account the views of providers and service users (including children). Here, it cannot be assumed that conceptual and administrative materials that categorize need can simply be "plugged in" and accepted by service users and other agencies. Thus, as we describe below, it was essential to engage providers and local people in the operation of assessment concepts and their presentation in the assessment tool so that the design was "owned" by key participants. It was also essential to engage providers and public in the selection of indicators and thresholds in order to take note of any local and/or cultural issues (particularly the Welsh language) that might influence our understanding of need and the process of assessment itself. Aspects of language and other areas of potential discrimination within assessment thus received close attention (Burke & Harrison, 2000; Robinson, 1998; Rojeck, 1988).

To repeat, the thresholds of concern that were linked to each of the six assessment categories (above) comprised mild, moderate or serious concerns. These thresholds were operationalized in relation to definitions of children in need within the *Children Act 1989*, s.17:

> "Mild concern could, for example, refer to families that were not receiving support universally available from statutory providers but otherwise would not need additional assistance and while this matter would be attended to, a referral to social services would be unlikely.
>
> "Moderate concern would refer to circumstances where a child was "unlikely to achieve or maintain or have the opportunity of achieving or maintaining a reasonable standard of health or development without the provision of services" (CA 1989 s17). "Here a referral is assumed but might not be considered an immediate priority.
>
> "Serious concern would address concerns that "a child's health or development is likely to be significantly impaired or further impaired without the provision... of services" (CA 1989 s17). Here an immediate referral would be expected."

Fleshing out these broad notions in relation to indicators of parenting capacity and key areas of child development was the subject of initial consultation with key stakeholders. This was accomplished through a sequence of group exercises and training sessions with key players, including professionals from health, education, police, social services and the voluntary sector. Participation in such sessions has been found to reveal substantial areas of common ground between professionals from different disciplines, and thereby to be an important factor in strengthening the mutual trust between agencies upon which this project depends (Peel & Ward, 2000). Likewise, a focus group of parents from the research area commented and advised on the materials.

Gaining the views of children was a more delicate matter, and it was considered unlikely that the materials being developed would be readily accessible to most 0–9 year olds. Nor did we think it appropriate, for reasons of sensitivity and confidentiality, to request access to children who had recently been assessed and who might not easily make an informed choice about whether to participate. However, in matters of welfare, we all too often neglect the views of children, and we have much to learn about the way they perceive adults (especially "officials") and how this influences their readiness to trust and disclose feelings and experiences (Butler 1997). Consequently, we explored the availability of existing children's forums convened by the local authority in the research area that had a membership sufficiently mature to conceptualize issues around children's needs and good parenting. Here we used, as did Peel and Ward (2000), vignettes from popular television programs to generate discussion with a selection of youngsters about how they perceived a range of needs and good parenting in particular. Our assessment materials were adjusted and agreed in light of these events and we then embarked on a program of training local agencies in the purpose and function of the scheme.

Training

Developing the local provider system through a basic familiarisation with the aims, concepts and procedures of common assessment was an ongoing feature of the project. The first phase of training involved some 130 professionals (mainly health, education, voluntary sector) in small groups composed of agency-specific members attending half-day sessions.

Ad hoc training of mixed groups continued thereafter (which included housing and police), and over the study period some 250 people received instruction and guidance in undertaking common assessments and referrals. During training, the key issues that arose for trainees concerned the likely response of social services to assessments received; limited knowledge of what social services had to offer; time costs in completing the forms; know-how to undertake assessments for occupational groups that had little background in engaging with parents and seeking their consent; and referring reluctant parents to social services and related aspects of stigma. The benefits perceived by trainees included standardized approaches to assessment, shared standards and shared awareness of areas of concern.

Researching the impact of the scheme: Methodology and methods

Our methodological position was a careful mix of the comparative, the quasi-experimental and action research. We sought to evaluate events in an environment that we were seeking to change through training and through agreed amendments made to the materials as we moved along. We were not examining discrete phenomena that could be abstracted from their surroundings and measured with full confidence. The study therefore comprises an unavoidably partial snapshot of the impact of the scheme. While we believe the study has been as robust as feasible within the time and resources available, we do not claim to have determined all the effects (or null-effects) of the scheme, or to have accounted for other variables that may have affected referral and assessment activity in the study period.

The research comprised five key elements: consultation in the design and preparation of the assessment tool; training in the use of the tool; implementation; evaluation; report and dissemination. The key research questions we asked of the scheme were related to the following impacts, viz., whether implementation led to:

- evidence of enhanced joint working;
- congruence of pre-referral assessments; i.e., did agencies incorporate/switch to the protocol;
- more family and child involvement in pre-referral assessments;
- evidence of a transparent relationship between identified need and services provided—with particular reference to developmental issues for children;
- a drop in child concern referrals due to the protocol reducing inappropriate selection;
- no direct consequences for child protection referrals (which follow a different route) stemming from under- or over-reporting of child concern or used inappropriately for child concern cases in order to "win" quick responses or resources;
- better linking of referrals to initial assessments;
- better quality of referrals received by social services, thus easier to prioritize cases.

In order to evaluate the impact of the scheme, it was important to undertake a comparative research strategy that would take a "before and after" view of the scheme within the participating authority of Swansea and also to undertake a similar study in a comparator local authority in Wales. Such an authority was identified where no similar scheme was being introduced but which shared similarity in service structure and had adopted the new Assessment Framework being introduced across Wales when the study commenced. The research design comprised a case-based analysis of 120 referrals in the 18 months before implementation and 120 referrals in the 18 months after implementation in both authorities, together with structured interviews with key stakeholders. We considered the sample size of referrals to be sufficient to allow SPSS manipulation and some statistical testing. An extensive audit tool (140 items) based on Assessment Framework domains and referral categories was applied to 120 referrals pre- and post-implementation across both authorities in order to identify whether there were discernible changes in the information provided and the impact of these changes upon cases.

The sample (before and after) was reasonably well matched by referring agency, age of child, family structure, and primary reason for referral. The ages of the children were 0–4 and 5–9 years. They were referred because of specific needs that were not, in the first instance, to do with urgent child protection and who were not re-referred as a pre-existing open case whereby recent assessment work would likely have already been undertaken. We did not include police referrals in our analysis because they were unable to engage in the scheme for operational and resource reasons, although they were able to participate in the Loughborough studies (op cit).

Key results: Pre- and post-implementation

With respect to Swansea referrals for children in need aged 0–4 and 5–9 that did not involve urgent child protection enquiries, there were a total of 480 referrals in the 12 months before implementation. In the 12 months post-phase, there were 448 referrals (not including police referrals). Looking therefore at non-police referrals (the majority were from health, education, courts and probation, local authority, housing, and voluntary sector) it can be seen that these declined 7% from the pre- to the post-period in the intervention site. The same type of referrals had gone up from 287 to 495 in the comparator site (by 72%), as was the case in other authorities in South Wales. As in the intervention site, this did not include police referrals.

Referrals from family and kin

During the same period there had been a reduction in referrals by family and kin (from 301 to 193), thus there would appear to have been no "knock on" effect whereby professionals might have (improperly but for reasons of expedience) encouraged service users to refer themselves directly. Accordingly, these professionals would not have had to spend time completing the assessment materials.

Child protection

It was important (a) to examine if there had been any increase in child protection referrals over the study period that might be linked in some way to the implementation of the scheme, and (b) to consider if any such increase may have been due to professionals using this route improperly as a means to "fast track" referrals and avoid completing the assessment forms. Across these two periods, there were no evident increases in child protection referrals from education, health and voluntary agencies as a consequence of collaborating in the scheme.

Referrals using the new forms

Initially, we sought to win cooperation and support over time from other agencies for the project. Over an 18-month period of piloting and data collection in 2003/4, some 169 referrals were received from referrers trained in using the assessment materials. Of these, 88 completed the common assessment materials and 81 did not, thus compliance with the project was not immediate and fulsome. However, as the scheme progressed the numbers not using the new materials fell markedly, and towards the end of the first 12 months most used the common assessment forms. Thus, our sample post-implementation was smaller than the 120 referrals we planned to accumulate but was adequate for broad comparative purposes.

Background information: Reduction in missing areas

When looking at essential assessment information missing from referrals pre- and post-implementation in Swansea, we can note the following reductions which are notable in some instances and which were not evidenced in the comparator authority.

Information area	Missing in referrals (pre)	Missing in referrals (post)
Ethnicity	27%	10%
First language	80%	46%
Religion	94%	85%
Parental responsibility	27%	9%
Had always lived with parent	73%	19%
Looked after or not	77%	27%
Registered as "disabled"	75%	23%
Child protection registrations	68%	23%
Parent/carer aware of referral	39%	7%
Consent noted	76%	17%

When looking at information entered about other professionals and agencies already involved with the family, it was possible to note a marked increase in this information from 110 entries in the Swansea pre-phase referrals ($n = 120$) compared with 228 entries in the post-phase referrals ($n = 88$). There were no marked increases in the comparator authority.

Children's views in common assessments

With respect to children's views entered or not before and after implementation, we noted little change across intervention and comparator sites and time periods. Children's views were entered in a small minority of instances (in Swansea pre-referrals 4% and in post-referrals 5%, and similar distributions were noted in the comparator authority).

Main referrers: Health and education

Perhaps unsurprisingly, health and education referrals using the common assessment tended to predominate. When looking at referrals from health, we can note relatively little change in Swansea across both periods in terms of information concerning immunizations, dental records, and type of assistance needed from social services. However, more information was entered on the child's developmental strengths (up from 10% to 24% of referrals post-implementation) and on the parent's capacity to meet the child's health needs (up from 3% to 24%). Regarding education, we can note much more information in Swansea referrals about the child's education strengths (up from 3% to 38%) and more on the child's education needs (up from 13% to 51%). As for assessment domains such as identity and social presentation, emotional and behavioural needs, or the child's family and social relationship needs, there was less change over the study period. The reasons for this are not clear; it may be that the more "interior" and less tangible nature of a child's emotional characteristics were areas where referrers had neither the training nor experience and conceptual skills to offer insights; most seemed more comfortable to describe the more visible aspects of a child's conduct or circumstances.

More emphasis upon strengths

There was much more information provided post-implementation in Swansea referrals about environmental factors likely to have an impact on the child and family. There was also much more information on parent/carer capacities to meet the needs of the child. Swansea referrals were much more likely than comparator referrals to comment on positives in the child and parent. Thus, in the post phase there was a marked increase of 30% or more in information entered on categories such as family history, housing deficits, social and community strengths, employment and income deficits, and 30% or more information with regard to parenting capacities such as basic care, ensuring safety, emotional warmth (strengths), boundaries (strengths), and stability (strengths). To repeat, a notable difference was the tendency for Swansea referrals in the post stage to give more emphasis to child and family strengths (more so than in the comparator authority). Out of a possible 15 referral categories and assessment domains in the audit tool that referred explicitly to strengths it was possible to note that all found some reference within the Swansea referrals and common assessments. By contrast, comparator referrals made reference to three of these 15 strengths only.

More information entered

In order to test whether change between the two periods and two sites could be subject to more rigorous examination, we collapsed the data and re-coded them into a binary score to indicate whether information was missing or present for each item on the audit tool. Comparisons were then made across intervention and comparator site to examine any differences in the proportion of missing data within each of the 140 audit items. These were assessed using the non-parametric Pearson Chi-Square test, suitable for such basic categorical data. Examination of pre-implementation data for both sites revealed no significant differences in the proportion of missing information for the vast majority of the audit items, indicating that the standard of completion was not very dissimilar at the outset. No significant differences were evident when the pre- and post-audit data for the comparator site were analyzed.

In contrast, the Swansea audit data showed significant statistical differences on 31 items between pre- and post-implementation. For five of the items there were more missing data at post- than at pre-implementation. For the remaining 26 items, however, the audit data at the post-stage yielded more information than obtained at pre-stage, and for all except two items the decrease in missing data was dramatic. It would seem likely, therefore, that the implementation of the common assessment did have an impact, and that statistically this was at a significant level for a substantial number of items across referral categories and assessment domains.

Further action on referrals

It was important to detect if there had been any change in further action as a consequence of the referral and common assessment being made. The following potential outcomes were examined as indicators of work being better focused. Thus, a reduction in advice and information giving was thought a likely outcome of referrals being more focused around needs. Here we can note that in Swansea in the post-phase, fewer referrals received advice only, down from 35% to 28%. Also, there was a reduction in referrals not receiving a service and being "posted" on to other agencies, down from 15% to 7%.

By contrast, more cases were allocated for social services intervention, up from 17% to 26%. There was also a reduction in "no further action" as an outcome, which fell from 47% to 38%. Initial assessments rose from 33% to 44%, which suggests that referrals may have assisted in identifying needs with more effect. In the comparator authority there were no similar changes; rather, there were increases in the proportion of referrals defined as "no further action" and proportionately fewer cases passed to social services teams for intervention.

Professionals' views on using the forms

Individual taped interviews were conducted with a purposive sample of health, education, police and social services staff ($n = 20$) who had completed one or more assessments and referrals. There were negative responses from professionals due to perceptions that the forms were repetitive and time consuming. Initial resistance from some agencies stemmed from a belief that it was the role of social services to assess in detail and not the job of the referring agency. Respondents from health and education acknowledged that the scheme provided an opportunity to learn more about family functioning while focusing on the needs of a child as an individual. It also provided an opportunity to encourage the family to have their say and to be involved in the decision making around appropriate services tailored to individual needs. Here, some referrers pointed to the way some families were guarded throughout the assessment; some families were not interested and felt the process to be frustrating given, in their view, the need for an immediate response to their circumstances. Referrers were also concerned that the assessment would raise expectations of services being available to meet the needs that were identified during assessment. Referrers were unsure to what extent they should specify in the referral the sorts of services that could best meet the child's needs.

Health workers seemed more comfortable than other referrers with the idea of seeking consent from parents/carers in making a referral. Most respondents could see some potential in relation to family empowerment, and a more constructive stress on "positives" in family capacities that arose in the format of the common assessment. Most referrers saw significant value in the way the forms provided indicators and thresholds for locating and describing their concerns.

Social workers in the local authority who received the common assessments found them useful and were keen for the scheme to continue subject to adjustments that would help streamline and delete areas of repetition. They found the common assessments helped them prepare for their encounters with families and offered a valuable starting point in identifying and understanding specific needs. These social workers also recognized that improvement in their feedback to referrers was needed if the scheme was to maximize support and cooperation from referring agencies.

Conclusion

We consider the scheme to be a qualified success. It is acknowledged that the pre-referral common assessment materials are in need of adjustment and streamlining. It is also acknowledged that better feedback is needed from social services to referrers in order to provide essential information and to generate a sense of reciprocity so as to elicit support for and compliance with the scheme. However, the scheme demonstrates potential that is well worth developing further via an amended common assessment protocol. The local authority recognizes this and there are now plans to introduce the scheme across the authority for all age groups of children and young people, and for child protection referrals as well. This will generate a more inclusive pre-referral assessment mechanism that will support the local authority's aim to offer a more integrated approach to child and family support.

References

Burke, B., & Harrison, P. (2000). Race and racism in social work. In M. Davies (Ed.), *The Blackwell encyclopaedia of social work* (pp. 282–283). Oxford: Blackwell.

Butler, I. (1997). Used and abused: Engaging the child in child protection, pp. 15–27. In A. Pithouse and H. Williamson (Eds.), *Engaging the user in welfare services.* Birmingham: Venture.

Cleaver, H., & Freeman, P. (1995). *Parental perspectives on suspected child abuse.* London: Her Majesty's Stationery Office.

Department for Education and Skills. (2003). *Every child matters* (Cm5860). London: The Stationery Office.

Department for Education and Skills. (2004). *Consultation: The common assessment framework*. Cheshire: The Consultation Unit, DfES

Department of Health, Department of Education and Employment, Home Office. (2000). *Framework for the assessment of children in need and their families*. London: DoH.

Department of Health & H. Cleaver. (2000). *Assessment recording forms*. London: The Stationery Office.

Hardiker, P., Exton, K., & Barker, M. (1996). *The prevention of child abuse: A framework for analysing services*. London: The National Commission of Enquiry into the Preventon of Child Abuse.

Hudson, B., Hardy, B., Henwood, M., & Wistow, G. (1999). In pursuit of interagency collaboration in the public sector: What is the contribution of theory and research? *Public Management: An International Journal of Research and Theory, 1*, 235–260.

Lloyd, M., & Taylor, C. (1995). Developing a holistic model of social work assessment in the 1990's. *British Journal of Social Work, 25*, 592–610.

Meyer, C. (1993). *Assessment in social work practice*. Columbia University Press.

Millner, J., & O'Byrne, P. (1998). *Assessment in social work*. London: MacMillan.

National Assembly for Wales. (2000). *The Assessment Framework – Consultation March 2000*. Cardiff: NAfW.

Peel, M. (1999). *North Lincolnshire Parenting Project: Training materials* (unpublished). University of Loughborough.

Peel, M., & Ward, H. (2000). *North Lincolnshire Parenting Project: Report to Area Child Protection Committee*. Loughborough University.

Pithouse, A., Batchelor, C., Crowley, A., Ward, H., & Webb, M. (2004). *Developing a multi-agency pre-referral common assessment approach to the identification of children in need in the community*. A report for the Wales Office of Research and Development for Health and Social Care, Grant Number: SCR01/1/009. Cardiff, Welsh Assembly Government.

Rojeck, P. (1988). *Social work and received ideas*. London: Routledge.

Robinson, L. (1998). Social work through the life course. In R. Adams, L. Dominelli, & M. Payne (Eds.), *Social work: Themes, issues and critical debates* (pp. 78–87). London: Macmillan.

Smith, C. (2001). Trust and confidence: Possibilities for social work in "high modernity." *British Journal of Social Work, 31,* 287–306.

Ward, H., & Peel, M. (2002). An inter-agency approach to needs assessment. In H. Ward & W. Rose (Eds.), *Approaches to needs assessment in children's services* (pp. 281–293). London: Jessica Kingsley.

Ward, H., & Rose, W. (Eds.). (2003). *Approaches to needs assessment in children's services.* London: Jessica Kingsley.

Waterhouse, L., & McGhee, J. (2002). Social work with children and families. In R. Adams, L. Dominelli, & M. Payne (Eds.), *Social work: Themes, issues and critical debates* (pp. 267–286). (Second edition). London: Macmillan.

Welsh Assembly Government. (2004). *Making the connections: Delivering better services for Wales.* Cardiff: WAG.

CHAPTER 22

Implementing Looking After Children as a collaborative practice and policy framework in Victoria, Australia

Ruth Champion and Gabrielle Burke

Introduction

In May 2002, the implementation of Looking After Children (LAC) was announced as part of the 2002/2003 Budget of the State Government of Victoria, Australia. The authors, who had each been advocating for many years for the full implementation of LAC throughout Victoria, both had key statewide roles in what followed from this announcement. Ruth Champion became the LAC implementation project manager within the head office of the Department of Human Services (DHS). Gabrielle Burke had a major role in developing the LAC training strategy, initially as the LAC practice consultant at Berry Street Victoria, one of the largest Victorian Community Service Organizations (CSOs), and then from September 2003 until June 2004 within DHS. This paper discusses our experience to date in implementing Looking After Children (LAC) as a collaborative practice and policy framework for those who share the parenting responsibility when children and young people are in out-of-home care.

Context

Australia has a federal system of government with powers and responsibilities shared between the Commonwealth (national) government and the six Australian States and two Territories. Child protection and care is a State/Territory responsibility. Victoria is the third smallest in geographic area of the eight States and Territories of Australia. It covers an area of 227,416 km^2 on the southeast corner of the Australian mainland, and accounts for just under 3% of Australia's total area.[1] However, it is the second most populous state (after New South Wales), having a population of just over 5 million, which is nearly 25% of the total Australian population of 20 million. Most Victorians live in the greater metropolitan area of

Melbourne (3.6 million) or in regional cities such as Geelong, Ballarat, Bendigo and Wodonga. Australia's Indigenous people are Aboriginals and Torres Strait Islanders. As a result of continuous immigration, Victoria has a culturally and linguistically diverse population, especially in the urban areas.

Historically, most welfare services (including orphanages and foster care) were established in Victoria by charities and churches ahead of government involvement. Consequently, the responsibility for the delivery of family support, child protection, and out-of-home care services is still shared between the government and community-based sectors. In Victoria, out-of-home care services are delivered by community-based organizations we call community service organizations (CSOs), which are authorized, funded and monitored by the State Government Department of Human Services (DHS). CSOs are responsible for providing out-of-home care services such as foster care and residential care services for children and young people and for ensuring that their respective needs are met while they are in care. DHS is directly responsible for providing child protection services. DHS operates through eight (previously nine) separate regions: there are five rural regions and three (previously four) in metropolitan Melbourne.

There were 8,628 Victorian children in out-of-home care in 2001/02.[2] The rate of children placed away from home for every 1,000 Victorian children aged 0 to 17 years was 3.4. Of the total 8,628 children and young people in out-of-home care in Victoria in 2001/02, 5,154 were in foster care (or other home-based care) and 924 were in residential care, making a total of 6,008 in placements provided by CSOs. The remainder were in kinship care (1,595) or permanent care (945). Overall, the number of children in out-of-home care is growing at a rate of 2% per year, but the trend to more kinship care placements means that the number in CSO placements is decreasing. Our most recent available annual throughput data[3] indicate that CSOs are currently providing out-of-home care placements for 4,623 children and young people over a 12-month period. Aboriginal children currently comprise 13% of those in out-of-home care, although only 1% of the Victorian population aged between 0 and 17 years are Indigenous.[4]

The decision to implement LAC in Victoria

Although the Victorian protection and care system—with responsibility shared between the government and community sector—is quite different from that in other places, many of the needs of children and young people being looked after away from home are similar the world over. For some time, those responsible for the protection, care and well-being of Victorian children in out-of-home care had expressed concern regarding the experiences provided to these children in terms of the quality of their care and their well-being outcomes. Therefore there was considerable Victorian interest in LAC, as a way of addressing these concerns, expressed very soon after LAC was first developed in the United Kingdom. However, the decision to implement LAC in Victoria was a long time in gestation. The first trial of LAC materials by a Victorian CSO (Kildonan Family Services) commenced in the early 1990s.

In 1994, CSOs began meeting with DHS to discuss potential benefits of LAC for Victoria. In 1996, the then Children's Welfare Association of Victoria—CWAV (now Centre for Excellence in Child and Family Welfare)—initiated a project with funding from the Stegley Foundation and DHS to pilot the LAC Assessment and Action Records in the Eastern Metropolitan Region of Melbourne. It involved 50 children and young people in care. Following this pilot, there was strong advocacy from within the community services sector, led by the CWAV as the peak body, for government support to implement LAC as a better way of meeting the needs of children and young people in out-of-home care.

In 2000, Berry Street Victoria, a major out-of-home care provider, decided to implement LAC within their own agency across four regions of Victoria, using funding from the ANZ Trustees. In 2001, another CSO, Orana Family Services, also decided to implement LAC. Hence, the State government decision to fund the establishment of LAC throughout the whole of Victoria in the 2002/03 Budget was welcomed as a response to a longstanding desire from the entire out-of-home sector to implement LAC as a way of improving the quality of out-of-home care. The nature of the Budget funding provided some significant challenges: it only provided non-recurrent establishment funding; there were short timelines for such a significant change that would affect many people; and we were introducing an approach that had been developed in another country. However, we had the advantage of implementing something that the sector wanted to do. We also had the benefit of drawing on the experiences of others who had implemented LAC ahead of us.

Building on the experience of others

Because LAC had been implemented in other places before Victoria, we were in a position to learn from their experience. There were three key themes that consistently recurred in a number of articles concerned with the evaluation of LAC implementation in New South Wales, Western Australia, Canada and the United Kingdom. These themes were thus adopted as principles that informed the initial implementation efforts in Victoria.

1. Successful implementation requires a well-coordinated "whole of organization" commitment, led by management within the organization who are convinced of the value of LAC.

2. Initial hesitation to LAC can be overcome through emphasizing its benefits and acknowledging staff skills and expertise.

3. Better results are achieved if the whole of LAC is used and it is essential that LAC replace—not duplicate—current ways of working.

Implementation features

Partnership

The implementation of LAC throughout Victoria was undertaken collaboratively by DHS and the CSOs providing out-of-home care services in Victoria. A Statewide LAC Reference Group was established at the beginning of the implementation process with representation from CSOs and DHS. Each of the 43 (now 39) CSOs providing out-of-home care services agreed to implement LAC and has continued to participate fully in this process at all levels. This includes the five Aboriginal agencies that provide out-of-home care services in Victoria.

Care Team

LAC is being used to support greater collaboration between all those involved in out-of-home care. In Victoria, LAC is not just a casework methodology for social workers. It provides the consistent framework for all those who share the complex parenting responsibilities when children and young people cannot live with their own families: birth parents, carers, CSO placement agency case workers, and DHS child protection workers. LAC is being implemented as a way in which people can work together to address the needs of children or young persons while they are in care. It refocuses on those things that good parents would do in order to achieve better outcomes for their own children.

Strengthened role of CSOs

Although we must emphasise that DHS and CSOs are jointly responsible for the out-of-home care that children and young people receive in Victoria, it must also be acknowledged that the roles of DHS and CSOs do differ. Broadly speaking, CSOs have the primary responsibility for the provision of day-to-day care; it is the DHS child protection workers who must assess and act upon the risk issues that are to be addressed in order to determine whether the child can safely return home. The implementation of LAC has provided the opportunity for CSO case workers to take a more proactive care and placement planning and review role. Copies of LAC records are expected to be given to all those involved in developing them, including child protection workers, but it is the CSO workers who have the primary responsibility for completing the LAC records. The LAC records are also being implemented to provide a consistent out-of-home care client information system for CSOs in Victoria. However, this has meant that so far we have not been in a position to implement LAC with those children and young people in kinship care and permanent care placements not supported by a CSO.

Use of existing materials

The initial implementation in Victoria has used a set of LAC records modified for use in Victoria from the original UK materials by Barnardos Australia and the University of NSW LAC Project.[5] Although not perfectly applicable to the Victorian context of shared DHS and CSO responsibilities for out-of-home care, it was decided that they were suitable enough for initial use. Using these existing materials enabled implementation to commence immediately. All Victorian CSOs and DHS entered into individual End User Agreements with the Barnardos Australia/University of NSW LAC Project to access the licensed materials. Most CSOs are using the paper-based version only, although 12 CSOs are using the off-line word processing version known as LACES. It has always been planned that DHS would obtain its own Commercial LAC licence from the UK and develop our own revised set of Victorian LAC materials (based on our initial implementation experience for use in the second phase of LAC).

Clarification of LAC processes in Victorian context

Because the Victorian context is significantly different from both the UK and NSW, LAC processes and records did not fit neatly with Victoria's division of responsibilities and the statutory child protection case planning processes. Considerable work was required to clarify how the LAC records would be made to fit with these processes, at least during the initial period of implementation. Discussion papers about the implementation options were prepared and discussed with the Statewide Reference Group. The expectations about how the records would be initially used in the Victorian context were then communicated by the Statewide Reference Group, Regional Implementation Groups, the training strategy, the DHS website (www.dhs.vic.gov.au/lac-victoria), and DHS Practice Bulletins and Instructions.

Statewide implementation

The implementation in Victoria is an ambitious, large-scale change management exercise. Because of the lengthy lead time prior to this implementation (which included several small pilots), we were in a position to roll out LAC for all children and young people in out-of-home care across the whole statewide service system at the same time. This has the advantage that we did not need to maintain dual systems and that we can simply say that LAC is "the way we do things around here." However, it has the disadvantage wherein it is easy to think "we did LAC last year" and expect instant takeup without acknowledging the considerable ongoing effort that will be required over many years before LAC is fully embedded in our daily work with all children and young people in care.

Regional implementation process

Most of the implementation effort in Victoria has been based in the nine (now eight) regions. Each region established Regional LAC Implementation Groups (known as RIGs) that took on significant implementation responsibilities. RIG members are senior managers from DHS and every CSO providing out-of-home care in the region. Each DHS region provided experienced DHS workers to act as regional LAC coordinators and support the RIGs. The RIGs were charged with the preparation of joint DHS and CSO regional implementation plans and were also given the responsibility for determining how best to use the funding allocated centrally for regional implementation. RIGs selected experienced practitioners to be trained as LAC trainers and managed the regional LAC training program. They also undertook the compilation of regional implementation monitoring data and the comprehensive consultation process to inform the revision of the LAC records. Some RIGs have also established LAC lead practitioners groups to support good practice and complement the more strategic coordinating role of the RIGs. More than two years after their establishment, all RIGs are still actively supporting the continuing implementation of LAC in each region.

Investment in training

Because the Budget Initiative for the establishment of LAC was non-recurrent and had to be spent during 2002/03, it was decided to invest the majority of this funding in saturation training of the whole sector to support the LAC implementation over the long term. The LAC training strategy is discussed in more detail below.

Additional contributions to LAC by DHS and CSOs

Modest establishment grants were provided by DHS to each CSO to cover some infrastructure costs and the initial licence fees charged by the Barnardos/University of NSW LAC Project for access to LAC materials. Because of the commitment to LAC and the shared ownership of its implementation, DHS (centrally and regionally) and all CSOs have made significant additional contributions in cash and in-kind to support LAC. Since July 2003, there has been no additional designated funding allocated for LAC. All ongoing implementation by both DHS and CSOs is using resources already allocated for out-of-home care. The limited resources have nonetheless created some difficulties because LAC raises expectations about what should be possible. As well, LAC highlights deficiencies in the capacity to meet the more clearly identified needs of children and young people in care.

Training strategy

The LAC training strategy has been pivotal to the implementation of LAC across Victoria. It was fortunate that Berry Street Victoria had already developed an excellent LAC training package as part of their agency-based LAC implementation, which commenced just prior to the announcement of Government funding for statewide implementation. DHS decided to commission Berry Street Victoria to extend their LAC training package into a train-the-trainer training approach, which would support a regionally based, statewide intensive training program.

The implementation of this training has been separately reported on by Berry Street Victoria (2004).[6] This paper will therefore provide only an overview of the main features of this training strategy.

Consistent statewide training package

The training package emphasized the following: skillful use of the LAC records and processes to support good practice; collaboration by all those responsible for good care; and doing the things that a good parent would to address the needs of children and young people while they are in care.

Regional trainers recruited from experienced practitioners

Each region selected experienced practitioners from CSOs and DHS to become LAC trainers, deliver the training sessions in their region, and be a permanent resource person for LAC implementation in their region after the initial training was completed. Each region had a team of between three and eight trainers, depending on the numbers of people to be trained in each region.

Train-the-trainer training

Overall there were 48 practitioners who were given either four or six days of intensive train-the-trainer LAC training, depending on whether they had previously attained competency in Training Small Groups. Of the 48 trainers nominated by the RIGs, 47 were assessed as competent trainers at the completion of the Train Small Groups-accredited, competency-based component of the training. These 47 LAC trainers were then provided with ongoing support while they delivered the training back in their own regions, including a mid-point training review day, a help line, and distribution of responses to FAQs.

Regional delivery

Regional training sessions comprising two days of training a week apart were delivered by a team of two LAC trainers co-training at a time. Between February and June 2003, nearly 3000 participants completed LAC training, which represented nearly 80% of all those who had been identified as requiring LAC training by their RIGs. The training modelled the experience of participation in the care team by training together at the same time a mix of foster carers, residential care workers, placement agency case workers and other CSO workers, child protection workers and other DHS workers involved in out-of-home care. This was the first time this group of people had ever been involved in joint training in this way. One feature of the training involved senior managers at the beginning and end of every training group; they provided leadership and support to the implementation commitment to LAC at all levels. The feedback from this training was overwhelmingly positive.

Follow-up training

In general, once the initial basic LAC training was completed at the end of June 2003, the approach for further training has been to expect that LAC principles will now be incorporated in all future induction processes and ongoing professional development. None the less, some additional LAC training initiatives have also been undertaken. Under the auspices of the then CWAV (now Centre for Excellence in Child and Family Welfare), train-the-trainer Care and Placement Planning training was provided for two of the LAC trainers from each region. These trainers then provided at least two sessions of this training in their region for those CSO workers responsible for coordinating the LAC Care and Placement Planning process. This training, entitled "More than a Meeting,"[7] acknowledged the fact that CSO workers wanted more resources to enable them to develop their role through LAC in working with birth families, carers, and child protection to develop care and placement plans for children and young people in care. The basic LAC training was also delivered to the central Child Protection Professional Development Unit for incorporation into their subsequent induction and other courses for child protection workers, and to TAFE (Technical and Further Education) providers of competency-based community services training for incorporation in their future training courses for residential care workers.

Monitoring implementation

From July 1, 2003, all CSOs in every region commenced implementing LAC with all children and young people who came into care after that time. They also undertook to phase in LAC by progressively completing LAC records retrospectively with those children and young people already in care at that time. The use of LAC records and rates of participation in LAC processes during the first six months of implementation were closely monitored by CSOs themselves, RIGs, and the central DHS LAC project team using a consistent set of monitoring tools that that addressed three key implementation questions:

1. To what extent are the LAC records being used?

2. Who is participating in the various LAC processes?

3. Is the expected information being exchanged between DHS workers and CSO out-of-home care services to support LAC implementation?

Three separate feedback sheet templates were prepared to collect information to answer each of these questions, along with a fourth sheet for recording more general comments about the implementation process. There was 100% return rate for this monitoring data in that every CSO in every region submitted monitoring data using the standard templates. This reflects the commitment of all Victorian CSOs to LAC implementation and the self-monitoring process.

Of the 3,342 children and young people for whom these LAC monitoring data were collected:

- 2,563 were in full-time placements;
- 779 were in respite placements.

These monitoring data cover nearly 90% of the children and young people in full-time placements and 66% of those who were in respite placements during this period. The central DHS LAC project team undertook the collation and statewide analysis of all the LAC implementation monitoring data. In brief, the main findings were as follows.

Use of LAC records

At least one LAC record was used with nearly 80% of all children and young people newly referred for full-time placements in the first six months of implementation. In addition, at least one LAC record was used with nearly 50% of the "backlog" of children and young people placed prior to July 2003. LAC records were rarely used in the initial implementation period for respite placements.

The majority of children and young people in out-of-home care only had the early information records, i.e., Essential Information Record Part 1 (EIR1) and the Placement Plan Part 1(PP1). There was a much lower take-up of the Care Plan and the Placement Plan Part 2 (C&PP2) (34% of new placements). Nonetheless, where placements lasted for three weeks or longer, 51% of the children in both new and pre-existing placements had a C&PP2 (including more than 70% of new placements lasting three weeks or longer). An important implementation issue identified through this monitoring process was the tendency for C&PP2 records to be held up by an understandable desire to get it absolutely right.

The takeup of the Review of Arrangements (RoA) record (13%) and the Assessment and Action Record (AAR) (9%) was higher than expected in the first six months. This was due to the amount of time needed to elapse before these records could be completed. In particular, it seems that many carers and others involved in out-of-home care were very keen to start using the AARs even before the first six months had elapsed.

Participation in LAC processes

The monitoring data provided evidence of a genuine commitment to the principles of inclusion and participation in the LAC processes by foster carers, residential care workers, child protection workers, and the CSO placement agency case worker. The high level of participation by carers (73% of all C&PP2 processes) was not entirely unexpected, given the enthusiastic response that LAC has received from Victorian foster carers in particular. The participation rates by child protection workers (63% of all C&PP2 processes) reflect the challenges of competing priorities of child protection and also provide an acceptable baseline from which to build greater collaboration in future. None the less, the outstanding achievement highlighted by the monitoring data was the extent to which birth parents were actually participating in these processes (63% of all C&PP2 processes) in the first six months on implementation, since this constituted a significant change from previous practice whereby CSOs and foster carers were unlikely to collaborate directly with birth parents.

Children and young people were also participating in their own LAC processes most of the time (50% of C&PP2, 42% of RoA and 71% of AARs). This is encouraging since some children are too young to participate and others may choose not to.

Exchange of information

The monitoring data identified important information exchange issues during the initial implementation period. There were concerns about the quality of the placement referral information provided by DHS using the LAC formats. The implementation strategy, whereby DHS completed the EIR1 and provided additional information required by the CSO to complete the PP1, is difficult to implement. The data also highlighted that CSOs did not routinely provide copies of completed LAC records to DHS as expected, and that the necessary systems to support this had still to be created by CSOs.

Revision of LAC records for next phase of implementation

As already indicated, it had always been planned that existing LAC materials would only be used for the initial implementation of LAC in Victoria, and that revised materials would be developed based on the initial implementation experience to make LAC more relevant in the Victorian context. Therefore, DHS has obtained its own commercial licence from the UK copyright holders to develop revised materials of our own from the UK source documents.

Consultation process

In November 2003, Aboriginal CSOs providing out-of-home care were consulted about the applicability of LAC records for their work. This process reaffirmed both the commitment of these agencies to implement LAC processes and the need to revise LAC records to improve their cultural relevance. During March and April 2004, RIGs conducted a series of extensive regional consultations with participation from foster carers, residential care staff, CSO workers experienced in using the LAC records, and child protection workers. CREATE, the Victorian organization representing young people who are or have been in care, also facilitated consultation sessions with their members. These consultations provided detailed feedback on features of LAC records to be retained and desirable changes to better support practice in the Victorian context. Additional feedback—provided in the form of comments on the data monitoring sheets—was also used to inform the revision process.

Issues being addressed

There was considerable agreement about what needed to be addressed in the revision, including:

- the need to develop better placement referral records which DHS can provide to CSOs, and which also contain the information that carers need at the start of a placement;

- the desirability of a separate Placement Agreement (or set of agreements) to be used by CSOs to record agreements with allocated CSO case worker, carer, child/young person, birth parents, and medical consents, etc.;

- the need to consolidate all the essential information into the one ongoing record;

- the need to simplify the Care Plan and the Placement Plan Part 2 and differentiate LAC Care and Placement Planning responsibilities from Statutory Case Planning responsibilities of child protection workers;

- the need to refocus the Review of Arrangements as a Review of the Care and Placement Plan; and

- the need to keep the language user friendly and prompt good care.

The consultation indicated that it was too early to provide much useful feedback about the Assessment and Action Records. Those who had used them were generally happy to keep using them in the current format.

IT development context

It has always been intended that LAC records would eventually be developed in Victoria into an interactive electronic client information system. It is somewhat fortuitous, however, that the implementation of LAC has occurred at the same time as the development of a new client information system known as CRIS (Client Relationships Information System) and CRISSSP (CRIS for Service Providers). CRIS involves several different client information systems (Disability, Early Intervention Specialist Services, Juvenile Justice, Child Protection and Care) and is scheduled to fully replace the current DHS Child Protection client information system (known as CASIS) in 2005/06. The capacity for CSOs to also access this client information system for their own clients via CRISSP is a significant IT partnership development.

Link to quality assurance and future outcome monitoring capacity

New Victorian residential care standards were developed in 2002 and new home-based care standards were developed in 2003. Following this, and in parallel with the LAC implementation, DHS has been developing a new Quality Assurance strategy in partnership with all out-of-home care service providers and the Centre for Excellence in Child and Family Welfare. The strategy is designed to ensure that implementation of LAC provides the basis for CSOs to demonstrate compliance with out-of-home care standards and document quality improvement. At the same time, one of the requirements for revising the LAC records is to ensure that compliance with applicable standards is prompted and documented throughout the records. In addition, we have also been conscious of the opportunity to use data collected in the course of good practice to improve our capacity to monitor client outcomes in out-of-home care in future. Therefore, the importance of ensuring that key outcome information is recorded has also informed the revision process.

Links with cultural planning for indigenous children and young people

All Aboriginal and Torres Strait islander children and young people are expected to have a Cultural Plan at the start of a placement that records how their cultural, community and family links will be maintained while they are in out-of-home care. The revised LAC records need to take account of the relationship between Cultural Plans and LAC Care and Placement Plans and ensure that LAC records support and build on the Cultural Plans that take priority over LAC processes.

Links with education planning processes

At the same time that LAC is being implemented, a complementary initiative is also being set in place. This is the Partnering Agreement between DHS and the Department of Education and Training (DE&T), which is focused on improving the school participation rates of children in out-of-home care. The revised LAC records provide an opportunity to prompt more effective links between LAC processes and the new Partnering Agreement processes.

Development of revised records

The process so far for the development of revised LAC records for next phase implementation in Victoria has been informed by the consultation feedback, our IT context, our quality assurance and improvement context, and our need to link LAC with other related planning processes for children and young people in care. Our revision has also drawn on the revised format for LAC records in the UK as incorporated in their new Integrated Childrens' System exemplars.

At this stage we have developed a new Placement Referral record to support LAC processes and three new draft revised LAC records for pilot testing from September 2004:

1. "Essential Information Record"—which will replace the current EIR2;

2. "Care and Placement Plan"—which will replace both the current Care Plan and the PP2;

3. "Review of the Care and Placement Plan"—which will replace the current RoA record.

The new Placement Referral record being developed in CRIS will eventually replace the current placement referral process based on the EIR1 and PP1.

The six age-related AARs (Assessment and Action Records) have not yet been revised. Current AARs will be used until a full set of revised records is available, based on further consultation during 2005. Further consideration will also be given during 2005 as to whether a new Placement Agreement record for CSOs is necessary.

Pilot process

The new Placement Referral record and the three revised LAC records are currently being built in an interactive electronic format within CRIS and CRISSP for pilot testing in Southern metropolitan region from February 2004.

We have also developed word processing versions of the three revised LAC records. These are being made available for preliminary testing by Victorian CSOs that choose to do so from September 2004. Ongoing access to the paper based version of the Barnardos Australia/University of NSW LAC Project materials is also being arranged for all Victorian CSOs until a complete set of revised LAC records is available for use in Victoria.

Feedback will be sought from both the word processing version pilot and the CRIS and CRISSP pilot in mid 2005 to inform the next version of the records to be developed in CRIS and CRISSP. The full set of revised LAC records for use in Victoria will be submitted to the LAC copyright owners in UK for approval under our licence agreement prior to completion.

Achievements and challenges

Collaborative ownership

We are pleased to be able to say that LAC was not only introduced in 2002/03 as a joint initiative of DHS and all the CSOs providing out-of-home care in Victoria; more than two years later, this partnership continues because it is still something that the whole sector wants to do. RIGs have harnessed the active ongoing commitment of DHS and CSOs to LAC as demonstrated in the 100% return of monitoring data and its subsequent use to identify and then address implementation issues. The whole care team of foster carers or residential care workers, CSO case workers, child protection workers and birth families are participating in LAC processes with the majority of all children and young people in care. This is a rare example of partnership where the practice matches the rhetoric, although we would be the first to warn that there is room for much more improvement in future—especially as it takes a lot of time and effort to work together effectively to address all the needs of children and young people in out-of-home care. The more we do, the more we realize we still need to do if we are to improve the outcomes for children and young people in care.

Training strategy

We are especially proud of our LAC training strategy and its implementation during 2003. In just five months, nearly 3000 foster carers, residential care workers, CSO workers involved in out-of-home care, and child protection workers and other DHS workers involved in out-of-home care participated in a saturation training process. This collaboration resulted in the development of a shared framework for working together—the same way a good parent would—to address the needs of children and young people in out-of-home care. This was a big logistical exercise that was only achieved with a significant effort from those involved at all levels. The feedback from this training was almost universally positive. Virtually everyone enjoyed the training experience, saying things like, "This will help us to focus on the things we always wanted to do for the children and young people in our care."

The train-the-trainer process provided us with some excellent LAC trainers who continue to provide a sustained resource in their agencies and regions. However, it has still proved a challenge to provide sufficient ongoing support in practice. Many of the LAC trainers have moved on to other positions, left the region, gone on maternity leave, and so on. Others have found it difficult to be released from their other responsibilities to provide further practice leadership. Nonetheless, each RIG and many CSOs have developed a range of strategies to overcome these challenges to provide continuous practice leadership for LAC. Some of the individuals who have played a practice leadership role in their regions have been acknowledged with LAC Achievement Awards, which enabled them to attend the Ottawa conference and return with further resources to contribute to the ongoing implementation process.

We have been reluctant to provide ongoing formal LAC training, not only because we have no additional LAC training resources, but also because we do not want to give the message that there is the real work and then there is the extra that LAC involves. However, our strategy of training virtually the whole workforce and foster carers at one time, and then expecting LAC to be incorporated into all future induction processes and ongoing training provided by DHS, external training providers and CSOs, has proved to be only partly successful. There has been a high turnover of CSO workers and child protection workers in particular since the training was completed. There has been a delay between completion of LAC training and its incorporation into Child Protection induction training and other professional development. CSOs have limited resources for in-house induction and professional development, and there have been few opportunities for workers to attend external training that incorporates LAC principles. No work has been done to incorporate LAC within our university-based social work courses at this stage. We have provided a lot of effective LAC training in a very short time, but there is still much more that could be done.

Extending protective focus to good care focus

We have come a long way using LAC to broaden the focus of our out-of-home care sector as a whole. It reaches beyond merely ensuring the protection and safety of children and young people in care, to include working together to provide good care that addresses their needs in the way that a good parent would.

The nature and complexity of the needs of children and young people in care mean that we have struggled to fully engage child protection workers in this process. Given the competing priorities of preparing statutory reports for the courts, and responding to the many crises that are a feature of child protection work, it is tempting for child protection workers to sometimes think that the others in the care team are managing the LAC processes well enough to provide good care without needing much child protection input. All the same, there are many examples where there has been a high level of child protection participation in LAC processes and many good news stories where this made statutory case planning easier, with fewer subsequent setbacks.

Systems integration

The out-of-home care service system in Victoria (as in many other places) is necessarily very complex, and it has been very challenging to integrate LAC processes within existing DHS, CSOs and other systems. We developed new placement referral processes to support LAC processes for the initial implementation and subsequently hope to improve these in the second phase of implementation. We developed practice guidance about sharing personal information in out-of-home care with those who need to know such information in the best interests of the child. These procedures protect the confidentiality of that information and comply with privacy legislation.

We are linking LAC processes to our out-of-home care quality assurance and quality improvement processes. We successfully negotiated with Barnardos Australia to enable their version of the EIR1 to be built within our current Child Protection electronic client information system (CASIS) to enable information held elsewhere in CASIS to be merged into this document and the rest of the EIR1 to be completed electronically by DHS workers within CASIS itself. We are part way through a more ambitious strategy to fully integrate LAC within CRIS and CRISSP as a component of a new and much larger client information system. Systems integration remains a constant challenge.

Engagement with birth families

An early achievement of the LAC implementation has been the unexpectedly higher levels of participation by birth families in the decision-making processes that determine how their child's needs will be met while they are in care. The implementation monitoring data show that, in the first six months of implementation, birth parents participated in the majority of LAC care and placement planning and review processes. This is remarkable because, although birth parents routinely participate in statutory case planning processes that relate to the need for their child to be in out-of-home care, it has not been common for CSO workers to have much direct involvement with them. Some informal policies in the past have prevented any contact at all between birth parents and carers. Although there are still situations where contact between carers and birth families is either inappropriate or impractical, this practice turnaround has already led to many positive impacts for the children and young people in terms of maintaining family connectedness and promoting better stability, permanency and resilience outcomes.

Indigenous cultural relevance

The existing LAC materials have not been developed to be culturally relevant for Indigenous children and young people in out-of-home care in Victoria. However, all five Aboriginal CSOs that provide out-of-home care in Victoria decided to implement LAC using the existing materials. This was possible because the implementation emphasised that these records are tools to support good practice and must be skillfully used, not rigidly adhered to. An Aboriginal worker was selected as one of the LAC trainers and contributed to the cultural relevance of the training package and the train the trainer strategy. The consultation with Aboriginal workers implementing LAC in Aboriginal CSOs and input from workers in the DHS Indigenous Initiatives Unit has informed the revision of the LAC records. Practical advice about what needs to be to considered when planning for Aboriginal and Torres Strait Islander children and young people in care has been incorporated throughout the revised LAC records, as have prompts to consistently link cultural planning with LAC processes. It remains to be seen how far we have progressed in making the LAC records more culturally relevant, and we will continue to seek assistance from our Aboriginal colleagues with his task. We are also trying to identify better ways of using LAC processes to support cultural, community and family connections for Aboriginal children in out-of-home care who are in non-Aboriginal placements.

Partnerships with schools

At the same time that LAC is being implemented, a complementary initiative also being set in place is the Partnering Agreement between DHS and the Department of Education and Training (DE&T) for children in out-of-home care to improve their school participation rates. There is a need to clarify the relationship between Individual Education Plans expected by the DHS/DE&T Partnering Agreement and the LAC Care and Placement Plans, to allay fears about duplication of effort. However, the concurrent initiatives provided the opportunity to promote complementary collaborative processes and build better relationships between carers, CSO case workers, child protection workers, birth parents and school personnel such as principals, teachers, student welfare coordinators, year level coordinators, and specialist Aboriginal educators.

Extending LAC to kinship care

We regret that we have not been in a position to introduce LAC with most of the kinship care placements. Because kinship care placements are managed directly by Child Protection and rarely receive support from a CSO, it was not practicable for the Child Protection worker to use LAC processes in addition to their other statutory case planning processes. If additional resources were to become available for kinship care placement support provided by CSOs, it would be a straightforward matter to extend LAC to these placements. In the meantime, since LAC records are being incorporated within CRIS and CRISSP, we intend to explore how our revised LAC records might also be used to supplement the statutory case planning records to more effectively address the needs of those children and young people in kinship care placements. The new UK Integrated Children's System exemplars, which extend the LAC framework to also incorporate social and environment factors and parenting capacity of carers, might also provide us with a basis in the future for developing new tools to better support kinship care placements.

Conclusion

The implementation of LAC in Victoria is an ambitious, significant, and long-term change management project. We feel we can be justifiably proud of our achievements in such a short time, thanks to the extraordinary contribution made by so many people across the whole sector. At the same time, we also acknowledge that we are only just beginning. We still have a long way to go. So much more remains to be done before we can fully harness and document all the benefits of the implementation of LAC in Victoria through demonstrably better outcomes for children and young people in our care.

References

Barnardos Australia and University of New South Wales (2003 and onwards). *The LAC Project Looking After Children Victorian Version Materials.* Retrievable (by licensed end-users only) from the LAC Project Web site: www.lacproject.org/

Berry Street Victoria. (2003). *LAC Training Package: Building the picture.* Self-published. Melbourne, Victoria.

Berry Street Victoria. (2004). *Looking After Children in Victoria: Training implementation final report.* Retrievable from Berry Street Victoria Web site: www.berrystreet.org.au/

Centre for Excellence in Child and Family Welfare. (December 2003). *LAC Training Package: More than a meeting.* Self-published. Melbourne, Victoria.

Clare, M. (1997). The UK Looking After Children Project: Fit for out-of-home care in Australia? *Children Australia, 22,* 29–35.

Department for Education and Skills (2003). *Integrated Children's System exemplars.* London, UK: DfES.

Department of Human Services. (2002). *Minimum standards and outcome objectives for residential care services in Victoria.* Melbourne, Victoria: Government publication.

Department of Human Services. (2002). *Discussion paper: Implementing Looking After Children in out-of-home care in Victoria.* Retrievable from LAC Victoria Web site: www.dhs.vic.gov.au/lac-victoria

Department of Human Services. (2003a). *Child protection and care practice instruction: PI-2003-03 placement referral process.* Retrievable from LAC Victoria Web site: www.dhs.vic.gov.au/lac-victoria

Department of Human Services. (2003b). *Child protection and care practice instruction: PI-2003-10 sharing information in out of home care.* Retrievable from LAC Victoria Web site: www.dhs.vic.gov.au/lac-victoria

Department of Human Services. (2003c). *Child Protection and Care Practice Bulletin: PB –2003-03 Looking After Children implementation information for child protection and placement coordination teams.* Retrievable from LAC Victoria Web site: www.dhs.vic.gov.au/lac-victoria

Department of Human Services. (2003). *Public parenting: A review of home based care in Victoria.* Melbourne, Victoria: Government publication.

Department of Human Services. (2003). *Minimum standards and outcome objectives for home based care services in Victoria.* Melbourne, Victoria: Government publication.

Department of Human Services. (June 2004). *The LAC implementation monitoring report.* Retrievable from LAC Victoria Web site: www.dhs.vic.gov.au/lac-victoria

Department of Human Services. (July 2004). *Placement referral record: Pilot version.* Government publication (limited distribution). Melbourne, Victoria.

Department of Human Services. (August 2004). *Revised LAC Records (pilot versions): Essential Information Record, Care and Placement Plan and Review of Care and Placement Plan.* Government publication (limited distribution). Melbourne, Victoria.

Dixon, D. (2001). Looking After Children in Barnardos Australia: A study of the early stages of implementation. *Children Australia, Volume 26, No 3.*

Donavan, D., & Ayres, M. (1998). Implementing Looking After Children in an English Local Authority. *Children and Society, 12,* 247–248.

Jones, H., Clark, R., Kufeldt, K., & Norman, M. (1998). Looking After Children: Assessing outcomes in child care: The experience of implementation. *Children and Society, 12,* 212–222.

Kufeldt, K., Vachon, J., & Simard, M. (Eds.) (2000). *Looking After Children in Canada: Final report submitted to Human Resources Development Canada.* Fredericton, NB: University of New Brunswick.

Ward, H. (Ed.) (1995). *Looking After Children: Research into practice*

---

1 Data source: Australian Bureau of Statistics Victoria Office (2002). Geography and Climate, Chapter 2 in *Victorian Year Book* (Number 114). Melbourne, Victoria, Australia. More information can also be retrieved from the Australian Bureau of Statistics Web site: www.abs.gov.au/ausstats/

2 Data source: Department of Human Services (June 2003). *Public Parenting: A Review of Home-Based Care in Victoria,* Melbourne, Victoria, Australia.

3 Data source: Department of Human Services unpublished data for 12 months: April 1, 2003 to April 30, 2004.

4 Data source: Department of Human Services Indigenous Initiatives Unit (2004).

5 More information about these materials can be retrieved from the Barnardos Australia/University of NSW LAC Project Web site: www.lacproject.org/

6 The LAC Training Report can be retrieved from the Berry Street Victoria Web site at the following link: www.berrystreet.org.au/. Sheree Limbrick, Berry Street Victoria also presented on the Berry Street LAC training project at the International LAC Conference Ottawa, 2004, *Setting Strong Foundations: An Implementation Experience of Looking After Children.*

7 More information about this training package can be obtained from the Centre for Excellence in Child and Family Welfare, Melbourne, Victoria, Australia. Centre staff can be contacted via their Web site: www.cwav.asn.au/

Promoting resilient outcomes in Australia with the Looking After Children Electronic System (LACES)

Deirdre Cheers and Jude Morwitzer

Background

Australia is a federation of six states and two territories, an island nation characterized by vast geographical distances. A large proportion of the total population of approximately 20 million people lives on the eastern seaboard and in the capital cities of Sydney in the state of New South Wales (NSW), and Melbourne in Victoria. With 20,000 children and young people reported as being in out-of-home care as at June 30, 2003 (Australian Institute of Health and Welfare), this constitutes an average rate of 4.2 children in care per 1000 Australian children. As in other parts of the world, indigenous children are vastly over represented in the Australian care system, making up almost one quarter of the total number of children in care, with a proportional rate of 22.8 per thousand. Over 95% of Australian children in the out-of-home care system are in family-based foster care placements, with less than 5% in residential or group home care.

Attempts at developing a national care and protection agenda for Australian children are affected by the fact that both federal and state/territory legislation in Australia has impact on children's daily lives. For example, immigration laws are a federal government responsibility, as is Family Law Court jurisdiction dealing with marriage, divorce, and child custody issues in relation to the breakdown of adult co-habitative relationships and requirements for child maintenance and decision-making regarding place of residence. The Australian federal government does provide some funding to the territories and states in domains such as education and homelessness services; however, the actual legislation governing these services is state based. Child protection laws (i.e., those laws concerning child abuse and neglect), and arrangements for the provision of out-of-home care, are governed by discrete state and territory legislation. The federal government has to date had no direct involvement, let alone interest, in this domain. Not surprisingly, there is an absence of a national Australian agenda for children in care, and no consistently applied standards for out-of-home care service provision.

Data collection within the Australian care system is problematic because the means and methods of counting children in care vary between states. Definitions are not consistent: for example, NSW counts and reports (to the Australian Institute of Health and Welfare) all children on Court Orders as being "in care," even if they are living at home with their own parents or extended family members, whereas other Australian states do not count children in care in this way. Not only is there a lack of standardization and practice consistency requirements for out-of-home care systems between the Australian states, but even within individual states and territories inconsistencies occur. Gilbertson and Barber (2004) report findings from a study in South Australia that indicate variable compliance by Family and Youth Services case workers with many of their statutory agency's out-of-home care practice standards.

Barnardos Australia and Looking After Children

Barnardos Australia is a large non-government child and family welfare agency. It provides a wide range of support services to families, including out-of-home care placements for approximately 1,200 children each year. These placements are predominantly in foster care. Short- and long-term foster care is organised by specialist out of home care teams; foster carers are professionally assessed, trained and supported; and matched place ments are provided whereby children are matched to appropriate carers according to individual need. Barnardos works proactively to promote sibling placements, such that siblings are virtually always placed together in care, and unrelated children are rarely placed together in the same foster home. A lengthy history of agency commitment to initiating best practice solutions for children, young people and their families is assisted by collaborative research relationships that have developed with Australian universities and teaching institutions over more than 20 years.

The concern on the part of Barnardos to improve outcomes of care and increase resilience for children and young people in the care system led to an agency decision to implement the UK Looking After Children (LAC) system in all Barnardos out-of-home care teams, commencing in 1997 (Dixon, 2001). The strong focus of LAC on the measurement of developmental outcomes for children and young people in care via the Assessment and Action Records makes it relatively easy to identify positive turning points in their lives. By situating the measurement of children's individual attributes within the overall social context, the assessment of pathways to the development of resilience is assisted (Gilligan, 2001). LAC directly assists in the development of resilience for children in care by:

- focusing attention on what should happen next for a child in care, rather than what has previously occurred;
- identifying important networks for children and young people in care;
- encouraging multiple social roles; and
- building and tracking the development of identity.

When the agency first implemented LAC, there were 12 teams of agency foster care caseworkers and two residential care teams. Foster Care teams comprised on average a Team Leader and six professional field staff, residential care teams with a Team Leader, and eight to twelve direct care staff, including casuals. In its first year, LAC implementation in Barnardos involved a total staff complement of approximately 100 professional workers and managers, over 400 foster parents, and approximately 1,200 children and young people in care.

Development of the LAC Project Australia

As awareness of the initial research and development of the LAC system spread outside the UK, pilot research project implementations of the LAC Assessment and Action Records were undertaken in the Australian states of Western Australia (Clare, 1997) and Victoria (Wise, 1999; Clark & Burke, 1998). This was assisted by connections between researchers and university academics on opposite sides of the world. These pilot LAC implementations were largely greeted with enthusiasm by Australian case workers and managers in the out-of-home care system, and also by foster parents and youth in care advocacy networks such as the Create Foundation Australia. The possibilities of large-scale implementation of LAC looked promising when the Western Australian statutory government child welfare department announced an intention to fully implement the system in August 2001. At that time, LAC was also already being used by several non-government out-of-home care agencies in NSW in addition to Barnardos, as well as the national capital ACT (Australian Capital Territory), the latter having implemented LAC in all agencies following a care system review.

Overall progress made in Australia-wide implementation of the LAC system has been slowed due to the lack of an Australian national agenda for child protection and out-of-home care, as already described. Although interest in LAC has remained on individual state and territory agendas, Australian governments have until quite recently been largely hesitant to commit sufficient time and resources to implementing LAC. Non-government agency levels of interest have continued to be high; however, many believe they can only make a decision to introduce LAC if a guarantee of government resourcing is indicated.

In 1997, Barnardos Australia and Dr. Elizabeth Fernandez, from the School of Social Work at the University of New South Wales, commenced a successful collaborative research project to adapt LAC materials to NSW state and Australian federal legislation and to implement the full LAC system with all Barnardos children and young people in care. This collaboration developed into the formal arrangement now known as the LAC Project Australia. The arrangement was initiated when Barnardos' Board of Directors saw the potential of the LAC system to have an impact on the lives of all Australian children and young people in care, thereby assisting the mission of Barnardos to improve the lives of all Australian children. Once the initial work of adapting LAC materials for NSW had been completed, the LAC Project consulted with expert out-of-home care practitioners in each Australian territory and state, all of them with a good working knowledge of state-specific care and protection legislation. A LAC Commercial Licence from the UK then enabled the LAC Project to provide the Looking After Children system throughout all of Australia. Currently in 2004, six out of eight Australian states and territories are using the LAC system with children and young people in care—five of these six via the provision of materials, initial training and ongoing support by the LAC Project Australia.

Assessment tool or case management system?

The early Western Australian and Victorian pilot LAC implementation projects, as already mentioned, involved only the assessment component of the system (the Assessment and Action Records—AARs), as did other early-stage international LAC research projects, for example, in Canada (Kufeldt, Simard & Vachon, 2000). In considering the reasons for this use of only the LAC AARs, it is important to recognize that these assessment tool components of the LAC system were in fact the first to be developed, in addition to being the most clearly recognizable research tool for measuring outcomes for children over time. The UNSW/Barnardos Australia three-year LAC research project initially addressed this issue via an analysis of all components of the LAC system, including Planning and Placement materials as well as Assessment and Action Records. This analysis indicated the importance of recognizing the connections between information collection, care planning, ongoing assessment, and review of the circumstances of children and young people in care. Although Barnardos care teams already had good systems for collecting information and planning care prior to the implementation of LAC, these were individual systems developed by teams, and very little consistency throughout the agency was in evidence. By embracing all components of Looking After Children in its implementation strategy, Barnardos saw the opportunity to address the issue of standards for children in care, not only within the agency but also throughout the states and territories—in other words, through all of Australia.

The question of LAC "full system" implementation such as described, versus partial implementation, has not featured prominently in Australia beyond the initial research pilots of LAC AARs in Western Australia and Victoria. Subsequent use of LAC by both Australian government departments and non-government out-of-home care agencies has involved the complete LAC case management system, including both Planning and Placement (including Care Plan and Review) materials and Assessment and Action Records. The fact that Australia has no legislatively sanctioned and enforced national standards for out-of-home care can be seen as an influencing factor for agencies deciding to use the full LAC case management system, as it is well recognized that the lack of agreed standards for care in Australia is problematic and that LAC can assist in filling this gap. The recognition of associated problems regarding the lack of standard definitions and the collection of out-of-home care data can also be seen as a contributory factor to agencies' adopting "full system" LAC.

The provision of LAC to care agencies by the LAC Project Australia has therefore been on the basis of a complete case management system rather than solely as an assessment tool for children and young people. In this respect, Barnardos and other key players such as foster parent groups and youth in care advocacy networks have advocated strongly for implementation. The advantages for children and young people when the LAC Assessment and Action Records are used within a comprehensive planning and review system lie in the fact that the assessments conducted are situated within a system that uses a consistent theoretical framework. There are standardized time frames for practice requirements such as placement visitation, and the seven well-researched and well-documented developmental dimensions contained in the AARs are connected with the ongoing process of care planning and review. Used in this way, LAC becomes a guided practice tool that helps to translate research findings into direct welfare practice, and bridges the gap that so often exists between theory and what is understood as best practice, and the application of best practice within the field.

While the early development of LAC in the UK focused heavily on the research components of the system, practice agencies learned much from the experience of implementation itself, in addition to the outcome data on children provided by the research. In the UK, the original LAC system has been built upon and enhanced—initially by the research into Children in Need and the development of the Framework for the Assessment of Children in Need and their Families; and most recently, by the publication of the Integrated Children's System (see Jones, chapter 24, this volume). In Australia, there have been two projects to date on implementing the UK Assessment Framework: in Victoria (Wise, 2001; Wise, 2003a), and by Barnardos in NSW and ACT (Fernandez & Romeo, 2003).

Social welfare practice, information technology (IT) and LAC

Social welfare has been generally slow to take advantage of the rapid progress made in the area of information technology. Whereas in other fields (e.g., business, finance, health, education) IT has had a major impact on the development of new areas of professional expertise, most social workers have tended to do little more than use word processing skills in their day-to-day work and professional lives. However, as the use of IT develops in social welfare, new challenges arise. In a comparative review of the UK child protection inquiries into the deaths of Maria Colwell and Victoria Climbié, children born more than a generation apart, Parton (2004) highlights the role of information technology in communication systems. Parton asserts that whereas 30 years ago communication about children was principally via verbal exchange and written records, today the issue is made more complex by "... the whole system of exchanging information and the way information is collated and gathered on a variety of sophisticated yet inadequate information systems." (p. 88) Whereas in the 1974 report into the death of Maria Colwell the problems highlighted were primarily in relation to communication between social workers, the 2003 Laming report concerning the death of Victoria Climbié considered the complex issue of system failure in not just sharing but also managing information. "The growth of information technology, the increasing hypercirculation of knowledge and communication and the need to try to manage this have all become important organisational issues over the last 30 years" (Parton, 2004, pp. 88–89).

While early development of the LAC system assisted practice agencies to both learn from the implementation experience and to monitor developmental outcomes for children over time, it also led to a highlighting of the gaps between policy and practice in out-of-home care. Barnardos consequently looked at how these gaps could be reduced, to the benefit of both social workers and management systems, via the use of information technology.

The potential was apparent for the use of IT to assist in the integration of practice knowledge and wisdom with research results, gained as a result of using an electronic version of the LAC system, in order to impact policy development. This focus on the integration of research, policy and practice was a key aspect of the development by the LAC Project Australia of the Looking After Children Electronic System—LACES. The information technology and processes underlying LACES facilitates the ready and immediate analysis of data on children and young people in care: LACES is a powerful data management tool built on the guided practice LAC case management system. LACES integrates IT with social work practice and avoids costly work duplication and repetition of social work tasks. It provides for "live" guided practice via the computer screen, with prompts and alerts to remind practitioners of research information concerning outcomes for children as a result of particular social work and care interventions. Because social care workers themselves input data relating to children in care into LACES, they have immediate and constant control not only over the way in which information is collected, but also over its impact on facilitating good outcomes for children and young people. The database functions embedded into LACES enable case workers as well as managers to readily call up individual and aggregate reports on children and young people in care, immediately and at any point in time.

LACES—Looking After Children Electronic System

The LAC Project and Barnardos' service specification and design criteria for the LACES database included the following:

- LACES must be user friendly, intuitive, easy to use, and immediately applicable to social work practice.

- LAC and LACES forms and materials must look like what care workers were already familiar with and completing; i.e., they had to look just like the LAC forms already in use in hard/paper copy, not a database format (traditionally not user friendly).

- Caseworkers using LACES should be able to access immediate and useful information on their own clients and not have to wait until data entry occurs elsewhere at some other point in time, in order to be able to collect individual and aggregate client outcome results.

- Managers should be able to access information readily and instantaneously for purposes of staff supervision and program evaluation and planning.

Comprehensive and accurate data are critical for the dual purposes of case management and service evaluation, and challenges exist in setting up an IT system that maximizes the opportunities for internal/inbuilt quality control. Therefore, it was also an essential criterion for the development of LACES that case management tasks be supported by data entry and management, rather than the reverse. This meant ensuring that case workers, who have control over data entry into LACES, are not only comfortable with the system but also easily able to understand the connections between the information they record about children in care and the outcomes achieved by these children as a direct result of intervention via the care system. Translating Looking After Children into a data system needed to encompass total integration of case management with data entry and quality control.

In Australia, as in many other parts of the world, the requirement for service evaluation is increasingly part of funding contracts and is part of broader government and organizational requirements. Rarely is service evaluation separately or independently funded, other than via research grants. The challenge exists therefore to use current and future ongoing developments in information technology to integrate service, project and program evaluation into day-to-day social work practice, partly to ensure that services remain responsive to client need, but also to satisfy funding requirements. Service evaluation systems frequently rely on a dual focus on output and outcome criteria to measure success. To facilitate the interface between policy and practice, dynamic and interactive service evaluation systems are generally more useful at an organizational level. And a key issue in using the information made available from evaluation is who should have access to the data in order to maximize their utility in a sustained way.

Following on from this recognition, additional LACES database software design criteria were as follows:

- A standard set of reports should be developed for the dual purposes of case management and service evaluation.

- Access to aggregated data reports should be given to all levels of management, not just to senior levels.

- Reports on individual children and young people should be immediately available to, and readily able to be generated by, case workers and managers, at any time.

Using LACES to enhance opportunities for an Australian out-of-home care database

Lack of consistency in the available data on Australian children in care is well recognized, as is the fact that a "whole of government" approach to out-of-home care is likely to be more successful to a reform or system change agenda than individual initiatives made by Australian territories and states (Clare, 2003). Not only is the consistency of Australian care data poor (due to variations from state to state as to what constitutes the definition of out-of-home care), but difficulties also exist in reporting mechanisms as well as data retrieval in individual systems. There are no uniform mechanisms for organizing the way in which Australian out-of-home care data are collected, nor a corresponding Australian national research agenda for child protection and out-of-home care. In order to routinely monitor service effectiveness and measure outcomes for children and young people in the Australian care system, a consistent means of data collection is needed; LACES offers a way forward in this respect.

A recent article in a special research edition of *Children Australia* (Wise, 2003b) discusses the opportunities provided by the growing Australia-wide use of the Looking After Children system. Wise advances the argument that LAC is a well-recognized system already in such widespread use in Australia that it provides a unique opportunity to have a centralized means of data collection, in addition to providing the ability to track the movements of children in care.

If LAC is to be used to provide aggregate data on the Australian out-of-home care population, then LACES can play both an integral as well as crucial role. Already, in the southern-most Australian state of Tasmania, the LACES database system is almost fully implemented across both government and non-government sectors, covering all children in care. This means that by mid-2005, easily accessible and widespread data aggregation will be readily available via LACES. Out-of-home care practice and research possibilities will be rapidly expanded as increasing numbers of Australian welfare organizations implement LAC and LACES.

As of August 2004, the LAC and LACES systems were being used by 68 out-of-home care agencies in Australia. Thus, 8500 children were being case managed via the LAC system, constituting over 40% of the total number of Australian children in out-of-home care. Incorporating advances in information technology into LAC is providing an unprecedented opportunity in Australia to bridge the gap between practice, policy and research, thereby enhancing service capacity to build resilient outcomes for children and young people.

The way ahead...

The Barnardos commitment to advocacy for children and young people has led the practice field in new directions regarding what is possible for Australian agencies providing out-of-home care, via the initiative of the LAC Project Australia and the development of the LACES database system. For the first time, the possibilities of a national database are a realistic agenda issue, and a "whole of system" consistent approach to data collection is a real and available possibility. A recently appointed government minister for Child Safety in the state of Queensland, among others, has called for a national strategy on child care and protection, reinforcing the voices of national peak bodies such as the National Foster Care Association and the Child and Family Welfare Association of Australia. Such an initiative needs to be grounded in a commitment to reducing data duplication, addressing service gaps to facilitate seamless service delivery, and an injection of complementary resources to maximize outcomes for these most vulnerable children in our community: those in out-of-home care. Good data that are able to provide real information about children in care are required in order to further develop this agenda. The use of a system such as LACES points out the way ahead.

Concern to improve good outcomes for children in care has provided the underpinnings for the ongoing development of the LAC Project Australia, and spurred the development of the Australian Looking After Children Electronic System. Known in Australia for its strong focus on better and best practice and producing excellence in outcomes for children and families, Barnardos saw in Looking After Children, and the development of LACES, the opportunity to extend and connect research with policy and practice. The development of an electronic database software product has been a most innovative development in the practice of Australian child welfare. LACES currently provides a unique opportunity in Australia to assist in the development of a national data collection agenda with respect to children and young people in care.

References

Australian Institute of Health and Welfare (2004). *Child Protection Australia 2002-2003*. Child Welfare Series No. 34. Canberra: Australian Government. http://www.aihw.gov.au/publications/index.cfm/title/9771

Clare, M. (1997). The UK 'Looking After Children' project: Fit for 'out-of-home care' practice in Australia? *Children Australia, 22*(1), 29–35.

Clare, M. (2003). 'Good enough parenting' when government is 'the parent'. *Children Australia, 28*(4), 19–24.

Clark, R., & Burke, G. (1999). *Looking After Children: An evaluation of the Victorian pilot program.* Melbourne: Deakin Human Services Australia & Children's Welfare Association of Victoria Inc.

CREATE Foundation Australia. http://www.create.org.au/

Dixon, D. (2001). Looking After Children in Barnardos Australia: A study of the early stages of implementation. *Children Australia, 26*(3), 27–32.

Fernandez, E., & Romeo, R. (2003). *Supporting children and responding to families: Implementation of the framework for the assessment of children and their families.* Sydney: School of Social Work, University of New South Wales.

Gilbertson, R., & Barber, J. (2004). The systematic abrogation of practice standards in foster care. *Australian Social Work, 57,* 31–45.

Gilligan, R. (2001). *Promoting resilience: A resource guide on working with children in the care system.* UK: British Agencies for Adoption and Fostering.

Kufeldt, K., Simard, M., & Vachon, J. (2000). *Looking After Children in Canada: Final report.* Submitted to Social Development Partnerships, Human Resources Development Canada. St. John, NB & Québec, QC: University of New Brunswick & Université Laval.

Parton, N. (2004). From Maria Colwell to Victoria Climbie: Reflections on public inquiries into child abuse a generation apart. *Child Abuse Review, 13,* 80–94.

UK Department for Education and Skills. *Integrated Children's System.* http://www.dfes.gov.uk/integratedchildrenssystem/index.shtml

Wise, S. (1999). *The UK Looking After Children approach in Australia.* Melbourne: Australian Institute of Family Studies.

Wise, S. (2001). *How should family services respond to "children in need"?.* Melbourne: Australian Institute of Family Studies.

Wise, S. (2003a). The child in family services: Expanding child abuse prevention. *Australian Social Work, 56,* 183–196.

Wise, S. (2003b). Using Looking After Children to create an Australian out-of-home care database. *Children Australia, 28*(2), 38–44.

CHAPTER 24

The Integrated Children's System: A resilient system to promote the development in children in care

Helen Jones

Introduction

> *Caregivers, teachers and social workers should remember that the detail of what they do with children counts… It is important not to…(lose) sight of crucial details of what can sustain the positive development of this child today*
>
> (Gilligan, 2000).

Resilience theory, with its growing literature, identifies a number of important ways of working with vulnerable children. Less attention seems to have been paid, however, to issues of resilience in relation to child welfare *systems* (but see Masten, chapter 1, this volume, for a notable exception.) Resilience is generally understood to be a framework for conceptualising positive adaptations of children and young people who have experienced adversity. It is essential that the most vulnerable children be provided with resilience-oriented policies and interventions, to ensure they will have the necessary opportunities for improved outcomes.

This chapter describes work undertaken in England and Wales to develop the Integrated Children's System (ICS), which provides an integrated approach to the management and practice of child welfare cases in local authority social services departments.[1] The work has built upon the earlier development of Looking After Children (Parker et al, 1991, Ward, 1995) and the Framework for the Assessment of Children in Need and their Families (commonly known as the Assessment Framework) (Department of Health et al., 2000). The lessons learned from the implementation of Looking After Children and the Assessment Framework have also served to increase the resilience of ICS. The latter is the product of close collaboration between researchers, policymakers and practitioners, the importance of which in delivering improved outcomes for children has been described elsewhere (Jones, 2003).

ICS provides a conceptual framework, a practice discipline, and a business process to support practitioners and managers in undertaking the key tasks of assessment, planning, intervention and review, based on an understanding of children's developmental needs in the context of parental capacity and wider family and environmental factors. It encompasses the processes required to be undertaken for children in receipt of social services (i.e., mainly child welfare services, in the present context), from referral to case closure. It also extends the use of the domains and dimensions of the Assessment Framework to work with all children in need, their families, and carers, including those in need of protection and looked after children. Its functionality is supported by an electronic information system.

Ensuring that services are needs-led and that provision is based upon the best possible assessments is key. Important elements of an effective system are conceptual clarity, transparent processes, including those for audit and review. and a user-friendly delivery mechanism. The lessons learned from research on and implementation of Looking After Children and the Assessment Framework have been used to increase the effectiveness of the new system and are described herein

Also discussed in this chapter is the role of ICS as a central element in the delivery of current government policy for children, which is centred on improving outcomes for all children and young people. England and Wales are currently developing and implementing a major change programme for all children's services, known as *Every Child Matters,* in England (DfES 2003), and *Children and Young People: Rights to Action,* in Wales (Welsh Assembly Government, 2004). The priority placed on early intervention through greater integration of services and local accountability that is reflected in *Every Child Matters* provides an important context to understanding ICS.

Resilient children and resilient systems

Although ICS is for all children in receipt of social services, the particular focus of this chapter will be on children looked after (i.e., children in care) in England. Recent evidence (Newman, 2004) suggests that children are being affected by an absolute increase in serious problems, accompanied by a reduction in capacity for natural resilience. Over the past few decades, developed countries have seen a decline in children's psychosocial well-being, while child welfare services have become more preoccupied with risk factors than the positive promotion of their welfare. Promoting resilience is therefore an important strategy for reversing this trend and supporting a focus on factors that promote well-being. These issues have particular relevance for looked after children, who have all experienced considerable adversity and disadvantage, resulting in developmental impacts and thus a particular need to focus on long term well-being.

For children who have experienced fragmented home lives, Gilligan defines resilience as "qualities which cushion a vulnerable child from the worst effects of adversity in whatever form it takes and which may help a child or young person to cope, survive and even thrive in the face of great hurt and disadvantage" (Gilligan, 1997). Masten (2001) provides a resilience framework for interventions that incorporates risk and asset-focused approaches aimed at decreasing children's exposure to adversity and increasing the protective factors in their lives, carers, and environment. Recently, a third element has been introduced to this model–the concept of process-oriented models of practice which attempt to modify developmental systems themselves, rather than solely the factors that influence them. "These approaches go beyond risk- and asset-focused models in an attempt to change the way systems work to protect and promote positive development" (Masten, 2004).

Within a process-oriented approach to resilience, interventions are designed to promote positive developmental outcomes through targeting key developmental tasks and monitoring progress towards success. Key to achieving these tasks are assessments that address the developmentally appropriate components of competence. However, in this paper we argue that children in care need not only resilience-promoting interventions but *systems* for delivering these interventions that are resilient. The levels of disadvantage, difficulty, and poor outcomes experienced by looked after children are well documented (Parker et al, 1991; Social Exclusion Unit, 2001), and the organisations, services, and systems intended to promote the welfare of the most vulnerable children too frequently compound their difficulties. The weaknesses or risk factors within all layers of child welfare systems are well documented in England (Utting 1997; Laming, 2003). They include poor interagency communication, a failure to listen to the views of children themselves, high staff turnover and severe staff shortages leading to discontinuity of practice, a lack of attention to the detail of children's daily lives and experiences, poor record keeping, and limited capacity for storing, retrieving and sharing information. Such systems are unlikely to be able to promote children's development effectively.

Policy context

Considerable attention has already been given to improving outcomes for looked after children and wider groups of children in need, and Looking After Children has played an important role in this. The more recent initiative referred to earlier, however, has set an even more far-reaching agenda for improving outcomes for children. *Every Child Matters: Change for Children*, published in December 2004 (HM Government, 2004), describes how these improved outcomes for children, young people, and families can be delivered and sets out wide ranging local authority-led change programmes. It sets an ambitious agenda for integrating services for children, both nationally and locally, to reduce the risk of the most vulnerable children falling through the net between services. *Every Child Matters* (DfES, 2003) sets out five outcomes identified as key to well-being in childhood or later life:

- be healthy
- stay safe
- enjoy and achieve
- make a positive contribution
- achieve economic well-being

Achieving these outcomes requires effective partnerships across health, education, social care, and wider partner agencies to meet the needs of children and their families. Local authorities are being required to put in place children's trust arrangements to bring together all services for children and young people under one commissioning body in a local area. There are four key elements underpinning the new strategy, including integrated common processes, an integrated strategy for planning and commissioning, and inter-agency governance. The fourth element, a single inspection framework and Joint Area Reviews of children's services, will ensure that the five outcomes remain the focus of activity across the spectrum of services for children.

The Children Act 2004 provides the legislative spine for the reforms, supporting:

- a sharper focus on safeguarding children, with statutory Local Safeguarding Children Boards replacing the current Area Child Protection Committees, and a new duty laid on all key agencies to safeguard and promote the welfare of children;

- partnership: local authorities working with other services through children's trust arrangements are to agree on local priorities for improving services for children, young people and parents;

- accountability: local authorities appointing Directors of Children's Services who will have responsibility for education and children's social services and designating Lead Members (Councillors) to provide vision and impetus.

- ICS will play a key role in ensuring that children in need receive the services and interventions which they require to make the five outcomes a reality for them.

Background to development of ICS

The development of ICS has benefited from the research and evaluation undertaken in relation to its predecessors, Looking After Children and the Assessment Framework. A research and development programme (Ward, 1995, Cleaver & Walker, 2004), focused evaluations, and a wide range of consultative events identified weaknesses in the systems and barriers to their effective use.

The first limitation was a lack of congruence between the two systems. The conceptual framework for Looking After Children was developed by a working group set up to consider how to improve outcomes for children in care. The working group produced an approach that was focussed on assessing children's developmental needs and strengths, identifying areas where additional actions or services were required, and reviewing the effectiveness of those interventions. Looking After Children also concerned only those children who were in care, about to enter care, or about to leave care (Parker et al., 1991). The materials form a complete package for assessing, planning, and recording the experience and progress of all children looked after by local authorities. On the other hand, the Assessment Framework was developed five years later and was intended for use with children living in families with which there were concerns about parenting and child safety. The Assessment Framework added two additional domains to that of a child's developmental needs, parental capacity and wider family and environmental factors (Department of Health et al., 2000). A disjunction between the two systems became evident at the point of entry to care. Looking After Children was predicated on there being little information about a child available at the beginning of a care episode, such that it collected basic data at the point of entry to care–information now collected at a much earlier stage by the Assessment Framework. Also, with Looking After Children, the development of plans to meet children's needs was introduced only for those who were looked after.

Five years after the comprehensive introduction of Looking After Children, a major review was undertaken of both content and implementation. Drawing on three years of annual audits of participating authorities (Moyers, 1997; Peel, 1998; Scott, 1999), the review included focussed workshops with local authorities, foster carers and stakeholders concerned with disabled, black, and minority ethnic children and young people. A number of difficulties and challenges emerged. Most fundamentally, it was not sufficiently clear to users whether the Looking After Children materials were a practice or research tool. Was the system for practitioners to use with children, families, and carers, or was it primarily for collecting data? A second significant weakness was its dependence on high-quality and consistent manual recording of information, never social workers' favourite activity and a major difficulty, given the workload pressures on front-line staff. Related to this was a lack of success in converting Looking After Children to an electronic format. While some word-processing versions were developed, they were not linked to an electronic information system and thus did not have the capacity to deal with data transfer and migration across records. This resulted in significant duplication of basic information in relation both to individual children and more particularly to sibling groups.

A key barrier to effective use of the Looking After Children system was the lack of evidence about children's progress before entry to care. This highlighted the necessity of collecting baseline information about a child's development where complex needs and circumstances have been identified, so that progress or the impact of services over time can be measured. The development and implementation of the Core Assessment within the Assessment Framework provides the opportunity for this to happen. The Core Assessment gathers baseline information on children who are usually still living in their families, while the Assessment and Progress Records, which replace the original Assessment and Action Records, are designed to monitor the child's progress. Where appropriate, questions within the Assessment and Progress Record for children in care are the same as those in the Core Assessment, to support the measurement of change over time.

The Looking After Children audits, conducted as part of the managed implementation programme, showed that although the Care Plan frequently recorded services or interventions to be delivered, it was not always possible to identify whether these had actually been received or, if they had, for how long. Also, recording was often restricted to those services provided by child welfare services, even though it is important to know the whole range of interventions being received, including, for example, those from Child and Adolescent Mental Health Services. Another consequence of partial recording of information is that it is not possible to cost services or make judgements about the effectiveness of one course of action versus another.

The research underpinning the Assessment Framework showed that while a lot of information was collected during an assessment, the quality of analysis was often poor, leading to plans which did not relate to the children's developmental needs and circumstances. Although the research demonstrated that the conceptual framework was robust, it also revealed barriers to implementation similar to those which had compromised the implementation of Looking After Children (Cleaver & Walker, 2004). In addition, evidence from the audits showed that information recorded about children's needs was often out of date or inaccurate. Consistency and accuracy are vital if the most appropriate services are to be provided.

All these issues demonstrate the importance of resilient systems being in place to assess accurately children's developmental needs, predict the level and type of service required by children, families, and carers, identify gaps in services provision, co-ordinate services more effectively across agencies, and ensure that children have access to a range of effective services appropriate to their needs. These issues have informed the structure of ICS.

The Integrated Children's System

An essential feature of ICS is that it is able to help the most vulnerable children achieve the five outcomes already highlighted as a government priority. The conceptual framework is provided by the use of the domains and dimensions of the *Assessment Framework,* while the practice processes are supported by a structured recording system.

ICS exemplar records for assessment, planning, intervention, & review

Paper versions of the exemplars and an electronic demonstrator disc have been produced as part of the development and implementation of the system, to show how information can be gathered for different purposes and transferred across to other records to reduce duplication and repetition. The exemplars provide a structured framework within which practitioners record information, decisions, actions, and plans at each stage of work with children and their families, in order to:

- build up a picture of children's needs, within the context of their families and the communities in which they live;

- facilitate the processes of information–gathering, collation and analysis at each stage;

- support the development of plans that include clear objectives and measurable outcomes for children;

- provide accurate information that can be linked to the costs of services delivered; and,

- facilitate review processes that monitor the child's progress and the effectiveness of interventions (Department of Health, 2002).

The exemplars are divided into four types: information records, assessment records, plans, and reviews. Information records contain factual details such as the request for service from another agency or the information which a foster carer needs immediately in order to care safely and appropriately for a child who is being placed. A particularly important example of an information record is the chronology. Public enquiries into child deaths, such as that into the death of Victoria Climbié, and serious case reviews have all highlighted the lack of an effective chronology to capture cumulative information which could help to identify patterns or significant events in a child's life (Laming, 2003). Within ICS, a chronology can be derived as an output from information already recorded and can be structured either as a straightforward narrative of all events or divided into different areas such as legal events, placement history, etc. Outputs from ICS are discussed in more detail later in the chapter.

The assessment records gather information about a child and family from a range of sources, including other professionals and agencies. They provide a structure for analysing the information and coming to an understanding of what is happening to the child and family, a view about their needs, and the action to be taken. As part of this, it is essential that the child and family be involved in the assessment and their views recorded. Assessment records include the Core Assessment, for children in complex circumstances who may be at risk of significant harm, and the Assessment and Progress Record, completed for children in care and building on the information recorded in a Core Assessment to monitor the child's developmental progress since entry to care. Materials have been commissioned to support the participation of children in their assessments to accompany ICS (Hutton, forthcoming).

All plans for children in need identify the specific actions to be taken in relation to the developmental needs identified in the assessment. Each new plan created if a child moves into more intensive services builds on previous plans. A Child's Plan, completed following a Core Assessment, thus revises and replaces the Initial Plan. Similarly, the Care Plan for a looked after child builds on and replaces the Child's Plan that obtained when the child was still living at home. The Care Plan will form the basis of the information to be presented to the Court in family proceedings and so on.

The Care Plan first records the child's developmental needs and strengths, describes how these will be responded to, and records the frequency and length of service to be provided. The person or agency responsible is clearly identified, as is the date the service is to commence. Most important, the planned outcomes of the service are recorded. This enables the review process to record the actual outcomes against the planned outcomes, throwing light on the effectiveness of the service or intervention. Recording the start date, frequency, and length of the service enables the total cost of the service to be calculated, once the service costs are known. Separate work is underway to provide standardisation of particular unit costs related to social care activity (Ward, Holmes, Soper, & Olsen, 2004; Selwyn et al, 2003).

Review records contain the information already recorded in the Care Plan about a child's needs and evaluate the child's developmental progress over a particular period. In England and Wales, there are legal requirements for reviews to be undertaken for all children in need who are looked after or on the child protection register at statutory intervals. The review considers the progress of the child, whether the planned outcomes have been achieved, and any revisions required to the plan.

If a secure base is an important contributor to resilience for a child, the capacity for improving the quality of care planning and implementation of the care plan to achieve permanence for the child must be essential features of a resilient system. ICS is designed to support high-quality permanence planning and to identify timescales for action through structuring social work processes. The Care Plan articulates the chosen permanence plan and the intended outcomes, which can be measured against actual outcomes in the review process. A significant development is the inclusion of an assessment of attachment to parents or current carers for under-fives, which provides important information for identifying the next appropriate long-term plan. As well as focusing on the achievement of longer term plans for children, social workers are also helped to monitor and improve the quality of the child's day to day care, building on strengths and resilience factors identified in the assessment as suggested by Masten's (2004) process-oriented model. The system also aligns processes for supporting children in need living in their families with those for children in care, to support smooth transitions into different parts of the child welfare system. ICS also improves the quality and use of information obtained about the child and the family at each stage of the work. Many looked after children return home but may remain vulnerable in the community. It is important that actions to meet a child's developmental needs identified while the child is looked after are not lost simply because of a change in legal status.

ICS Electronic Information System

Information Systems in current use in children's social services, whether computer- or paper-based, are generally designed more for recording information than for retrieving it, especially in daily practice. This severely limits their usefulness and reduces the quality of the data they contain—users of a system who get nothing out of it are unlikely to care much about what they put in.

(Gatehouse, Statham, & Ward, 2004)

The development of ICS as an electronic system has been supported by wider developments in policy and practice in relation to information technology (IT) and, in particular, the government requirement for the implementation of e-social care records by 2005. It is intended that this will be the most resilience-enhancing feature of the new system.

Fundamentally, it is the volume and complexity of information required for the practice and management of child welfare cases and the expectations of an information age which requires that ICS, unlike its predecessors, be underpinned by an electronic information system. However, as Gatehouse and colleagues (2004) correctly point out, the system must support all aspects of modern social work practice and management.

Managers and others responsible for the delivery of child welfare services rightly regard IT as a tool to facilitate their work, without the need to understand the complexities which lie behind the screen. Those responsible for both commissioning and delivering the IT system need a detailed understanding of the information requirements and the inter-relationship between them. For their core business, all child welfare agencies have to undertake the same tasks and require the same set of reporting information to assist in the management of individual cases, the aggregation of need-related data to inform future service development and delivery, the provision of internal quality assurance, and the achievement of local and national performance targets.

In partnership with local authorities, system suppliers and academics, work has been undertaken to define a common set of 'core' information requirements to support the delivery of children's services. The completed work comprises:

- A *Process Model*, which sets out the core processes for delivering children's services based on the statutory requirements. Each discrete process is accompanied by a statement of the data management requirements.

- *Process Flow Diagrams*, which are diagrammatic representations of the flow of operations within core case management.

- A *Logical Data Model* (aimed at technical staff), which expands on the definitions and attributes of the data items identified in the Process Model and maps the logical connections between them. Its purpose is to ensure that the required functionality is built into the system.

- An *Entity Relationship Diagram* (for technical staff), which models the logical core information requirements expressed in terms of discrete entities and their attributes.

- A *Glossary of Terms,* which provides a clear and concise description of any terms used in the documentation.

All the activities carried out within ICS are represented in the Process Model, and the data collected through those processes are represented in the Logical Data Model. The Core Information Requirements alone, however, will not support improvements in the use of information systems to support the management and practice of child welfare cases. The key to increasing the resilience of a system for improving the outcomes for children and their families is what comes out of the information system–the outputs–and how they are used. An Outputs Framework has therefore been published to ensure that information captured within the system is used effectively (Gatehouse et al., 2004).

The outputs framework identifies a 'virtuous circle' of information management that provides rewards for frontline staff to encourage greater use of the system and greater accuracy of the information entered. This has major implications for system development and design, to ensure that electronic information systems provide pre-populated forms, quick location and look–up, lists, summaries, chronologies, alerts, and so on. In particular, the system must be able to identify which children are reaching certain targets and which are not, in order to make sense of performance indicators and highlight their relevance to individual children.

The new policy agenda for service integration and multi-agency working brings new requirements for information-sharing and the transfer of information across systems. Within the new Children Act 2004, there is legal provision for an information hub to be developed that contains a small amount of basic data about every child in a local authority area. This is to ensure that children in need of services can be identified at an early stage and that professionals with concerns about a child will know which other agencies are already involved.

Of particular relevance to ICS is the development of a Common Assessment Framework (CAF) and improved understanding of information-sharing to enable practitioners across settings which provide services to children–schools, early years programs, health services, child welfare–to identify the additional needs of individual children and ensure timely referrals to appropriate services. Early examples of a common assessment have been developed in some local authorities (see Pithouse, chapter 21, this volume), and the experience of North Lincolnshire has already provided valuable lessons (Jones, Chant, & Ward, 2004).

Figure 1 shows how the central spine of information to be collected about all children can be connected to agency specific systems that will hold information at a much greater level of detail.

Figure 1. The leaves and stem model of information systems

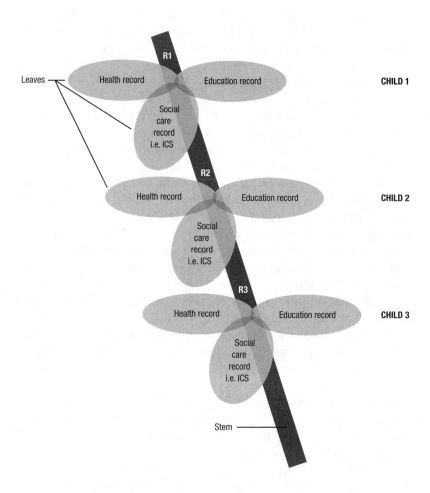

Importance of resilient implementation of ICS

As with any new system, road testing is key. Funding has been obtained to conduct two separate pilots of ICS as an electronic system (Cleaver et al, forthcoming; Bell et al, forthcoming). The first report will be an evaluation of the impact of ICS on aspects of inter-agency working. In the context of a wider agenda of developing a common language and common assessment processes across agencies, the ICS multi-agency pilot will examine the effects of implementing ICS on inter-agency working, collaboration, and information-sharing. Work in three English councils and one Welsh council involves scrutinising documentary evidence from agencies working with children, interviewing service providers from health, social services, education, youth justice services, and the police, and the completion of questionnaires, case-file audits, and interviews with children and young people and their carers. The second pilot (Bell et al, forthcoming), in two English and two Welsh councils, is looking at the coherence of the system within child welfare agencies through all the processes from referral to case closure. This study is over-sampling disabled, black, and minority ethnic children, to ensure that the system can meet their particular needs appropriately. A further strand of this study will evaluate the extent to which the system supports permanence planning for children.

Councils in England have been asked to have the functioning system in place by January 2007, as part of government requirements for the introduction of e-social care records. The electronic demonstrator disc referred to earlier includes 'dummy' cases to show how the information about an individual child, once entered, can flow across records. It is being used for training purposes and to support the development of the IT system. Implementation is also being supported through a capital grant for electronic system development and a regional development programme.

Future developments

As discussed earlier, a key feature of a resilient system is that it minimises repetition of processes and supports the use of common information in as many fields as possible. As part of the continuing process of developing the system, consideration is therefore already being given to bringing additional child welfare processes into the ICS framework. An area of continuing difficulty in England concerns the relationship between the child's care plan developed by child welfare and the court care plan required by the family justice system in family proceedings. At present, the child's care plan does not contain all the information required by the Court for consideration of whether to make an order (i.e., crown wardship, in Canada), and work will now be undertaken with practitioners from the family justice system to align the two plans within ICS.

A further area of work, related to the policy desire to improve the timeframe within which looked after children find a permanent new family if they cannot return home, is adoption and fostering. A report from the system is currently being developed for family placement services, including adoption. These services use the developmental assessment already undertaken to consider the implications for the type of family the child will need.

Such reports are currently produced as a separate process. As a further extension, it is hoped to test the applicability of the domains and dimensions of the Assessment Framework to the assessment of foster and adoptive parents. If this proves possible it will enable reports on applicants to be framed in terms of their parental capacities and wider family and environmental factors, both in terms of strengths and potential difficulties. Framing the report on the child in terms of his or her developmental needs and the one on the applicants in terms of their capacities will improve matching of the child to the most appropriate family. The intent would be to increase placement stability and anticipate, at an early stage, areas where carers will need additional supports and services.

A set of studies on the costs and effectiveness of services for children in need has recently been completed. Studies within this initiative have developed unit costs for social care processes, such as finding a first and subsequent placement for a looked after child, developing a care plan, and undertaking a review (Ward et al., 2004). Further work is currently being undertaken to link the costing software to ICS so that eventually it should be possible to calculate the cost of each element in a care episode. The development of similar unit costs for processes undertaken by other agencies, such as health, education and juvenile justice, will eventually make it possible to calculate the costs of providing a range of services to individuals and groups of children over particular time periods, and to relate these to outcomes.

Conclusion

This chapter has discussed the importance of creating resilience within child welfare systems in order to promote resilience in children in care. ICS provides a conceptual framework to improve the recording, analysis, and use of information gathered through the core processes of assessment, planning, intervention and review, to ensure that children's developmental needs are identified and met. The system supports practice and performance improvements on the individual case-management and strategic-planning levels. The use of a conceptual framework based on children's developmental needs is key to modifying the developmental process and increasing resilience. For looked after children, ICS is designed to enable the identification of an appropriate long-term plan for permanence and ensure that the important detail of what is happening to the child in the everyday is captured, thereby increasing the likelihood that opportunities for promoting resilience *now* will be acted upon. The key challenge is to achieve resilient implementation of ICS within child welfare agencies in England and Wales.

References

Bell, M., Shaw, I., Sloper, P., Sinclair, I., Claydon, J., Mitchell, W., Walker, C., Ashworth, M., & Dyson, P. (forthcoming). *The Integrated Children's System: the social services evaluation. A pilot study to evaluate the impact of the Integrated Children's System from the perspectives of the social service providers and the children and families involved.* York, England: University of York.

Cleaver, H., & Walker, S. (with Meadows, P.). (2004) *Assessing children's needs and circumstances: The Impact of the Assessment Framework.* London, UK: Jessica Kingsley.

Cleaver, H., Ward, H., Pithouse, A., Rose, W., Scott, J., & Walker, S. (forthcoming). *A pilot study to assess the development of a multi-agency and integrated approach to the delivery of services to children and their families.* Report to funders. Royal Holloway, University of London, Loughborough University, Open University, & Cardiff University.

Department for Education and Skills. (2004). *Every Child Matters: Next Steps.* London, UK: Department for Education and Skills.

Department of Health, Department for Education and Employment, and the Home Office (2000). *Framework for the assessment of children in need and their families.* London: The Stationery Office.

Department of Health. (2002). *Working with children in need and their families.* Consultation document. London, UK: Department of Health.

HM Government. (2003). *Every Child Matters,* Cm 5860. London, UK: The Stationery Office.

HM Government. (2004). *Every Child Matters: Change for Children.* London, UK: Department for Education and Skills.

Gatehouse, M., Statham, J., & Ward, H. (2004). *The knowledge: How to get the information you need out of your computers and information systems.* London, UK: Institute of Education.

Gilligan, R. (2000). Adversity, resilience and young people: The protective value of positive school and spare time experiences. *Children and Society, 14*(1), 37-47.

Gilligan, R. (1997). Beyond permanence: The importance of resilience in child placement, practice and planning. *Adoption and Fostering 21*(4), 12–20.

Hutton, A. (forthcoming.) *Say it your own way: Listening to children in assessment.* Ilford, Essex, UK: Barnardo's.

Jones, H. (2003). The relationship between research, policy and practice in delivering an outcome-led child welfare service. In K. Kufeldt & B. McKenzie (Eds.), *Child welfare: Connecting research, policy and practice.* Waterloo, ON: Wilfrid Laurier University Press.

Jones, H., Chant, E., & Ward, H. (2004). Integrating children's services: A perspective from England. In N Trocmé, D. Knoke, & C. Roy (Eds.), *Community collaboration and differential response: Canadian and international research and emerging models of practice.* Ottawa, ON: Centre of Excellence for Child Welfare.

Laming, H. (2003). *The Victoria Climbié inquiry*, Cm 5730. London, UK: The Stationery Office.

Masten, A.S. (2001). Ordinary magic: Resilience processes in development. *American Psychologist, 56,* 227–238

Masten, A.S. (2004). Introduction. In T. Newman (Ed)., *What works in building resilience.* Ilford, Essex, UK: Barnardo's.

Meltzer, H., Gatward, R., Corbin, T., Goodman, R., & Ford, T. (2003). *The mental health of young people looked after by local authorities in England.* London, UK: The Stationery Office.

Moyers, S. (1997). *Report of an audit of the implementation of looked after children in year 1: 1995/96.* Totnes, UK: Dartington Social Research Unit.

Newman, T. (2004). *What works in building resilience.* Ilford, Essex, UK: Barnardo's.

Parker, R., Ward, H., Jackson, S., Aldgate, J., & Wedge, P. (1991). *Looking After Children: Assessing outcomes in child care.* London, UK: Her Majesty's Stationery Office.

Peel, M. (1998). *Report of an audit of the implementation of Looking After Children in year 3: 1996/97.* Leicester, UK: University of Leicester.

Scott, J. (1999) *Report of an audit of the implementation of Looking After Children in year 3: 1997/98.* Leicester, UK: University of Leicester.

Selwyn, T., Sturgess, W., Quinton, D., & Baxter, C. (2003). *Costs and outcomes of non-infant adoptions.* Report to the Department for Education and Skills. Bristol, UK: Hadley Centre for Adoption and Foster Care Studies, University of Bristol.

Social Exclusion Unit. (2001). *Preventing social exclusion.* London, UK: The Stationery Office.

Social Exclusion Unit. (2003). *A better education for children in care.* London, UK: Office of the Deputy Prime Minister.

Utting, Sir W. (1997). *People like us: The report of the review of safeguards for children living away from home.* London, UK: The Stationery Office.

Ward, H. (1995) *Looking After Children: Research into practice.* London, UK: Her Majesty's Stationery Office.

Ward, H., Holmes, L., Soper, J., & Olsen, R. (2004). *The costs and consequences of different types of child care.* Report to the Department for Education and Skills. Loughborough, UK: Centre for Child and Family Research, Loughborough University.

Welsh Assembly Government (2004). *Children and young people: Rights to action.* Cardiff, Wales: Welsh Assembly Government.

---

1   The Integrated Children's System has been developed through collaboration between academics in the UK from Royal Holloway College, University of London, Loughborough University, the Open University, and the University of Wales, Cardiff, and policymakers at the Department for Education and Skills.

CHAPTER 25

A synthesis of research findings and practice and policy suggestions for promoting resilient development among young people in care

James G. Barber

Introduction

This book and the conference that spawned it have fundamentally been about the promotion of human development. The term "human development" may roll off the tongue easily enough, but except in narrowly biological terms, it is no simple matter to define it. After all, what is so distinctly *human* about our development, and what is the optimal outcome of the process? Humans change over time, that is certain, but surely not all of it can be called "development." Just ask the nursing home resident who needs help to feed herself. So how does *change* over the life cycle add up to *development* in the sense of progress toward a goal? When we interpret change as development, are we not engaging in a value judgement? Are we not implying that earlier is inferior to later, that the infant is inferior to the adult? Moreover, if life cycle change truly is about development, what are we developing into? What is the endpoint of this progression? Death? How can development mean progress if that is its objective?

The central thesis of Richard Dawkins' (1989) book, *The Selfish Gene*, is that the popular interpretation of Darwinism, which holds that life is about the survival of the species, is actually a gross distortion of the facts. Life, according to Dawkins, is about nothing more than the struggle of individual organisms to propagate their own genetic material. The organism entrusted with this task is of no intrinsic importance; it is designed merely to provide genes with their best chance of survival and reproduction. From this viewpoint there is nothing to separate humans from any other living organism: birds, cockroaches, fish, or even pond slime and geraniums. (Indeed, it is a sobering fact that the genetic material of all living things is fundamentally identical.) Dawkins does not even grace us with the epithet "human being." He prefers the term "survival machine" because it conveys our true purpose and because it applies to all living things equally. Quite clearly, the survival machine is not where the action is. It is tossed away, like a polystyrene cup, when its work of launching genetic material into the future is done. If Dawkins is right, where is the sense in a notion like "human development"? The very term distracts us from our primary purpose, which is about *perpetuation*, not change. And even if we could justify the idea of human development from this radically reductionist point of view, surely there can be no development, no progress after the stage of transmitting genes has ended. When one's children reach independence, there is only degeneration, decay and the flagrant waste of resources on superfluous, clapped-out survival machines.

A dramatically different view is taken by developmental psychologist James Garbarino (1992), who tells us that, "the study of human development is literally a science of miracles" (p. 331). The fact that babies emerge from near nothingness to make language, art, science and music is a source of wonderment and joy for Garbarino. To quote him once again, "From infant organism to cultured person, human development is a series of miracles, one after another" (p. 331). So what *does* it mean to become human? The question may be elusive, but the often grim daily experiences of child welfare workers mean that most will confront the issue at some time in their careers. The profoundly disabled, the violent, the hopelessly addicted— sooner or later one of them will press the question: "What is the point of this human life"? One proposition on which Dawkins and Garbarino might be able to agree is that being human involves the capacity to think, feel and choose. But both authors also recognize that such capacities do not mark us out from other animals. Monkeys, for example, are perfectly capable of communicating their ideas and their needs with language and symbols. They also display a wide range of emotions, from joy and anger, to love and jealousy. And it is not just primates that have these capacities. Many animals display an acute awareness of loss and death, for example. Elephants grieve when their family members die and they linger for hours on end over the bones of long-dead relatives.

Resilience and the ecological environment

Complicating the issue is the fact that the Ottawa conference was about a particular kind of human development—the *resilient* kind—and it is clear that not all presenters used the term in the same way. While some at least tacitly conceived of resilience as an attribute possessed to a greater or lesser extent by the child, Christopher Lalonde, among others, explicitly rejected this idea. For Lalonde, resilience is a process that includes but also transcends the individual and he went out of his way to avoid slipping into what he called "the trait trap." Like Lalonde, Ann Masten, who was the keynote speaker at the conference and is one of the leading thinkers in the field, also avoids the trait approach by directing attention to developmental outcomes rather than inputs (traits). For Masten and her colleagues, resilience can be recognized in positive social adjustment despite sustained stress or adversity, and in successful recovery following a serious ordeal of some kind.

To the extent that resilience refers to processes that are *manifest* in individuals, if not actually possessed by them, the pioneering work of Uri Bronfenbrenner (1979) lights the way. He wrote of the need to understand the "ecological environment" inhabited by the developing child. He conceived of the ecological environment as a set of nested structures extending far beyond the immediate situation experienced by the child. Equally important are connections between other persons present in the setting and their indirect influence on the child through their effect on those who deal with the child first-hand. To capture this idea, Bronfenbrenner employed a diagrammatic representation of concentric structures, each contained within the next as shown in Figure 1.

Figure 1. The Ecological Environment

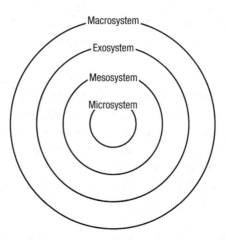

Macrosystem

Exosystem

Mesosystem

Microsystem

At the lowest level of analysis is the *individual.* Clearly, all efforts to promote resilience must begin with a thoroughgoing assessment of the individual child and, where possible, with that child's view of the situation. Beyond the individual is the *microsystem,* or the pattern of activities, roles and interpersonal relations experienced by the developing child in a given setting. To put this another way, the microsystem is the child's phenomeno-logical field. It contains all the individuals and settings with which the child has a direct relationship, such as the foster family, the school, friendship networks, and so on. In order to understand the world from the child's viewpoint, then, we need to understand the interconnections between the child and others within his or her immediate setting. Beyond the microsys-tem is the *mesosystem*, or the interrelations among two or more settings in which the developing child actively participates. At this level of analysis, a child welfare worker would examine relationships between the microsys-tems that comprise the child's life, such as the relationship between foster home and school, or between foster home and family of origin. At a level beyond mesosystem analysis is the *exosystem*, which refers to one or more settings that do not involve the child as an active participant, but within which events occur that affect what happens in settings that do contain the child. Exosystem analysis often involves the assessment of social policies impinging on the child's situation. For example, the implementation of Looking After Children (LAC) will have profound implications for chil-dren in care even if they have never heard of the term. The final level in Bronfenbrenner's model is the *macrosystem*, or consistencies in the form or content of lower-order systems (micro-, meso-, and exo-) that exist at the level of the subculture or culture. An example of a macrosystem issue rele-vant to child welfare would be Jay Belsky's (1980) point that child maltreat-ment will persist so long as societies continue to regard children as the property of their parents.

So the ecological perspective forces us to recognize that the promotion of resilience is about much more than individuals; it is a product of the interaction between psychological traits, innate biological imperatives, and inconstant social forces. It is therefore impossible to understand how chil-dren grow into adaptive adults without examining the proximate and dis-tal forces acting on them, and on which children act in return. One advantage of this multilevel analysis is that it encourages child welfare workers both to promote the child's personal adaptiveness while simulta-neously searching for ways to increase the responsiveness of the social envi-ronment. The ecological perspective is therefore perfectly capable of accommodating Christopher Lalonde's emphasis on the dynamic, interac-tive nature of resilience while also recognizing that the attributes children possess do matter in determining whether the outcomes articulated by Ann Masten will actually be achieved. Louise Legault and Shaye Moffatt hit the nail on the head with their proposition that "the positive outcomes associ-ated with resilience are generally (attributable) to factors at work in the environment as well as resources within the individual."

This latter point is precisely the emphasis conveyed in Ann Masten's chapter, which carries the subtitle, "A general framework for systems of care." In addition to its emphasis on positive outcomes rather than merely the avoidance of negative ones, resilience theory, according to Masten, "can be applied to any living system or to a human organization," and she acknowledges Looking After Children for incorporating both emphases within its Assessment and Action Records. Masten also recognizes that resilience theory has so far limited its attention mainly to individual and microsystem processes and that the influence of the higher system levels represented in Bronfenbrenner's framework is in need of research attention. A number of the chapters following Masten's either provide some of that research evidence or explicate key aspects of the "adaptation systems" advocated in her paper.

Resilience and multiple ecological levels

Beginning in the centre of Figure 1, Robbie Gilligan explored the subjective experience of children who are removed from home and placed into care. His presentation argued that entry to care always involves loss, as does the transition out of care. He also reminded us that when all is said and done, it is in the microsystem—the mundane experiences of daily life—that children actually live their lives, and he directs our attention to some of the microsystem attributes he regards as foundational for a satisfying childhood. Among these are supportive relationships at home and at school; hobbies; a sense of agency; placement permanence; and the sense of coming from somewhere, of continuity with a family history. Ross Klein, Kathleen Kufeldt and Scott Rideout widened the lens on positive environments with their examination of resilience from multiple system levels—individual, family, school and neighbourhood. These authors pointed out that the Assessment and Action Records from LAC provide a framework both for identifying such factors and, as Bronfenbrenner's model directs, for involving children as active participants in their own development.

Christopher Lalonde drew our gaze even further outward by examining resilience at the level of culture (the macrosystem). He presented intriguing data that suggest a novel but very plausible explanation for the wildly fluctuating suicide rates in Canadian Aboriginal communities. In brief, Lalonde argued that one common characteristic of the suicidal communities in his sample is that they fail to promote a sense of "personal persistence," by which he means the capacity to conceive of continuity in identity over time. Without this protective cultural factor, Lalonde claims, the developing individual is cast adrift, without meaningful aspirations or a normative frame of reference. Among Lalonde's proposed remedies are the promotion of traditional cultural practices and self-governance, including in matters related to child welfare. This latter strategy is, of course, consistent with the now voluminous research evidence demonstrating the close and positive association between attributions of personal control and health outcomes generally.

Evelyn Khoo, Lennart Nygren and Ulf Hyvönen focused on the macro- and exo-systems with their examination of the Swedish and Canadian child welfare systems. According to these presenters, there is a stark contrast between Sweden's welfare orientation to children and Canada's protection-oriented approach. Khoo and her colleagues suggested that this difference in culture results in need being the ultimate justification for state intervention in Sweden, while child welfare in Canada is narrowly directed at risk management. Although the broader mandate of child welfare in Sweden allows child welfare workers to be more intrusive than is the case in Canada, Khoo et al. claimed that child welfare is much less forensic in Sweden. In support, they pointed to the far greater proportion of Swedish children who are in care under voluntary agreements than happens in Canada. The provocative conclusion these presenters reached was that by substituting need for risk, Sweden has demonstrated greater commitment to the notion of a resilient society than Canada has.

Ivan Brown, Sophie Léveillé, and Pamela Gough's report of the panel discussion held toward the end of the conference deals mainly with the exosystem and opens with a discussion of the elevated objective (some might say "sacred cow") of placement permanence. The panel explored three dimensions of the idea: (a) emotional permanence; (b) physical permanence; and (c) legal permanence, and went on to consider which of these dimensions is the most important. In this context, the panel emphasized the need to work more intensively than most jurisdictions normally do with families of origin because most of the children who leave foster care return home. Among the other policy problems identified by panelists were: the tendency to over-simplify and over-generalize the findings of sometimes flimsy research evidence; the appetite that policy-makers sometimes have for arbitrary administrative benchmarks; and the rapidly shrinking pool of foster carers. In their lucid and helpful summation of the panel discussion, Brown and his colleagues identified a number of themes that they consider point the way forward in alternative care policy. The authors argue that these themes, taken together, speak of the need for individualizing care planning, enhancing social networks, and expanding the range of support services available to children in care. Among the strongest

423

messages to emerge from this discussion was the recommendation to policy makers that they not pressure agencies to turn permanency into an end in itself. This message was repeated in presentations by Marie Drolet and Melissa Sauvé-Kobylecki and by the author and Paul Delfabbro. We presented data from an Australian tracking study of children in foster care. These data suggest that whether or not placement impermanence is harmful depends on the inter-related factors of how long it continues and why it occurs. In the early stages of care, there are often good reasons for moving children from one place to another, such as to return to a former school or to live with a more suitable foster parent, but serious problems arise when children are evicted from foster care due to their behaviour. Although these children do not benefit from being in care, they tend to remain there longer and to bounce from one placement to another.

Looking After Children and resilience among young people in care

Notwithstanding this group for whom resilience is seriously compromised, the research findings from around the world that were presented at this conference provide some grounds for being sanguine. Elizabeth Fernandez conducted interviews and administered standardized instruments 18 months apart to 59 Australian foster children between 2 and 15 years of age, their carers and caseworkers. In her chapter, Fernandez reports that the experience of foster care was generally a positive one, with children reporting a high level of satisfaction with their carers and displaying improvements in social and emotional functioning over the period. Both findings were replicated in the author's and Delfabbro's work with an unrelated Australian sample of foster children. Importantly also, Fernandez's interviews with foster children leave no doubt that foster children do yearn for a stable home life and therefore that, all things being equal, it is always better not to disrupt a placement. Placement stability was also highest on Mike Stein's list of priorities because of the connection he sees between permanence and the development of secure attachments. This message was repeated by the 14 social workers in Marie Drolet and Melissa Sauvé-Kobylecki's study referred to earlier.

In one of a series of presentations emanating from the Ontario Looking After Children project, Robert Flynn, Annie Robitaille and Hayat Ghazal confirmed Fernandez's finding of high levels of satisfaction among children in out-of-home care. Flynn and his colleagues' sample consisted of around 430 mostly foster children who rated their satisfaction with placement more highly than children in group homes did. In a multiple regression analysis of placement satisfaction, the child's relationship with the female caregiver dominated the model, highlighting the importance to the developing child of a nurturant maternal figure. This message was repeated in Angela Dumoulin and Robert Flynn's presentation showing that the quality of the child's relationship with the female caregiver was related to the child's level of hope and coping skills and to the foster parent's self-reported nurturance. It is encouraging that this study also found that the self-reported level of hope among the children in care was similar to that of children from the general population.

Among other components of the child's microsystem that were found to be associated with positive outcomes in care were the self-declared parenting practices of foster carers. These data were presented by Julie Perkins-Mangulabnan and Robert Flynn who found a statistical association between four self-reported measures of psychosocial adjustment in foster children and the parenting behaviour of foster parents. As in general population studies, however, the authors also found that parenting practices account for relatively small amounts of variance in child adjustment. Moreover, the cross-sectional nature of the study begs the question of causal direction. On balance, then, Perkins-Mangulabnan and Flynn's findings are consistent with the conclusion frequently reached in parenting research: while parenting practices obviously matter, children are adaptable creatures and most can accommodate variations in parenting preferences provided those practices fall within reasonable bounds. Robert Flynn, Julie Deaulac and Jessica Vinograd's presentation contributed further to the examination of the microsystem with their finding that involvement in structured voluntary activities—sports, dance or art classes, hobbies, clubs, etc.—is statistically, if rather weakly, associated with positive psychosocial outcomes. Importantly, the strength of this association increased when the risk factor of substance use was examined as a moderator of the association.

Based on a slightly expanded Canadian Looking after Children sample, Louise Legault and Shaye Moffat investigated the positive life experiences of approximately 900 Canadian children and young people in out-of-home care. Their goal had been to understand what children themselves considered had helped them to cope with the dual stresses of being removed from home and whatever it was (usually maltreatment) that led to the removal. It may be surprising to some that the researchers found that maintaining relationships with families of origin was of critical importance to the children. Legault and Moffat also found that being in care was regarded by children as an important positive experience, although the obvious demand characteristic of a procedure that involves a joint interview between child, foster carer and child welfare worker does caution against making too much of this particular finding. Like Flynn and his colleagues, Legault and Moffat's children also nominated various activities and events as being helpful to them—activities like vacations, sports events, camps and entertainments. Finally, and to a lesser extent, children said school helped alleviate the stress of removal from home.

Implementation of innovative approaches in child welfare

At the level of program development, the conference heard of some promising approaches and of the successful implementation of LAC around the world. In her paper on foster care services for children affected by prenatal drug exposure, Lenora Marcellus indicated that the ecological perspective was the inspiration behind a novel program in the Canadian province of British Columbia. In her "Safe Babies" program, services are targeted at the microsystem and mesosystem levels and consist of interventions to train and support foster families as well as to enhance the child's mesosytem by creating and connecting families with community support services. Simon Nuttgens described the efforts of his agency to move from a "deficit paradigm" to a "strength-based perspective." After describing the key elements of this strengths-based perspective, Nuttgens briefly highlighted some of the organizational challenges involved in making the shift. Andrew Pithouse described the implementation of structured need assessment within the Swansea authority in Wales. This "pre-referral common assessment" is compatible with the Assessment Framework and Looking After Children and engages service providers and clients in the systematic examination of six domains of child welfare: health; education; identity and social presentation; family and social relationships; emotional and behavioural development and self care; and physical and social environment. In a quasi-experimental evaluation of this initiative, Pithouse reports some encouraging, though not yet conclusive, results on the instrument's effectiveness.

Raymond Lemay, Beverly Ann Byrne and Hayat Ghazal told a similarly positive tale of organizational change. Their presentation described how one Children's Aid Society was able to convert dissatisfaction with their existing service into a comprehensive and carefully planned organizational change strategy. Lemay and colleagues described how their Ontario-based agency modified and then implemented Looking After Children and, in the process, they provided a roadmap for organizational change that begins with pilot-testing, and moves through the tasks of establishing an implementation working group, training workers, and revising agency partnerships. Policy makers and agency managers will find Lemay and colleagues' tips for the journey to be an invaluable source of practice wisdom. Among their suggestions, for example, is to act decisively and not to over-plan, and to develop communication and feedback strategies that keep stakeholder fully apprised of developments. Importantly, and perhaps most impressively, the authors did not begin until they had secured the funding and the expertise that was necessary to ensure that all their actions were based on sound research evidence and their successes and failures were carefully evaluated. Bravo to these colleagues! Let's hope the funders and policy makers read your chapter.

Like Lemay and colleagues, Ruth Champion and Gabrielle Burke's presentations showed just what can be achieved in the child welfare field when political will and agency leadership pull together. Champion and Burke's presentation described how the Australian State of Victoria moved its entire child welfare jurisdiction to Looking After Children with a truly masterful implementation strategy. The process began when the leadership of Victoria's Department of Human Services succeeded in having the State Government commit publicly to Looking After Children in the Budget Speech of 2002/03. Once this financial commitment had been made, the Department and its non-government partners moved swiftly into action, building partnerships, establishing infrastructure, and winning hearts and minds through a carefully conceived staff training and devel opment program. One of the many outstanding achievements of this proj-ect was the attention that was paid to implementation fidelity, which was monitored through a statewide survey of almost 3500 cases. As Looking After Children moves into its next phase, LAC records are being revised on the basis of workers' experiences with the system and, even more impres-sively, Victoria's entire child welfare IT system is being remodeled to create interactive, electronic LAC records. LAC procedures are being modified for cultural appropriateness, links are being revitalized with service providers from other sectors, LAC training materials are being revised and institu-tionalized, and LAC itself is being extended into kinship care. This has undoubtedly been a triumph of service planning and all that remains now is for the Department to implement its evaluation strategy.

As Victoria redesigns its electronic systems, it is to be hoped that they will consult with the other Australian States of New South Wales and Tasmania where the "Looking After Children Electronic System" (LACES) is now oper-ational. Deirdre Cheers and Jude Morwitzer's chapter describes the partnership between the University of New South Wales and Barnardos Australia in the development of this powerful data management tool for the storage and analysis of LAC data. In her presentation on the Integrated Children's System (ICS), Helen Jones also showed how IT can be used to enhance the developing child's ecosystem. Following certain implementation problems experienced with Looking After Children and the Assessment Framework, the ICS was designed to harmonize the two systems, aid clinical decision making, and provide a repository of administrative and research data. For their part, Lisa Holmes and Harriet Ward provided the conference with a methodology for identifying the full cost of placing children in care that could be readily incorporated into the electronic databases under construction. This methodology derives from Holmes and Ward's specification of eight processes entailed in the care of "looked-after" children. Sarah Pantin, Robert Flynn and Vivien Runnels cast further light on the organizational aspects of successful program development with their presentation on worker perceptions of the usefulness of LAC's Assessment and Action Records (AARs). In a nutshell, this study highlighted the importance of agency supervision practices. Not only was the frequency with which supervisors discussed the AAR with caseworkers the single best predictor of the AARs' perceived utility, but this variable also mediated the effect of the other predictors in the model: amount of experience in the AAR, and amount and quality of LAC training. Marie Drolet and Melissa Sauvé-Kobylecki's qualitative study of 14 social workers also dealt with workers' attitudes toward AARs and reported that their respondents were positively disposed to LAC in general and to the AAR in particular. Caseworkers felt that the AAR promoted careful case planning and review, but that the tool was not without limitations. Of particular concern to respondents was the fact that AAR raises expectations among workers and children that existing resources are often ill-equipped to meet.

Mike Stein's presentation occurred early in the conference, but his discussion of children leaving care is an ideal way to round out this discussion of the practice and policy implications of the conference. Stein emphasized the vital importance of preparing children for what, by today's standards, is a very early transition to adulthood by most children in care. Much of his analysis dealt with the UK's exosystem-level initiative of the *Children (Leaving Care) Act 2000*, which aims to ensure that children are adequately prepared for leaving care and are provided with emotional and material transition support. The Act was responsible for the creation of "leaving care" specialists to give effect to these objectives and, according to Stein, the early results are encouraging, although much remains to be done to adapt the fledgling service to the needs of children with disabilities.

Conclusion

At its core, human development is merely the study of how society raises the children to take its place. This may be an unromantic notion, but it does capture a fundamental truth about the purpose of our lives and how they should be measured. By this standard, resilient societies cannot be judged solely by the happiness and prosperity of its members, but also by the extent to which they contribute to the generations coming behind them. But for the qualifier "human," such a definition of development can be applied equally to all species. It can also be applied to gay couples and couples without children because they are just as involved as any parent in creating the future. Developmental accomplishments are therefore inherently social, both in origin and purpose. We will therefore recognize the extent to which we have promoted resilience in child welfare by the kind of world our clients create for the generations coming behind them.

References

Belsky, J. (1980). Child maltreatment: An ecological perspective. *American Psychologist, 35,* 320–325.

Bronfenbrenner, U. (1979). *The ecology of human development: Experiments by nature and design.* Cambridge, MA: Harvard University Press.

Dawkins, R. (1989). *The selfish gene* (2nd ed.). New York: Oxford University Press.

Garbarino, J. (1992). *Children and families in the social environment* (2nd ed.). New York: Aldine de Gruyter.

Author index

Subject index[1]

[1] Please note that ff (e.g., in the expression 52ff) means the page mentioned (here, page 52) and the following few pages.